PLAYA DEL CARMEN, TULUM & THE RIVIERA MAYA

Hidden World

A COMPLETE GUIDE

FIRST EDITION

Playa del Carmen, Tulum & the Riviera Maya

Joshua Eden
Hinsdale

The Countryman Press
Woodstock, Vermont

We welcome your comments and suggestions. Please contact Great Destinations Guide Editor, The Countryman Press, P.O. Box 748, Woodstock, VT 05091, or e-mail countrymanpress@wwnorton.com.

ISBN-13: 978-1-58157-032-8
ISBN-10: 1-58157-032-5
ISSN 1558-8785

Maps by Mapping Specialists Ltd., © The Countryman Press
Book design by Bodenweber Design
Text composition by Melinda Belter
Cover photograph of Playa del Carmen by Jeremy Woodhouse
Interior photographs by the author unless otherwise indicated

Published by The Countryman Press, P.O. Box 748, Woodstock, VT 05091

Distributed by W. W. Norton & Company, Inc., 500 Fifth Avenue, New York, NY 10110

Printed in the United States of America

10 9 8 7 6 5 4 3 2 1

This book is dedicated to my ever-supportive parents and my beautiful wife, Andrea.

Acknowledgments

I am forever grateful for my friends, family, and total strangers who have directly or indirectly led to or assisted with this project:

My mother, a self-proclaimed Italian urban gypsy, introduced me to *Jonathan Livingston Seagull*, Willie Nelson, the beach, and a sense of wonder and delight with life. She encouraged me to explore the world, took motorcycle riding lessons with me when I was 15, cried when I left for college, and always made coming home a warm and wonderful experience.

My father taught me to water-ski, play baseball, and understand the stock market. He took me fishing, learned scuba so we could dive together, validated my wanderlust, and always led by example. He taught me that you can have an exciting life and still be responsible.

I met Andrea in Austin, Texas, and took her to Playa del Carmen hoping she'd fall in love with me. She travels with me when she can and understands that I still need to go when she can't. I carry her in my heart wherever I am. And when I return, she reminds me why there's no place like home. She is the most patient, most supportive, and most beautiful person I could ever know.

Thanks also to my first dive buddies, Eric "Rico" Andrews, Keri Kennerly, Chris Glisan, Ellen Lock, and Amanda Miller; my firefighting friend and dive instructor, Davis Graham; my ninth-grade Spanish teacher, Mrs. Milby; the Villalobos family, my hosts in Costa Rica; my Cancún companion, Michelle Craft; my ranch rebel, Shana McGuyer; my colleague and friend George Hunter; Sandy Welch; fellow dreamer Chip Rankin, who encouraged me to write this book; my good-times friend Derek Palisoul; Barry Diller; Jimmy Buffett; Willie Nelson; and everyone I've ever been to Mexico with or met while there.

I am thankful for the kindness, support, and assistance of the hundreds of hoteliers, restaurant owners, tour operators, and others who I visited during my research. Thanks to the hotel associations, tourism boards, and other official organizations that offered information and support. Thanks also to my faceless friends on online message boards and e-mail discussion groups who shared their thoughts and feelings about the destination. And thanks to the people of the Riviera Maya, who smiled at me as I walked the beaches and streets of their hometowns.

Finally, thanks to Dr. John E. Anderson, University of Manitoba, for his contributions to chapter 5, Mayan Ruins.

OVERVIEW: THE RIVIERA MAYA

GULF OF MEXICO

Río Lagartos

El Cuyo

Isla Holbox

Holbox

Laguna de Yalahán

Chiquilá

Isla Contoy

Isla Mujeres

Cancún Puerto Juárez

Tizimín

YUCATÁN

180

307

Central Vallarta

Puerto Morelos

Tres Ríos

Punta Bete

Playa del Carmen

Ferry

180

Pisté

Valladolid

Chichén Itzá ▲

Cobá

Cobá ▲

Xpu-Ha

Xcaret

Paamul

Puerto Aventuras

San Miguel de Cozumel

Isla Cozumel

Akumal

Xel-Ha

Tulum

Boca Paila

CARIBBEAN SEA

QUINTANA ROO

307

Punta Allen

Bahía de la Ascensión

Sian Ka'an Reserve

N

295

184

Felipe Carrillo Puerto

307

0   30 miles

0   30 kilometers

Limones

307

Bahía de Chetumal

Mahahual

Chinchorro Banks

Laguna Bacalar

Chetumal

186

MEXICO BELIZE

© The Countryman Press

Contents

3
The Riviera Maya—South of Playa del Carmen
185

4
Activities
231

5
Mayan Ruins
261

FOREWORD

When I was asked to write a foreword to this guidebook, I thought about how I could spend 10 years traveling through Mexico, with each day bringing a sense of discovery, new faces, and plenty of surprises. I have been visiting Mexico for more than 30 years and love it so much that I make my home in Los Cabos, where I run the Cabo Wabo Cantina, hang out, drink tequila, and jam with friends. Whether I'm down there or across the country in Playa del Carmen and the Riviera Maya, it's always great to be in Mexico.

Many people have discovered the charms of Mexico during the past 30 years, but I find that some things never change. I can still get the thrill of being the only gringo in a back-street cantina and find adventure and exploration around every corner. Often, a sunrise means my day is ending, not beginning. For me, Mexico is a magical and mystical place. There is a timelessness and sense of a deep-rooted folklore that is personified in the people.

Most of all, I love the white-sand beaches, the music, the food, the fiestas, and enjoying time with family and friends. It's a place where the warmth of the sun is equaled by the warmth of the people. My family and I try new food, meet new people, and generally kick back on the world's greatest beaches. Mexico inspires me. It might mean a new song, a new idea, or a renewed outlook on life. Whatever it does to you, Mexico will remind you to enjoy life.

See you on the beach!

Sammy Hagar

Introduction

My parents first traveled to the Riviera Maya in 1980, when it was known only as the not-so-catchy "area south of Cancún." They went to Xcaret when it cost 25 cents and the road was yet to be paved. They went to Xel-Ha and Garrafon, in Isla Mujeres, and marveled at the tropical fish and the deserted beaches. They ate lobster on the beach in Cancún and snorkeled the virgin reefs of Cozumel. When they came home, they showed me their pictures and talked of their adventures, and I knew I'd go there one day.

My first experience with the Caribbean was in Belize, when I was 16. I went diving at Turneffe Island and was blown away by the color of the water, the number of fish, and the relaxing island lifestyle. A year later, I went on a dive trip to Cozumel with a group of friends from school. I loved the food, the freedom, and the excitement. We took the ferry to the then-tiny town of Playa del Carmen and could hardly find a place that was open to eat lunch.

For each of the next 10 years, I went to Mexico every chance I could, eventually leading group trips, selling travel packages, and making friends around the country. In college, I spent a year at the University of Costa Rica, studying Spanish and traveling around. After graduating from the University of Texas, I went to work for a Mexico-based tourism developer and worked on the early stages of the creation of Playacar.

I moved to Cozumel, worked in a hotel, and traveled the region extensively. I later moved to Cancún, worked for the *Cancún News* (the English daily newspaper, now closed), and made frequent trips to Playa del Carmen. In 1993 I visited the construction site of the Robinson Club (now the Royal Maeva) in Xpu-Ha for a photo shoot, but I could never have imagined the development that would follow up and down the coast.

Over the years, I stayed active in the Riviera Maya community, splitting my frequent trips between Cancún, Cozumel, and Playa. As many others have, I've watched the area boom and grow, amazed with each trip at the new hotels, restaurants, and other attractions.

The region continues to draw me, almost magically, to its sandy beaches, backstreet cantinas, secret fishing holes, and buzzing nightspots. It is in my soul and has become a large part of who I am. I love being there, I love talking about it—and I love sharing it with other travelers.

Mike Stone

History of the
Playa del Carmen Region

*"In the beginning all was invisible. The sky was motionless. There was only water, the quiet
ocean, the silence, the nights. Then there came the word."*

—From the *Popol Vuh*, sacred Mayan scriptures

Playa del Carmen owes its growing popularity to the nearby resort town of Cancún, just 40
miles to the north, and Cozumel Island, just 12 miles to the east. The influence of these two
towns has helped shape Playa since the days of the Mayans.

Playa del Carmen is named for Our Lady of Mount Carmel, who is the patron saint of
Cancún. She was named for a town in Italy, which was the first place where a chapel was
built in her honor, in 1263, before her ascension into heaven.

The first recorded visitors to the beaches of what is now Playa del Carmen came during
the Early Classic Period (A.D. 300–600) of the Mayan civilization. Then called *Xaman-Ha*,
or "waters of the north," Playa was a rest stop of sorts for travelers making their way from
the great cities of the Mayan world to the island of Cozumel. These travelers readied their
dugout canoes and prepared for the journey across the straits on the same shores that now
house the restaurants, hotels, and nightspots of modern-day Playa del Carmen.

Cozumel, called *Ah Cuzamil Petén*, meaning "island of the swallows," by the Mayans, was
a sacred site and home to Ix-Chel, the goddess of fertility and wife of Itzámna, the god of
the sun. Young women across the Mayan empire, from present-day Yucatán, Honduras,
Belize, and beyond, journeyed to Cozumel on a sacred pilgrimage to pay homage to Ix-Chel
and pray for fertility and healthy childbirth.

In return for the dozens of shrines and temples that the Mayans constructed, Ix-Chel is
said to have gifted the people with the graceful swallow, or *cuzamil*, which led the Mayans
to give the island its name. Many of the temples for Ix-Chel have survived, including San
Gervasio, which can still be visited today.

Meanwhile, on a sheltered sandbar known to the Mayans as *Kankun*, or "nest of
snakes," the temples of El Rey were constructed as a ceremonial site and resting place for
the society's nobles. The site is adjacent to a golf course and across the highway from what
is now the Hilton Hotel, making it a popular destination for visitors to Cancún who want to
experience the Mayan ruins but are not able to get to the more major sites in the region,
such as Tulum, Cobá, or Chichén Itzá.

Cancún did not have many other sacred sites because it was so narrow and did not have good access to the mainland, though the ocean breezes and proximity to various shallow lagoons did make it a nice place to live for the natives who fished along its shores and harvested food from the mangroves.

During the post-Classic period (A.D. 1000–1500), the area around Playa del Carmen, Cancún, and Cozumel served as a major trade route and religious center, and the Mayan culture flourished and prospered. At its height, the walled city of Tulum contained splendors beyond belief, and the nearby town of Cobá was a spiritual center of the entire Mayan empire, with a population of nearly fifty thousand. Near the end of this period, the populations dwindled as the natives dispersed due to storms and wars and to seek gentler climates.

Juan de Grijalva, a Spanish explorer, passed close to Playa del Carmen in 1518 and then discovered Cozumel while en route to Cuba, several hundred miles to the east. He didn't stay for long, but word of his find traveled fast, and his countryman Hernan Cortez returned the following year, bringing Catholicism and not much of an appreciation for the Mayan way of life. Cortez and his men demolished Mayan temples and built a Catholic church, and he also brought something else with him when he landed on Cozumel—smallpox. The disease spread quickly within the island's close-knit community, and the population was decimated, dropping from 40,000 to less than 200 within 50 years.

Where Did My Bathing Suit Go?

If you continually misplace something on your trip, don't blame your traveling companion— it may be an *alux* (pronounced "aloosh") playing pranks.

Aluxes are, according to Mayan superstition, mischievous elfin or childlike creatures who live in the tropical jungle and play tricks on people who do not believe in them or give them the respect they deserve. Some stories claim that the aluxes were originally clay or stone carvings that were placed in the Mayan religious temples and then later came to life.

Many Mayans and other locals claim to have had run-ins with aluxes. They can cause the phone to ring at odd hours of the night, and when it's answered, no one is on the other end. They can move objects around the room and sometimes even steal bits of food. To curry the favor of the aluxes, many people build them little houses or shrines on their property. Once appeased, the aluxes become good luck charms, helping to ensure a good harvest, bring about good fortune, and protect the believers from other dangers.

Many hotels in the Riviera Maya, even some large and well-established ones, have homes for the aluxes on-site, in hopes that appeasing them with a comfy dwelling will encourage them to be friendly, though they rarely talk about it. Ask your waiters and housekeepers, though, and chances are they'll know what you're talking about—and will probably have a story of their own to share.

The first European settlement in the region was at Xel-Ha, just a few miles south of Playa del Carmen, which had been a Mayan outpost and is now an ecotourism theme park. Over the next two hundred years, the Spanish traveled throughout the Playa del Carmen area and the Yucatán, spreading Catholicism and disease as they went. Many Mayans resisted the new religion, and small communities retained their traditional ways and their sacred cultures. During the 1700s and 1800s, pirates set up shop on the nearly deserted shores of Cozumel, using it as a base for their marauding forays across the channel to Playa del Carmen and elsewhere around the region.

A single taxi awaits arrivals at the Cancún airport in 1970.

Meanwhile, trade continued in and around Playa del Carmen, given its location midway between the port city of Veracruz to the north and Honduras to the south. Local commodities, including salt and honey, were bartered for goods imported from other regions, giving the area a taste of the diversity, commerce, and—yes—tourism that would eventually secure its place in the Mexican economy.

John L. Stephens and Frederick Catherwood passed through the Riviera Maya in 1842 as part of their expedition to the Mayan ruins, which was documented in their excellent book, *Incidents of Travel in Yucatán.* In the book, Stephens writes about what they saw and the people they encountered while Catherwood presents exacting drawings of the ruins. The book is incredibly precise and detailed, and it's still used by scholars, archaeologists, and Mayan enthusiasts today.

In 1848 the Mayans and various Spanish refugees began to resist the Spanish occupation more aggressively, leading to an uprising known as the War of the Castes. During the struggle, a large group of the oppressed set out from the Yucatán town of Valladolid and traveled across the peninsula, settling in Cozumel, which led to a regrowth of the island's population. Other natives took cover in the ruins of Tulum, which made a great fortress given its walled perimeter. The town of San Miguel de Cozumel was officially established in 1840, and several years later, U.S. President Abraham Lincoln pondered using the island as a place to send the freed American slaves and even went so far as talking to the Mexican government about purchasing it.

Due to the remote location and its dense, inhospitable jungle environment, Playa del Carmen and the surrounding area kept a low profile for the rest of the 1800s. In 1902 the region was finally granted status as a territory of the country of Mexico, and it was named after Gen. Andreas Quintana Roo, of the Mexican army. Cozumel was used as a base by the U.S. Navy during World War II and was then abandoned again until the 1960s, when scuba adventurer and documentary film producer Jacques Cousteau visited the island with an

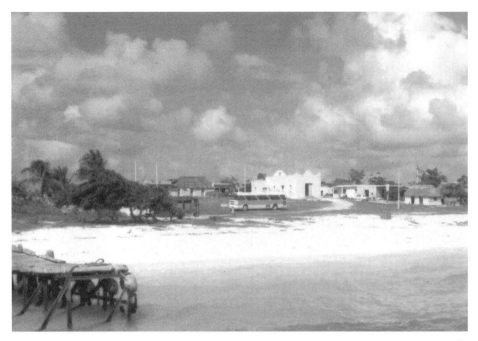

Playa was a tiny outpost in the 1970s. The church in the background is still there, at the northwest corner of the town square.

underwater camera crew and began to show the world the beauties of the Great Mayan Reef (second in size only to Australia's Great Barrier Reef), which runs between Cozumel and Playa del Carmen for hundreds of miles.

The single most important factor in the development of the region came in 1967, when the Bank of Mexico and the country's tourism development commission identified Cancún as the location for one of its mega-development projects (along with Ixtapa, Los Cabos, Loreto, and Huatulco). In the original government documents, the area was called "Kan Kun," which quickly morphed into the more Spanish "Can Cun," and then eventually shortened to just "Cancún."

Bridges were built, sewer lines were laid, and electrical poles sprang up. The first hotels, opened in the early 1970s, were the Palacio Maya, Playa Blanca, Cancún Caribe, Camino Real, and Club Med. In 1970 a wooden boat dock was built on the central beach in Playa del Carmen, and shortly thereafter, ferry service started to Cozumel. In 1974 Quintana Roo was granted Mexican statehood and the Cancún International Airport opened for business, with a bamboo and palm air-traffic control tower and a single taxi waiting for arriving planes. Two years later, the city's Pok-Ta-Pok golf course opened with 18 holes, many with views of the ocean and minor Mayan ruins. Over the next 10 years, Cancún grew from a coconut jungle visited only by traveling fishermen and a few loco gringos to a world-class tourist destination. The local population boomed as workers from across the country poured into Ciudad Cancún to find jobs and establish their families.

Cozumel experienced a growth spurt of its own as recreational scuba diving became more popular and affordable and more and more divers came to witness for themselves what they had been able to see only on the Jacques Cousteau television show.

Local Lingo

CENOTE: A rare geological feature of the Yucatán, a *cenote* is a freshwater sinkhole formed when the limestone ground caves in and fills with water from underground rivers.

COLECTIVO: A sort of taxi-bus combination, a *colectivo* is a van or similar vehicle used for local transportation. It has semi-fixed routes and is cheaper than a taxi.

COSTA MAYA: The coastline south of the Riviera Maya (which officially ends at Tulum).

FEDERAL: Used when referring to Highway 307, a federal highway.

HA: Mayan for "water." You'll see it used every-where.

MOLE: A chocolate-based sauce made with dozens of herbs and spices, used in traditional Mexican cooking.

MUELLE: Spanish for "dock," it's commonly used when referring to the ferry landing.

NOPALES: Sliced cactus from the nopal tree, it's used locally in breakfast juice and can be served grilled or sautéed with any meal of the day.

PALAPA: Thatched palm used to make roofing in the Riviera Maya. The tight weave keeps out rain and has to be replaced every couple of years. The word is also used generically to refer to any structure that has a thatched-palan roof.

PAN DULCE: Literally, "sweet bread," it's used to describe a variety of delicious locally made breakfast pastries. For a quick start to your day, order a *café con pan dulce.*

PARADA: Spanish for "bus stop."

PLAYA: Meaning "beach" in Spanish, this is the short name used locally when referring to Playa del Carmen.

PLAYACAR: A name created in 1992 to refer to the tourist development located just south of First Street and the ferry dock.

PROPINA: Spanish for "tip." Make sure you check your bill to see if tip has already been added: *propina incluida.*

QUINTA: Spanish for "fifth," it's the name used for Fifth Avenue, the main tourist strip in Playa del Carmen.

RIVIERA MAYA: The name used to refer to the area from just south of Cancún to Tulum. The actual boundaries tend to change a little bit, depending on whom you talk to. The phrase was coined in the early 1990s. The English version, "Mayan Riviera," is sometimes used, also.

TACOS AL PASTOR: Pork tacos cooked on a verti-cal spit, seared with licking flames and served with pineapple slices.

TIEMPO COMPARTIDO: Spanish for "time share." If a deal is too good to be true, like a Jeep rental for $20 a day, chances are it's part of a *tiempo compartido* offer.

Despite a few bumps along the way, including lack of airline support, the devaluation of the peso, and a series of hurricanes, Cancún and Cozumel continued to grow and prosper. Somehow, though, Playa del Carmen lagged behind, as the city to its north and the island to its east developed more quickly. As the growth went on around it, Playa del Carmen was still known only as the ferry landing for boats traveling back and forth between Cozumel and the Quintana Roo mainland. A handful of fishermen lived in huts on the beach and a few optimistic entrepreneurs sold tacos and handicrafts to the hurrying travelers, but tourists and locals moved quickly through town on their way to the more established locales.

In its hippie heyday, Playa del Carmen's visitors would while away the day along the beaches south of town. The small cove now occupied by the Gran Porto Real hotel was close enough to the town square to be convenient but just out of sight of the ferry dock, making it the preferred place for those who liked to sunbathe au naturel. At night, tourists

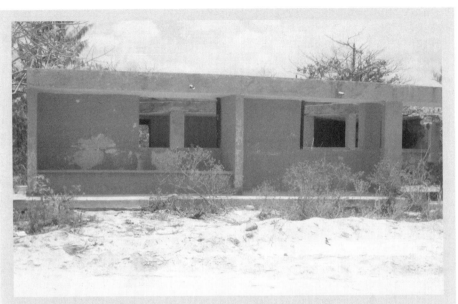

Hurricane Gilbert damaged many homes and businesses, such as this restaurant, which was abandoned.

Hurricanes of the Riviera Maya

1951, Hurricane Charlie: Made landfall in the Riviera Maya with 125 mph winds.

1967, Hurricane Beulah: Came ashore as a category 2, causing widespread damage.

1980, Hurricane Allen: Weakened as it approached the region, sparing it from harm.

1988, Hurricane Gilbert: Smashed into Cozumel with 170 mph winds and a 15-foot storm surge, caused more than $80 million in damage on the island alone, stranded a 125-foot Cuban freighter (the *Portachernera*) on the beach in Cancún, and killed more than three hundred people after it crossed the Yucatán and hit northern Mexico.

1995, Hurricane Roxanne: Slammed into the Riviera Maya with 115 mph winds.

1998, Hurricane Mitch: This massive storm was expected to hit the area but curved away. An American tourist was killed in a boating accident near Cancún related to the rough water.

2003, Hurricane Claudette: Skirted the area with tropical storm–speed winds before continuing on to Texas.

2004, Hurricane Ivan: Made a beeline for the Yucatán, causing heavy rains and high waves along the coast, before curving north and slamming Florida.

2005, Hurricane Emily: Struck Cozumel as a category 4 storm, then crossed the Riviera Maya near Puerto Aventuras, causing widespread damage, some severe, though the area quickly cleaned up and recovered.

2005, Hurricane Wilma: Just 3 months after Emily, Wilma became the most intense hurricane ever in the Atlantic Basin. The eye lingered over Cozumel and Cancún for nearly a day, causing severe damage to waterfront areas and flooding much of the region.

returned to the beach for the freewheeling and ultracasual nightlife under the stars, a refreshingly unpretentious antidote to the pulsating discotheques that were becoming so popular in nearby Cancún. During a full moon, locals and tourists alike congregated on the beach for a ceremonial "lunata" celebration, complete with bonfires, cold Coronas, and skinny-dipping—a tradition that must have made the Mayan gods smile (especially Ix-Chel, the goddess of fertility!).

But starting in the early 1980s, little by little, street by street, the tiny fishing village and ferry town began to grow. New shops, restaurants, and even a couple of hotels opened their doors, luring the passing visitors to stay a while. The first hotels were built of bamboo and palm fronds, with slatted wood doors—not to keep out thieves, but to prevent the wild pigs from entering and looking for food.

Disaster struck in September 1988 when Hurricane Gilbert slammed into Cozumel and the Riviera Maya with 170 mph winds, blowing the roofs off hotels, pulling trees out by their roots, smashing windows, and flooding the streets. Inside the storm, the barometric pressure was 26.23 inches, the lowest sea-level pressure ever recorded in the Western Hemisphere. The hurricane caused more than $80 million in damage in Cozumel alone, and it changed the face of the region for years.

In the early 1990s, Playa del Carmen became a regular stop for the cruise lines, exposing Playa to a new breed of revelers. Soon after, the outdated Cozumel ferry boats were replaced with sleek and modern jet-powered watercraft, which made the trip from the island faster and easier on the stomach and brought in even more visitors.

Guadalajara-based tourism giant Grupo Sidek purchased thousands of acres of land along the shoreline just south of the ferry landing, dubbing the development "Playacar." First came the Continental Plaza (in 1992, now the Playacar Palace). Later that year, the Diamond Resort (now the Allegro Occidental) was inaugurated, marking the first opening of

The "Riviera Maya" name was coined in the early 1990s.

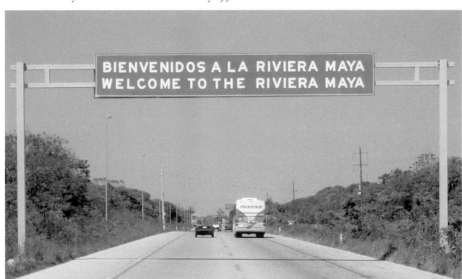

Hurricane Emily: An Unwelcome Guest

At 5 PM on July 17, 2005, management at the Moon Palace announced an immediate termination of alcohol sales and room service and instructed guests to stay indoors until further notice. Earlier in the day, the staff had lashed down all the outdoor furniture and plucked all the coconuts from their trees. The guests, many from the northern United States, Canada, and Europe, were complete strangers to tropical weather and immediately lost any romantic notions of hurricane parties or the amusing thrill of riding out a storm. It was an ominous sign of what was to come as the largest Atlantic hurricane ever recorded in the month of July was bearing down on the Riviera Maya.

Just after midnight, Hurricane Emily, a category 4 storm, ripped across the southern tip of Cozumel Island, enveloping the Punta Sur lighthouse in the eerie calm of the eye. The hammocks at the Reggae Shack swung wildly until the wooden poles supporting them collapsed in a heap, followed by the *palapa* roof of the bar. Up the east side of the island, angry waves licked at the walls of Mezcalito's restaurant as wind-driven rain lashed into the kitchen. A 160 mph gust of wind tore at the roof, pulling it apart bit by bit and spitting it into the ocean. Hundreds of trees along Rafael Melgar Boulevard, the main road along the western beachfront, fell, almost in unison, as the storm continued east. At 1 AM the clock tower in the town square clanged a single time, but the howling wind and distant sirens made it impossible for anyone to hear it.

As the eye moved across the Cozumel channel, the normally ubiquitous ferry boats were nowhere to be seen. The angry storm stirred up massive waves as it traced a path for Puerto Aventuras, hungry for the luxury yachts docked at the marina. Waves crashed over the bulkhead, flooding into shops, restaurants, and hotels. The roof of the Copacabana hotel came crashing down, exposing the lobby to the full force of the storm. Luckily, all the guests were huddled in the relative safety of the hotel's ballroom. A huge metal navigational buoy broke free from its anchor and barreled toward shore, beaching itself in front of the Riu Palace in Playacar. Concrete and wooden utility poles across the region snapped like twigs while billboards along Highway 307 advertising XX Beer and Xcaret Park were crumpled like paper in a fist.

Thousands of people hunkered down in shelters from Cancún to Tulum. Several hundred sought refuge in the convention center at the Mayan Palace, thousands more crowded into the Playa del Carmen municipal gym, and some six hundred others waited and prayed from inside the concrete walls of a bordello on the outskirts of town. Locals and visitors in Cancún rode out the storm together in the tiny rooms of an elementary school. When one room flooded, the group had to brave the elements and run to another. Shortly thereafter, the door to that room was torn from its hinges.

The eye passed right by Paamul, rumbling the mobile homes and testing their window seals with driving rain. Palm trees were gouged from the ground, and rain-soaked sand whipped into the trailers, sounding like thousands of BBs being shot into beer cans.

As the night wore on, bloggers tapped away on computer keyboards in sheltered Internet cafés, updating Internet users around the world of the storm's progress. Their missives grew less frequent as

an all-inclusive resort in the Riviera Maya. A golf course opened in September 1994, and then hotel after hotel rose from the jungle, changing the face of the community forever.

On the other side of the ferry dock, development continued as well, but government-imposed density restrictions kept away large-scale hotel projects, and small, family-run inns dominated the landscape. From 1990 to 1997, the local population grew from 2,000 to 20,000, and 100 new families were moving to town each month, establishing Playa del Carmen as Mexico's fastest-growing city, a title it still holds today.

powerlines fell and connection became impossible. A key Tel-Mex cell phone tower swayed in the wind, then bent and fell, cutting off yet another mode of communication.

It was still drizzling when dawn broke, but the heavy winds were gone and the furious sea had calmed. Locals and visitors alike crept from their shelters and spilled into the streets to survey the damage. Along Quinta Avenida in Playa, many shops suffered from broken glass and ruined merchandise. Water was nearly waist deep along Constituyentes. Many homes in the humble residential area north of the tourist zone had collapsed and lay in ruin, and distraught locals sat on the beach and on the street, numb from shock and unsure of where to go. Swimming pools were filled with sand and debris, street signs littered the streets, the beaches were full of trash, *palapas* were torn down, and uprooted or stripped trees outnumbered healthy ones.

The National Guard arrived early to begin clearing the streets and cleaning up the heavily touristed areas, including Quinta. There were widespread power outages, but some stores were open, selling food, water, and other supplies. Hotel guests and staff worked side by side to clear broken glass, sweep out flood waters, and repair damages.

It quickly became apparent that things were not nearly as bad as they could have been. Though powerful, the storm was compact and fast moving, so it did not cause as much damage as it could have. Cozumel, Puerto Aventuras, and Akumal were the hardest hit, with thousands of trees downed and many roofs torn off and buildings flooded. The beach in Playa Paraíso was badly eroded, but in Tankah, just down the coast, there seemed to be more sand than before. Two gas stations lost their roofs and were in shambles, but no fires had broken out. Local farms suffered greatly, with the summer's corn, papaya, and citrus crops enduring major losses.

It was clear that the Riviera Maya had learned the hard lessons since being caught severely underprepared for Hurricane Gilbert in 1988. The large-scale evacuation effort had worked. A convoy of 500 buses had moved 60,000 tourists to safety in less than 12 hours. Some hotels in the Riviera Maya sent guests to sister properties in Cancún, while others were sent to shelters in Vallodolid, Mérida, and elsewhere. Hundreds of petrochemical workers were evacuated from rigs and oil platforms in the storm's path.

The storm claimed the lives of four people in Jamaica, and two men working on oil rig evacuations were killed when their helicopter crashed in the Gulf of Mexico. A German dive instructor living in Playacar also died when he was electrocuted as he prepared his home for the storm. Miraculously, no other major injuries or deaths were reported.

The airports in Cancún and Cozumel opened the day after the storm, and hotels and restaurants opened as quickly as they could. Some were back in business in days, while others took weeks or even months before they were ready again. The people of the Riviera Maya kept their faith, helping each other make it through the hard times. New palm trees were planted, *palapas* were constructed, signs replaced, homes built, and lives repaired. No doubt Hurricane Emily was strong, but she was no match for the determination, the will, and the community spirit of the Riviera Maya.

The main road paralleling the beach, Quinta Avenida, or Fifth Avenue, became the town's principal street and was lined with restaurants, shops, hotels, and other businesses catering to the tourist trade. Favored by European backpackers and U.S. and Canadian budget travelers, Playa del Carmen began to make a name for itself on the international travel scene. Known as the place where the hippie lifestyle was not only accepted but celebrated, "Playa," as the in crowd called it, had arrived.

A damaged rooftop, courtesy of Hurricane Emily

A Date with Emily

*Contributed by Franco Spina, Playa resident and owner
of SeaMonkeyBusiness.com and Sealife Divers*

The days before the hurricane were exhausting. I prepared my house on Fifth Avenue and 28th Street by boarding up some of the windows and removing everything from the balconies. Halfway through I ran out of plywood, but the stores in Playa were sold out, so I taped up the windows and hoped for the best. After taking care of the house, my dive shop, Sealife Divers, was next on the list. I took everything out and stored it in my home and took the boats to Puerto Aventuras, which was sup-posed to be safer than Playa.

When my personal things were taken care of, I reported for duty at the local fire station. The fire department is one of the best in the Riviera Maya, but it is not as well equipped as we would like. Along with two other firemen, I set out with a truck, an electric chain saw (which promptly broke), three machetes, an axe, some rope, a two-way radio, and a list of homes that needed tree branches removed. For the next 10 hours, we cut branches away from the homes in an effort to prevent dam-age. That night, I crumpled into bed and slept for four hours before getting up to get back to work. The hurricane was supposed to arrive at about 2 PM, but it took until 5 PM for the ocean to begin growling and the winds to pick up. There was nothing else we could do, so we went to the beach and looked at the ocean, where I said *adios* to the dive shop, never expecting to see it again.

By the late 1990s, Quinta had extended more than a mile north of the ferry dock, and much of it was closed to vehicular traffic, creating a pedestrian-friendly walkway that developed a unique character unknown in other parts of the world. In the early 2000s, Quinta stretched past Constituyentes Boulevard (between 18th and 20th Streets), and the area was dubbed "La Nueva Quinta," sometimes called "Little Italy," "Upper Playa," or

By about 7 PM the wind had picked up, and the sand blowing on the beach felt like needles on your skin. On the walk back to my house 2 blocks from the beach, I saw a construction site with some workers in it. I told them that this site was not safe and they should leave. They told me that they did not have anywhere to go and had been sleeping at the site each night after work. I radioed the fire department to send help to evacuate the workers, and the police came with their trucks, and a tour company loaned us their all-terrain vehicle, which carries up to 20 people at a time. To my surprise, when I told them to come down and form a line, there were 120 workers. Within an hour, we had managed to take them all to a nearby shelter.

At 9 PM, I bolted the door of my house and started the long waiting period with my girlfriend and a friend of ours who was living alone. We lost electricity, shut down the gas, and had no water. We were getting hungry, so we had an impromptu cookout in our hallway with a portable gas grill. The nasty part of the hurricane began at 11 PM and lasted until 2:30 in the morning. The exciting part was at 1 AM, when the drains in my balcony became clogged with leaves and water started to come into the house. Water was about a foot deep in the balcony, and we were mopping up the water that was coming in with all the towels. When I got tired of squeezing towels, I decided to go outside and see if I could do anything about the drains. I put on a wet suit and a dive mask, opened one of the windows, and crawled outside. I spent the next hour making sure the drains were unplugged and flowing smoothly. I have never felt rain hit me so hard in my life and wind swirling like it did. I could hear things banging everywhere. My satellite dish was flapping against the roof, and it almost flew away. I remember wishing it would, because all the banging was threatening to cave in the roof.

Finally, at 4 AM the wind and rains slowed down, and we all got some sleep. At first light, I climbed to the roof and looked around. What I saw amazed me. It was as if one thousand gardeners had come by and decided to take all the leaves from the trees and scatter them around the neighborhood. Then, I looked at the beach and saw that our dive shop was still standing, and I could barely believe it. I drove around Playa and saw a lot of trees down, but not much major structural damage. Some power poles were split in half, and there were twisted signs everywhere. The military, police, fire department, and anyone who had an axe or machete was out cutting trees and clearing debris from the roads. That afternoon, I met up with a group of 15 friends at our local coffee shop and sat around sharing stories and drinking red wine to celebrate the departure of Emily and that we had all made it through.

We were lucky, and I had expected a lot worse. The eye of the hurricane had passed less than 50 miles away, and I can't even imagine what a direct hit would have been like. Electricity was restored the following day, and Internet, water, and phone were also turned back on. I was proud that everyone worked to put my town back together again so quickly. One of our two boats sunk in Puerto Aventuras, but we were able to raise it up and repair it. A couple of days after the storm, we were taking divers to the reefs again and getting on with our lives.

I learned a lot from Hurricane Emily and am thankful that it wasn't worse.

simply "The New Playa." Italian-style cafés stood next to taco stands that stood next to gourmet steakhouses, creating a town with a truly eclectic and international flair. The beach north of Constituyentes also saw some changes. A second ferry dock was built, two Porto Real hotels were constructed, and a couple of beach clubs sprang up, offering food and drink service, *palapa* and chair rentals, and towel service for the cruise passengers, day-trippers, and guests from hotels that aren't on the beach.

Hurricane Wilma—Mexico's Costliest Natural Disaster in History

Three months after Hurricane Emily tore through the Riviera Maya in July 2005, Tropical Storm Wilma formed in the Atlantic Basin and churned and sputtered for a couple of days without much strengthening or fanfare. On Wednesday, October 19, though, things changed quickly. Within 24 hours, the storm had developed into a massive category 5 hurricane, reaching a minimum central pressure of 882 millibars and sustained winds of 175 mph, making it the most intense hurricane on record in that part of the world. The U.S. State Department issued an urgent evacuation notice for all U.S. citizens in the region. By the morning of Thursday, October 20, the MTV Latin Music Video Awards in Xcaret had been canceled and music performers and celebrities crowded the Cancún airport with thousands of tourists, all trying to get a flight back home. Meanwhile, the storm was poised offshore, forecast to veer to the east and spare the region, but not yet showing signs of the turn.

By late afternoon, winds from the outer bands of Hurricane Wilma began lashing the coast of Cancún and the Riviera Maya. Palm trees were bending and the waves were crashing, even though the storm was still 150 miles offshore. At dawn on Saturday, October 21, 10-foot waves were pounding into the seawall on the western shore of Cozumel, shooting sprays of water 30 feet into the air. The outer bands were tearing at the trees and rooftops and some signs had already blown down. Up and down the Riviera Maya and Cancún, hotels prepared for the worst and visitors and residents were bused to shelters while the military patrolled the streets, ensuring everyone had a place to ride out the storm. As the hurricane's eye neared the coast, the area braced for a direct hit, with landfall predicted to be somewhere between Playa del Carmen and Cancún.

At 10 AM on Friday, Cancún police reported the city's first death. A local woman was on her roof cleaning debris and a power line fell and electrocuted her. At 2 PM, the wall of the eye passed over the northern tip of Cozumel, while all across the region, the situation deteriorated rapidly. Gary Walten, an Akumal resident and owner of LocoGringo.com, was seeking shelter in his home while talking on the phone to CNN, which broadcast the conversation to the world. Wolf Blitzer asked him to hold his phone near the window so the audience could hear the sound. The noise was howling at a near-deafening volume, described by one survivor as "one thousand cats, screaming in pain." Water was washing across the main street through the Cancún hotel zone, and Quinta Avenida in downtown Playa del Carmen was a shallow river, with whitecaps cresting between storefronts. Most of the windows were boarded up; the ones that weren't were shattered. Cars were washing down the street in downtown Cancún and in the back streets of Playa and Puerto Morelos.

By sundown, the eye had stalled over the Cancún hotel zone, creating the worst-case scenario for the region, as the rainfall continued relentlessly. The wind created a 50-mile-long wall the strength of a Force 2 tornado, and the storm surge inched higher and higher. Reports of an exploded gas tank and associated injuries made their way across the Internet, with readers praying for the safety of their loved ones, stranded in shelters across the area. Water was waist-deep along the Cancún hotel zone and had completely washed out the road leading from Tulum to Punta Allen. Through the night, things only got worse. Witnesses in Playa del Carmen reported seeing 200-gallon water tanks, stoplights, plate glass, and even automobiles flying through the air. Water had washed completely over Kukulcán Boulevard in Cancún, connecting the ocean and the lagoon and making one solid sea of water.

At sunrise on Saturday, October 22, weary-eyed residents and tourists, many of whom were kept awake by the screeching winds and rising waters, peeked out the windows and were horrified by what they saw. The devastation was worse than anyone had imagined. Mexico's President Vincente Fox had already declared the entire region a disaster zone. To make matters worse, the storm was still stalled, meaning the misery would last at least another 12 hours. Nearly every hotel in Cancún had lost dozens, if not hundreds, of windows, while the ocean in Playa del Carmen had risen to meet Quinta Avenida, forming a sea of water 3 feet deep along the town's main tourist district. By 3 PM, the winds had receded to below hurricane strength for the first time in 24 hours, though the conditions were still too severe for anyone to leave the shelters. Food and water were running scarce and reports of looters being arrested in Cancún did little to calm any fears. Across the entire region, waves of up to 25 feet continued to crash ashore, ripping apart everything in their path.

By Sunday, rumors of "total devastation" swept across the Internet, while Hurricane Wilma left the Yucatán and made a beeline for the Florida coast, where it went on to cause $11 billion in insured damages. Back in the Riviera Maya, thousands of travelers were stranded, with no way to get home. The Cancún airport was damaged, and some tourists paid up to $400 for a taxi to Mérida to catch a plane out. Tour operators scrambled to take care of their passengers and get them home. Some stranded survivors waited in line for two hours to use a payphone to tell their loved ones that they were alright. Over the next week, the Mexican government passed out roofing materials for rebuilding houses and thousands of bottles of water and also cleared the streets. Generous locals prepared food for hungry tourists. Residents and visitors banded together to start cleaning up.

Within weeks, most of the damaged buildings had been cleared or were in the process of being rebuilt. The Capitan Lafitte, just north of Playa del Carmen, was declared a total loss. Cozumel's beachfront and Cancún's hotel zone took the brunt of the storm, with some hotels having to replace hundreds of windows and replace soft goods in all of their rooms. But over the following months, the beaches regained their natural splendor. Restaurants along Quinta in Playa put on fresh coats of paint and rebuilt their *palapas* (open-sided dwellings with thatched roofs). The large all-inclusive resorts along the Riviera Maya built back bigger and better than ever.

Thankfully, Hurricane Wilma claimed only five lives in all of Mexico. Once again, the region proved itself to be incredibly resilient, even in the face of great challenges. By 2006, the crowds were returning in droves, proving that the Riviera Maya is not only a destination full of history and stories of a splendid past, but also a world-class travel destination with unlimited potential for the future.

Puerto Morelos rebuilds after Hurricane Wilma.

The End of the World—Or Just the Beginning?

The Mayan calendar ends at 11:11 AM on December 21, 2012 (the winter solstice), which coincides with an extremely close alignment of the path of the sun and the galactic equator (the Milky Way's midpoint). The Mayans did not necessarily foretell the "end of the world," but they did say that on this date, the world as we know it will be complete, and a new "Golden Age" will begin. Mayan scripture reveals that the ancient peoples predicted that our society will have great advances in technology, that time and money will become meaningless, and that human beings will be upgraded from the center of the galaxy. The event is even cryptically captured in images carved into the walls of Mayan sacred temples.

Modern astronomy and archaeology researchers have recognized the amazing accuracy of the Mayan calendar and its ability to calculate and forecast the movement of the stars, and they have confirmed that the alignment will indeed happen as predicted. Whether it will have any great impact on life on Earth is yet to be revealed.

Next time you're in Playa, at least you'll have a good excuse to celebrate life, so wake up early to get the best beach chairs, order the surf and turf at dinner, and savor an extra top-shelf margarita.

As the upscale all-inclusive hotels of Playacar introduced the town to more affluent travelers, the tone of the village continued to change. The thatched-roof bus station was rebuilt with electric displays and molded plastic seats. Across the street, McDonald's opened up, and up and down the coast, more and more resorts were carved from the jungle. Renovations began on Quinta as work crews buried the utility lines and paved the gravel road with cobblestones, giving the road a bit of colonial inspiration to go along with its nouveau chic attitude.

Hurricanes Emily and Wilma, both devastating storms with deceivingly demure names, tested the region's will in the summer and fall of 2006 when they sliced similar paths across Cozumel, Cancún, and the Riviera Maya. Emily raged with sustained winds of 135 mph, shearing off rooftops, leveling trees and signs, shattering windows, rearranging beaches, and sending sixty thousand tourists scrambling for shelter. Wilma completed the one-two punch by hammering the area three months later with 150 mph winds and a storm surge topping 11 feet in Cancún. Tourists were confined to shelters for days, and it took some nearly two weeks after the storm to finally get a flight back home. Hotels in Cancún were hit the hardest, though all along the Riviera Maya there was extensive flooding and wind damage. Some hotels closed for days, while others took weeks or even months to reopen. The region bounced back, though, as the communities worked together to rebuild and restore the splendor of the area.

By 2006 the Riviera Maya was celebrating its status as one of the top international tourist destinations in the world. Expatriates from 46 countries around the globe call Playa del Carmen home, and the town seems to thrive on the notoriety. And through it all, Playa has stayed true to its roots, somehow preserving its almost magical charm and exceptional character. It is still a place where travelers from around the world come together to lounge on the beach, toast the day with a cold beer, sip a hot cappuccino, and celebrate life. And in a town where backpackers from crowded hostels, newlyweds from fancy all-inclusives, and European trendsetters from chic new condos all cozy up to the same bars, it's easy to understand why Playa so easily works its way into your heart.

The ruins of Xaman-Ha can still be seen in modern-day Playa del Carmen. The main temple is along the beach just south of the Playacar Palace hotel and is now a popular spot for wedding ceremonies. Many other shrines dot the Playacar development, including the golf course. And though it may be hard to envision a time when the Mayans carved their dugout canoes from local trees and plied the waters to Cozumel, today's visitors to Playa will undoubtedly feel a sense of the grand history, the sacred importance, and the incredible natural beauty that have lured visitors to its sandy shores for thousands of years.

As one longtime local resident puts it, "No one knows what makes Playa so special, but everyone seems to return."

Philip Gammon

Practical Information

Travel should be easy, it should be carefree, and it should be comfortable. Unfortunately, that's not always the case. Getting around, having the proper paperwork, and making sense of unfamiliar rules and regulations can cause a fair amount of stress during any vacation, and travel to the Riviera Maya is no different.

An old adage that scuba divers use is "plan your dive and dive your plan." This concept should be applied to vacation travel as well. Taking some time before your trip to learn a bit about the region where you are traveling and to create a plan for how you're going to get around is essential to enjoying your vacation to the fullest. After all, wouldn't you rather use your vacation time relaxing on the beach rather than visiting the consulate, searching for maps, or asking everyone you see for help?

A Note about Geographical Terms and Addresses

This book focuses heavily on the town of Playa del Carmen, which is in the geographic center of the Riviera Maya (Mayan Riviera) and is home to the largest concentration of hotels, medical facilities, grocery stores, restaurants, and tourist services south of Cancún. The town's name translates to "Carmen's Beach," though it is always referred to by its Spanish name. The shortened version, favored by locals, is simply *Playa* (pronounced ply-a, with an accent on the first syllable). There is also substantial coverage of the surrounding villages and tourism developments of the Riviera Maya, including the towns of Cancún, Puerto Morelos, Akumal, Puerto Aventuras, and Tulum. Unless otherwise noted, "downtown" refers to the central business and tourism district of Playa del Carmen.

The main pedestrian street through Playa del Carmen is Fifth Avenue, which, in Spanish, is Quinta Avenida, or just *Quinta* (pronounced keen-ta, with an accent on the first syllable), as it's known locally. In this book, all references to this road will be made using the local term, to help travelers get accustomed to using it.

Addresses in Playa del Carmen do not follow the standard that many travelers are accustomed to. Many streets do not have lot numbers, and if they do, they are seldom used. The most common—and easiest way—to identify and find a specific location is to use the nearest intersection or list the nearest cross streets. A restaurant may list an address of Tenth Avenue at 6th Street if it is on or very close to that intersection. If it is in the middle of the block, the address would look more like: 15th Avenue between 8th and 10th Streets. Though this system doesn't specify the precise location or on which side of the street a particular business can be found, the blocks are generally fairly short, and it's easy to find what you're looking for once you go to the location given. After all, it's part of the charm of Third World travel.

Arrival by Air

Most international visitors get to Playa del Carmen and the Riviera Maya by flying into the Cancún International Airport (CUN), which is 45 miles north of Playa and 10 miles south of the resort city of Cancún.

The Cancún airport was inaugurated in 1974 but has had regular renovations, leaving it in excellent condition. There are two terminals, each with several gates. Planes either pull up to the Jetway or stop short and allow passengers to exit down the stairs and onto the tarmac, which provides a delicious first taste of the warm tropical air.

There is a food court in terminal two, where most flights depart, with a Burger King and TGI Friday's, plus several local eateries and fast-food counters. Terminal one handles mostly charter flights and does not have quite the same level of services, though both terminals have multiple souvenir shops, money exchange counters, ATM machines, public phones, and duty-free centers with jewelry, liquor, tobacco, chocolates, and other goodies.

Starting in 2007, it is mandatory that all Americans have a valid passport to enter Mexico. Prior to arrival on an international flight, visitors will be required to fill out a tourist card (good for up to 90 days) and customs form. These are usually handed out on the plane, though they are available at the airport as well. After landing you will be funneled through the main airport departure lounge (don't wander off) and then downstairs to the immigration room. Depending on how many flights are arriving, the wait can be a couple of minutes to nearly an hour. Have your proof of citizenship and your forms ready, and then remember to save your copy of the tourist card, which the agent will return to you with your proof of citizenship, as you will need it when you depart. If you lose it, it will cost you $40 to replace it, plus you could be in for a bit of an interrogation at the airport when you leave.

Once through immigration, you will enter the baggage claim area, which can get a bit crowded. Once you claim your bags, if you checked any, you will proceed to the back of the room to the customs checkpoint. Hand your customs form to the agent standing next to the vertical traffic light mounted on a pole about chest high. You will be asked to push the button. Green means "go," and red means your baggage will be opened and inspected.

The customs area leads to the main exit, where the atmosphere transitions from neat and orderly to frenzied and chaotic. Rental car counters and local transport agencies line the walls, and women in colorful dresses pass out coupon books and advertising flyers. There are some good coupons and free maps available, so it may be worth the trouble to take what's offered.

Restrictions on Importing Items Into Mexico

- Gifts of no more than $300 in value
- One video camera and one regular camera per person, plus 12 rolls of film
- Two bottles of liquor or wine
- 400 cigarettes or 50 cigars
- Perfume and cologne limited to personal use only

Airport Transportation

If you're on a package trip or you have hotel transportation prearranged, you can look for your name on a placard or for the representatives holding signs with the names of the tour group. Though there is lots of scurrying to and fro, the reps all seem to know each other and are generally willing to help point you in the right direction.

If you don't have transportation prearranged, you will find several options for getting to your hotel or wherever else you may want to go. The primary options are taxi, shuttle bus, city bus, or car rental.

TAXIS

Taxi service from the airport is heavily regulated. Only specially licensed cabs are allowed to pick up passengers, and as a result, fares from the airport are higher than for the return trips to the airport. Taxi fares, which you can pay in dollars or pesos, are paid in advance at one of the counters in the exit area. You will then take your receipt out to the curb, and you will be directed to the next available cab. The official fare at press time from the airport to the Cancún hotel zone is $40, and a trip to Playa del Carmen will run you $62. Fares are good for up to four passengers, so feel free to look for ride-share partners if there aren't enough people in your own group to fill the cab.

A taxi to the area between the airport and Puerto Morelos is $34, and a cab to the Puerto Aventuras area will run you $90. To Tulum and nearby hotels, the fare is $115. Any local taxi can be hired for a return trip to the airport. Fares from Playa del Carmen run around $40, with areas farther south costing more. Negotiating can sometimes get you a better rate. For larger groups, Suburbans and vans can be hired to transport five to eight passengers. The fare to Playa is $85, and a trip to Tulum would be $140.

If you don't find a cab on the street, try Taxi Stand (984-873-0032), Quinta at 10th Street.

SHUTTLE BUSES

Shuttle buses, called *colectivos*, are available for $18 for each passenger to Playa del Carmen. You will ride with other travelers and stop at other hotels along the way, but it can be a good way to save a few pesos. If your group has kids, you can often bargain for a discount for the younger passengers. For the return trip, you can arrange for pickup through your hotel or at one of the various kiosks located on Quinta, in downtown Playa. It is best to do it the day before your departure, and remember to keep your receipt, as you will need it to board. A shuttle to Cancún is $9 per person; to Puerto Morelos is $16; and to Tulum is $50 per person.

Private Shuttle (Accommodates up to 10 passengers)		
Location	One-Way	Round-Trip
Cancún hotel zone	$35	$65
Downtown Cancún	$35	$65
Moon Palace	$35	$65
Puerto Juárez	$40	$75
Puerto Morelos	$50	$95
Playa del Secreto	$55	$105
Mayan Palace	$55	$105
Playa del Carmen	$60	$115
Puerto Aventuras	$65	$125
Xpu-Ha Beach	$70	$135
Akumal	$75	$145
Xel-Ha	$85	$165
Tulum	$100	$190

CITY BUSES

There is public bus service between the Cancún airport and the main terminal in Playa del Carmen (Quinta and Juárez), which is a short walk or taxi ride to most Playa hotels. Tickets

The main Playa bus station at the town square

can be purchased on board the bus for $7, and it departs from the east end of the parking lot in front of the domestic arrivals terminal. Any local will point the way, but make sure you are getting on the right bus, and don't be talked into paying an additional fare for a different service. Return trips can be arranged at the same station where you are dropped off, and the rate is the same. The fare is $7, and no advance purchase is required. The service runs from 10 AM to 8:30 PM.

Buses going from the Cancún airport to Playa del Carmen leave at 10:30 AM, 11:45 AM, 12:45 PM, 1:45 PM, 3:00 PM, 4:45 PM, 5:45 PM, 7:00 PM, and 8:30 PM. Buses going from Playa del Carmen to the Cancún airport leave at 8:00 AM, 9:00 AM, 10:30 AM, 11:45 AM, 1:00 PM, 3:00 PM, 4:00 PM, 5:00 PM, and 6:15 PM.

Buses also run from the Cancún airport to the Cancún bus station in downtown. They leave every thirty minutes from 9 AM to 10 PM, and the fare is $1.50 each way.

CAR RENTAL

If you plan to do much local exploring and you prefer to have a self-guided trip rather than go on planned excursions, renting a car may be your best option. And since the price of car rental for a day is about the same as taking a taxi from the Cancún airport to Playa del Carmen, it usually makes sense to pick up the car at the airport and drop it off on your way back. Alternatively, you can choose to get your car once you're at your hotel or drop it off early at one of your rental agency's offices in the Mayan Riviera.

Most of the American chains have offices at the Cancún airport, and cars can be reserved through the companies' toll-free numbers or web sites. There are usually plenty of rental cars available, though you may have to check with a couple of companies before finding one. Most do not honor the U.S.-based frequent renter clubs, so brand loyalty may not be as much of an issue, anyway.

When renting a car in Mexico, it is important to investigate your insurance options. You are required to carry at least liability, and it will be clearly marked on your rental contract. Collision and comprehensive add-ons are available and can add 50 to 100 percent to the price of the car rental. Verify in advance whether your existing car insurance or even credit card contract provides for rental car coverage, and double-check to ensure that the coverage extends to vehicles rented in Mexico, as many times it will not. For peace of mind, it sure is nice to have full coverage, especially if you plan to drive the car in remote areas or leave it unattended/unsecured overnight. Most rental contracts also specify that taking the car off paved surfaces (down dusty beach roads, for example) will void your insurance. I have heard of stories where a car will develop a flat tire while on a rock-strewn back road, and the driver will have the car towed back to the asphalt before calling the rental company.

Renters are also advised to check their rental contract as it relates to whether or not the car must be returned full of gas. Some companies (Hertz, Avis, and maybe others) require the renter to prepurchase a tank of gas, which means that the car need not be refueled prior to returning it. The flip side to this benefit is that any gas left in the tank is essentially a gift from you to the rental agency, with no refund given for the amount of fuel with which the car is returned. Many drivers prefer to not prepay the gas and to fill up the tank on their own just prior to turning in the car. Since almost all rental offices are located in urban areas, finding a nearby gas station is never an issue. If you are returning your car to the Cancún airport, there is a station just south of the exit, so you'll hit it on the way from Playa to the airport.

If you have reserved your car in advance, you should check in at the company's rental desk near the airport exit. The agent will take your information, then point the way to the company's main office, most of which are just across the street from the main airport parking lot. The process will probably take a bit longer than you're used to, but while you wait, you can skim through the available maps and chart your course to your destination. Though popular late-model SUVs, Jeeps, and sedans are available, most of the budget cars will be names that you're probably not familiar with, such as the Dodge Atos, Verna Ikon, or VW Pointer. Cars are available in manual or automatic transmission and with and without A/C, stereo, and other options. Choose your car based on what you expect your need to be. The lower-end cars can be substantially cheaper, if you're willing to sacrifice a bit

Go Hog Wild in the Riviera Maya

For some travelers, taking a guided trip in a tour bus or even setting out on their own in a rental car is just too tame. For these intrepid travelers, renting a Harley Davidson may be the best way to visit the ruins, discover hidden beaches, and make a style statement, all while getting a tan. Playa Harley Davidson, located on Highway 307 between Playacar and Playa del Carmen, offers 883 Sportsters, 1200 Customs, and Softtail Fat Boys for $125, $175, and $225 per day. Eaglerider Cancun (Km 13.5 Kukulkan Blvd., 801-783-4274 [US] or 998-885-0626 [Cancún]; www.eaglerider cancun.com) Electra Glide, Road King, Heritage Springer, and Yamaha Road Star bikes for $185 per day. Customized travel maps and tour suggestions are available at both locations. Riders are encouraged to exercise extreme caution while riding along busy sections of Highway 307 and any unpaved roads they may encounter.

of luxury and space. Economy cars cost about $40 a day, while SUVs, vans, or four-wheel drives can cost up to $120 a day.

Prior to leaving the rental lot, an agency employee will give you a quick checkout on the car, pointing out the spare tire and jack, the gas tank, and the trunk release. The agent will also do a thorough inspection of the exterior and mark any damages on a checkout sheet that you will be asked to sign to verify that all damage has been marked. It's a good idea to ensure that all damage is reported, including minor paint scratches, since you could be held liable for any new damage when you return the car. Of course, if you have purchased the comprehensive insurance, this won't apply since you're covered no matter what happens to the car. It is smart to check the tire pressure and wiper fluid and have the agent make any adjustments you want before leaving the lot.

Parking can be a bit hard to find, particularly near the busy sections of Quinta in Playa del Carmen. A pay lot is available on Tenth Avenue at Eight Street and free parking can usually be found along Constituyentes, between the beach and 20th Street, which provides walking access to most of the town's attractions. Parking along the curb is generally allowed, as long as the curb is not painted yellow, and never on Quinta.

Return Trip to Cancún Airport

Getting back to the airport is slightly less expensive than inbound transfer. Taxis cost $35 from Playa del Carmen to the Cancún airport, and you can also take the city bus from the bus station across from the town plaza for $4. In addition, many companies offer airport transportation in vans and Suburbans that will pick you up at your hotel, with a couple of stops along the way at other hotels. Most hotels can arrange this service, or it can be purchased through one of the many travel agencies around town. One convenient agency, Cenote Azul (984-803-2880), is located on 12th Street between Quinta and 10th. The rate is $15, though some hotels charge an additional commission.

Hit the Road

Thankfully, finding your way around Playa del Carmen and the Riviera Maya is relatively simple. The main federal thoroughfare, Highway 307, provides a direct route all the way from Puerto Juárez, north of Cancún, through Puerto Morelos, Playa del Carmen, Tulum, and on down to the Costa Maya and toward the border with Belize. The road is four lanes from Cancún to Xcaret and then narrows to two lanes all the way to the Belizean border. The speed limit averages about 50 mph, with up to 65 mph in more rural areas. Most of the hotels in the Riviera Maya have well-marked entrances from the highway (some are quite elaborate), and the ones that don't are generally easy to find, with at least a few directional signs to help guide you.

When turning left from the highway into some resort entries, drivers first veer to the right, where the road curves and intersects the main road, so you can wait out of the moving lane of traffic for cars to clear before crossing the road. In other spots, an open center lane is available for making turns. To reach the hotels in downtown Playa del Carmen, you will enter into town on either Avenue Constituyentes or Avenue Juárez, depending on whether your hotel is on the north or south side of town. Access to Playacar is through Avenida Juárez or one of the direct-access gated roads on the east side of Highway 307, marked by the ornate flowers and stone carvings.

PLAYA COMMUTER FLIGHTS

There is a small airfield in downtown Playa del Carmen, just a few blocks behind the Playacar Palace hotel. It is used mostly by private aircraft, but public flights are available to Cancún (25 minutes), Cozumel (10 minutes), and occasionally Cobá (40 minutes), Chichén Itzá (45 minutes), or other nearby destinations. The planes are turboprops with limited seating. The Cozumel plane seats only four passengers and can be a real adventure, but it is worth it just for the sight-seeing. The main airline, AeroCaribe (987-872-0877), has an office on the street in front of the landing strip.

THE COZUMEL FERRY

If you hit the ferry schedule just right, getting to Playa del Carmen from Cozumel can take even less time than arriving through Cancún. The Cozumel International Airport is smaller than the Cancún airport and has only two runways and a small terminal. As your plane slows to a stop on the

Cozumel Ferry Schedule

COZUMEL TO PLAYA DEL CARMEN	PLAYA DEL CARMEN TO COZUMEL
5:00 AM	6:00 AM
7:00 AM	8:00 AM
8:00 AM	9:00 AM
9:00 AM	10:00 AM
10:00 AM	11:00 AM
noon	1:00 PM
2:00 PM	3:00 PM
4:00 PM	5:00 PM
5:00 PM	6:00 PM
6:00 PM	7:00 PM
8:00 PM	9:00 PM
10:00 PM	11:00 PM

Catch the Cozumel ferry from the municipal dock. Philip Gammon

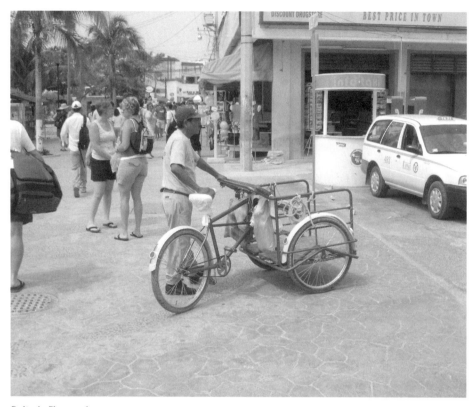

Pedicab, Playa style

runway, you will think the wingtips are about to snip the treetops off the palm trees that line the strip, but it is a safe and modern facility, even if it lacks the pretensions of the newer and more recently renovated Cancún airport.

Just as in Cancún, taxi service at the Cozumel airport is regulated, and taxi fare or shuttle service must be paid for at a kiosk in the airport. Visitors with little luggage who are looking to save a few bucks can walk off the airport grounds and hail a taxi on the street. An official taxi will cost you $12 to the ferry landing, while a taxi hailed on the street will set

Exploring is fun, but so is knowing where you are. CancunMap.com sells exhaustively researched and individually produced maps covering Cancún, Cozumel, Isla Mujeres, Playa del Carmen, and the Riviera Maya. The fold-out maps highlight hotels, restaurants, nightspots, activities, and other attractions and include personal comments and recommendations from the creators, an American couple who has been traveling around the region for years. One of the owners, known as Map Chick on Internet message boards, is happy to answer specific questions that buyers may have. The maps, especially the Riviera Maya one, are highly recommended for travelers who are planning on renting a car and doing their own adventuring. They sell for $8 each and come with a money-back guarantee.

you back only $5 or so. Either way, the ride is only 10 minutes and will take you through a quick tour of the town of San Miguel before letting you out at the base of the ferry landing, or *muelle*, as it's called in Spanish.

Ferry schedules are clearly posted, and you will have your option from a couple of different boats. Each boasts to be the newest and fastest, though any differences in the times are almost negligible. The boats seat more than two hundred passengers and have air-conditioning, snack bars, rest rooms, and both indoor and outdoor seating, plus a lower deck with TVs showing funny videos, cartoons, and promotional tourism ads. The ride takes from 30 to 45 minutes, depending on the boat and the water conditions. On windy days the ride can be a little rough, so it's recommended that you use the rest room prior to boarding or before departure, in case it's too rocky to safely move around. Fares can range from $5 to $9 each way, depending on how many boats are available.

To verify ferry schedules, you can contact the ferry office directly at 987-872-1588 or visit their web site, www.crucerosmaritimos.com.mx.

Upon arrival in Playa del Carmen, you will walk down a metal ramp and onto the wide concrete pier. If you've checked bags, they will be delivered to you on the dock, near the bow of the ferry boat. Tricycle taxis are available to help carry you and/or your bags to the street to catch a proper taxi or all the way to your hotel, if you're staying in the immediate downtown area. A taxi to a downtown hotel should cost $2–3; to Playacar hotels, $5–6; and to Puerto Morelos, $30. To get to hotels in the southern Riviera Maya, you will pay $20–40.

A new ferry dock was constructed in 2005 in front of the Porto Real hotel, about a mile north of the old one. It is embroiled in a legal debate since not all of the permits were correctly acquired. It is, however, sometimes used by one or more of the ferry operators.

Sample Taxi Fares around the Riviera Maya
From Playa del Carmen to:
Punta Bete: 4 miles, $6
Xcaret: 4 miles, $6
Paamul: 11 miles, $10
Puerto Aventuras: 11 miles, $11
Akumal: 20 miles, $17
Puerto Morelos: 20 miles, $17
Xel-Ha: 30 miles, $21
Cobá: 35 miles, $50
Tulum: 39 miles, $27
Cancún: 42 miles, $35

GETTING AROUND IN PLAYA

The hotels in Playa del Carmen proper are nearly all within walking distance of Quinta, the town square, the ferry dock, and most major in-town attractions. Taxis are readily available and charge only a couple of dollars for in-town treks.

Another option for getting around Playa is the communal taxis, or *colectivos*, which crisscross the downtown area and will get you to your destination for a cheap price, if not always as quickly as you like. They are white vans with red lettering, and they regularly pass by the basketball court on Second Street and 20th Avenue.

Bike Rental

Renting a bike is a great way to get around Playa del Carmen. Todo Yellow, located on 6th Street between Quinta and 10th Street in front of Hotel Casa, offers bikes by the hour ($1.50), morning to evening ($7), 24 hours ($9), or week ($35). Bike & Scooter Rental

(984-803-2880), located on 12th Street between Quinta and 10th Avenue, offers mountain bikes and Cripton scooters for rent.

Regional Bus Travel

There are two bus stations in Playa del Carmen. The original terminal is on Quinta and Avenue Juárez and offers frequent service to Cancún and Tulum, usually departing every 15 to 30 minutes. Fares are $3–4 each way, in an air-conditioned bus with rest room and TVs. It also offers trips to Campeche, Chetumal, Chichén Itzá, and other regional destinations.

Bus Fare Samples
From Playa del Carmen to:
Cancún: 1 hour, $4
Tulum: 1 hour, $3
Cobá: 2½ hours, $4.50
Felipe Carillo Puerto: 3 hours, $8
Valladolid: 3 hours, $18
Chetumal: 4 hours, $15
Chichén Itzá: 4½ hours, $14
Mérida: 4½ hours, $21
Campeche: 7½ hours, $30
San Cristóbal: 18 hours, $60
Mexico City: 24 hours, $90

A regional and long-distance terminal is located a half mile away (20th Avenue between 12th and 14th Streets) and offers service to other destinations around Quintana Roo and other Mexican states. The buses are generally in good condition, with air-conditioning, rest rooms, uniformed driver, and TVs, though the audio is in Spanish.

Car Rental in Playa del Carmen

Even if you didn't choose to pick up a car at the airport, you can still rent one in town. They can be rented by the day or week and can usually be dropped off at a different location (such as at the airport or in Cancún) for no additional fee.

The following are some local car-rental offices:

Alamo: Plaza Antigua, 984-873-1118
Avis: downtown, 984-873-3842
Budget: downtown, 984-873-2772
Executive: Playacar Palace, 984-873-2354
Hertz: downtown, 984-873-1130
National: Porto Real, 984-873-0360
Payless: downtown, 984-873-1072
Thrifty: downtown, 984-873-0119

A *colectivo* shuttle van departs downtown Playa from Second Street between 15th and 20th Avenues and drops passengers off anywhere along the way between Playa and Tulum for $2, even if your destination is off the main road. The van fits eight people and departs as soon as it is full, from 7 AM–8 PM.

City Orientation & In-Town Driving

Playa del Carmen is laid out on a grid system. Cancún is due north, Cozumel is due east, Tulum is due south, and the Quintana Roo interior is due west. Avenue Juárez is the main road into town, cutting through 15 blocks of dumpy hotels, convenience stores, car repair shops, clothing stores, and fruit stands as it carves its way west to east from the highway to the beach. The road is closed to normal traffic a block from the beach, forcing all cars to turn north, except for taxis and buses, which can continue on down to the beachfront.

The streets to the north of Juárez are numbered evenly and go up as you move away from the center of town. For example, Second Street is 1 block north of Juárez, Fourth Street is 2 blocks north of Juárez, and 10th Street is 5 blocks north of Juárez. The streets to the south of Juárez are numbered with odd numbers and also go up as you move farther from town: First Street is 1 block south of Juárez, Third Street is 2 blocks south of Juárez, and Ninth Street is 5 blocks south of Juárez.

The beach is the zero point for the roads traveling north–south. The first block from the beach is First Avenue, though it starts only at 10th Street and heads north. The next road inland from First (and the first road inland when you're south of 10th Street) is Fifth Avenue, or Quinta Avenida (Quinta), which is the main pedestrian walkway through town. The 20-block portion of Quinta (from the town plaza to 40th Street, where it ends—for now) that is closed to vehicular traffic is by far the busiest tourist zone of Playa. Moving westward and farther from the beach, the roads go up in increments of five, so 10th Avenue is just west of Fifth, 15th Avenue is just west of 10th, and so on.

Most streets in Playa del Carmen are one-way, and not all of them are clearly marked. If you do head down the road the wrong way, expect to hear jeers and friendly hollers from the locals, who make a pastime of watching the tourists do silly things. Most of the traffic around town continues on at a fairly slow pace. The town is relatively small, and no one is in that much of a hurry. Local police direct traffic at the busiest intersections and are known to be quite polite to tourists. Though most do not speak English, they will try to help you if you need assistance or directions.

Driving beyond Playa del Carmen

As mentioned before, Highway 307 will take you almost anywhere in the Riviera Maya you want to go, from Cancún, through Playa del Carmen, and on down to Tulum. What used to be a narrow two-lane road encroached by jungle and seldom driven is now two lanes each way and, in some places, even three. The speed bump marking the Puerto Morelos turnoff is now a traffic light, and turning lanes have been added at the major intersections. At Xcaret and other key attractions, left turns are made by exiting to the right and then curving around perpendicular to the highway, allowing drivers to wait for a clear path while safely off the roadway. Of course this also means you have to cross all lanes of traffic to turn, rather than just waiting for a pause in the oncoming traffic, but it does serve to keep cars out of the center of the road, which can help keep things safe for passing traffic.

Drive slowly, even on back roads.

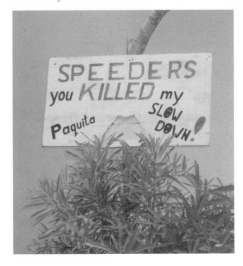

Construction seems to be ongoing, and in many parts there is a soft shoulder. Attempts are being made to grade the median and plant palm trees and flowering plants, which has been done close to

Cancún but is lagging behind in other areas. The highway is notorious for the many large trucks heading from Cancún to Chetumal and back. Drivers are encouraged to use extreme caution during heavy traffic as some others on the road do not drive as defensively as American drivers are typically taught. Though fender benders are a daily occurrence and urban legends of honeymooners crashing in their Jeeps can sound horrific, the road is usually traversed without incident. Seatbelts are required by law, and drinking and driving is just as illegal and ill-advised while on vacation as it is back home.

Federal police, infamously known as the *Federales,* patrol the highway and occasionally pull drivers over for speeding or other infractions. Fines can usually be paid at once and range from $10 to $100, depending on how good of a negotiator you are and whether you did anything to deserve being pulled over in the first place. Stories of police torture and abuse are way overexaggerated, and the vast majority of the time, drivers pulled over will be back on their way in a matter of minutes, with only a small fine assessed. Any hints of alcohol or drug use, though, may very well lead to seizure of your vehicle and a ride to the main police station downtown, where the fines and the hassle go up considerably, especially if any drugs (including marijuana) are found. Remember, the Mexican constitution declares that if accused of a crime, you will be considered guilty until proven innocent, which puts detainees in a very different position than those in the States. If you get into serious trouble, a U.S. consulate should be notified, but they will not necessarily be able to help, especially if you are legitimately accused of committing a crime.

Traveling through the Riviera Maya is supposed to be fun, and driving yourself can be a rewarding way to discover the area on your own timetable. So don't be afraid to pack up a cooler, bring some snacks, turn up the radio, and get exploring. Driving your own car lets you see and do many things that you just can't experience on public transportation. In remote stretches, you'll see iguanas, snakes, and even tarantulas (some so large you'll swear you can see their fur) crossing the street. Look closely and you will spot homemade signs placed to mark the trail leading to someone's home. Some use an old shirt tied to a tree, while others paint a family name on a tire and hang it from a branch or cut the bottom from a plastic jug and fit it over the top of a plant. You will see people walking or on horseback in the most remote areas where you would think that nothing is around, but the jungle just beyond the roadside treeline holds many secrets, and you're never as alone as you think you might be.

There are so many things to see that you could spend an entire day driving around, never traveling more than 50 miles away from downtown Playa, and see Mayan ruins, freshwater lagoons, deserted beaches, caves, hidden snorkeling spots, traditional cantinas, fresh seafood restaurants, and many other attractions.

Stopping for Gas

The federal government's oil refinery and gasoline distribution company, Petroleos Mexicanos, operates all of the country's gas stations under the name Pemex. Prices are heavily regulated, and the stations are dispersed throughout the country. The only areas where you really need to make sure you fill up before heading out are south of Tulum, where there is a long stretch without gas before you arrive at a gas station near the Mayan ruins of Kohunlich—if you take the highway or, in Punta Allen, if you take the beach road. It's best to fill up here if you're heading farther south, to the interior of Sian Ka'an or the towns near the Belizean border. Also, if you're heading west across the peninsula, past

Chichén Itzá and toward the Uxmal ruins, it's best to fill up whenever you come across a gas station since service stations in that part of the Yucatán are few and far between.

All stations are full service. It's a good idea to check which side your tank is on before pulling in, especially if the station is busy, or you're likely to lose your spot if you're forced to turn around so the hose can reach. You can pay with cash or credit card, though cash is recommended, especially if you're in a rush. Gas is priced by the liter and is generally a bit more expensive than it is in the States. Tips are not mandatory, but they are definitely appreciated. Just like in the States, most gas stations also have convenience stores. Unlike the States, though, you will need to repark your car away from the pumps after filling up, since there are fewer pumps at each station and yours will soon be needed by another driver.

CALLING HOME

Don't dial direct from your hotel room! That's the first lesson for any visitor to the Riviera Maya, as even a quick call home from your hotel can carry a charge of $25 or more, due to high connection fees and even higher per-minute tolls. Most hotels offer local calls for around $1 each, about the same as in the States, but long-distance calls—especially inter-national—are a completely different story. Your best option is to buy a prepaid phone card and make all calls with it. Even then, it's best to make the calls from a public phone to ensure you won't be billed a connection fee, which is common even for "toll-free" calls. The cards, called LADA cards, or *tarjetas LADA*, are available at nearly every pharmacy, gro-cery store, and convenience store in town and can be purchased in denominations ranging from $2 to $20. A call to the United States or Canada is charged at 50 cents a minute. Since many U.S.-based phone services offer inexpensive calling to Mexico, it can work out great to call home and then schedule a time for your party to call you back at the hotel, since you won't be charged to receive a call in your room.

Many shops in Playa offer inexpensive local and long-distance calling stations, where the attendant will dial your number and then assign you to a semiprivate booth to take your call. Calls are charged by the minute, and you will pay the attendant at the completion of the call. Rates are comparable to using the LADA card. One such place is Phone Home (Quinta between 10th and 12th Streets, Playa del Carmen), which offers private booths for long-distance phone calls. They charge 40 cents a minute to the United States or Canada.

If you have some extra pesos jingling in your pockets, you can also use a public phone on the street or in the hotel lobby to place a direct call home. Rates vary depending on the phone owner, but they are generally substantially less expensive than direct-dialed calls from your hotel room. Don't be fooled by the stickers placed on many public phones or printed on flyers advertising discounted credit card calls to the United States. Though they do have English-speaking operators and will effectively place your calls, they often charge exorbitant rates. The same goes for services offering to assist in placing collect or third-party calls.

Mobile phones are booming in popular-ity in Mexico, and most U.S.-based carriers offer service in the Riviera Maya through

Numbers Game	
Country code for the United States:	01
Country code for Mexico:	52
Area code for Cancún:	998
Area code for Playa del Carmen:	987
Prefix for dialing Mexican mobile phones:	044

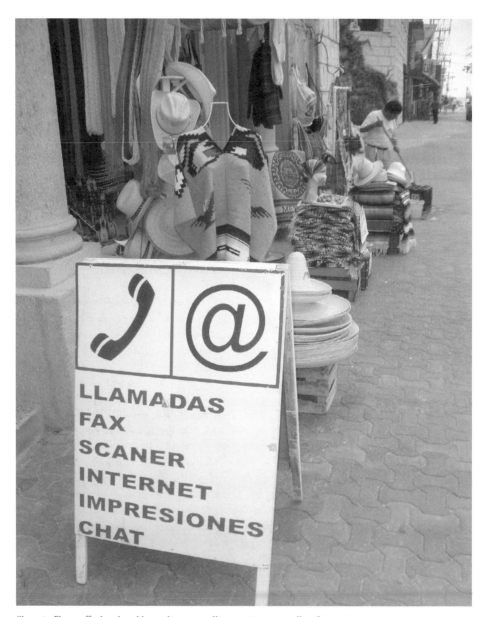

Shops in Playa offer local and long-distance calling stations, as well as Internet access.

roaming contracts with the local providers. Rates vary according to your calling plan and aren't always cheap, but the convenience factor of making and receiving calls with your own phone can count for a lot. Callers from back home will simply call your number like they normally do, and it will ring wherever you are. Call your provider before starting your trip to make sure your international calling is turned on and ask about the rate plans available.

Though service is not available throughout the region, it is more and more common to have a sufficient signal. You'll know you're in a coverage area when the name of the local provider shows up on the display of your phone.

If you're making an in-country call to a Mexico-based mobile phone, you will need to add 044 before the area code. This is because in Mexico, the caller—not the one receiving the call—pays for the cost of the call. This is the deft strategy that the Mexican cellular companies have used to help keep costs down for local users.

The other option, albeit the most expensive, is to rent or purchase a satellite phone, which will work in almost any spot on the globe and ensure that you're never out of touch.

INTERNET ACCESS

Finding Internet access in downtown Playa del Carmen is as easy as looking down the road. Nearly every block has at least one Internet café, or "cyber" as they're called here. Most are small affairs, with four to six computers, a couple of phone booths, and a young attendant playing PC games in between customers. Prices range from $1 to $5 per hour, depending on location and the number of tourists who frequent it. Some of the cybers along Quinta are located in full-service restaurants and allow the user to sip a beer or even enjoy an entire meal while checking the web or sending e-mail. Farther from the beach, the prices drop and the number of locals increases. It's not uncommon to find most stations occupied by friends of the attendant surfing for free, though they willingly relinquish their seats to paying customers.

Most locations have acceptably fast access, though there are a few with slow or sporadic connections. You may have to try a couple of shops before settling on one that works for you. Most cybers also have an extra line available for customers who bring their laptops and just need a connection. Sometimes, a bit of configuration is required on your computer to adapt the network settings. If you'd rather not mess with that, try the next spot. The fee is the same, whether you use their computer or your own. Some locations use an installed program to record your usage times and fees, while others have numbers taped to the sides of the computer and the attendant keeps track with a watch and a pad of paper. Either way, it's best to monitor your own time to ensure you are not overcharged.

The vast majority of Internet cafés you come across will have the software you need pre-installed, including popular word processing and spreadsheet programs. You will also find AIM, MSN Messenger, and Yahoo Messenger already there. If you need a freeware program that's not installed, most computers have administrative access, so you can usually download it and install it without missing a beat.

Always remember to log out of any instant messenger programs and to erase any passwords that may have been saved. It's best to clear your Internet cache and also the cookies in case the computer is set to store your information for the next user. It's not a bad idea to change your passwords when you return home, just to make sure any data you have unintentionally left behind doesn't come back to haunt you.

The following are a few Internet cafés in downtown Playa del Carmen:

The Point (10th Avenue between Second and Fourth Streets). This is an Internet café with an attitude—but a good one. It's more like a reggae lounge, with 10 computer stations, carpeted floor (the only one around), cold air-conditioning, free coffee, scanning/printing

Surf Before You Snorkel

Try these free online resources for more information about the Riviera Maya:

LocoGringo.com. This superb source for detailed aerial photos, virtual tours, and high-quality photos and descriptions of hotels, attractions, and beaches covers Playa del Carmen, the Riviera Maya, and surrounding areas. You can make reservations for hotels, condos, and villas as well as participate in its active message boards.

MayanHoliday.com. A regularly updated blog covering Playa del Carmen and the Riviera Maya.

RivieraMaya.com. The Riviera Maya tourism board's site has hotel and restaurant lists, plus attractions, travel stats, and tour info. Hotel reservations can be made online or by phone in the United States at 1-877-7-GO-MAYA (877-746-6292).

Playa.info or PlayadelCarmenInfo.com. This site offers active message boards, detailed hotel reviews from recent travelers, a live webcam, and real estate information.

PlayaMayaNews.com. A community site for people living in or visiting Playa del Carmen, it provides local movie schedules, classified listings, human-interest stories, health advice, culture, and community action. It makes an entertaining and interesting read whether you're actively planning a trip or just learning more about the area.

PlayaManiac.com. Its message boards cover a wide variety of topics, including living in Playa, all-inclusive hotels, traveler meet-ups, real estate, classifieds, and destinations in and around the Riviera Maya. Browse through the information, or post your question and get responses from recent travelers and Playa regulars.

PlayadelCarmen.com. A commercial site devoted to area hotels, condos, photos, destination guides, and message boards.

TripAdvisor.com. This site has user reviews, candid photos, price comparisons, message boards, and reservations information for hotels throughout the Riviera Maya. The site is not specific to the region, so you will need to search to find your specific hotel.

Travel.State.Gov. The U.S. State Department provides a wealth of travel information covering documentation requirements, health, safety, and overseas services.

service, and long-distance phone booths. Music posters decorate the walls, and each computer and phone has its own name and theme—from Bono to Lenny, from Jimi to Frank, and from Bob to Jim. If you don't know who all these people are, you're still welcome to hire their service, but you'll appreciate it more if you do.

The Point (Quinta at 24th Street). This travel-themed Internet café has fast connections, a pleasant atmosphere, good air-conditioning, a scanner and a copier, private booths for long-distance calls, and free coffee.

24 Hour Internet (24th Street between Quinta and First Avenue). This aptly named Internet café offers all-day and all-night Internet access, color printing, scanning, copying, and long-distance phone calls. Free coffee and water are available, and there are also sodas and candy bars for sale.

ELECTRICITY

Electrical power is the same as it is in the States: 110 volts AC. The outlets are the same size, and most U.S. plugs will work without any problem. Some hotels do not offer polarized plugs (where one prong is slightly larger than the other), so if your important electronic gadget has a polarized plug, you may want to pick up an adapter at your local hardware or discount store. Adaptors are very inexpensive and could save the day if you have the misfortune of having an uncooperative outlet at your hotel.

OFFICIAL TOURISM OFFICE

The state-run tourism office can provide free area maps, promotional information, tour recommendations, safety tips, and lists of approved vendors at its in downtown Playa del Carmen on Avenue Juárez at 15th Avenue.

POST OFFICE

The main post office (984-873-0300), on Avenue Juárez between 15th and 20th Avenues, is open 8–5 Monday through Friday and 9–noon Saturday. Postcards are cheap and always appreciated by the folks you left back home. It can take weeks for mail to arrive, however, so don't mail home instructions on how you're to be picked up at the airport in a few days, or you will end up waiting on the curb for a ride that never shows. Stamps can be purchased at many convenience stores or hotel gift shops.

To send anything quickly or of any value, it is recommended that you use a private courier, as the Mexican postal service is not generally recognized as being efficient or reliable. Estafeta is Mexico's largest document and package delivery company. A FedEx-sized package sent two-day air express to anywhere in Mexico is only $10. Overnight service within the country is $18. Deliveries to the U.S. start at $30. Estafeta is located on Fourth Street between 30th and 35th Avenues, across from the Social Security Hospital. It is open Monday through Friday from 8–5. There's also a shipping agent located on 12th Street between 10th and 15th Avenues that can handle orders for FedEx, DHL, and UPS, with guaranteed international delivery.

NEWSPAPERS

The *Miami Herald* prints a Cancún edition, which features local news, weather, and tourism features in English. It is distributed free of charge and is available in the lobby of the major hotels and at some coffee shops downtown. The *New York Times* and *USA Today* are available at the larger convenience stores and hotel tobacco shops. Many smaller hotels have subscriptions to the TimesFax news service, which allows them to print mini-versions of the *New York Times* on a computer printer and distribute them to their guests.

MEDICAL CARE

The vast majority of visitors to Playa del Carmen and the Riviera Maya never need to think about medical care during their visit, but accidents do happen—even while on vacation—so it's good to know a little about the area's medical services before heading out on your trip.

Medical facilities in Cancún, Cozumel, Isla Mujeres, and Playa del Carmen are modern and more than sufficient for most moderate emergencies and standard medical care. Most are operated by the Red Cross, or *La Cruz Roja*, and truly are first-class facilities, by any standard. Many of the doctors are U.S. trained and can provide care equivalent to what can be received at an average facility of a similar size in the United States or other First World countries. The emergency medical responders are especially well trained and equipped, and they are well versed on procedures related to scuba-diving accidents, falls, car wrecks, animal bites, broken bones, and other common incidents. There are also many private clinics with English-speaking doctors who can treat nonemergency cases and make house calls to hotels or other locations.

The major facilities have 24-hour pharmacies supplying all necessary medications. There are also numerous pharmacies in town where all manner of medicines can be purchased, with—and frequently without—a prescription. Cancún, Cozumel, and Playa del Carmen each have a hyperbaric chamber, used to treat decompression sickness, or "the bends," which can happen while scuba diving. Most dive operators charge a mandatory $1 chamber insurance fee for each dive trip, which helps keep the chambers operating and provides for free care for affected divers. Divers who want to be extra cautious should investigate the Divers Alert Network (DAN) (www.diversalertnetwork.com) before their visit. For a reasonable yearly fee, DAN provides information about diving safety and also offers air-evacuation insurance should a diver need to be airlifted back home for treatment of a diving-related injury.

The farther you travel from the main cities, the fewer medical facilities you will find available. In Akumal, Puerto Aventuras, and Tulum there are small clinics, though emergency services lag behind those of the larger cities in terms of quality and reliability. If heading way south, toward Kohunlich or Sian Ka'an, travelers should not expect to depend on the availability of nearby medical assistance and may need to go to the nearest city, such as Chetumal, for medical care.

Common sense and common precautions will prevent most accidents, and taking good care of yourself, including drinking plenty of water and moderating your alcohol intake, will reduce your chances of getting sick. After all, even though the medical facilities are generally quite good, they're not as nice as the beach.

LAUNDRY

There are laundry facilities in Playa every few blocks anywhere other than Quinta, since the rent is too high. Many offer fluff-and-fold services, button sewing, and related services. Chic Lavandaria on Avenue Constituyentes between 10th and 15th Streets even offers free delivery.

MONEY

The Riviera Maya plays prominently in the history of money in our civilization. One of the first forms of payment in the New World was the cocoa bean, which the Mayans crafted into a sweet drinkable beverage they called *xocoatl*, which is the origin of the word *chocolate*. They would harvest the cocoa from trees and then transport it by canoe to other villages, trading it for goods not native to the Yucatán. They also bartered for supplies and trinkets with each other and with members of neighboring tribes, using shells, baskets, cotton, and corn as items of trade.

One of the key times that money and trade were important was prior to a wedding ceremony, when tradition called for the family of the groom to bestow gifts upon the parents of the bride. A common form of payment, and a highly prized one, was a live chicken. Depending on the status of the couple, the amount could be as high as a dozen birds. The Mayan word for *chicken* is one that Americans use on a daily basis, probably without ever even knowing it. These feathered fowl were known to the Mayans as *k'aash*, and the word has stuck with us in its current American form: *cash*. Apparently, in the days of the Mayans, credit was not an option.

Society has changed dramatically since then, and the official currency of Mexico, even for the remaining Mayan population, is now the peso. The value fluctuates daily against the U.S. dollar, though it is much more stable than it used to be. Visitors will rarely notice any official change in the

Banks & ATMs in Playa del Carmen:

Banamex (984-873-2947), 10th Avenue at 12th Street

Bancomer (984-873-0402), Avenue Juárez at 25th Street

HSBC (984-873-0404), Avenue Juárez at 10th Street

Banco Serfin (984-873-2900), Plaza Playacar

Cajero Automatico, Quinta at 16th Street

Money Exchange Locations in Playa del Carmen:

Quinta between Second and Fourth Streets

Quinta between 12th and 14th Streets

Quinta between 22nd and 24th Streets

Eighth Street between Quinta and 10th Avenue

10th Street between Quinta and the beach

Plaza Marina, at the ferry dock, behind Señor Frog's

value during their trip. The symbol for pesos is the dollar sign ($)—the same as the U.S. dollar—which can cause a bit of confusion since some businesses list prices in dollars and others list prices in pesos. This book will use the dollar sign ($) to signify U.S. dollars and the word *pesos* to refer to the Mexican peso. American dollars are almost universally accepted in the Riviera Maya, though change will almost always be given in pesos. American coins are not accepted.

There are many banks in downtown Playa del Carmen, which are noticeable by the presence of an armed guard, dressed in Army green and casually holding an automatic rifle at his side. Banks are open 9–4 daily, and it's perfectly acceptable to enter wearing short pants, a T-shirt, and beach sandals. Banks offer money exchange at the official bank rate and without commission, though lines can be long since you sometimes have to wait in the same line as the locals doing their everyday banking or paying bills.

Many hotels offer money exchange at the front desk, and while the exchange rates are not always the best, the convenience can frequently make up for it. Most visitors opt to change money at one of the many public exchange houses, or *casas de cambio*, that can be found every few blocks in the tourist-laden downtown area. These tiny offices are usually painted white and feature the exchange rate on red or black letters hanging from the wall. Different exchange houses offer slightly different exchange rates (up to 5 percent variations are common), so it may help to shop around if you're changing large quantities. Restaurants, bars, and shops can also set their own exchange rate for purchases made in dollars, and some even lure customers in with the promise of a favorable exchange. When in doubt, if you're paying in dollars, always ask in advance to ensure a reasonable exchange rate. Some out-of-the-way locations have been known to offer an exchange rate of up to 15 percent less than the official bank rate, though this is not common.

At any money exchange location, the "buy" price is the rate that they will pay in pesos for your dollars. The "sell" price is the rate they will exchange your pesos back in, should you change too much money. As you'll notice, there is about a 10 percent difference, which should encourage you to exchange only as much money as you will need so you don't have many pesos left over when your visit ends. You can change as little as $5 at a time, so it's always best to exchange too little than too much, since you can always go back for more. Just slide your dollars in the little window and the cashier will slide your pesos back out, along with a printed receipt showing the exchange rate and the number of pesos you should have. Always check the numbers and count your pesos in front of the clerk, and do not be shy about asking for your due if the amounts don't add up.

The *casas de cambio* at the airport, whether at your originating airport or at your arrival airport, will always charge a commission on money exchange transactions. What may look like a good exchange rate often is negated when the commission is factored in. Don't be lured by offers to charge pesos at an airport exchange house on a credit card, since the transaction is treated not as a purchase but as a cash advance, which will carry steep finance charges from your credit card company.

Traveler's checks are generally treated like cash, though smaller businesses do not like to accept them since it requires a trip to the bank to get their cash. Some exchange houses will give a slightly lower exchange rate for traveler's checks than cash, but banks will always give full value. If you are traveling with traveler's checks, remember to always keep the check numbers recorded somewhere separate from the checks themselves since you will need the numbers to make a claim if the checks are stolen or lost. Also remember to bring along a photo ID, which is required when countersigning your check to validate it.

Credit cards can be a great solution for making purchases since the charge will post in pesos and then will be converted to dollars at the official exchange rate, which is frequently higher than the shop or restaurant normally gives on cash purchases. Most tourist-oriented businesses will accept credit cards, though it is not safe to assume that they will. For the establishments listed in this book, we mention credit cards only if they're not accepted. Otherwise, you can assume that they are. If you do not have the cash to cover a purchase, always ask to make sure your credit card will be accepted, or you could end up *lavando los platos* (washing the dishes).

ATM machines (*cajeros automático*) can be found at the entrance to nearly every bank and also in some stand-alone locations in Playa del Carmen. After hours, some machines are secured within locking glass entrances and can be accessed only by swiping your card through the locking mechanism. Amazingly, most working ATM cards will open the lock, allowing access to the machine. Most ATMs allow the user to select dollars or pesos, which will be exchanged at the official bank rate. Keep in mind, your home bank will most likely charge you a service fee for using your card at a nonaffiliated bank, so you may consider taking out as much as you need all at once rather than making multiple small withdrawals.

Outside of Cancún or Playa, ATM access is somewhat scarce. Some of the larger hotels have machines available, though it's advisable to get as much cash as you need before leaving town, because the nearest machine may be miles away.

If you're short on cash and don't have an ATM card, there's still hope. A Western Union office is located at Avenue Juárez and 15th Avenue in downtown Playa del Carmen. A passport of government-issued ID is required to collect any wired funds.

It is considered rude in Mexico for a waiter to bring your bill before you request it. This is definitely true in Playa, where lingering over meals is the norm and it's not rare to pass two to three hours savoring dinner, drinks, dessert, and post-meal conversation with friends. To get the bill, ask for *la cuenta* or just gesture to your waiter with a scribbling motion in the air. Tax is frequently factored in to the cost of meals, but gratuity is extra, unless your tab specifically lists *servicio* after the tax.

Tipping is expected for waiters and is appreciated by just about everyone else. Ten to 15 percent is sufficient at restaurants, and $1 for each round of drinks is a nice gesture at a bar. Massage therapists, tour guides, dive guides, and others providing extended service should be tipped around $10, depending on the nature of their service, as gratuities often make up a large percentage of their compensation. Bellhops get 50 cents to $1 per bag, room attendants get $1 a day, and grocery baggers, rest room attendants, and other personal-service providers should be tipped at your discretion. Taxis do not require tips for standard service, particularly local fares. Extraordinary service, though, such as assisting with bags, making multiple stops, providing valuable recommendations, singing mariachi songs, or teaching you naughty phrases in Spanish, does warrant a bit of a gratuity.

Fun for Kids

You don't have to leave the kids at home to have a fun vacation in the Riviera Maya. Many resorts have special facilities for kids, including playgrounds, kid-friendly meals, activities programs, and complimentary child care. In-room babysitting can be arranged through hotel concierges, who maintain a list of recommended caretakers. Smaller hotels can often arrange for a housekeeper to look after the kids while the parents enjoy a tour or day trip. At the beach, kids enjoy collecting shells, watching the pelicans dive for fish, and building sand castles. In most areas there is little wave action, so introducing kids to the ocean is a breeze. In 2005 a playground was added to the town square in Playa del Carmen, complete with a sandy play area, jungle gym, monkey bars, slides, and a great ocean view.

WHAT TO BRING

The Mayan Riviera is not considered a remote location. You're never more than 30 to 45 minutes from a grocery store, pharmacy, clothing boutique, electronics store, hair salon, or even hardware store. Contrary to what you may have heard or read before, all standard batteries are easy to find, film is not exorbitantly priced, and mosquito repellent can be purchased almost anywhere.

Packing for a trip to Playa and environs is all about comfort and bringing what you want to have with you to make you more content and your trip more enjoyable. Unless you're planning on a serious camping trip to Sian Ka'an or a long-distance jungle hike, preparing

Sample Packing List for a Five-Night Trip (Male):

• 5 pairs of underwear
• 5 pairs of socks
• 3 pairs of shorts
• 1 bathing suit
• 4 T-shirts
• 4 nice shirts for nightlife
• 1 pair of light slacks
• 1 pair of jeans
• Toothpaste and toothbrush
• Shaving supplies
• Antiperspirant/deodorant
• Baseball hat
• Sandals/water shoes
• Walking shoes/evening shoes
• Medicines, sunscreen
• Camera, film, batteries (or digital camera and charger)
• Book, magazines
• MP3 player and travel speakers
• Dive mask and snorkel
• Passport, driver's license, credit card, cash
• Backpack

Sample Packing List for a Five-Night Trip (Female):

• 5 pairs of underwear
• 5 pairs of socks
• 1 pair of shorts
• 2 pairs of capri pants
• 1 pair of jeans
• 3 tank tops
• 2 bathing suits
• 1 swimsuit cover-up
• 1 pair of sandals
• 1 pair of walking shoes
• 1 pair of evening shoes
• 1 resort-wear outfit
• Toothpaste and toothbrush
• Shaving supplies
• Antiperspirant/deodorant
• Shampoo, conditioner, facial soap
• Body lotion
• Sun hat
• Cosmetics, medicine
• Camera, film, batteries (or digital camera and charger)
• MP3 player and headphones
• Book, magazines
• Travel journal
• Dive mask and snorkel
• Passport, driver's license, credit card, cash
• Beach bag

for your trip should be thought of not as survival packing but more in the way of luxury packing. What you need to bring is largely determined by where you are staying and what you plan on doing.

For instance, if you're staying at a five-star all-inclusive hotel, you will need to bring resort wear for your evening meals. If you're going to be horseback riding, you should bring jeans and closed-toe shoes. If you're going to play tennis or golf, make sure to bring the proper attire and footwear. If you plan on scuba diving, you'll want to bring whatever gear you don't want to rent.

All visitors will want to bring a pair of beach sandals, walking shoes, walking shorts, lightweight breathable clothing, plenty of underwear and socks, a bathing suit, toiletries, medicines, hat or sun visor, sunglasses, electronic gadgets, and proof of citizenship. Almost all hotels offer soap, and most come standard with shampoo, conditioner, and even body lotion. If you have sensitive skin or prefer to use your usual brand, bring it along. Most beachfront hotels have beach towels available, so there is usually no need to bring your own unless you are staying at a budget hotel, and even then you can usually sneak your bath towel from your room and use it at the beach, unless you're really looking to spread out on the beach and not get sandy. If you plan on sending postcards, don't forget to bring your addresses.

STAYING SAFE

Playa del Carmen is no longer a sleepy fishing village where everybody knows each other and nobody locks their doors. It is still a happy little town, though, where a lot of people know each other and not everyone locks their doors. Petty theft is the main problem, and tourists are advised to watch their belongings, lock their hotel rooms, and not leave valuables unattended on the beach or elsewhere.

For the most part, Playa is quite safe. It is best to not be on remote parts of the beach late at night, as incidents have been reported. Leave your jewels at home and, like anywhere else, don't flash large amounts of cash or be too showy with expensive equipment or electronic gadgets. Use the hotel safe whenever possible and do not leave valuables in plain view in your hotel room or rental car. Report suspicious activity at your hotel to the front desk and be alert of your surroundings. Men should carry their wallets in their front pockets on crowded streets, and women should ensure their bags are fully closed and not swinging freely.

The Tourist Police are happy to help.

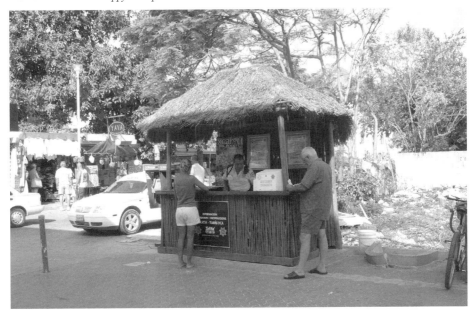

There have been reports of drug running, gang activity, and associated crime and violence in the area. If you go looking for trouble, you'll have a better chance of finding it. Visitors are strongly advised to keep their noses clean and to stay well away from any obvious trouble or precarious situations. Do not travel into the destitute neighborhoods, especially at night. Do not associate with questionable individuals, and stay away from problem areas.

The Tourist Police hut, at Quinta at 10th Street, is manned nearly 24 hours a day and is the base for Playa's tourist police force. Most officers are bilingual and can help with any problems you have. They patrol the beach and the main roads in town and are well respected by the locals.

WEATHER

Month	High Temp.	Low Temp.	Ocean Temp.	Rainfall
January	80°F	66°F	75°F	3.75 inches
February	81°F	67°F	76°F	2.25 inches
March	83°F	70°F	77°F	1.75 inches
April	84°F	72°F	78°F	1.75 inches
May	87°F	76°F	80°F	4.75 inches
June	88°F	77°F	83°F	7.75 inches
July	89°F	77°F	85°F	4.25 inches
August	89°F	76°F	85°F	4.25 inches
September	88°F	75°F	84°F	9.00 inches
October	86°F	73°F	82°F	8.50 inches
November	83°F	71°F	81°F	3.75 inches
December	81°F	68°F	79°F	4.25 inches

Playa del Carmen lies just north of the tropics, which start at 20° north latitude. It's actual coordinates are 20°36'30" N, 87°04'30" W, making its official designation subtropical. Don't let that fool you, though—the weather is definitely what most would consider to be tropical. Hot sunny days, sporadic rain showers, high humidity, balmy evenings, and warm ocean breezes are the norm. Summertime highs sometimes reach 100°F with 90 percent humidity, while evenings in the low 60s are common during the winter months, especially when the north winds bring down the remnants of cold fronts across the Gulf of Mexico.

June, September, and October are the rainiest months, when it seems to shower almost every day. The monsoonlike rains can come down quite hard, though the showers usually come and go, rarely washing out a whole day of fun in the sun. On the contrary, the rains are welcomed, since they tend to drop the sometimes-stifling temperature a few degrees. Hurricane season is June through November and usually passes without incident, though it's always best to watch the forecast and change your plans accordingly, because being stuck in a foreign land during a serious storm is a scary thing. Most hotels track the weather and will advise guests several days in advance of an approaching storm.

The Cancún airport has had to shut down on several occasions due to high winds and driving rains, leaving tourists to settle in and batten down the hatches with the locals. As long as the storm isn't too serious, though, tourists and locals alike turn the storm-motivated camaraderie into a genuine hurricane party.

A storm brews over Playa.

Travel to the Riviera Maya is not as seasonal as in some resort destinations, since it attracts such a varied base of travelers. That said, hotel occupancy rates and prices do tend to fluctuate during the year. The year starts off in high season, which lasts from January to April, as Americans get tired of the cold weather back home and head south for a tropical vacation. Low season is May and June, when European travel is at a minimum and most Americans are enjoying comfortable warm weather at home. This is the least expensive time to travel and there are the most singles and student travelers at this time.

July and August are the months when many Americans take their summer vacations, diminishing room availability and driving up prices. A second low season starts in September and lasts through the middle of December. The most expensive time of year is the winter holiday season, starting in mid-December and lasting through the New Year holiday. Prices at hotels can fluctuate 50 percent or more, as high demand elevates prices during high season. In general, though, prices for meals, tours, and transportation do not fluctuate.

Whenever you go, you'll notice that temperatures on the beachfront are a few degrees cooler than they are a couple of miles inland. If you have a trip planned to the interior for horseback riding, hiking, jungle exploring, or visiting the ruins, you'll feel noticeably hotter than you do at your beachside hotel.

TIME ZONE

The Mayan Riviera and the entire state of Quintana Roo are on Mexico Central Time, which is GMT -6 hours. This is also the same as U.S. Central Time. The country of Mexico honors daylight savings time on the same schedule as the United States. It starts the first Sunday in April, when clocks are moved forward by one hour, and ends the last Sunday in October.

CancunValet: Helping You Use Your Vacation Time Wisely

If you're staying at a condo and would rather spend your time on the beach than in the grocery store, consider using CancunValet to do your shopping for you. Through an online ordering process, select your groceries (including beer, liquor, and other miscellaneous goods) and have them delivered to you for a fee.

Visitors can also rent strollers, boogie boards, coolers, VCRs, DVD players, wheelchairs, high-chairs, and cribs. In addition, the company rents mobile phones. Numbers can be assigned before your trip, so you can give your number to your contacts back home before you leave.

Log on to www.cancunvalet.com for more information and online transactions. Daily minimums and delivery fees apply.

EMERGENCY NUMBERS

Police, fire, or ambulance: 066 (free call from any phone)
Red Cross: 984-873-1233 or 065
Cancún Hyperbaric Chamber: 998-884-1202
Playa del Carmen Hyperbaric Chamber: 984-873-1365
Playa del Carmen Fire Department: 984-879-3670
Medica de Carmen Hospital: 984-873-0885
American Hospital in Playa del Carmen: 984-884-6133
Ameri-Med Ambulance Service: 984-881-3400
Playa del Carmen Police: 984-873-4000
Highway Police: 998-884-1107

Other Helpful Numbers:

Directory Assistance: 020
Cancún Airport: 984-873-0804
Bus station: 984-873-0109
Cozumel Ferry Office: 984-803-5581

U.S. Consulates

Cancún (998-883-0272), Plaza Caracol Two, second level, No. 320–323, Boulevard Kukulkán, km 8.5, Zona Hotelera.

Cozumel (987-872-4574), Plaza Villa Mar en El Centro, Plaza Principal (Parque Juárez between Rafael Melgar and Fifth Avenue), second floor, Locales #8 and 9.

Medical problems require immediate attention, whether you're on vacation or not. If trouble strikes when you're in Playa del Carmen, visitors can call on Emergencias Medicas del Caribe for 24-hour emergency medical care, ambulance service, outcalls, and clinic care. The company provides free care in most situations, though there are fees for seeing a specialist. The hotline number is 984-879-4745. The clinic is located next to Highway 307 on Constituyentes Avenue at 45th Street.

Another ambulance service, Akumal Medical Service, promises 24-hour emergency response to hotels, villas, and condos throughout the Riviera Maya, along with care provided by English-speaking Dr. Nestor Mendoza Gutierrez. The urgent care number is 044-984-806-4616. The clinic is located in Akumal.

Distance Chart
(NOTE: All distances are expressed in miles.)

	Cancún	Puerto Juárez	Punta Sam	Puerto Morelos	Playa del Carmen	Xcaret	Puerto Aventuras	Akumal	Xel-ha	Tulum	Cobá	Chetumal	Chichén Itzá	Mérida	Uxmal	Isla Mujeres	Cozumel
Cancún	0	3	7	22	42	46	54	66	76	82	108	239	111	178	28	3	45
Puerto Juárez	3	0	4	26	46	49	58	69	79	85	111	242	114	181	231	3	48
Punta Sam	7	4	0	30	50	54	62	73	84	89	116	246	119	186	236	3	53
Puerto Morelos	22	26	30	0	20	24	32	43	54	59	86	216	114	181	231	29	19
Playa del Carmen	42	46	50	20	0	4	12	23	34	39	66	196	134	201	251	49	11
Xcaret	46	49	54	24	4	0	8	19	30	36	62	193	138	204	267	53	15
Paamul	51	54	59	29	9	6	6	14	25	31	58	188	143	209	259	58	20
Puerto Aventuras	54	58	62	32	12	9	0	11	22	28	55	184	146	213	263	61	23
Kantenah	60	63	68	38	18	14	6	6	16	22	49	179	151	218	268	66	29
Yalku	61	64	69	39	19	16	7	4	15	21	48	178	153	219	269	68	30
Akumal	66	69	73	43	23	20	11	0	11	16	44	173	157	224	274	72	34
Chemuyil	68	71	76	46	26	23	14	3	8	14	41	171	159	226	276	74	37
Xcacel	74	78	82	52	32	29	20	9	2	8	35	164	166	233	283	81	43
Xel-Ha	76	79	84	54	34	31	22	11	0	6	33	163	168	234	284	83	45
Tulum	82	85	89	59	39	36	28	16	6	0	28	157	173	240	290	88	51
Cobá	108	111	116	86	66	63	54	43	32	26	0	129	199	266	316	114	77
Chichén Itzá	111	114	119	114	134	138	165	176	187	193	219	353	0	67	117	118	156
Mérida	196	199	203	205	218	222	232	243	254	259	286	419	67	0	50	184	223
Uxmal	246	249	253	254	268	272	282	293	304	309	336	469	117	50	0	234	273
Isla Mujeres	3	3	3	26	46	49	58	69	79	85	138	242	114	181	231	0	36
Contoy	22	20	15	44	64	68	76	88	98	104	156	261	133	200	250	19	55
Holbox	41	39	34	63	83	86	95	106	117	123	175	279	152	219	269	38	74
Cozumel	45	48	53	19	11	14	23	34	45	51	77	145	156	223	273	36	0

LANGUAGE

Spanish is the official language of Mexico and is the primary language spoken in the Riviera Maya. Playa del Carmen has developed into a very international city, though, and it's quite common to hear French, Italian, German, and other languages spoken on the street, in the restaurants, and on the beach. People from all over the world have fallen in love with Playa and have chosen to make it their home. Many of the best restaurants are owned and operated by foreigners, who have brought their cuisine with them. During your visit, you'll have the opportunity to meet and make friends with people from all over, which is one of the things that makes Playa so great.

Many natives, particularly those originally from the Yucatán or Quintana Roo, still speak the ancient language of the Mayans, though most locals in the area are recent transplants from elsewhere in the Republic, with many coming from Mexico City, Veracruz, Guadalajara, and other cities where Mayan is not spoken. English is taught in schools, and most tourism employees have at least a rudimentary ability to speak it. The larger hotels offer English classes to all employees, who at least learn the basics. Don't expect your average cab driver, hotel maid, or police officer to be fluent, though, so if you have something important to convey and you are not proficient in Spanish, you may need to enlist the help of a translator. Remember that you're in their country, so the onus is really on you to find a way to effectively communicate.

If you're in town for a week or more, you may want to take some Spanish lessons. International House (984-803-3388; www.ihrivieramaya.com; 14th Street between Quinta and 10th Avenue, Playa del Carmen) is primarily an English school for locals, but Spanish classes are also offered. Playalingua (984-873-3876; www.playalingua.com; 20th Street between Quinta and 10th Avenue, Playa del Carmen) is a well-respected local school offering crash courses in Spanish, cultural immersion opportunities, customized learning programs, scuba certification, home stays, and comfortable and affordable lodging on-site at its well-maintained inn with pool, courtyard, hammocks, art room, library, cafeteria, and Internet station. Weeklong courses run about $250. At Solexico Spanish School (984-873-0755 or 1-877-266-8988 [U.S.]; www.solexico.com; 6th Street between 35th and 40th Avenues, Playa del Carmen), as its slogan states, you have the chance to "learn Spanish in paradise." Founded in 1997, this language school offers all levels of instruction, with a maximum of five students per instructor.

As a sign on the wall of the Señor Frog's bar says, WE DON'T SPEAK ENGLISH, BUT WE PROMISE NOT TO LAUGH AT YOUR SPANISH. Not only is learning a bit of the local language a good way to win the favor of the locals you meet, but it can also be a lot of fun. You'll be amazed at how friendly the locals are, especially if you're trying to speak to them in their own language.

In Playa, Americans are usually referred to as "gringos." Though it may sound a bit harsh to some Americans' ears, and in some Latin American countries it does have a negative connotation, it is not at all meant as a derogatory in Mexico, so don't take offense. To the Mexicans, using the word *Americanos* is confusing and a bit offensive, since all residents of North, Central, and South America could be considered "Americans." Also, since the full name of the republic of Mexico is Los Estados Unidos de Mexico, or the United States of Mexico, it's also not quite adequate to use the textbook translation of *estadounidiense*, which is essentially "United Statesian," for citizens of the USA. Americans are sometimes referred to as *norteamericanos*, which means "North Americans," but that's not quite

Words and Phrases

ENGLISH	SPANISH
Another one	Otra
ATM	Cajero automático
Bathroom	Baño
Beach	Playa
Beef	Carne de rés
Beer	Cerveza
Big	Grande
Boat	Lancha
Bottled water	Agua en botella
Breakfast	Desayuno
Bus	Autobús
Car rental	Renta de autos
Check/bill	La cuenta
Chicken	Pollo
Coffee with milk	Café con leche
Dinner	Cena
Downtown	El centro
Drunk	Borracho
Eat	Comer
Fishing	La pesca
Goodbye	Adiós, hasta luego
Good morning	Buenos días
Good night	Buenas noches
Happy	Felíz
Hello	Hola
How much	Cuánto
Ice	Hielo
I want	Yo deseo
Lime	Limón
Lobster	Langosta

ENGLISH	SPANISH
Luggage	Equipaje
Lunch	Comida
Money	Dinero
Money exchange	Cámbio de dinero
More	Más
My name is	Me llamo
Nice to meet you	Mucho gusto
Orange juice	Jugo de naranja
Please	Por favór
Post office	El correo
Rain	Llúvia
Scuba diving	Buceo
Shrimp	Camarón
Shuttle bus	Colectivo
Sick	Enfermo
Silly tourist	Turista loca
Small	Pequeña
Sunscreen	Bronceadora
Swim	Nadar
Swimsuit	Traje de baño
Tax	Impuestos
Thank you	Graciás
Tip	Propina
Towel	Toalla
Waiter	Mesero
Walk	Caminar
Why	Porqué
You're welcome	De nada

TRY A LITTLE MAYAN

Hello, what's up?	Ba'ax ka wa'alik?
What's going on?	Bix a bel?
I'm fine.	Ma'alob.
See you later.	Taak tu lakin.
I'm just looking.	Chen tin wilik.
How much is it?	Bahúux leti'?
Tastes good.	Ki'.

Hot pepper	Lik
Juice	K'aab
Where	Tu'ux
Plaza	K'íiwik
Thank you	Dios bo'otik
You're welcome	Mixba'al

accurate either since it fails to distinguish between the United States and Canada, and the latter's citizens are known simply as *canadienses*. So, embrace your inner "gringo" and don't consider it a negative label.

In this book, the word *American* is used to refer to residents of the United States.

RELIGION

The primary religion in the Riviera Maya is Catholicism, though many of the ancient rituals of the Mayans are alive and well, oftentimes intermingling with traditional Catholic practices, giving the region a bit of its own religion and associated customs. Services are offered in various denominations, and the larger hotels maintain a list of current services and worship schedules. Tourists are welcome at all ceremonies, provided they dress and act appropriately and show respect for the local customs.

TRAVELING WITH PETS

Mexico allows the temporary importation of dogs and cats into the country, provided that the owner has an official letter from a veterinarian stating that the animal is healthy and current on all vaccinations. Most vets have a standard form that they can provide for such uses. Each airline has its own regulations, so it's best to check ahead if you are compelled to bring your pet on your trip.

Even if you figure out how to do it, taking your pet on a trip to the Riviera Maya may not be a great idea, anyway. Few hotels are equipped to accommodate travelers with pets, there are stray dogs that could carry disease, the weather can be quite hot, and unless you're able to babysit your pet at all times, you could run into trouble.

WEDDINGS IN PARADISE

If your idea of the perfect wedding is exchanging vows during a beachside ceremony with the sun going down, tropical flowers forming the aisle, a Mexican trio providing romantic music, and your guests dancing the salsa while they sip tequila, then getting married in the Mayan Riviera may be for you.

Though most weddings in the region are fairly casual outdoor affairs, the facilities and services exist to put on a spectacular formal ceremony for hundreds of guests, complete with all the traditions and comforts of a wedding in your own hometown. Both civil and religious ceremonies can be planned, depending on the preference of the bride and groom.

There are several independent wedding planners in town, in addition to the on-staff planners at the larger hotels.

Top Five Places to Pop the Question
- The cliffs at the Mayan ruins of Tulum
- On a private sailboat in Soliman Bay
- On the beach at Playa Maroma
- On top of the rocks at the Xaman Ha Beach in Playacar
- In the canals of the Sian Ka'an Biosphere

(List courtesy of Brenda Alfaro, owner of Ajua Weddings in the Riviera Maya. To plan your wedding, call 512-351-4557 in the United States or 984-803-1118 in Playa del Carmen. For more information log on to www.ajuaweddings.com.)

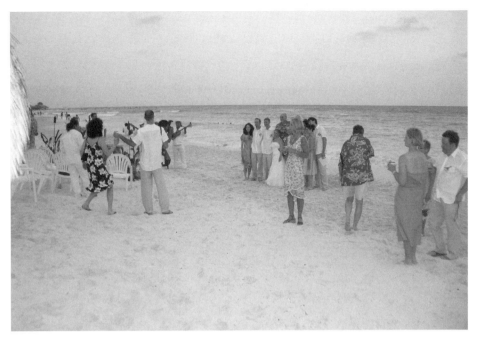

Las Palapas beach is an ideal spot for a casual wedding ceremony.

They can assist with all of the details, from cakes to flowers, from hotels to photography, and from rehearsals to receptions. Due to the legal requirements for foreigners getting married in Mexico, it is recommended that the couple arrive in Playa del Carmen at least three business days prior to their wedding day to file the necessary paperwork.

Legal Requirements for Getting Married in Mexico

At least two days before the ceremony, the couple must go to the local courthouse and present:

1. A valid tourist card (your temporary visa, issued at the airport).
2. A notarized copy of each person's birth certificate (must have a raised seal).
3. An official Spanish translation of the birth certificate (should be done locally by a court-approved translator).
4. A health certificate certifying blood type and AIDS/STD status. (The tests must be performed and certified by a court-approved facility.)

Top Five Places to Host a Wedding Reception or Other Special Event

Ajua Maya Lobster & Steak House, Playa del Carmen: Great food, playful waiters, live music (see chapter 2)

Hotel Básico, Playa del Carmen: Choose the patio seafood restaurant or the exclusive rooftop terrace (see chapter 2)

Kartabar, Playa del Carmen: A trendy spot for food and drinks in the middle of Playa's party zone (see chapter 2)

Maroma Resort & Spa, Punta Maroma: Hosts upscale events that your guests will be proud to attend (see chapter 1)

Rancho Punta Venado: A private beachfront ranch with all the necessary facilities (see chapter 4)

(continued on next page)

5. The proper court documents if either person is divorced or widowed.

6. Two witnesses, with valid passports showing name, age, address, and nationality.

7. Basic fees, which total about $475.

Beach Etiquette

All of the beaches in the Riviera Maya and throughout Mexico are federal property. No hotel can restrict access to the beach (from the water) or make up their own regulations about what you can and can't do. That being said, hotels do not have to allow you to cross their private property to get to the beach, and they can prevent access to the hotel from the beachfront. Many hotels set up a cordoned-off area or supply beach chairs or shade umbrellas for the exclusive use of their guests, and this is allowed by law.

Going nude or even topless is not permitted by Mexican decency laws. Topless sunbathing is tolerated by the local police in many areas, though, and many visitors to Playa del Carmen and the Riviera Maya—particularly Europeans—enjoy this freedom. To avoid any trouble with the law, it is best to restrict such European-style sunbathing to times and places when there are other people doing the same. In Playa del Carmen, for instance, the beaches adjacent to the ferry dock are popular with local families and children, and tourists should be respectful of the local customs and refrain from going topless in these areas. Farther south of the dock, closer to the Porto Real hotel, topless tanning becomes more of the norm, and visitors should not have any problem, except for an occasional passing gawker. To the north, most of the beaches are topless-friendly, though it is more uncommon in front of the more family-oriented hotels.

Elsewhere in the Mayan Riviera, the local attitude will dictate whether or not topless sunbathing is acceptable. On most beaches it is no problem, though in some areas it is frowned upon. The general rule is that the more locals or families, the less appropriate it is to go topless. Full nudity is generally frowned upon in all but a few specific areas, namely in front of the nude resorts, such as Hidden Beach, Caribbean Reef Club, and Playa Secreto.

The Mayan Riviera still has some relatively deserted beaches, accessible only by a four-wheel-drive vehicle and a bit of courage. Though these beaches do see occasional patrols from the Mexican Army or local police, discreet travelers can generally enjoy the freedom of being one with nature, however they choose to define it.

Yearly Events Calendar

January 1, New Year's Day.

January 6, Day of the Three Kings. A traditional day of Christmas gift giving, marking the Christian holiday of Epiphany, and the day when the three wise men arrived to give gifts to the baby Jesus.

January 10, Constitution Day for Quintana Roo. Banks are closed, but not much else happens.

January 11, anniversary of the reinstatement of Quintana Roo as a territory.

February 5, Constitution Day. A federal holiday, but there's not much social celebration.

February 14, Day of Lovers and Friends. Similar to Valentine's Day in the United States. Street vendors sell flowers and balloons; restaurants offer special romantic meals for couples.

February 24, Flag Day. A ceremony is held in Cancún and Cozumel at the site of their super-size flags.

February–March, Carnaval. Fluctuates with the Christian calendar. It's mostly celebrated in Cozumel, where schoolchildren dress in colorful costumes and parade through the streets. Other towns have live music, dances, and parades.

March 20 or 21 (depending on the year), vernal equinox. This marks the first official day of spring, when daylight and night are the same length. It's celebrated at Chichén Itzá, where the shadow of the serpent Kukulkán snakes down the side of the temple when the sunlight hits it just right.

March 21, birthday of former president and reform movement leader Benito Juárez. Juárez's name pops up frequently in the Riviera Maya, in street names, building names, and statues. The name of Playa's main highway connector road, for instance, is Benito Juárez Avenue. All banks and government offices are closed, but most tourist businesses stay open.

March or April, Easter and Holy Week. This is a very popular travel time for Mexican families since schoolchildren get two weeks' vacation. The holiday, which celebrates Christ's resurrection, is traditionally celebrated even more than Christmas.

April 21–May 2, Sol a Sol Regatta. Yearly sailboat race from St. Petersburg, Florida, to Isla Mujeres, north of Cancún. Live music, street festival, and celebrations.

May 1, Labor Day. National holiday.

May 5, Cinco de Mayo. Celebration of Mexican independence from France during the 1862 Battle of Puebla. Not as widely celebrated as the September 16 holiday marking independence from Spain.

May, Cancún Jazz Festival (date varies). Annual music festival sponsored by the Cancún Hotel Association.

June 1, Navy Day. Honors sailors lost at sea. Celebrations vary by municipality.

Last weekend of June, Playa del Carmen Sportfishing Tournament. This major fishing tournament helps to fill the hotels and restaurants, but the town doesn't get too involved.

July, Reggae Fest (date varies). Reggae bands from Mexico and around the world meet in Playa for a weeklong beach party, with concerts, food, and drink.

August, Dia de la Asuncion Festival, Oxkutzcab, Yucatán (date varies). Weeklong Assumption Day celebration near Loltún Cave, about three hours from Playa del Carmen.

Second weekend of August, Italian food festival (date varies). Restaurant specials and a yearly "largest pizza in the world" exhibition, where restaurants on Quinta pitch in to create (and then serve) a pizza that spans some 6 blocks through town.

August 17, Isla Mujeres Founding Day. Locals celebrate the date of their town's founding with parades, parties, live music, and street dancing. Underwater ceremony at Los Manchones Reef, where a large bronze cross is attached to the coral.

September 1, Presidential State of the Union Address. Mexicans love politics, and many stay riveted to their TVs to watch the speech. Bars and stores are not allowed to serve alcohol until it's over, but it usually turns into a party afterward.

September 16, national holiday marking Mexico's independence from Spain in 1821. Widely celebrated with parades, fireworks, and street parties. Much more important to locals than Cinco de Mayo.

September 22 or 23, autumnal equinox. Marks the first day of fall. Date varies according to the year.

September 27–October 13, Fiesta de Cristo de las Ampollas in Mérida. Religious festival honoring a sacred relic housed in the main cathedral.

October 12, Dia de la Raza, or Columbus Day. Celebrated throughout Mexico as a day to honor the many types of people that make up the country's population.

October, Isla Mujeres International Music Festival (date varies). Twelve-day event with music and dance performances featuring locals and invited guests from around the world.

October 31, All Souls' Day. Festivities inspired by the American Halloween celebration.

November, Latin Jazz Fest (date varies). This three-day festival brings together jazz musicians from around the world for concerts, dancing, and all-night parties.

November 1–2, Day of the Dead. Mexico's larger Halloween-time holiday to honor the dead. Friends and relatives gather at the graves of loved ones to celebrate their lives and honor their deaths.

Some Things Are Cheaper South of the Border

Though the price of meals, drinks, and many everyday purchases are relatively close to what you'll find back home, some services are still a bargain south of the border. Here's a few ideas of how you can save some money while you're in the Riviera Maya:

Get new eyeglasses. Bring a written prescription or even a pair of well-calibrated glasses, and the technicians at area eyewear shops can match your prescription in a wide variety of frames and lenses for a fraction of what you'd pay at home.

Manicures and pedicures. Want acrylic nails or just need a fresh mani/pedi? Prices are half or less of what you'd pay back home at salons catering to locals.

Watch repair. If you have an old watch that needs fixing and you've been putting it off, bring it on vacation. Drop it off one day and pick it up the next, and it'll be ticking like it was new. Watch shops in Playa are common a few blocks back from the beach, and the skilled craftsmen can fix almost anything.

Shoe repair. Shoes falling apart? Stop by a local shoe repair shop, and you can have new soles, heels, or other repairs done while you're away enjoying the ruins at Tulum. The price will be significantly less than back home, and the craftsmanship is top-rate.

November 20, Mexican Revolution Day. Marks the 1910 Revolution of Mexico. It's mostly a federal holiday, with little local observance.

December 8, Feast of the Immaculate Conception. Religious holiday celebrated through-out the Riviera Maya.

December 24, Nochebuena, or Christmas Eve. A religious and social holiday with parades and street parties.

December 25–January 2, Christmas week. Weeklong festival with candlelight proces-sions, Catholic mass, nightly parties, and religious ceremonies.

December 31, New Year's Eve. Many bars offer drink specials and all-you-can-eat spe-cials. At the stroke of midnight, it is good luck to eat 12 grapes, one for each month of the new year. Nightclubs stay open until dawn.

IMPORTANT TELEPHONE NUMBERS

Lost credit cards:
American Express, 1-800-333-3211 (U.S.)
MasterCard, 1-800-307-7309
Visa, 1-800-847-2911 (U.S.)

Long-distance service:
AT&T, 1-800-288-4472 (U.S.)
MCI, 1-800-021-8000 (U.S.)
Sprint, 1-800-877-8000 (U.S.)

Airlines:
Aerocaribe, 998-884-2000
Aerocozumel, 998-884-4000
Aeromexico, 1-800-021-4000 (U.S.) or 998-287-1860
Allegro (charter), 998-887-3459
American, 1-800-904-6000 (U.S.) or 998-886-0086
British Airways, 998-866-0554
Magnicharters (charter), 998-884-0600

THE RIVIERA MAYA—
NORTH OF PLAYA DEL CARMEN

The cities and towns of the Yucatán Peninsula and the Riviera Maya are covered in this book following a north-to-south orientation. Many of the locations are found along Highway 307, which parallels the coastline as it traverses the region from Cancún to the north down to Tulum and beyond in the south. Whenever possible, addresses are given using Highway 307 as a primary reference point, which is especially useful for self-guided travelers who choose to explore the region on their own.

The region north of Playa del Carmen is highlighted by the islands of Isla Holbox, Isla Contoy, and Isla Mujeres, plus the resort city of Cancún and the growing town of Puerto Morelos, which marks the official start of the Riviera Maya and is the midway point between Cancún and Playa del Carmen. Isla Cozumel is also included in this section, though the island's main town, San Miguel, is located due east of Playa del Carmen.

Most travelers to the Riviera Maya arrive via Cancún, which is one of the world's most popular mega-resorts. The small islands to the north of Cancún offer an abundance of relaxation, sunshine, and pristine beaches without the crowds so often associated with tropical vacations. Cozumel, meanwhile, is a scuba diver's dream, where shore dives, wall dives, and night dives can all be done in a single day.

Isla Holbox (105 miles northwest of Cancún)

Holbox, a long, narrow island 7 miles off the northern coast of the Yucatán, is one of the region's lesser known and underappreciated destinations. It has a year-round population of only 1,500, including descendants of the island's original eight families. It is said to have been settled by pirates who used it as a hideout and then ended up making friends with the local population and decided to stay.

The island is a come-as-you-are hideaway for ultracasual vacationing. If you consider the Riviera Maya to be the land of *mañana* (tomorrow), then Holbox would be sometime next week. It's doubtful that anyone has ever worn a tie here, unless it was some kind of joke. Most locals don't even wear shoes since the roads are powdery sand.

Since the island faces the Gulf of Mexico, it does not have the turquoise water that is common in the Riviera Maya. It is more of a greenish murky color, though there are some areas clear enough for snorkeling. Because of the currents and the island's location, thousands of shells wash on shore at each high tide. Many of them are complete, with no breaks, making them highly prized for gatherers.

The island has no cars, just electric carts, bikes, and mopeds. Locals operate the handful of restaurants, bars, and inns. Others go fishing and lobstering and sell their catches each day at the beach. There are no banks or ATMs, and most businesses accept only cash. From May to September, whale sharks pass by just offshore of the island, and tour boats can take you close enough to see them frolic in the water, or you can even don your mask and snorkel and swim right with them. Tourists while away the day on the beach or go windsurfing, sailing, fishing, snorkeling, and diving; several dive sites are reachable via a short boat ride. Local dive and fishing guides can be hired at the boat dock, and rental equipment is available.

Yalahao Lagoon, on the sheltered side of the island, features a mangrove swamp, flamingos, schools of dolphins, and a freshwater spring just up from the beach. It is a popular gathering spot for locals and tourists alike. In the times of the Mayans, it was believed to have curative properties, and natives would come from miles away to rejuvenate and refresh.

Holbox was hit particularly hard by Hurricane Wilma, which pounded the tiny island for hours when it slammed through the region in late 2005. The hotels, restaurants, and shops were flooded and the wind damage was extensive.

GETTING THERE

The island of Holbox is about a three-hour drive from Cancún and then 7 miles offshore. If you're lucky enough to fly there, the airstrip is just a few blocks from the town plaza. (For more information about plane tours to Holbox, log on to the web site for Aerosaab, which has an office in Playa del Carmen, at www.aerosaab.com.) Otherwise, you must first get to the village of Chiquila and then take a ferry to the island. Chiquila can be reached by bus or car from the Riviera Maya. If you're in your own car, a secured lot is available for only $2 a day.

To drive to Chiquila from Riviera Maya, go north on Highway 307, which parallels the coast. Once you pass through Cancún, take Highway 180 west to the town of El Ideal, and then start watching for signs to Holbox, which will lead you to an unnamed road going north to Chiquila.

If you're traveling there by bus, buses depart from the main Cancún bus terminal for Chiquila daily at 8 AM, 12:30 PM, and 1:30 PM. Once you've reached Chiquila, ferry service to Holbox is available at 6 AM, 8 AM, 10 AM, noon, 2 PM, 4 PM, 5 PM, and 7 PM. Return trips to Chiquila depart at 5 AM, 7 AM, 9 AM, 11 AM, 1 PM, 3 PM, 4 PM, and 6 PM. The trip takes 30 minutes and costs $4 per person. A water taxi is available also and costs $20 for up to seven passengers, departing whenever you want.

LODGING

Accommodations in Holbox are not luxurious. If you're looking for Italian sheets, cold air-conditioning, a Jacuzzi in the bathroom, and a terry cloth robe, you're best off just visiting the island as a day trip and then returning to Cancún or the Riviera Maya. But if you're comfortable sleeping on a hammock and taking quick showers before the water runs cold, you'll do just fine in Holbox.

The cheapest way to stay the night is to rent one of the Mayan-style beach *palapas* available on the island's north side. For around $10, you can get a place to put your things and a hammock to sleep in, either under the stars or in a small hut. Bathrooms are communal and not in the best of shape. Another low-budget solution is to rent a room in a local house. To go this route, just ask any cab driver or waiter or pretty much any local, and they are sure to know someone who has a room for rent. The cost for doing this ranges from $15 to $25 and includes a private room, shared bathroom, and usually a meal or two with the host family.

Amigo House

Two blocks from the beach, by the volleyball courts

Opened in 2004, this bright and cheery house features king or double beds, air-conditioning, ceiling fans, color TV with DVD player, and shared kitchen. Rates: $40 a night.

Esmeralda Hotel

Playa Blanca

It faces the beach, has air-conditioning, and averages $60–110 a night.

Hotelito Casa Las Tortugas
Playa Blanca

On the beach, it has air-conditioning and clean rooms. Rates: average $65 a night.

Hotel Puerto Holbox
On the beach, 3 blocks from town

This lodging has four simple rooms, hot water, air-conditioning, and a balcony. Rates: $80 a night.

Villa Flamingos
Playa Blanca

On the beach, Villa Flamingos is composed of 10 thatched-roof bungalows with ceiling fans, double beds, and private bathrooms. There is also a pool, kayaks, and bikes for guest use. Rates: averages $90–150.

Xaloc Resort
800-508-7923 or 1-800-728-9098 (U.S.)
Playa Norte

With 18 rustic rooms and a public living room, Xaloc also has air-conditioning and a pool. Rates: range from $80 for a standard room in low season up to $180 for an ocean-view room in high season; include breakfast

DINING

Edelyn
On the main tourist street

If you're looking for lobster, Edelyn is the top place in town. It is known for having the freshest and best, nearly year-round. Moderate.

Pinocchio's
On the main plaza

Popular with the island's European, Canadian, and American ex-pats, this restaurant serves grilled steaks and fresh seafood. Moderate.

Viva Zapata
On the main tourist street

This two-story open-air restaurant has a thatched roof and serves lobster, whole fish, shrimp, and traditional Mexican fare. Inexpensive.

Isla Contoy (25 miles north of Cancún, by boat)

This bird sanctuary and wildlife refuge is offshore from the northeastern tip of the Yucatán Peninsula. There are no bars or restaurants, no hotels, no roads, and very few facilities. A small group of Mexican marines runs a lighthouse, museum, lookout tower, and outpost, but there are no other full-time inhabitants. It is a popular nesting ground for sea turtles, and occasionally naturalists will camp out and care for them and watch for poachers, backed by the marines. There are a few rolling hills and a long deserted beach, ideal for strolling and snorkeling. Visitors can arrive by private boat or with a tour group.

Isla Mujeres (15 miles north of Cancún, by boat)

Once a sacred pilgrimage site for the Mayan natives, 5-mile-long Isla Mujeres is now a top spot for travelers seeking sunny days, pristine beaches, good food, tropical bars, and a casual lifestyle that you just can't get on the mainland. The island was named by Spanish conquistador Francisco Hernandez de Cordoba, who visited the island in 1517 to look for gold and other riches. Though he didn't find precious metals, he did discover a large

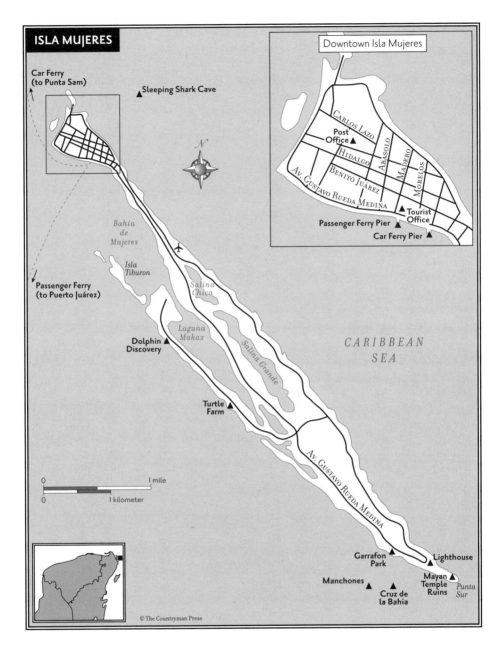

ISLA MUJERES

Car Ferry
(to Punta Sam)

Sleeping Shark Cave

Passenger Ferry
(to Puerto Juárez)

Bahía
de
Mujeres

Isla
Tiburon

Salina
Chica

Laguna
Makax

Dolphin
Discovery

Salina Grande

CARIBBEAN
SEA

Turtle
Farm

0   1 mile

0   1 kilometer

Av. Gustavo Rueda Medina

Garrafon
Park

Lighthouse

Manchones

Mayan
Temple
Ruins

Punta
Sur

Cruz de
la Bahia

© The Countryman Press

Downtown Isla Mujeres

Carlos Lazo

Post
Office

Hidalgo

Abasolo

Benito Juárez

Madero

Morelos

Av. Gustavo Rueda Medina

Tourist
Office

Passenger Ferry Pier

Car Ferry Pier

number of Mayan statuettes of women, which had been used in religious ceremonies. It
was then that he named the spot Isla Mujeres, which translates to "Island of the Women."
Other visitors included pirates, among them Jean Lafitte, and then later the island was
discovered by hippies and bohemians who used it as a place to get away from civilization
and commune with nature and all it has to offer. Today, the island's few narrow roads are
best explored in golf carts, which are available for rent by the hour or by the day. The top

tourist attraction is Garrafon Park, a snorkeling paradise with a shallow protected cove and a coral reef heavily populated with fish and other marine life. Other draws include a Spanish fort, a museum, the town square, shopping boutiques, and tranquil beaches. Snorkeling, fishing, and diving are the main activities, and boats leave from the municipal pier throughout the day on various excursions. The island was partially destroyed by Hurricane Wilma in 2005. The infrastructure was badly damaged and the entire island was incommunicado for nearly a week. It has been rebuilt and is once again welcoming guests to its tropical shores.

There is an HSBC Bank across from the ferry dock, and there are several ATMs and money-exchange houses in the downtown area. There is a clinic near the town square (Centro de salud, 998-877-0117), and the Red Cross provides ambulance service throughout the island (998-877-0280).

GETTING THERE

Ferries depart from Puerto Juárez to Isla Mujeres every 30 minutes from 6:30 AM to 8:30 PM, and again at 11:30 PM. They return from Isla Mujeres to Puerto Juárez every 30 minutes from 6 AM to 8 PM, and again at 9 PM. The cost is $3.50 per person. The boat departs from the main dock in Puerto Juárez, 5 miles north of Cancún.

LODGING

Casa de los Sueños
998-877-0651 or 1-866-705-1691 (U.S.)
www.casadelossuenosresort.com
On the road to Garrafon, Isla Mujeres

This exclusive property offers eight rooms with ocean views, private terraces, air-conditioning, premium bedding, and original decorations. There is a gym, yoga instructor, bicycles for guest use, pool, snorkeling, kayaking, and hiking. The on-site Spa Zenter offers a range of traditional and regional treatments, including an aloe vera body wrap, a seaweed detox wrap, and a nourishing ocean mud wrap. Rates: start at $240; include complimentary morning coffee delivered to your room, continental breakfast, and a stocked minibar.

Cielito Lindo Beach Studios
998-877-0585
78 Rueda Medina

Right across the beach and just 4 blocks from the ferry dock, Cielito Lindo, once a private residence, is divided into two separate guest apartments, each with air-conditioning, satellite TV, ceiling fans, living room, kitchenette, coffeemaker, and ocean-view balcony. It's a great place if you want to stay a while and don't want the hassle of dealing with a standard hotel. Rates: $60–100. Three-night minimum; cash only.

Hotel & Hostel Posada del Mar
998-877-0044
www.posadadelmar.com
Avenue Rueda Medina, #15

If you're looking for a beachfront hotel but don't need anything big and fancy, try the Posada del Mar. It has 50 contemporary-style rooms with bright tropical decor, air-conditioning and fans, phone and TV, private balcony, and in-room safe. There's even a pool and beach club with *palapa* bar. The on-site Pinguino's restaurant serves three meals per day. Rates: start at $50 per night. The hotel also operates a few rooms a couple blocks away as a hostel, with safe rooms for budget travelers for $9 per person per night.

Hotel Bucaneros

998-877-1222
www.bucaneros.com
Downtown Isla Mujeres

With only 16 rooms, Bucaneros is a friendly inn with a local feel. The staff is helpful and friendly and is happy to recommend restaurants and bars located nearby. The beach is a 10-minute walk from the hotel. Rooms are simple, but they are attractive and clean, and some have air-conditioning. The on-site restaurant serves quality Mexican food and seafood. Rates: $40–70. Recommended for budget travelers.

Hotel Na Balam

998-877-0058
www.nabalam.com
Calle Zazil-Ha, #118, Playa Norte

Na Balam, which means "house of the jaguar" in Mayan, is an exclusive beach-front hotel with 28 rooms decorated as traditional Mayan cabañas. Rooms are located around the pool or next to the beach and have air-conditioning, ceiling fans, safes, and private balconies or terraces. The hotel gardens offer shade from the Caribbean sun and hammocks ideal for napping in the warm breeze. An on-site restaurant serves local and regional specialties. The hotel specializes in weddings, yoga retreats, and other special groups. Rates: $125–250.

Hotel Osorio

998-877-0294
Madero Avenue near Benito Juárez Avenue

This family-run downtown hotel is a block from the beach and offers budget accommodations that are clean, but not luxurious. Rooms have ceiling fans, private bathrooms, and a place to hang your hammock. Rates: $27 per night.

Hotel Secreto

998-877-1048
www.hotelsecreto.com
Punta Norte

On a secluded cove of Halfmoon Beach with a great shoreline, this upscale Mediterranean-style boutique hotel offers luxurious accommodations and a sense of privacy and exclusivity that can be hard to find on Isla. Rooms feature original artwork, air-conditioning, CD players, satellite TV, safes, and refrigerators. Each room has an outdoor terrace with patio furniture. Great spot for a romantic hideaway. Rates: $180–225. Recommended.

Hotel Villa Rolandi

998-877-0500
www.rolandi.com
East beach

Your stay starts off with a trip across the Cancún straits in a private yacht. Once at the resort, you'll be treated to uniquely decorated rooms with air-conditioning, satellite TV, contemporary furnishings, superior linens, private balconies, and ocean views. There is an infinity pool overlooking the beach and a gourmet restaurant on a dock over the ocean, where meals can last for hours as you savor a glass of wine or cup of coffee and watch the stars after your meal. Tony Blair stayed here on his last visit to Mexico. Rates: $250 and up. Highly recommended.

Villa Las Brisas

www.villalasbrisas.com
2½ miles from Playa Norte

This seaside bed & breakfast has six rooms and caters to adults only. The house offers a relaxing respite from the hurried world and has no phones, TVs, or alarm clocks, but the rooms have ocean views, air-conditioning, ceiling fans, and minibars. The common areas include a spacious open-air living room, a terrace with hammocks, a swimming pool, and a bar. From May to July, sea turtles nest on the hotel beach. Rates: $80–225, depending on the room and time of year; breakfast included. Recommended.

DINING

Casa O's
998-888-0170
www.casaos.com
Playa Sur, near Garrafon

One of the top restaurants in town, Casa O's has waterfront dining, candlelit tables, a garden courtyard, and a boat dock for diners arriving by water. The service is excellent, and the tables face west, affording views of the sunset and the lights of Cancún. The kitchen serves mainly seafood, with shrimp and squid ceviche, lobster bisque, and grilled shrimp. There is also steak and a wide assortment of after-dinner drinks. Moderate.

Chi-Chi & Charlie's
Playa Norte

Isla's traditional spot to watch the sunset, Chi-Chi & Charlie's serves burgers and Mexican snacks, along with ice-cold beers and cocktails. Inexpensive.

Chiles Locos
Avenue Hidalgo, downtown

This hot spot has affordable lunches and dinners, plus live music nightly. The rather simple menu is highlighted by burgers, tacos, and fajitas. Inexpensive.

La Adelita
Avenue Hidalgo, downtown

Open for dinner and drinks, La Adelita is the spot to sample your choice of 150 tequi-las. For dinner try the grilled shrimp, steak, or fajitas. Moderate.

Rolandi's
998-877-0500
www.rolandi.com

This gourmet restaurant is on a dock behind the Villa Rolandi hotel. The Cancún elite are known to boat over just for dinner on occasion. The menu features seafood, steak, shrimp, and Mexican specialties. There are also selections from around the world and an excellent wine list. Expensive.

Zazil Ha Restaurant
998-877-0058
www.nabalam.com
Calle Zazil-Ha, #118, Playa Norte

This romantic spot under a large *palapa* roof serves vegetarian and regional specialties, including shrimp, rice and beans, and grilled chicken. Inexpensive.

NIGHTLIFE

Buho's
Avenue Carlos Laza, Playa Norte; by the Maria del Mar hotel

Isla's happy-hour bar, popular with locals and tourists, has a *palapa* roof and swinging bar stools. It is known for cocktails made with tropical fruit, and the bartender is happy to mix-and-match to create your own unique drink. The music is a mix of reggae and American rock, with an occasional Mexican standard thrown in to spice things up.

Mamacita's
Avenue Hidalgo at Matamoros Street

Isla's party crowd packs Mamacita's after dinner for drinks and live music.

OM Bar
Matamoros Street, downtown

A Playa del Carmen native, OM Bar offers beer, wine, and cocktails along with live jazz music and an upscale lounge atmosphere.

Sergio's
Adjacent to the town plaza

This sports bar is a popular hangout when there's a big game on. Other times, visitors munch on burgers or tacos and play pool.

ATTRACTIONS

Garrafon Park
www.garrafon.com
Punta Sur, km 6

On the southeast tip of Isla Mujeres, Garrafon is the easternmost point in Mexico. Each New Year's Day, locals flock to this spot to be the first of their countrymen to see the sun in the new year. The park also has the Yucatán Peninsula's highest cliff, which leads down to the beautiful Caribbean. Visitors arrive by the boat on day trips from Cancún or can arrive by land from downtown Isla. The park gets its name from the Spanish word for "canister," either because the site was once used as a fuel depot or because the bay off the coast is shaped like the curved neck of a water bottle, depending on which version of the story you believe. The park has several restaurants, souvenir shops, an ice cream parlor, a swimming pool, a protected snorkeling area, a sundeck, and a hammock area, and there is also a museum and an ancient Mayan lighthouse relic. Visitors can rent clear-bottom kayaks ($6) and a Snuba ($39) or Sea Trek ($39) suit to experience the underwater realm. The park is open 9–5 (until 6 in the summer), and the entrance fee is $15 for adults and $8 for children (5–12 years old). For $29 for adults and $15 for kids, the trip includes a round-trip cruise to Cancún, admission, and a downtown tour, and for $54 for adults and $27 for kids, you can also get unlimited food and drinks. Snorkeling gear is available for rent for $10.

Cancún (45 miles north of Playa del Carmen)

Though officially it is too far north to be considered a part of the Riviera Maya, many visitors choose to stay a night in Cancún for a taste of the world-class shopping, great restaurants, powdery beaches, and over-the-top nightlife. The hotel zone is about 14 miles long, with dozens of hotels and every tourist service imaginable. There is a less commercial downtown area with great local restaurants, a large bus station, many Internet cafés, shops, and nightspots. The main tourist area is at the elbow of the 7-shaped tourist strip, near the convention center. Within a short walk, there are two malls, a Hard Rock Café, 20 restaurants, more than a dozen nightclubs and bars, pharmacies, cigar shops, grocery stores, souvenir shops, and—yes—even strip clubs. An 18-hole waterfront golf course is just a few minutes away, and there are even some impressive Mayan ruins just miles from the convention center.

Hurricane Wilma battered the hotel zone with 150 mph winds, 25-foot waves, and an 11-foot storm surge when it stalled out over the city for nearly 12 hours in late 2005. The beachfront resorts suffered major damage and there was some serious beach erosion, but

CANCÚN

0   3 miles
0   3 kilometers

Puerto Juárez

Ferry (to Isla Mujeres)

Bahía de Mujeres

Ferry (to Isla Mujeres)

Av. López Portillo

Av. Bonampak

To Chichén Itzá

180

Blvd. Kukulcán

Av. Kabah

Blvd. Kukulcán

Bull Ring

Av. Tulum

La Boom Disco

Convention Center

Punta Cancún

Dreams Cancún Resort & Spa

Pok-Ta-Pok Golf Club

The City

Pok-Ta-Pok Ruins

Señor Frog's

Coco Bongo

Laguna Bojórquez

La Isla Mall

Fiesta Americana Grand Aqua

Laguna de Nichupté

307

Blvd. Kukulcán

Fiesta Americana Grand Condesa

Aqua World/Sub See Explorer

Del Rey Ruins

Cancún Hilton

Laguna Río Inglés

CARIBBEAN SEA

Cancún International Airport

Blvd. Kukulcán

Nizuc Park

Punta Nizuc

Gas Station

307

To Playa del Carmen

Moon Palace Resort

© The Countryman Press

the hotels immediately went to work to rebuild and Mexico's number-one tourist town has reemerged.

LODGING

Carisa y Palma Condos
998-883-0211 or 1-866-521-1787 (U.S.)
www.carisaypalma.com
Boulevard Kukulcán, km 11, Cancún hotel zone

If you're on a budget but want to be close to the action of Cancún's main tourist center, Carisa y Palma offers a good value. The beachfront buildings are showing their age a bit, but if you just need a place to crash that's walking distance from Señor Frog's, Coco Bongo, and dozens of other restaurants and bars, it may be worth it. Rooms have air-conditioning (not the best) and kitchenettes, and there's an on-site restaurant, tennis court, swimming pool, convenience store, and gym. Rates: $70–80; breakfast included.

Dreams Cancún Resort & Spa
998-848-7000 or 1-866-237-3262 (U.S.)
www.dreamsresorts.com
Boulevard Kukulcán, km 10, Punta Cancún

Known for its great location, this large-scale all-inclusive resort is on the beach and is walking distance to the convention center and main tourism entertainment district. It was badly damaged during Hurricane Wilma in late 2005 but reopened again in early 2006. It's one of the few resorts in Cancún where you could pass a week without getting in a car or bus and still get to see some of the town's main attractions. Of all the hotels within the convention center area, it has the best beach, which is hidden in a sheltered cove next to the Hyatt Regency. There is no easy public access to the beach, making it especially safe and relaxing. Though it's all-inclusive, guests are not required to wear wristbands and instead sign all meals/drinks to their room. There are several restaurants and bars, including a seaside sushi bar, an air-conditioned buffet, a seafood grill, and a

The Dreams resort, at the northeastern tip of Cancún Courtesy of Dreams Resorts & Spas

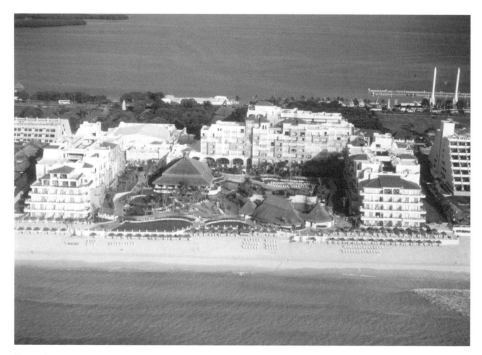

Fiesta Americana Grand Condesa Cancún Courtesy of Fiesta Americana

beach bar. There are nightly themed shows and meals, including a Mexican fiesta complete with mariachi bands and folkloric dancers. Accommodations include all food and drinks, nonmotorized water sports, gym, business center (including Internet access), stocked minibar, and even 24-hour room service. The staff goes out of their way to provide great service, even though tips are included in the room price. Highly recommended. Rates: $300–$550 per night, double occupancy, all-inclusive.

Fiesta Americana Grand Aqua
998-840-6010
www.fiestaamericana.com
Boulevard Kukulcán, km 13

Located a couple of miles from the central tourist area and on a perfect beach, the Grand Aqua is a new concept for the Fiesta Americana brand, normally known for its traditional Mexican-style resorts. The hotel is thoroughly contemporary in every way, from the aromatherapy kits available in each room and the 24-hour lounge music to the phosphorescent pillows at the beachside lounge. The rooms are spacious and feature premium bedding, marble bathrooms, and private balconies with an ocean view. The on-site restaurants feature celebrity chefs and have become the hip spots in town for the see-and-be-seen crowd. Guests, however, get preferential reservations. The hotel lost nearly every ocean-facing window during Hurricane Wilma in 2005 but reopened within a few months of the storm. Rates: start at $250.

Fiesta Americana Grand Condesa Cancún
998-881-4200
www.fiestaamericana.com
Boulevard Kukulcán, km 15.5

With the tallest *palapa* in all of Cancún, the Condesa (named for the chain's hotel on

DOWNTOWN CANCÚN

Condesa beach in Acapulco) is hard to miss. It was recently renovated, giving it a slick mix of traditional Mexican hacienda decor combined with a bevy of local accents and upgrades. The lobby is cooled with ocean breezes, and the beach is composed of flourlike sand. The buildings are reminiscent of a Mexican village, with subdued earth-tone colors and cool stucco. There is a great Mexican restaurant on-site, plus several pools, a hip lobby bar, and a modern fitness center. For those who complain that Cancún has lost its charm, the Fiesta

Americana Condesa may make them change their mind. Rates: begin at $210, double occupancy.

Moon Palace Golf & Spa Resort
998-881-6000
www.palaceresorts.com
Highway 307, km 338

Most flights out of the Cancún airport fly over the all-inclusive Moon Palace, which gives everyone a view of the magnificent beach and huge lagoon pools. It's the closest resort to the Cancún airport and is about 30 minutes from the main Cancún hotel zone. It's a massive complex, with nearly 2,000 feet of beachfront, 123 acres of jungle, more than 2,100 rooms, 10 restaurants, 7 bars, 6 tennis courts, 2 basketball courts, and 2 gyms, giving it a sort of Las Vegas–on–the– beach feeling. The rooms are housed in three-story villas, most with an ocean view, and all with air-conditioning, satellite TV, private balcony, in-room safe, minibar, coffeemaker, and liquor dispenser. Accommodations include all meals and drinks, local and imported liquor, nonmotorized water sports (such as snorkeling, kayaking, and paddleboating), activities program, volleyball, mini golf, bicycles, and even a daily round of golf at the resort's 18-hole Jack Nicklaus golf course. The resort provides complimentary transportation to the Cancún hotel zone, where guests have privileges at the other Palace resorts. At night, guests head to the on-premises theater for live entertainment, then to the dance club, where everything is included. Rates: start at around $330 per night.

DINING

La Habichuela
998-884-3158
www.lahabichuela.com
25 Margarita Street, downtown Cancún

Though the indoor air-conditioned dining room is quite pleasant and suitably upscale to impress any date, the true joy of this place is the back patio, where the trees, plants, Mayan replicas, and twinkling lights create a majestic setting for a long, slow meal. The specialty of the house is the Cocobichuela, which features a coconut stuffed with lobster in a cream sauce. It has a unique flavor and goes great with ice-cold beer. The restaurant also has a respectable wine list. Expensive.

Lorenzillos Lobster House
998-883-1433
Boulevard Kukulcán, km 13

Built on stilts over the water in the Nichupté lagoon, across the main road from the beach, Lorenzillos advertises its lobster all over town, and it lives up to the promotion. Choose from tails or whole live lobster and pick your meal from the tank. It's a great place to watch the sunset, and at night you can see the city lights and the stars at the same time. The dining room fills up nearly every night, so go early or call ahead if you want one of the coveted waterside tables on the outer deck. In addition to lobster, there are some great fish and shrimp dishes. Blown to bits by Hurricane Wilma in 2005, this long-time Cancún favorite rebuilt quickly. Expensive.

Pericos
998-884-3152
www.pericos.com.mx
Yaxchilán 61, downtown Cancún

Okay, so it's not really an authentic Mexican cantina, but the fiesta that Pericos throws every night sure is fun. There are folkloric dancers, funny skits, conga lines, a live mariachi band, and even dancing masked midgets. The menu features a selection of Mexican standards, including fajitas, tacos, enchiladas, and grilled steak or shrimp. Moderate.

The Plantation House
998-883-1254
Boulevard Kukulcán, km 13

Seafood specialties are served up in style at the Plantation House. The waitstaff has a well-practiced Southern sense of service, and the food is prepared fresh. Top dishes include grilled shrimp and lobster. Adjacent to Lorenzillos, it offers a more buttoned-up approach to the over-the-water dining experience. Expensive.

NIGHTLIFE

Coco Bongo

998-883-5061
www.cocobongo.com.mx
Boulevard Kukulcán, km 10.5

Located across from the convention center, this is one of the city's top nightspots. But to call Coco Bongo a bar would be woefully inadequate—to even call it a nightclub is somewhat of a joke. It's more like an entertainment center, where travelers congregate to celebrate life and get a little bit crazy. There's often a line wrapping around the corner, but it goes fast, and you can start making friends before you even get inside. There's a cover charge of $10 if you want to pay as you go, or pay $28 for all-you-can-drink. Once inside, you'll find a central bar area ringed by stadium-like seating, an upper deck with another bar and more seating, and an elevated stage, where most of the club's nonstop action happens. From celebrity impersonators and high-flying acrobats to live rock music, there's always something happening on stage or hanging from the rafters above the main bar. The atmosphere is very convivial, with a strong spirit of communal fun.

La Boom

998-849-7587
www.laboom.com.mx
Boulevard Kukulcán, km 3

Just across the bridge that joins the mainland to the hotel strip, La Boom is the party spot for the young and beautiful crowd. It's actually two clubs in one, with a rock 'n' roll bar on one side and a sophisticated dance club on the other. On the rock 'n' roll side, patrons dance on the bar and on the stage while the DJ plays a mix of American and Mexican music that keeps the crowd pumping all night long. On the dance club side, the atmosphere is more subdued, with waiters offering bottle service at reserved tables around the dance floor. The later it gets, though, the more the two clubs look alike as the crowds mix with each other and the all-you-can-drink crowd starts to get their money's worth.

Señor Frog's

998-883-1092
www.senorfrogs.com
Boulevard Kukulcán, km 9.5

This legendary bar keeps packing in the partiers, night after night. No matter what time of the year or what day of the week it is, you'll find a mix of young and old, locals and visitors, partying hard and dancing even harder. The bar host keeps things moving with games, contests, and sing-alongs, while the waiters and shot-girls make sure nobody goes thirsty. It's open for meals during the day, and then around 10 PM the tables get pushed back and the dancing starts.

Isla Cozumel *(11 miles from Playa del Carmen by boat)*

Isla Cozumel was once considered the sacred home of Ix-Chel, the Mayan goddess of fertility and childbirth, and Mayan women from around Mesoamerica would travel to pay homage and pray for their unborn children. Several religious shrines have survived over the years and can still be visited today. Measuring 28 miles by 10 miles, Cozumel is only 5 percent developed and is mostly open land, ripe for exploration on Jeep, horseback, or moped. It is a mecca for scuba divers and snorkelers, who revel in the amazingly clear waters, easily accessible reefs, and first-class dive operators.

ISLA COZUMEL

0 ————— 5 miles
0 ————— 5 kilometers

N

Ferry (to Puerto Morelos)

Ferry (to Playa del Carmen)

Punta Molas
Lighthouse

Isla de
la Pasión

Golf
Course

Av. Rafael Melgar

Cozumel
International
Airport

San Gervasio
Mayan Ruins

Ferry Dock

Cozumel Island Museum

San Miguel
de Cozumel

Plaza

Av. Juarez

Carretera Transversal

Paraiso
Reef

Atlantis
Submarines

Mescalitos
Cafe/Bar

Chankanab
Reef

Chankanaab
Park

El Cedral
Mayan Ruins

Chen Rio
Restaurant

Playa
San
Francisco

Yucab
Reef

Santa
Rosa
Wall

Palancar
Reef

Coastal Road

Reggae
Shack

CARIBBEAN
SEA

Colombia
Reef

Punta
Sur

Punta Sur
Ecological Park
Entrance

Punta Sur
Ecological
Park

Maracaibo
Reef

Punta
Celarain

Punta Celerain
Lighthouse/Museum

© The Countryman Press

The ferry from Playa lands at the town square of the town of San Miguel, the island's only town, which is on the island's western shore. From nearly every beach hotel on this side of the island, guests have a spectacular view of the sunset as it slowly goes down into the Caribbean. There are dozens of shops, restaurants, bars, and other attractions within an easy walking distance of the ferry dock. There are a few hotels downtown, and the rest are along the beaches to the north and south of the town square. The eastern side of the island faces the open ocean, and the water is much rougher, with less reef and much less development. Visitors can drive around the south side of the island, hugging the shoreline almost the entire way. This is a great way to get away from the crowds and feel like a real explorer, though you are never more than 15 minutes away from a cold beer and tasty plate of food. There are a few Mayan ruins that are run as federal parks, with information centers, gift shops, and certified multilingual guides.

Cozumel was heavily damaged during the dual hurricanes of 2005. Many of the street signs, *palapa* roofs, and light poles were blown down and the beachfront was severely flooded. More than a dozen dive-boat piers were ruined and two of the three cruise-ship docks were destroyed. The island received major assistance from the federal and state governments (the governor of the state of Quintana Roo was from Cozumel, which didn't hurt) and was rebuilt to match its pre-storm splendor.

LODGING

Cozumel Palace
987-872-9430
www.palaceresorts.com
Southern hotel zone, km 2.5

Once the site of the Plaza Las Glorias, Cozumel's famed dive resort, this hotel reopened in the summer of 2005 as the all-inclusive Cozumel Palace, which is about a 15-minute walk to town. A complete renovation spruced up the pool, guest rooms, lobby, restaurants, and all common areas. The hotel has 176 rooms; each is a junior suite with Jacuzzi tub, safe, air-conditioning, ceiling fan, satellite TV, stocked minibars, and private balcony with ocean views. Guests enjoy unlimited food and drinks, snorkeling gear, pool activities, and 24-hour room service. An on-site dive shop offers scuba tours, fishing excursions, and snorkeling trips. Though the hotel is right on the water, the shoreline is exposed reef, so the beach is built up above the rocks. Snorkelers and divers use ladders to get in and out of the water. The snorkeling is excellent right at the hotel, with barracuda, parrot fish, colored coral, sea anemone, sea urchin, lobster, and other things to see. Boats pick up guests from the hotel dock for excursions. A kids' club is available for children 4–12. Rates: $250–300. Highly recommended.

El Cozumeleño
987-872-9530 or 1-800-437-3923 (U.S.)
www.elcozumeleno.com
Northern hotel zone, km 4.5, Santa Pilar Beach

One of Cozumel's original hotels is still one of the most popular spots for families and others looking for an affordable, all-inclusive beach vacation. Guests enjoy unlimited meals, snacks, drinks, cocktails, and nonmotorized water sports. Recreational activities include mini golf, tennis, beach soccer, Ping-Pong, billiards, giant outdoor chess, two pools and two Jacuzzis, snorkeling, intro to scuba lessons, bicycle tours, windsurfing, aerobics, and volleyball. At night, guests head to the on-site nightclub for karaoke and DJ dancing. The resort's 252 rooms have spacious floor plans, air-conditioning, satellite TV, safes, and private balconies with ocean view. The Cozumel Country Club is just a couple of minutes away, and guests receive a 30 per-cent discount on fees. There is also an on-site workout room and dive and tour shop, where guests can schedule scuba diving, fishing, WaveRunner rental, parasailing, and other activities. A kids' club provides complimentary supervision and children's activities during the day. Rates: $170–$250.

Fiesta Americana Cozumel Dive Resort
1-800-FIESTA1 (U.S.)
www.fiestaamericana.com
Southern Coast Road, km 7.5

Located on the southern end of the island, this 224-room hotel is popular with fami-lies, serious scuba divers, and other guests who value ready access to the best dive sites over proximity to downtown, which is a 20-minute car ride away. The hotel is very casual and features traditional Mexican decor. There are two swimming pools, a beauty shop, massage service, and a video arcade and playground for the kids. The rooms have air-conditioning, coffeemak-ers, and an ocean or garden view. There are two restaurants and a popular bar, where guests congregate at night for live music, billiards, karaoke, and other entertain-ment. The beach is across the street from the main part of the hotel, where there is a swimming pool, restaurant, lounge chairs, and a boat dock, where divers, snorkelers, and anglers depart. Rates: start at $90.

Playa Azul Beach Resort
987-872-0033
www.playa-azul.com
Northern hotel zone, km 4, San Juan Beach

This beach and golf resort is just a few miles north of the town square. It has 50 rooms in a contemporary hacienda style, with a beachside swimming pool and plenty of beach chairs. The rooms feature tropical decor, living room, air-conditioning, satel-lite TV, coffeemaker, safe, and ocean-view

balcony or terrace. Guests receive unlim-ited play at the Cozumel Country Club golf course, just a couple of minutes away. Rates: start at $135.

Safari Inn
987-872-0101
www.aquasafari.com/safariinn.html
Rafael Melgar, between Fifth and Seventh Streets

Located behind the Aqua Safari dive shop, the Safari Inn is a favorite for divers and other guests who don't need to be on the beach but want the convenience of being near downtown and area nightlife. The hotel is about a five-minute walk from the town plaza and is across the street from a rocky beach. Guests use the Aqua Safari pier, across the street, for meeting boats for excursions. The hotel has 12 rooms with cold air-conditioning and spacious floor plans sleeping up to five guests. Rates: start at $40, depending on the season and occu-pancy. Highly recommended.

Sol Cabañas del Caribe
1-888-95-MELIA (U.S.)
www.solmelia.com
Northern hotel zone, km 5.1

Though it's owned by Grupo Sol, a major Spanish hotel chain, this 48-room beachside hotel retains its semirustic charm and small-town feeling. Its location near the northern end of the hotel zone gives it a sense of seclusion and privacy, making it a good spot for couples seeking a romantic hideaway. It's also popular with families, who appreciate the small-scale swimming pool near the rooms, ultracasual atmos-phere, and no-frills vibe. Much of the beach is rocky, but there is a 10-yard stretch where swimmers and snorkelers can walk right into the water from the sandy beach. The rooms are a bit spartan but are air-conditioned and clean, with traditional dark-wood furnishings and private balconies or terraces with hammocks and ocean views. An on-site water sports center offers windsurfing, sailing, snorkeling gear, scuba diving, fishing trips, and WaveRunners. Rates: average $70. Recommended.

Suites Colonial

987-872-9090
www.suitescolonial.com
North side of the town square, overlooking the plaza

If you want to be in the downtown area and near the ferry dock and you don't need to be right on the beach, the Suites Colonial is an affordable option. Rooms are not fancy, but they are clean and convenient to everything in town. Activities can be booked through any local dive shop, and arrangements can be made for hotel or pier pickup. The 28 rooms and suites all have air-conditioning, cable TV, and safes. Rates: $65–80; continental breakfast included.

DINING

Casa Denis

Town square, downtown Cozumel

If you're facing the clock tower with the ocean behind you, follow the walkway that leads straight back from the plaza on the right-hand side. The first restaurant you run into is Casa Denis. It has been there for more than 20 years and offers up some of the best food in town, particularly if you're looking for traditional Mexican fare. They have fish, tacos, enchiladas, shrimp, and steak. They also have *sopes*, a traditional dish from Acapulco served on thick, soft corn tortillas with lettuce, cheese, refried beans, and meat toppings. Inexpensive.

Chen Rio Restaurant

Seven miles up the coast on the island's east side

Most of the island's east side has rough water and somewhat less-than-inviting beaches, but at Chen Rio the reef is just offshore, which cuts down the waves and makes the water shallow and calm. There is a long stretch of white-sand beach, some small waves, tide pools, and a casual beachfront restaurant. The menu is limited, with fried whole fish the main specialty. The drinks are cold, and the shallow cove makes for a great place to take a dip and cool off from your journey. If you have packed a picnic lunch, you can just buy drinks at the restaurant and then lay out your blanket on the beach. Inexpensive. No credit cards.

Las Palmeras

Town square, downtown Cozumel

Located on the west side of the town square, facing the ferry dock, Las Palmeras is the traditional place to pass the time while waiting for the boat to Playa del Carmen. It is famous for its fishbowl margaritas, which are served ice-cold, potent, and delicious. The restaurant serves breakfast, lunch, and dinner and has seating indoors with open windows and walls, allowing the ocean breezes in and giving diners a great view of the waterfront and the bustle of the ferry dock. Moderate.

Mezcalitos

At the intersection of the cross-island road and the northern end of the road that goes along the eastern shoreline

This local favorite is the northeasternmost public restaurant on the island. If you take the southern route around the island, this is where you will turn left to head back to the town of San Miguel. If you take the eastern route, this is where you will turn right and start paralleling the coast. The restaurant serves Mexican dishes and snacks and has a full bar. There are tables in a shaded indoor area and also outside on the waterfront patio. The beach is not good for swimming, but it is great for exploring since it is undeveloped and natural. This is a great place to meet other travelers because everyone here is doing the same thing—cruising around the island. It's a nice way to get tips on hidden beaches and good places to go. The restaurant shares a parking lot with a couple of souvenir stands selling T-shirts, trinkets, Mexican blankets, and other goods. The restaurant was destroyed during Hurricane Emily but has since been rebuilt. Inexpensive.

Pasta Prima

Town square, downtown Cozumel

From the center of the plaza, take the walkway to the right that heads south, and Pasta Prima will be on the northeast corner of the first intersection. Owned by a native of Dallas, Texas, this Italian terrace restaurant is a favorite for visiting diving clubs, honeymooners, and even locals searching for an authentic Italian meal. Visitors enter from the street level and climb a stairway so narrow it seems like a replica from a Mayan ruin. The dining room is on an open-air patio overlooking the city streets, with the ocean just beyond. It bustles most nights, and there is frequently a wait for a table, though it is always worth the time. The menu features pastas, spaghetti, and a heavy dose of seafood, including live Caribbean lobster, prepared a variety of ways. There is also a respectable wine list. Moderate.

Pepe's Grill

One block south of the town square, downtown Cozumel

One of the fancier and more expensive restaurants on the island, Pepe's Grill is the traditional spot for a first or last meal during a Cozumel visit. The chef prepares tender steaks, fresh seafood, and Mexican specialties. It may be best known, however,

for its Mayan coffee, which contains a locally made orange schnapps called Xtabentun. The waiters make the after-dinner drinks tableside, and whenever one is being prepared, the whole restaurant watches as the liquor is lit on fire and poured into the coffee. Expensive.

Plaza Leza

Town square, downtown Cozumel

This casual outdoor café is on the south side of the main plaza, facing the clock tower. It specializes in fajitas and steak, and the smell from its grills will catch you as you walk by, if the waiters offering you a table don't. Take a seat at one of the covered sidewalk café tables or in the small indoor dining room. After dinner, linger a while with a cup of coffee or a tropical drink and watch the people walk by. On Sunday nights, this is a great place to watch the music and festivities that take place at the plaza's gazebo. Inexpensive.

NIGHTLIFE

Reggae Shack

Southern Coast Road, where the coastal road turns east at the southern tip of the island

This come-as-you-are beach bar has no electricity (and doesn't accept credit cards) and is rather ramshackle, but it is a must-see waypoint for travelers circumnavigating the island by Jeep or moped. It is at the southwest end of the island, where the highway reaches a stop sign and all traffic must turn to the left. Go straight instead and park along the street. Each day, the bartender brings a cooler of ice and drinks from San Miguel and serves them up cold and cheap to passing visitors. There are a few hammocks for snoozing and a couple of tables set up in the sand, right next to the water. The reef here is exposed and the water is rough, so there is no swimming. If you walk to the left, there is a deserted beach ideal for walking and tanning. There is a handmade NUDE BEACH sign, but it is not an official nude beach, and nudity is not recommended, though topless is generally fine. Though the facility was wiped out by Hurricane Emily, it was quickly rebuilt and is as popular as ever.

Señor Frog's and Carlos 'n Charlie's

South of the town square, by the new cruise-ship dock, where the overhead walkway empties into the shopping plaza

With one built right on top of the other,

these two main tourist bars make bar-hopping easier than ever. Just take the escalator down from Señor Frog's, and you're at Carlos 'n Charlies. Señor Frog's is more nightlife oriented, with a stage, dancing waiters, and full-time party atmosphere, while Carlos 'n Charlie's is more of a restaurant, with a more subdued atmosphere, at least until late at night, when it transforms into more of a bar. Depending on the day and how many cruise ships are in town, these tourist havens can be packed or empty, raucous or tame.They both serve consistently good Mexican food, seafood, and pasta.

ATTRACTIONS

Chankanaab Park
987-872-0914
www.cozumelparks.com.mx
Southern Coast Road, km 9.5

Created in 1980 to protect the marine life in the region, plus the flora and fauna along the shoreline, Cozumel's main beach and nature park is just south of the Fiesta Americana hotel on the coastal road. The water is crystal clear, with more than 100 feet of visibility on most days, making for excellent snorkeling and scuba diving. The beach offers easy water access, slow currents, and exciting shore dives, where statues of Christ and the Virgin Mary beckon from the shallows. There is a botanical garden with 60 species of palm trees, orchids, water lilies, and dozens of tropical flowers, plus birds and iguanas. An archaeology area features 60 Aztec, Mayan, and Toltec replica temples and a replica of a Mayan *choza*, or hut, where visitors can witness how the indigenous inhabitants of Cozumel and the Riviera Maya once lived and worked. There is also a dolphin and sea lion discovery lagoon where visitors can pay to swim with these creatures in their natural habitat. Underwater videos of the encounters are available for purchase. Open 7–6 daily. Admission is $12 for adults and $6 for kids 3–11.

Cozumel Island Museum
www.cozumelparks.com.mx
Rafael Melgar and Fourth Street

The island's history museum is on the coastal road just a couple of blocks north of the town square. Through a series of displays (re-creations, drawings, and artifacts) it tells the history of the island from the days of the Mayans to the 16th-century discoveries by Juan de Grijalva and Hernan Cortez, through the pirate years and the War of the Castes, and to the present day. There is a gift shop, library, and snack bar, and bilingual guides are available for hire. Open 9–5 daily. Admission: adults $3, kids eight and under free.

Punta Sur Lighthouse Park
987-872-0914
www.cozumelparks.com.mx
Southern Coast Road, km 27

This 100-hectare ecology reserve and beach park is at the southeastern tip of Cozumel
Island. It encompasses white-sand beaches, mangrove swamps, lagoons, and thick jungle.
The crowning feature is the Faro Punta Sur, the famed lighthouse where the former caretakers would host a weekly fish fry and invite everyone on the island—locals and tourists
alike—to the party. The $10 entrance fee (for all visitors nine and up) includes transporta-
tion through the park and access to the museum, lighthouse, and other attractions. There
is also a souvenir shop and snack bar. A catamaran tour is available for $3 extra. Open 9–6
daily.

San Gervasio Mayan Ruins
987-872-0914
www.cozumelparks.com.mx
Cross-Island Road, km 7.5

Located about halfway between the town square and the east side of the island and
Mezcalito's restaurant, San Gervasio is Cozumel's largest and most historically significant
Mayan site. It was inhabited from A.D. 200 until the Spanish conquest and was a major
political, spiritual, and social center for the natives; it was also an important pilgrimage
site for women who traveled to the island to pay homage to Ixchel, the goddess of fertility.
The site, which spans more than 2 square miles and has several different temples and
small pyramids, is home to many tropical birds and iguanas. Visitors can walk among the
ruins by themselves, reading the interpretive signs, or they can hire a guide. There is a
gift shop, bookstore, and snack bar. Open 7–4 daily. Admission is $5.50 for adults and free
for children under eight.

THE RIVIERA MAYA BEGINS

Puerto Morelos
(Highway 307, km 320; 20 miles north of Playa del Carmen)

If you want to know what Playa del Carmen was like 20 years ago, just take a look at
modern-day Puerto Morelos, which is the official beginning of the Riviera Maya and its
northern border. The quiet town square ringed by a few restaurants and shops, the natural
beach, the unpaved roads, the encroaching jungle—it's almost exactly how Playa used to be.
The road from the highway to town is a straight shot through 2 miles of scrub brush and
mangrove swampland before ending at the town square. Most of the development is within
a couple blocks of the square, which has a beachside restaurant, several open-air sidewalk
restaurants, a couple of Internet cafés, a coffee/pastry shop, and a few souvenir stores,
pharmacies, money exchange offices, and dive shops. Along the beach you'll see a leaning
lighthouse and a fishing pier where the boats dock when they're not pulled up onto the
beach. Less than a half mile offshore is the barrier reef, and you can see the waves breaking where the coral meets the surface, which indicates a great spot for snorkeling when the

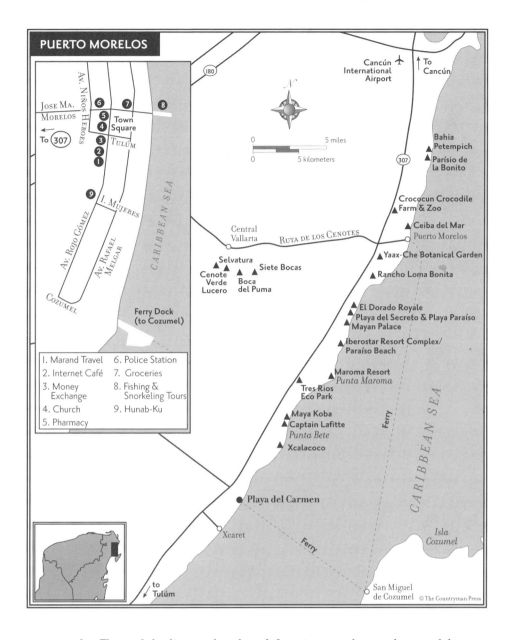

seas are calm. The roads leading north and south from town are dusty and unpaved, but they lead to some of the nicest natural beaches in the area. To the north are a collection of rental homes and small hotels, plus a couple of recently developed large-scale resorts. To the south the road curves behind an Army base and then a shipping and industrial area before meeting the beach again near the entrance to a laid-back budget hotel and a clothing-optional "lifestyle" resort.

The town was hit hard by Hurricane Wilma in late 2005. The storm pushed a thick layer of sand 200 yards inland, flooded the mangroves, tore down *palapas*, destroyed an elementary school, and heavily damaged most beachfront establishments. The town received

Souvenir shops line the town square in Puerto Morelos.

less government support than Cancún and struggled to regain its services. The towns-people worked together to clean up the mess and repair the damages. By the spring of 2006, tourists were returning in droves and the town marched onward.

A gambling-boat operator had petitioned to operate a casino boat from the port to take travelers to international waters, but the petition was denied, and the area retains its calming and relaxed feeling. A ferry transfers vehicles from Puerto Morelos to Cozumel at 5 AM, 10:30 AM, and 4 PM, with return trips at 8 AM, 1:30 PM, and 7 PM. For more information call 998-871-0008.

GETTING THERE

Puerto Morelos is located at the midpoint between Cancún and Playa del Carmen. The turnoff from Highway 307 was marked with just a speed bump only a few years ago, but now there's a traffic light, turning lanes, several shops, and even a road sign, so you can't miss it. Another road, just north of the Crococun Zoo, leads to the north end of town and the Secrets Excellence and Paradisus hotels. From there the road winds and turns as you head south, passing by private homes and small family-run hotels. In several spots, heavy marine rope has been laid across the street as a sort of makeshift speed bump. After a few miles, the road ends at the town square. There are frequent buses from the Cancún and Playa del Carmen bus stations that will drop you off at the crossroads, and from there it's a 2-mile hike to town or a $3 taxi ride. Though it may not be generally encouraged, it's also fairly easy to hitch a ride along the road that leads to town. Since the road basically goes to only one place, it's a pretty fair bet that anyone headed down that road is going somewhere close to where you are.

LODGING

BAHIA PETEMPICH

Azul Hotel & Beach Resort
998-872-0808
www.karismahotels.com
Highway 307, km 330

To get to Azul, go through the gated entrance to Bahia Petempich, and then turn left where the main road meets the beach road. Once in the gated entrance, you'll be met by a greeter and a glass of champagne. The Feng Shui–friendly hotel is an up-market all-inclusive boutique resort located on an idyllic beach just a few miles north of Puerto Morelos. The lobby has marble floors and minimalist decor, with lots of whites and blues, and calming music playing in the background. The hotel welcomes families and even has an activities program for kids. It has fewer than one hundred rooms, all of which are very close to the beach and have cold air-conditioning, minibars, coffee-makers, DVD players, and a private balcony or patio. There is a beautiful pool with attendants at the ready to bring you fresh towels, drinks, magazines, or whatever else you need. Since it's all-inclusive, guests can indulge all they like at a variety of on-site restaurants and bars. There is a special menu for kids, an all-lobster menu, a stylish sushi bar with tatami tables, and a healthy diet menu, plus 24-hour room service. Unlike many all-inclusives, the bars serve premium liquors. Rates: $300–400 per night, all-inclusive.

The courtyard of the Azul Hotel

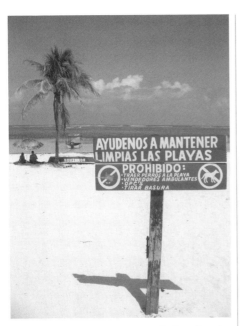

Keep Puerto Morelos clean—no "K-K" allowed on the beach! "K-K" is a Spanish play on the slang word "caca," in this case suggesting beachgoers clean up after their dogs.

Desire Resort & Spa

998-872-8280
www.desireresorts.com
Highway 307, km 326

Two minutes south of the town square in Puerto Morelos, the narrow road enters a swampy area renowned for its crocodiles and other wild animals. The aptly named Desire Resort sits on the ocean side of the moatlike swamp, connected by a wooden bridge. Songbirds fill the air, and the palm trees sway a welcoming wave. Once past the lobby, you'll realize that Desire is not for the prudish. In fact, if you're not a swinger or at least open to the swinger lifestyle, you're best off choosing another place to spend your vacation. If, however, you're into that kind of thing, this stylishly done resort deserves a serious look. It is known in the "lifestyle" circles as one of the best hotels around for swingers who enjoy traveling to the tropics to meet others, have

fun, and cast away their inhibitions, assuming they had any to begin with.

The 110-room all-inclusive resort accepts only adult couples, and minutes after arrival it's obvious why that is. Billed as "clothing optional," the hotel caters much more to the sexually liberated set than the run-of-the-mill nudist or "naturist." Public displays of affection, even extreme affection, are allowed and, in some designated areas, encouraged. And even though there's a strict "no means no" policy, it's clear that there are lots of yeses going on.

There is a great beach, and the local officials look the other way (literally), allowing guests to be on the beach in the buff, though it's generally frowned upon in most other areas. There are three restaurants, four bars, a dance bar, a fitness room, a beauty parlor, and a spa with steam room and several treatment rooms. There are two pools and a huge Jacuzzi with room for 30 people (I'm sure you could fit more if you tried), which seems to be the center of attraction most days. Next to the dance bar there is a "play room" where the most sexual activity takes place.

The rooms are spread out in low-rise thatch-roofed buildings, and each has a garden or ocean view, bathrobes and slippers, CD player, and fully-stocked minibar. Room rates include all meals, snacks, 24-hour room service, premium liquors, entertainment, and nonmotorized watersports. Rates: $310–360 per couple per night.

Paraiso de la Bonita Resort & Thalasso Spa

998-872-8300 or 1-866-751-9175 (U.S. reservations)
www.paraisodelabonita.com
Highway 307, km 330

The turnoff for Paraiso de la Bonita is a few miles north of the town of Puerto Morelos; there is a gated entry marked BAHIA PETEMPICH. The road to the resort is not paved,

Top 10 See-and-Be-Seen Hotels of the Riviera Maya Area

BLUE PARROT, PLAYA DEL CARMEN: With an open-air dance floor and fire dancers at your back door, you can't go wrong. (See chapter 2.)

FAIRMONT MAYAKOBA, PUNTA BETE: The huge stone entryway makes you wonder what's inside; only the privileged few know for sure. (See this chapter.)

FIESTA AMERICANA GRAND AQUA, CANCÚN: Cancún's one and only lounge hotel, with 24-hour DJ and luminescent bar pillows. (See this chapter.)

HOTEL BÁSICO, PLAYA DEL CARMEN: The prosperous days of 1950s Latin America glorified with a rooftop bar, oil-tank swimming pools, and rooms with neon lights. (See chapter 2.)

HOTEL DESEO, PLAYA DEL CARMEN: Up the unmarked stairs, it's the hip hangout for the Playa elite. (See chapter 2.)

HOTEL ESENCIA, XPU-HA: The former estate of an Italian duchess can be yours, for a price. (See chapter 3.)

MAROMA RESORT & SPA, PUNTA MAROMA: If it's good enough for Tom Cruise and Katie Holmes, you'll probably enjoy it also. (See this chapter.)

MEZZANINE HOTEL, NORTH OF TULUM PUEBLO: Swanky digs, topless beaches, and DJ parties in the shadow of the Tulum ruins. (See chapter 3.)

OCCIDENTAL ROYAL HIDEAWAY, PLAYACAR: Playacar's premier hotel proves all-inclusive resorts can be luxurious, too. (See chapter 3.)

PARAISO DE LA BONITA, NORTH OF PUERTO MORELOS: With a $3,000-a-night penthouse, you never know who you may rub shoulders with at the swim-up bar. (See this chapter.)

but it is fairly smooth, with no major pot-holes, though there are large speed bumps every quarter mile or so. When the road reaches the beachfront, turn left and head north a short spell, and you'll arrive at the entrance to the hotel. With fewer than one hundred rooms and suites, this very high-end, all-suite property has 1,100-square-foot standard rooms with ocean views. The service is impeccable, and the staff does an excellent job of making guests feel special. The architecture and decor are unusual, with a combination of African, Asian, Balinese, Caribbean, European, and Mayan inspirations. Guests enjoy a Jacuzzi, a sauna, tennis courts, a pool bar, and salt-water swimming pool. For an extra fee, there is a Mayan steam bath (*temazcal*),

sailing tours, and full-service restaurant. Room rates include complimentary airport transfers, yoga and Pilates classes, daily breakfast, and a welcome gift. The beach is raked clean, but the tides are full of sea-weed, making swimming less than pleasant. Rates: $600–$1,000; penthouse $3,000/night.

PUERTO MORELOS PROPER

Ceiba del Mar
998-872-8060
www.ceibadelmar.com
Highway 307, km 320

Halfway between the Cancún airport and Playa del Carmen, the Ceiba del Mar is a newer property spawned from the La Ceiba hotel in Cozumel, a longtime favorite of scuba divers. Along the beach just north of the town of Puerto Morelos, this 126-room resort is ideal for guests who want to get away from the city and the bustle of Cancún but don't want to be too far from the activities and fun of the Riviera Maya.

The architecture is a combination of traditional Mayan and contemporary Mexican. Set on a large plot of land surrounded by jungle, the resort is laid out with meandering paths in a sort of villagelike atmosphere, so guests never feel too crowded. There are two large, beautiful pools, rooftop sundecks, an upscale lobby, a gift shop, a beauty salon, and a European spa that uses organic spa-care products. Amenities include a water sports center, yoga classes, Jacuzzis, and a fitness center with free weights and exercise stations. There are three on-site restaurants and bars. Rates: $270, including continental breakfast; $370, including a food and beverage plan.

Secrets Excellence Riviera
998-872-8500
Highway 307, km 323; northern end of Puerto Morelos

The most direct route to get to this adults-only resort, the sister property of Secrets Capri, is to take the turnoff just north of Crococun and follow it to the beach. Designed as a place of tranquility and relaxation, with an emphasis on privacy, personal service, and romance, Secrets Excellence's 446 suites feature a Jacuzzi tub, coffeemaker, and stocked minibar, which can make spending time in the room just as enjoyable as venturing out. There are six swimming pools, a fitness center, three outdoor Jacuzzis, a beauty salon, and a 35,000-square-foot full-service European spa, which has indoor and outdoor treatment rooms and a soothing, gardenlike atmosphere. There are six theme restaurants (Mexican, Japanese, steak, seafood,

gourmet, continental), plus a buffet. There are also nine bars, including a coffee bar, piano bar, swim-up bar, lobby bar, *palapa* bars, sports bar, and show bar. Snacks and drinks are available 24 hours a day, and everything is included. Rates: $460–600 per couple per night.

SOUTH OF PUERTO MORELOS

El Cid
www.elcid.com
Highway 307, km 316; southern end of town

The 350-room El Cid sits on a beach a couple miles south of town on a sheltered cove, with a marina that offers mooring for up to two hundred boats. The resort is all-inclusive and will operate much like the chain's resort in Mazatlan, with a strong emphasis on time-share sales. Rates: $300–450 per person.

Hotel Ojo de Agua
998-871-0202
www.ojo-de-agua.com
Highway 307, km 321; Avenue Javier Rojo Gómez at the beach

On a northern beach between Bahia Petempich and the town square, Ojo de Agua serves as somewhat of a home base for beachfront activity. It has beach toys for rent, a swimming pool, a full-service restaurant, and an on-site tour office. The hotel's 36 rooms, decorated in contemporary Mexican style, have air-conditioning or fan and kitchenette. The hotel was devastated by Hurricane Wilma in 2005 but rebuilt and even improved its facilities. Rates: $40–45.

Rancho Libertad Sak Ol
998-871-0181
www.ranchosakol.com
Highway 307, km 318; southern end of Puerto Morelos, past the Army base and shipping facility

Sak Ol, formerly known as Rancho Libertad, offers an alternative to the large corporate-owned hotels for travelers who value simplicity and serenity over luxury and pampering service. There are 14 minimalist rooms with suspended beds, air-conditioning (downstairs units), purified drinking water, and a rocky yet calm and natural beach that is practically deserted—a good spot for more hotels. You can look to the north and see a half-sunken barge at the shipping facility that has been there for years. Rates: $65–110; includes a large buffet breakfast each day, plus wireless Internet access.

DINING

Café Finca
South side of the town square

Open for breakfast and lunch, this European-style café serves fresh coffee, crêpes, and homemade sandwiches. The staff can also prepare meals to go for excursions and tours. Moderate.

Caffetto
One block north of the town square

This small café serves coffee, crêpes, pastries, full breakfasts, and fruit and snacks. Open for breakfast and lunch. Inexpensive.

Cocina Economica
Northwest corner of the town square

This ultracasual restaurant, popular with locals and budget travelers, offers super-cheap lunches of typical Mexican and Yucatecan foods, including tacos, empanadas, and enchiladas. Inexpensive.

El Picudo Azul
South side of the town square

With an extensive menu for these parts, this casual eatery offers fresh fish, salads, steaks, enchiladas, and fish tacos. The bright and airy dining room is a nice spot to seek shelter from the sun. Moderate.

El Tio
Northeast side of the town square

Sometimes open, sometimes not, this hole-in-the-wall eatery offers typical local fare. It's good if you're in a pinch: The staff will wrap up your sandwich or tacos to go, if you ask. Inexpensive.

La Marina
On the Marina El Cid
998-871-0184

Offering a view of the luxury yachts docked at the marina, this casually elegant restaurant serves lobster, fresh fish, and other seafood specialties. It also has steak, chicken, and upscale Mexican food. Sit in the shaded indoor dining room or the al fresco patio. Moderate.

Le Café D'Amancia
Southwest corner of the town square

This small café, with a few tables in a small dining room, serves sandwiches, fresh breads, cheesecake, fruit, espresso, cappuccino, and coffee. Open 8–3 and 5–10 daily. Inexpensive.

Los Gauchos
Across from the church, near the town square

This sidewalk café serves pizza, pasta, empanadas, and continental breakfast. Inexpensive.

Monchis
Southeast corner of the town square

Monchis (get it?) sells coffee, sandwiches, ice cream, and other snack items, as well as a selection of T-shirts and other souvenirs. (You won't find items that are much different than at other area shops, but many of them are made locally, so you can feel good about your purchase.) There are a couple of small tables, but most diners get their food to go. Inexpensive.

Ojo de Agua Restaurant & Bar
998-206-9179
Avenue Javier Rojo Gómez; on a northern beach, close to Secrets Excellence hotel

This casual beachfront restaurant, bar, and beach club offers a daily breakfast buffet, fresh seafood, and Mexican dishes, as well as a daily happy hour from 3 to 4. Inexpensive.

The Old Fisherman
North side of the town square

This second-story restaurant offers fresh lobster, chiles rellenos, hogfish in butter, grouper, and other seafood dishes, plus grilled steak and chicken. The dining room is air-conditioned, and the waiters are longtime local residents who can give you advice on tours and activities. Moderate.

Pelicanos Restaurant
Southeast corner of the town square

The most prominent restaurant near the town square, it's also the largest. It offers a selection of Mexican and American breakfasts for less than $5, and for lunch and dinner, it's seafood or nothing. Try the fried whole fish, the shrimp ceviche, or the grilled shrimp, and you can't go wrong. There are tables inside, but there's no air-conditioning, so your best bet is to find an

empty *palapa*-covered table facing the beach to catch a bit of breeze. Moderate.

Porto Bello
South side of the town square

Good Italian food, including pasta, pizzas, salads, and lasagna, is served here in a fan-cooled dining room or at sidewalk tables. Open for lunch and dinner. Moderate.

Restaurante El Muelle
South of the town square, just west of the Army station

Turn back toward the highway instead of the ocean, and you'll find this bustling restaurant. It is popular with workers from the shipping facility and gets busy at shift change. Very inexpensive lunch items are served, including ceviche, chicken tacos, and rice and beans. Inexpensive.

Yax-che Restaurant
At the back side of the La Ceiba Hotel, facing the main street

A second location for the restaurant of the same name in Playa del Carmen, it offers traditional Mayan cuisine for lunch and dinner, including turkey, *tikin chic* (baked fish wrapped in banana leaves), and great steak. The upscale, relaxing dining room is decorated with replicas of Mayan relics, tropical plants, and carved stone. It's also one of the few places around with air-conditioning. Expensive.

SHOPPING

Alma Libre Bookstore
South side of the town square

This shop sells newspapers, magazines, used books, maps, regional books, and paperbacks.

Hunab-Ku
Half block south of the town square

Offering crafts, blankets, hammocks, T-shirts, and souvenirs, the shop is owned by a group of 18 families in a sort of co-op, where they work together on arts and crafts and then sell them direct to the public, without a middleman. You can watch the artists working on hammocks, jewelry, wood carvings, native clothing, and other creations.

GROCERIES AND SERVICES

ATM Machine
North side of the town square, next to Casa Martin

Casa Martin Groceries
North side of the town square

If they don't have it at the mini-super, they probably don't have it here, either. But at least it gives you some hope.

Internet Café
Southwest corner of the town square

They offer Internet connection for $1.50 an hour, long-distance phone calls to the United States and Canada for 50 cents, fax service, office supplies, and stationery.

Marand Travel
998-871-0162
www.puertomorelos.com.mx
Southwest corner of the town square

This full-service travel agency offers airline ticketing, hotel reservations, car rental, and flight confirmations. They can also book any of the tours in the area, including snorkeling, fishing, diving, Chichén Itzá, Xcaret, Xel-Ha, and Tulum. They have free local maps highlighting area attractions, plus a few computers with Internet access.

Mini-Super
Northwest corner of the town square

Open daily, it sells groceries, snacks, and basic supplies.

Money Exchange
Southwest corner of the town square

Open daily 8–6.

Pharmacy
West side of the town square

Sells snacks, over-the-counter and prescription medicines, sunblock, water, Gatorade, and batteries and film.

Police Station
Northwest corner of the town square

Puerto Morelos Church
West side of the town square

Service in Spanish only; service times are posted on the door. The doors are usually open for vistors; however, the church is fairly humble and without any historical significance, and it may not be of interest unless you're looking to attend a service.

TOURS

Fishing & Snorkeling Tours
Northeast side of the town square, next to the beach

The friendly folks at this tour office can arrange fishing and diving trips along the Puerto Morelos coastline, and because they have their own fleet of shaded 25-foot boats and local guides, they can custom-create a trip that suits your fancy. Basic tours include a four-hour fishing trip (including trolling and bottom-fishing), which includes beer, water, sodas, and all equipment and bait for $225 for up to four people. Common catches include dorado, white-fin tuna, barracuda, and even marlin and sailfish, if the timing is right. Snorkeling trips are $22 per person for a two-hour trip covering two different sites. For custom trips, the boats can be chartered for $40 an hour—which is common for sight-seeing and sunset cruises. It's preferred that you make your reservations the day before so the staff can get all the necessary equipment and supplies, though impromptu trips can be arranged as long as you're flexible.

Puerto Morelos Adventure Tours
998-884-2316
www.snorkelincancunrivieramaya.com

Operating out of the Ojo de Agua hotel, this tour company offers active tours in and around Puerto Morelos. Top trips include a two-hour snorkeling trip for $35, which includes lunch, beer, equipment, and a visit to a handicrafts market. An ATV tour ($58 for one ride, $48 each for two) departs each day at 9 AM, returning at 2 PM, and includes visits to two cenotes, a Mayan village, and a market; swimming; and lunch and beer. There's also a $69 cenote and reef snorkeling excursion, which includes visits to caves, cenotes, and a marine park, plus gear, snacks, and drinks. It departs at 9 AM and returns at 5 PM.

Playa del Secreto & Playa Paraíso
(Highway 307, km 308–312)
Playa del Secreto and Playa Paraíso combine to form one of the largest stretches of mostly undeveloped beach remaining in the area. Several spots along the shoreline are frequented by sea turtles, which lay their eggs in the balmy summer months. The area is dominated by the massive Iberostar resort complex, which includes four separate but connected all-

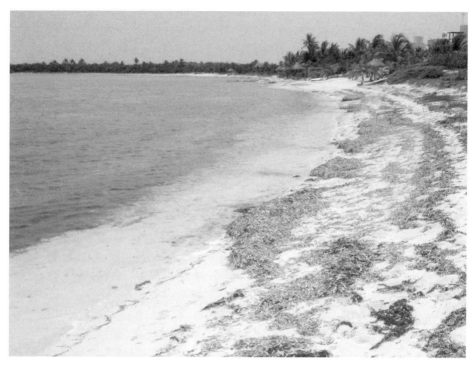

Dried seaweed lines some of the deserted beaches in Playa del Secreto.

inclusive resorts, totaling more than 1,200 rooms. There is a convention center operated by Iberostar and an 18-hole golf course, which opened in mid-2005, that features 18 holes designed by P. B. Dye, the son of renowned course designer Pete Dye.

LODGING

PLAYA DEL SECRETO & PLAYA PARAÍSO

El Dorado Royale—A Spa Resort
998-872-8030
www.karismahotels.com
Highway 307, km 312, Playa Paraíso

This 432-room, all-inclusive, adults-only resort bills itself as "laid-back luxury," and it seems to be an appropriate description for a resort best known for its in-room hot tubs and patio hammocks. Spanning 450 acres of prime beachfront land, the hotel has a mile-long beach (called Punta Brava) marked by white sand, a few rocks, and hundreds of palm trees. All rooms have indoor Jacuzzis, cold air-conditioning, private terrace with hammock and chairs, and a coffeemaker and stocked minibar. At meal time, guests choose from international, Italian, gourmet Mexican, Pan-Asian, or grilled cuisine. There are also six bars, ranging from secluded and romantic to lively and sociable. Recreation options include paddleboats, sauna, steam baths, yoga classes, fitness center, tennis, kayaking, or even free scuba clinics. The on-site European day spa offers a variety of traditional European and regional Mayan treatments. At night, guests can head to the outdoor *palapa*-covered discotheque for live entertainment and dancing. Rates: $350–400, double occupancy.

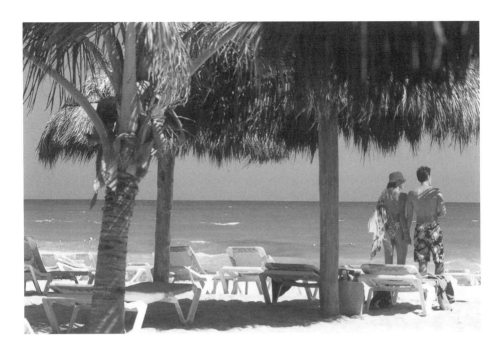

The beach in front of the Iberostar complex is one of the area's best.

Iberostar Paraíso Beach
984-887-2800 or 1-888-923-2722 (U.S.)
www.iberostar.com
Highway 307, km 309, Playa Paraíso

Part of the massive four-resort Iberostar complex, the Paraíso Beach property has 388 rooms and suites with satellite TV, stocked minibar, coffeemaker, and private balcony. There are six restaurants, two pool bars, lobby bar, cigar bar, sports bar, and a theater with nightly live shows put on by the staff. There is a huge meandering pool and large sundeck, and a kids' pool and kids' club keeps children ages 5–12 entertained during the day. Other activities include aerobics, archery, sailing, table tennis, tennis, volleyball, water polo, and windsurfing. Internet access, scuba diving (there is an on-site PADI dive school), spa services, and tours are available for an additional fee. This is the most affordable of the Iberostar properties, making it most popular with families and those seeking package deals. Rates: $230–480; package deals can bring the price down.

Iberostar Paraíso del Mar
984-877-2800 or 1-888-923-2722 (U.S.)
www.iberostar.com
Highway 307, km 309, Playa Paraíso

Stretched out along nearly a mile of idyllic beachfront, the 388-room Iberostar Paraíso del Mar is an all-inclusive resort popular with budget travelers who are looking for an active vacation full of fun water sports and tours, with plenty of relaxation mixed in. Since the resort is only 9 miles from Playa del Carmen, many guests go into town for shopping and nightlife, though with the nightly shows and on-site restaurants and bars, it's not really necessary. Rooms are housed in 11 low-rise buildings clustered along the beach, giving all guests ready access to the soft sand and clear water. There is a PADI dive shop, which offers diving and snorkeling trips to nearby reefs (for an extra fee). The grounds are amazing, with several pools emptying into a central canal. Amenities include tennis courts, a fitness room, a day spa, an outdoor Jacuzzi, and a swim-up bar. The main nightclub that services all the Iberostar hotels is at this resort. Rates: $230–480; package deals can bring the price down.

Iberostar Paraíso Lindo

984-887-2800 or 1-888-923-2722 (U.S.)
www.iberostar.com
Highway 307, km 309, Playa Paraíso

The Paraíso Lindo has 448 rooms and offers midrange lodgings for travelers looking for comfort, elegance, and beautiful surroundings. The all-inclusive accommodations include meals at the 12 restaurants (gourmet, Italian, Cajun, Asian, steak, and others), 14 bars (lobby, theater, pool, beach), plus 24-hour room service. Guests can also eat at any of the other Iberostar

resorts in the area. There is even a wave pool—the only one in the Riviera Maya. This property is a big hit for honeymooners, families, and singles. Rates: $280–550; package rates can bring the price down.

Iberostar Paraíso Maya

984-887-2800 or 1-888-923-2722 (U.S.)
www.iberostar.com
Highway 307, km 309, Playa Paraíso

The newest and most luxurious hotel in the Iberostar complex, the 432-room Paraíso Maya is laid out like a Mexican village, so guests never feel crowded. The rooms have TVs with DVD players, in-suite Jacuzzis, large marble bathrooms, and premium bedding. There are several pools, a lazy river tube slide, a large gym, a spa, a shopping plaza, and a kids' club. There are several specialty restaurants (Japanese, steak, Mexican, seafood), plus dining privileges at 16 others; 17 bars; and 24-hour room

The main pool at Iberostar Paraíso Maya Courtesy of Iberostar Resorts service. At night, guests head to the theater for live entertainment and then to the disco, located at the Paraíso del Mar. Rates: $450–750; package deals can help bring the price down.

Mayan Palace Riviera Maya

984-206-4000
www.mayanpalace.com.mx
Highway 307, km 310, Playa Paraíso

Home to what may be the largest and most impressive entryway of any hotel in the Riviera Maya, the aptly named Mayan Palace is equally inspiring once you're inside. With such a grand entrance, it's a bit surprising that the resort has only 336 rooms. Though the architecture may be inspired by the traditional Mayan building style, with thatched-palm roofs, low-rise buildings, and heavy use of local materials, the standards of luxury are significantly higher than even the Mayan gods could have imagined. The rooms are thoroughly contemporary, with tropical colors, soothing earth tones, cold air-conditioning, great views, bold artwork, and marble floors. The beach is beautiful but rocky, so be prepared to pick your way through the rough terrain if you want to go swimming. There is an on-site 18-hole Jack Nicklaus golf course, tennis courts, and an on-site kids' club, which provides complimentary child care in a fun environment. Since the property is so large, some guests complain about the walking distances from one attraction to another, but the landscaping and the natural beauty seem to keep most happy. Rates: $400–550, double occupancy.

PUNTA MAROMA

Six miles south of Playa Paraíso, quiet Punta Maroma has the kind of sugar-sand beach so often featured in postcards and travel agency brochures. The beach, more than 100 feet wide in many parts, is bordered by coconut palms and sea oats, and

there are very few rocks and light waves, making it a great place for swimming and snorkeling. There are a few upscale resorts, villas, and private homes, but it has an uncrowded, timeless, and faraway feel to it, making it an ideal spot for a tropical escape.

Club El Mandarin

984-873-4700
www.clubelmandarin.com
Highway 307, km 299, Xcalacoco

This 320-room all-inclusive resort has a private entrance from the highway. Once inside, guests enjoy a calm and isolated beach, a big pool and Jacuzzi, three restaurants, several bars, a nightclub, live entertainment, two tennis courts, a gym, pool tables, a fitness area, and spacious rooms with private balconies. A kids' club keeps children entertained during the day while parents relax by the pool or take a tour. Guests can take a free shuttle to Playa del Carmen. Scuba diving, shopping, and Internet access are available for an additional fee. Rates: start at $165 per person.

Maroma Resort & Spa

998-872-8200 or 1-866-454-9351 (U.S.)
www.maromahotel.com
Highway 307, km 305; enter through the Venta Club entrance

Recognized as one of the top hotels in the world, the 64-room Maroma Resort deserves its stellar reputation, with repeat guests making up a large percentage of the monthly reservations. The resort occupies some 200 acres of land, giving it an uncluttered and private feeling that can be hard to find in the area. Unlike many Riviera Maya resorts, Maroma is not the kind of place where visitors hang out in their cutoffs and tank tops, swilling margaritas and playing volleyball in the pool. Guests are much more subdued, and there is even a dress

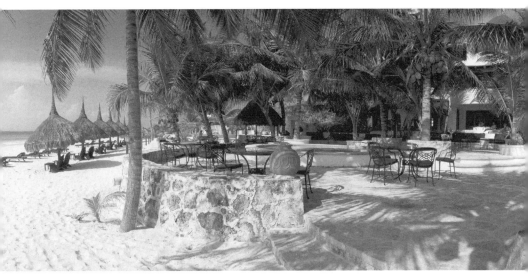

There's plenty of room to roam at Playa Maroma. Courtesy of Maroma Resort

code at the restaurant for dinner, with no jeans, sandals, or T-shirts allowed. Don't get the feeling that it's stuffy, though. It's definitely still relaxed, just classy.

The resort is down a gravel road and on an absolutely perfect beach. The jungle encroaches from all sides, and jungle animals seem ever-present, including iguanas, birds, and even arboreal turkeys, which call loudly from the trees at dusk. At night, a thousand candles line the walkways, giving the hotel a romantic and faraway feeling. The buildings feature thatched roofs, furniture made on-site from native hardwoods, and original artwork throughout. Rooms have hand-painted tiles, wool rugs, oversize tubs, and cold air-conditioning, which gives each room a blend of the old and the new, the traditional and the contemporary, the simple and the sublime. The beach is dotted with shaded cabañas, and a refreshing pool is next to the terrace, overlooking the beach. Sunbathing guests are tended to by a pool concierge, who is always ready with a cold drink, warm towel, or refreshing bottle of water. The on-site spa specializes

in Reiki, facials, mud baths, aromatherapy, body scrubs, crystal therapy, and other types of body treatments. Massages are also offered at a beachside hut or in the hotel's lookout tower, perched four floors above the jungle canopy, making it one of the tallest points around.

A beachside *temazcal* (sweat lodge) is the place to be at dusk, when guests are led through a 90-minute sweat-lodge ceremony, followed by a refreshing dip in the sea. Another treatment, a flotation chamber, allows guests to float weightless in a hyper-salted water tank. A 45-minute rest in the chamber is supposed to be equivalent

Celebrity Guests at Maroma Resort

TIM ALLEN • TONY BLAIR • TOM CRUISE • CLAIRE DANES • DANNY DEVITO • CAMERON DIAZ • MATT DILLON • MINNIE DRIVER • FARRAH FAWCETT • ENRIQUE IGLESIAS • BRAD PAISLEY • SEAN PENN • ROBERT PLANT • PRINCE CHARLES • SHARON STONE

The temazcal at Maroma Resort Courtesy of Maroma Resort

to an eight-hour sleep. An on-site gym has a full-time personal trainer, yoga and Pilates classes, and modern equipment. The restaurant, next to the beach, serves grilled fish, fresh seafood, lobster, salads, natural fruit juices, ceviche, and nightly specials. Try the *agua de chaya* for a refreshingly sweet alternative to water. Guests just give their room number when making purchases at the restaurant or other hotel installations, rather than signing a check each time.

Maroma has a variety of activities for guests to enjoy. From an early-morning nature walk (jaguars have been spotted in the past) and snorkeling and scuba diving to trips to area cenotes and Mayan ruins, the on-site tour desk can help you plan any activity. At the resort, there are tequila tastings, chili tastings, cooking classes, and a Spanish immersion program, in which guests receive a colored bracelet that lets staff members know to speak to them only in Spanish.

The resort is closed for upgrades each August. Rates: start at $340 and go much higher.

Mi Hotelito
998-872-8038
www.karismahotels.com
Highway 307, km 297

With only 24 rooms, including two spectacular honeymoon suites, Mi Hotelito is a very private resort, and it prides itself on offering personal service and luxurious accommodations. All rooms have an ocean view, plus minibar, coffeemaker, CD/DVD player, and private balcony or terrace with

Playa Xcalacoco
Some small Mayan ruins and a coconut grove mark the small, secluded beach of Xcalacoco, which is just south of Punta Bete. There are a couple of *palapa* restaurants that serve seafood and Mexican dishes, and campers can set up their temporary home at the Xcalacoco campsite, which has solar power and public showers.

hammock. Even though there are only two dozen rooms, there is a full-service restaurant and bar on-site serving international, Italian, and Asian food. Rates: $285–385 per person.

Secrets Capri
987-873-4880
www.secretsresorts.com
Highway 307, km 298

A lavish resort complex on 71 acres of pristine beach just south of Playa Maroma, the 285-room Secrets Capri is adults only and all-inclusive. It appeals to active couples who want to experience a broad range of recreational options while being surrounded in the comfort of a high-end resort. The architecture is a combination of Mediterranean and colonial Mexican, with graceful arches, tile work, and tropical plants throughout. Guests are welcomed into the lobby with a glass of champagne and a chilled towel and then descend a grand staircase to the pool deck area. There is a European day spa offering more than 30 different treatments, a swim-up bar, a poolside Jacuzzi, and drink service at the pool and on the beach. Rooms all have private balconies, jetted tubs, CD/DVD players, high-speed Internet access, coffeemakers, stocked minibars, and marble bathrooms. There are meeting and special-event facilities, plus a full-service business center with Internet access. This is a popular spot for weddings and honeymoons, and it offers a on-site wedding planner. All meals, drinks, and nonmotorized water sports are included. Rates: $380–480 per couple per night.

Punta Bete Region

Marked by the Capitán Lafitte hotel and the large wood-and-stone entrance of the Mayakoba megadevelopment, Punta Bete is just 4 miles north of Playa del Carmen, at km 296–298, making it popular for visitors who want to stay somewhere out of the way but still be close to the action of town.

LODGING

Fairmont Mayakoba
1-800-441-1414 (U.S.)
www.fairmont.com
Highway 307, km 297

Crowning the Spanish-owned Mayakoba development near Playa del Carmen, this family-friendly 401-room resort started taking reservations in December 2005. It features 90 two-story bungalows with only two to four rooms each, giving it a spread-out and spacious feeling. The decor is home-style Mexican, with dark wood, stone, and a palette of gold, soft reds, and oranges throughout. The rooms have air-conditioning, ceiling fans, premium bedding, oversize tubs, high-speed Internet access, LCD TVs, DVD/CD players, and private balconies. The property has two infinity pools, a great beachfront, and a 20,000-square-foot Willow Stream spa, with treetop treatment rooms, mineral pools, and steam rooms. Guests are shuttled through the resort on boats and in golf carts, and bicycles are also available for guest use. Mayakoba will eventually have six self-contained hotels, two golf courses, and private homes. The next project slated for completion is Laguna Kai (www.lagunakai.com), a very upscale condo project, developed by Rosewood Resorts. Others include

Banyon Tree, Viceroy, and La Casa Que Canta (of Zihuatanejo fame). Rates: start at $549.

Ikal del Mar

987-877-3000 or 1-888-230-7330 (U.S.)
www.ikaldelmar.com
Highway 307, km 294, Playa Xcalacoco (just south of Punta Bete)

To get to Ikal del Mar, follow Highway 307 south just past the Tres Rios ecology park and look for the turnoff to the left. The 1½-mile gravel road leads to the hotel entrance, and only registered guests are permitted access.

Small and very upscale, Ikal del Mar, whose name translates as "poetry of the sea," is one of the more likely places to spot a vacationing celebrity or business tycoon. Far from pretentious, though, the resort strives to harmonize with nature rather than completely shut it out. The hotel prides itself on the fact that no trees were cut down during construction. At night, tiki torches line the paths from the rooms to the restaurant and along the beachfront. Though the service, amenities, and price clearly place it in the luxury category, there are no marble bathrooms or video check-in kiosks. Here luxury is defined by the privileged setting, simple indulgences, and personal service. Poetry books top the carved-wood coffee table in the thatched palm pavilion at the hotel entrance that passes as the lobby, and the 30 guest rooms are housed in free-standing modernized versions of Mayan-style huts scattered along a winding sand trail that leads from the powdery white beach to the jungle. Rather than room numbers, each unit is assigned the name of a famous poet. The villas and furnishings are made from local stones and hardwoods. While the setting is exotic, don't expect iguanas and hermit crabs to sneak in between the thatched twig walls like they surely must have done in the days of the Mayans, however. Rooms are upgraded from the days of old with sealed walls, imported linens, private bathrooms, and—yes—even air-conditioning. Each villa also has a private terrace with splash pool and hammock.

The hotel beach is wide and cleaned daily. Guests relax under shady *palapas*, sipping tropical drinks and snacking on fresh ceviche. A long pier extends into the Caribbean, giving guests a shortcut to the good snorkeling spots. The pool and sundeck are just steps away. At meal times, the two-level gourmet restaurant serves a blend of Mediterranean and Mexican cuisine dubbed "Mexiterranean." There are also Asian-inspired selections and Mayan specialties. The wine list spans from French to Spanish to Italian.

The hotel spa is where the real pampering happens. It offers a steam room, a Jacuzzi, Swiss showers, and several treatment rooms. A local Mayan shaman leads guests in spiritual healing sessions at the beachside stone sweat lodge, called a *temazcal*. Other services include massage, facials, body scrubs, and yoga lessons. Rates: start at $525 a night.

La Posada del Capitán Lafitte

984-873-0214
www.capitanlafitte.com
Highway 307, km 296

Just north of Punta Bete and Playa del Carmen, this was one of the first hotels in the region, and it's still visited by longtime regulars who keep coming back for the premier location on a desolate beach, the high standards of personal service, and an atmosphere that is more laid-back than at many of the newer resorts. The entry from the highway is marked by a pirate ship, complete with wooden bow, steel mast, and tattered sails. The land was developed back when it was relatively inexpensive, so the complex is spread out over a wide area, with hundreds of feet of beachfront and a villagelike atmosphere. The 64 rooms aren't fancy, but they are comfortable and well maintained. Guests congregate around the pool during the day, savoring its view of the beach and the ocean beyond. There is a restaurant and bar, but since it's so close to Playa, many guests take a taxi into town during the evening. Rates: $140–200, depending on the time of year.

2

Playa del Carmen

Playa del Carmen is in the geographic center of the Riviera Maya and is the region's principal city. It is the seat of the municipal government and is home to the area's primary lodging, dining, nightlife, and shopping options.

Playa, as the locals call it, is the only town in the region whose development fills the land between Highway 307 and the beach. Within the past few years, it has even spilled onto the west side of the highway, an area that is seeing more and more development, including major shopping centers and housing developments for the local population.

No longer a sleepy fishing village, Playa has grown into a cosmopolitan beach resort, while somehow staying true to its roots, typified by its laid-back lifestyle, low-density development, international flavor, and casual come-as-you-are vibe. Visitors will find small local inns next to luxury villas, taco shacks next to steakhouses, and dusty cantinas next to stylish lounges. The mix of people and cultures, the variety of tourist offerings, and the welcoming spirit of the locals make it a unique travel destination, not just in Mexico, but in the entire world.

Looking toward Cozumel from Playa's lighthouse

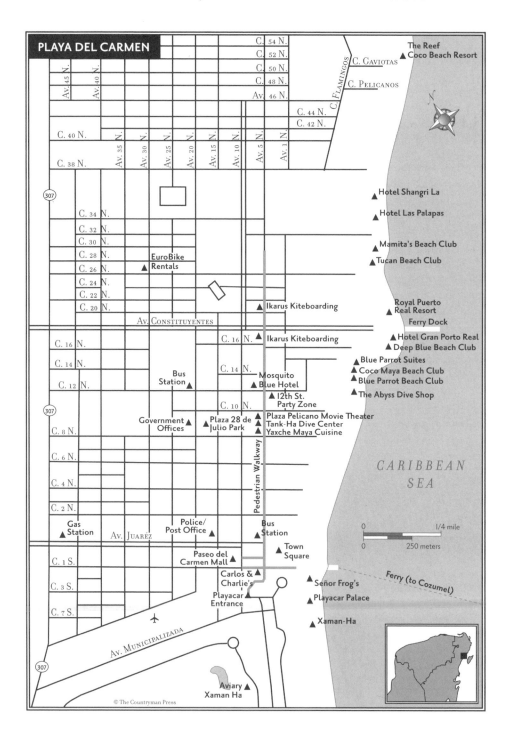

PLAYA DEL CARMEN

C. 54 N.
C. 52 N.
C. 50 N.
C. 48 N.
Av. 46 N.

C. 45 N.
Av. 40 N.

C. GAVIOTAS
C. PELICANOS
C. FLAMINGOS

The Reef
Coco Beach Resort

C. 44 N.
C. 42 N.

C. 40 N.

Av. 35 N.
Av. 30 N.
Av. 25 N.
Av. 20 N.
Av. 15 N.
Av. 10 N.
Av. 5 N.
Av. 1 N.

C. 38 N.

307

C. 34 N.

Hotel Shangri La

Hotel Las Palapas

C. 32 N.
C. 30 N.
C. 28 N.
C. 26 N.

EuroBike
Rentals

Mamita's Beach Club
Tucan Beach Club

C. 24 N.
C. 22 N.
C. 20 N.

Ikarus Kiteboarding

Royal Puerto
Real Resort
Ferry Dock

AV. CONSTITUYENTES

C. 16 N.

C. 16 N.   Ikarus Kiteboarding

Hotel Gran Porto Real
Deep Blue Beach Club

C. 14 N.

C. 14 N.

Bus
Station

Mosquito
Blue Hotel

Blue Parrot Suites
Coco Maya Beach Club
Blue Parrot Beach Club

C. 12 N.

C. 10 N.

12th St.
Party Zone

The Abyss Dive Shop

307

Government
Offices

Plaza 28 de
Julio Park

Plaza Pelicano Movie Theater
Tank-Ha Dive Center
Yaxche Maya Cuisine

C. 8 N.

C. 6 N.

C. 4 N.

CARIBBEAN
SEA

C. 2 N.

Gas
Station

AV. JUAREZ

Police/
Post Office

Pedestrian Walkway

Bus
Station

0   1/4 mile

0   250 meters

C. 1 S.

Paseo del
Carmen Mall

Town
Square

Ferry (to Cozumel)

Carlos &
Charlie's

C. 3 S.

Señor Frog's

Playacar
Entrance

Playacar Palace

C. 7 S.

Xaman-Ha

AV. MUNICIPALIZADA

307

Aviary
Xaman Ha

© The Countryman Press

LODGING

For some travelers, selecting a hotel is part of the fun of a visit to Playa del Carmen. There are more than 350 hotels offering some 25,000 rooms in the Riviera Maya, with many of them in the greater Playa area. Within a 2-mile radius, visitors can see more than 70 hotels, many of which, while not necessarily large, would be perfectly suitable for most needs. (Many of the area's hotels—about 75 percent—have 30 rooms or fewer.) Though many people choose to book a hotel prior to arriving, most of the year it's completely possible to show up without a reservation and take a stroll around town looking at different properties and current prices before making a final decision. Most hotel operators will happily give travelers a quick tour of their property and rooms, and sometimes they will be willing to negotiate a discounted price. Accommodations range from student hostels and inns with very few amenities that cater to budget travelers to large self-contained resorts with first-class facilities and services. There is also a new wave of "concept hotels," such as Hotel Básico and Hotel Deseo, which offer trendy accommodations in uniquely designed surroundings. Many hotels offer a wide range of room choices, with simple beach cabañas, modern hotel rooms, and luxury villas all at the same resort. The most important considerations are location (on the beach, on Quinta, or in town), budget, and desired atmosphere (romantic, singles, quiet, traditional). The selections in this chapter are organized into three different budget categories—budget, midrange, and luxury—and within each category there are a wide range of choices to please a wide range of tastes.

Budget Hotels

These properties are generally located a couple of blocks from the beach, between the town square and 30th Street. They are considered to be clean and safe but do not have many of the amenities that many travelers are accustomed to. Most do not have swimming pools, beautiful views, or on-site restaurants, and the rooms may not have in-room bathrooms, air-conditioning, or balconies. Prices range from $15 for a bed in a hostel dorm room to $65 for a well-kept room in a family-run inn with ceiling fan, purified water, and in-room safe. These hotels are popular with budget travelers, students, and short-term visitors who just need a place to stay for a couple of days while traveling through.

Antigua Posada Barrio Latino
984-873-2384
www.posadabarriolatino.com
Fourth Street between 10th and 15th Avenues

This is the namesake hotel for the Barrio Latino neighborhood from Second to Sixth Streets, between the beach and 30th Avenue. The area is reminiscent of the way that Playa used to be, with traditional hotels and a slower pace than the rest of town. The 16-room Italian-owned hotel is a popular home base for Europeans, student travelers, and others who may have money to stay at one of the more luxurious properties around town but choose to stay at a smaller hotel for the local charm, traditional character, and family-like service. The hotel is just 1½ blocks from Quinta, providing quick access to the town's restaurants and nightlife. Rooms are secure and clean, with private bathrooms, tile showers, ceiling fans, and in-room safes. Many also have air-conditioning. The owners can book most of the same tours that the larger tour agencies can, but they return their sales commission to their guests, resulting in a nice discount. An Internet station is located near the front desk, and complimentary

Antigua Posada Barrio Latino hotel   Courtesy of Posada Barrio Latino

wireless Internet access reaches most rooms. Rates: average $50 a night; include complimentary continental breakfast and a discount at the nearby Café de la Luna Italian restaurant. Highly recommended.

Copa Cabaña
984-873-0205
Quinta between 10th and 12th Streets

At the Copa Cabaña, located next to 100% Natural (see *Cafés and Light Fare*), sunning and working out are always in fashion. The rooms are built around a garden courtyard decorated with potted plants, tropical flowers, and Mayan-inspired artwork. The simple but comfortable rooms have air-conditioning, ceiling fans, and Mexican furnishings. There is a rooftop sundeck with Jacuzzi, hammocks, and a massage room. Rates: start at $60 per night.

Corto Maltes
984-873-0206
On the beach at 10th Street

Boasting 14 rooms that are the "Last of Old Playa," this classic hotel gives guests a taste of the way things used to be (and still are, in places such as Tulum). In a town where luxury condos are going up nearly every month, it's amazing that this place still exists. The Mayan-style huts have no air-conditioning, but they are clean and have private bathrooms and oscillating fans (to keep the warm air circulating). Each room has a hammock on the patio and a view of one of the best stretches of beach in downtown Playa. Rates: start at $65 per night.

Don Emilione
984-873-2073
www.donemilione.com
Quinta at Second Street

Opened in 1999, this 12-room, three-story hotel has a modern feel to it. The rooms are large and have air-conditioning, wicker furnishings, tile floors, safes, TVs, private bathrooms, and purified tap water. The hotel is just a block from the beach, and guests have seating privileges and dining discounts at a nearby beach club. The on-site Mexican restaurant has sidewalk tables and an indoor dining room, and the bar has a nightly happy hour from 5 to 7. Rates: $45–100, depending on the view (courtyard or beach) and the time of year.

Fiesta Banana
984-803-0201
www.fiestabanana.com
Quinta at 32nd Street

With less than 20 rooms, a common terrace, and a rooftop sundeck, this three-story inn has the feel of a large and friendly home. Its location near the northern end of Nueva Quinta puts it in the middle of the action, and it's just a couple of blocks from Nikki and Mamita's beach clubs. Rooms are spacious and offer traditional Mexican decor, air-conditioning, and tile floors. The staff is young and outgoing and can help provide local information and plan day trips. $40–$70. Highly recommended.

Hostel Playa
984-803-3277
www.hostelplaya.com
25th Avenue at 8th Street

Located about a half mile from the beach, this inexpensive alternative is a good spot for students and budget travelers who want a safe spot to stay but don't need much luxury. Rooms feature a natural wood motif and have mosquito netting, orthopedic mattresses, and clean bedding. There is a fully equipped kitchen for guest use, plus a common living room with sofas, TV, and DVD player. There is free coffee every morning and purified water all day long.

Peso-Pinching Activities

Traveling on a budget? Try these free and fun activities:

- Take free salsa lessons Tuesday and Thursday at 7 PM at La Bodeguita del Medio (see *Dining*).
- Walk along the interpretive nature trail at the back of the parking lot of the Las Palapas hotel (see *Luxury Hotels*).
- Visit the Xaman-Ha ruins in Playacar, just south of the Playacar Palace hotel (see chapter 3).
- Head to the beach and build a sandcastle in the shape of the great pyramid at Chichén Itzá.
- Get up early to watch the sun rise over the Caribbean. Some people like it even more than watching a sunset.
- Take advantage of the free appetizer/drink coupons offered by many restaurants along Quinta in Playa del Carmen.
- Stroll the park across from the municipal building and learn to count in Mayan from the educational displays.
- Grab your snorkel and take a dip in Manatee cenote, across from Blue Sky Resort in Tankah (see chapter 3).
- Watch the fire dancers perform their nightly show on the beach of the Blue Parrot bar (see *Drinks & Dancing*) at 11 PM or at the next-door El Pirata bar (see *Casual Drinks*) at midnight.
- Join the locals for a street party in Cozumel, complete with live music, each Sunday evening in the town square.
- Snorkel the protected cove at Akumal Bay and see moray eels, stingrays, and barracuda lurking in the shallows.

Rates: male, female, or mixed bunkrooms $10 per night; private rooms with double bed $25 per night; private rooms with two beds $35 per night. All guests receive a large locker with padlock. No credit cards; no children.

The Riviera Maya: A Land of Business Opportunity

Contributed by Brenda Alfaro

Great business opportunities abound in the Riviera Maya, and with careful consideration and planning, foreigners can invest successfully in this growth. Doing business in Mexico is not for the faint of heart, however. It requires moxie and experienced advice to be successful. Having a local on your side is always a plus, especially in Latin America, where polite business relationships guide you through the maze of paperwork, labor relationships, and license requirements. Patience is also a must-have virtue to survive the relaxing *mañana* Latin style.

Where do you start to create a business in Mexico? Well, not with the "slick talker and aggressive salesperson" attitude, would be my advice. First, look for someone who has been successful in a quiet way, who obviously has learned the ropes and has created the business and official relationships that have kept her in business. Seek her advice and be wise enough to listen to it.

Second, before stepping into the business community with a substantial investment, research and understand the legal system and labor relationships in Mexico. This is easily done on the Internet. Mexico laws are based on the Napoleonic Code, similar to the laws of France or Louisiana in the United States. Labor relationships are based on the "employee is always right" philosophy, and Mexican employees know their rights and use them effectively—as do the lawyers who represent them.

Third, understand the importance of a Mexican notary, which is a powerful appointed position in Mexico. Notaries create most of the official legal documents in Mexico, including establishment of corporations, buy-sell agreements, and real estate transactions. No transaction or legal agreement is considered legal in Mexico unless it has been officially registered. All parties to an agreement must sign it in front of a notary, and that agreement must be registered in the municipality's official records.

Fourth, before completing a business transaction, seek the advice of a person who is completely independent of the parties involved in the transaction and one you trust to translate the agreements to you accurately. I am always amazed when I hear that someone is using a lawyer or notary who was recommended by those who stand to benefit from the transaction, such as a seller or a real estate agent. A good rule of thumb is "If you would not do this in your country, you should not do it here."

Fifth, contract an accountant to keep you current with your tax filings and license requirements. Be careful whom you contract, and seek the advice of those who have experience here.

Hotel Alux
984-803-2482
www.hotelalux.com
14th Street between 10th and 15th Avenues

This small, 16-room, inn-style hotel has contemporary Mexican design and hacienda-inspired furnishings. All rooms have air-conditioning and private bathrooms. It's a good choice for visitors who don't mind being a couple blocks removed from the action. Rates: standard double rooms start at $35; rooms with kitchenettes and ceiling fans $40–50.

Hotel Azul
984-873-0562
www.hotel-azul.com
Quinta between 10th and 12th Streets

This hotel, in the center of the main tourist strip, has 20 rooms with private bathrooms and traditional Mexican ambience It may not be fancy, but you can't beat the location if you want to be near the action. There is no pool, but there is a shady courtyard, and the hotel is just 1½ blocks from the beach. Rates: average around $40.

Sixth, avoid all lawsuits and labor board actions. Swallow your pride or anger and settle with an employee who is leaving or involved in a legal situation. In the end, it will save you money and stress and allow you to focus on your business at hand and not on revenge or a compelling desire to "win." If you do end up needing a lawyer, find one who actually knows the law and has strong legal contacts as well.

Seventh, be polite and patient—always! Mexican people are intelligent and are part of a formal, polite society. Do not underestimate their abilities or insult them. Stop, listen, and think before you answer or react. Directness is not a business asset in Mexico. Talk, smile, and never argue or raise your voice. If you do, the costs will be great.

Eighth, follow the rules. It is so much easier when you are always in compliance, which means no extra favors need to be made to run your business. Remember, the person who receives a favor will be out of power in a few months or years, and the new official will expect the same or more—so why begin? And get your FM3, our resident work visa. Don't risk deportation.

Ninth, treat your employees with respect, learn the labor laws, and use employee contracts. Talk with business owners in your field and understand your employee base. Call for references before hiring someone. Find out who the "professional labor board employees" are who move from business to business to collect a labor settlement. Look prospective employees in the eye—if they do not look back or seem distrustful, do not hire them. Trust your instincts.

Tenth, enjoy the experience. When your patience begins to wear thin, escape to the beach to relax, recharge, and remember why you chose to live and work in this paradise in the first place.

BRENDA LONG ALFARO AND HER MAYAN HUSBAND, JORGE LUIS ALFARO MÉRIDA, ARE SUCCESSFUL RESTAURATEURS IN PLAYA DEL CARMEN. THEY OWN THE WIDELY ACCLAIMED AJUA MAYA RESTAURANT (SEE *Dining*), A SEAFOOD AND MAYAN GRILL; THE HACIENDA MAYA RESTAURANT (SEE *Dining*), FEATURING 19TH-CENTURY FRENCH-INFLUENCED MAYAN AND MEXICAN CUISINE; AND AJUA WEDDINGS, WHICH OFFERS CUSTOM-DESIGNED WEDDINGS AND EVENT SERVICES ON THE RIVIERA MAYA. THEY ALSO ESTABLISHED THE FUNDACIÓN AMÉRICA MAYA TO PROVIDE HEALTH CARE, EDUCATION, AND ECONOMIC PROGRAMS TO MAYAN FAMILIES AND CHILDREN.

Hotel Delfin
984-837-0176
www.hoteldelfin.com
Quinta at Sixth Street

A no-frills budget hotel in the heart of the older part of Quinta, the Hotel Delfin has simple but clean rooms with air-conditioning, TV, minibar, and safe. Rates: start at $45 in low season and go up to $80 in high season.

Hotel El Acuario
984-873-2133
www.elacuariohotel.com

25th Avenue between Second and Fourth Streets

Run by a local family, the Acuario offers budget accommodations in a safe and friendly neighborhood just a few blocks back from Quinta and the beach. Rooms have air-conditioning, ceiling fan, minifridge, and private terrace or balcony with hammock and table and chairs. Guests receive complimentary coffee each morning and have access to a grill for cooking their own meals. Rates: $45–75.

A Sunset Facing East?

Since the Riviera Maya faces east, it is not known as a good place to witness a tropical sunset. If your beach vacation just won't be complete without watching the golden orb disappear into the horizon, there's still hope. Try these five tips for catching a sunset in the Riviera Maya.

• Take a champagne sunset cruise aboard the Fat Cat 41-foot catamaran in Xaac Cove near Puerto Aventuras and watch the sun sink into the Caribbean (www.fatcatsail.com).

• Walk to the point at the north end of Playa del Carmen Cove, in back of the Porto Real hotel, and watch the sun go down next to the El Faro lighthouse.

• Climb to the top floor of the Moon & Sunset Bar in Paseo del Carmen and enjoy a rare sunset over downtown Playa and the jungle beyond.

• Take a day trip to Isla Cozumel and stay for sunset, then take a late ferry back to the mainland. Since the town's main beaches and town square face west, the sun sets over the ocean, just like in the postcards.

• For the ultimate unobstructed sunset view, schedule a sundown skydive and look down, not up, at the setting sun (see chapter 4).

Hotel Las Molcas

984-873-0070
www.molcas.com.mx
First Street at Quinta

This hotel is at the west end of the town square, making it especially convenient to the Paseo del Carmen mall and Quinta, as well as the ferry dock. There are 25 rooms with private bathrooms, air-conditioning, and minifridges. It is clean but a bit dingy and not especially charming. Rates: start at $45.

Hotel Plaza

984-873-2193
45th Street between 10th and 15th Avenues

No frills, but a great location. The Hotel Plaza has a pool, restaurant, convenience store, and rooms with air-conditioning and cable TV. Some rooms have nice views of the action on Quinta. Rates: $50–75.

Hotel Riviera Caribe Maya

1-800-822-3274 (U.S.)
www.hotelrivieramaya.com
10th Avenue between 28th and 20th Streets

This local-style inn is a budget hotel but doesn't feel like one. Its 22 rooms have contemporary design, air-conditioning, ceiling fans, cable TV, minifridge, and safe. There is also a pool, Jacuzzi, and restaurant. Rates: start at $55 for a basic room and go up, depending on room class and time of year.

Hotel Vista Caribe

984-873-0349
www.hotelvistacaribe.com
Quinta at Sixth Street

A longtime favorite for budget travelers, this 36-room hotel has a great location on Quinta and is only a block from the beach. All rooms have air-conditioning, ceiling fans, TVs, and safes for storing valuables. Some rooms have an ocean view, and others face the street. There is a small swimming pool and a flower garden. Rates: standard rooms range from $65–80.

Jungla Caribe

984-873-0650
www.jungla-caribe.com
Quinta at Eighth Street

Full of local charm, this hotel has been around a while and has developed a loyal following. Though it may not be trendy, it has a lot more character than many of the newer hotels. The winding staircases, shaded courtyard, small pool, and tile work all add to the ambience. The on-site Jaguar restaurant and bar serves Mexican dishes and seafood in a funky and fun setting overlooking Quinta. Rates: start at $30 for a single with no air-conditioning and go up to $60 for a suite with air-conditioning and private terrace. In high season the rates double.

La Ziranda
984-873-3933
www.hotellaziranda.com
Fourth Street between 15th and 20th Avenues

With its stucco walls, *palapa* roof, green grass, and stone walkways, La Ziranda charms from the moment you see it. There are 16 rooms with air-conditioning or ceiling fan and purified water. Each opens onto a grassy courtyard. Rates: $30–55, depending on the time of year. No credit cards.

Maya Bric/Tank-Ha Hotel
984-873-0011 or 984-873-0302
www.mayabric.com or www.tankha.com
Quinta between Eighth and 10th Streets

This family-owned hotel has two names and two web sites, but it's really the same place. Maya Bric is the original name of the hotel, and Tank-Ha is the on-site dive shop and the name that is used when marketing the hotel to divers. There is a shaded pool for basic dive instruction, and the 29 simple rooms have private bathrooms and air-conditioning. Divers can learn about area dives and book their trips at the dive shop, a good spot to meet other divers if you need a dive buddy. Rates: $50–60.

Pension San Juan
984-873-0647
www.pensionsanjuan.com
Quinta between Sixth and Eighth Streets

Pension San Juan

10 Tips for Enjoying Your Trip

Rent a car. Being mobile and free gives you a whole new perspective on a destination. You won't need it the whole time, but get one for a few days and explore the coast on your own. Pack a cooler, beach towel, map (freebies are available at the airport and most hotels), and mask/snorkel, and hit the road. Make sure to hit Tulum, hidden beaches, and lost-in-time villages.

Learn a little Spanish. A little goes a long way, and it helps you feel like you belong. It's also a nice gesture to make to your Mexican hosts, who will appreciate the effort and are usually happy to take some time to teach you new words. For bonus points, learn a little Mayan. Even saying "hello" or "thank you" in the native language is a sure way to get smiles from the locals, many of whom speak it fluently.

Take care of yourself. Don't get dehydrated or sunburned. Drinking plenty of purified water will keep your energy level up and can prevent serious illness. Don't be stingy with the sunscreen, either: a trip-ruining sunburn can happen in less than an hour if you're not used to the sun and you don't protect yourself. And while you're at it, put on insect repellent before heading out at night. While others are scratching their ankles, you'll be enjoying your margarita.

Order the whole fish. Native to the region, this dish has been a favorite for hundreds of years. The fish is scaled and gutted but left whole, and it is then lightly fried and usually served with tomatoes and onions. It's a good dish to share, with each diner forking off the pieces he or she wants. Even the skin is crispy and tasty, full of healthy fish oils.

Request a mariachi song. Sure, you can hear them playing at the table across the way, but there's nothing like being surrounded by the band as they play at your very own table. It makes for great photos, also, so request a song, try to sing along, and take some fun pictures. Remember to tip $3–5 per song.

This friendly, family-run, 12-room inn is located right on Quinta. Rooms have traditional Mexican decor, ceiling fans, safes, and private bathrooms, and some also have air-conditioning, TVs, minifridges, and a view of Quinta. There is an incredibly charming outdoor kitchen for guest use on a terrace overlooking Quinta, which gives you the sense that you're in your own private café. Rates: $30–60; include complimentary coffee and cooking supplies. Highly recommended.

Santa Barbara Hotel
984-873-1382
Fourth Street between 10th Avenue and Quinta

Across from the Ajua Maya restaurant (see *Dining*), this simple 18-room hotel has a great location close to the action. Wind your way through the maze of stairs, and you'll find the units are clean and bright—but they have cement floors and small showers, which can be a turnoff for some. Some rooms have air-conditioning and TVs, others don't. All have private bathrooms, and one has a private terrace. Rates: $30–80.

Siesta Fiesta
984-803-1166
www.siestafiestahotel.com
Quinta between Eighth and 10th Streets

There's always something going on at this hot spot in the middle of Playa's busy pedestrian walkway, which can be a good thing or a bad thing. There is a restaurant and bar in the cozy courtyard, featuring several hours of live music each night, plus

Check out the late-night scene. Sitting at a rope-swing bar stool and dancing under the stars is a longtime Playa tradition, and it's alive and well at the Blue Parrot (see *Drinks & Dancing*). The party gets going at around II PM, when the fire dancers put on their show, followed by DJ music and dancing on the wooden dance floor, on the beach, or in the chic *palapa*-covered lounge room. More into a relaxing scene? Linger over a glass of wine at the Glass Bar (see *A Classy Night on the Town*), savor a martini at Fly (see *Trendy Lounges*), or practice your lounging skills at Kartabar (see *Trendy Lounges*). Not tired yet? Head to Santanera (see *Drinks & Dancing*) and learn to dance like a local.

Stroll along the beach. Leave your sandals behind and take a long walk on the powdery white-sand beach. If you're staying in Playacar, head south toward Xcaret and follow the beach until a rocky point bars your way, and you'll find a secluded and picturesque spot to rest before heading home. If you're staying near Quinta, head north past Mamita's Beach Club all the way to the Reef Club hotel and the deserted beach beyond (Playa Chun-Zumbul).

Visit a cenote: These freshwater sinkholes, unique geographical features, are a whole lot of fun. The refreshingly cool water feels great after a day in the sun, and the virtually unlimited visibility makes you feel like you're floating in space. Hidden World (see chapter 4) is the most expensive, but it's also the best.

Snorkel or scuba dive on the Great Mayan Reef. Take the plunge for a chance to see colorful corals, tasty-looking lobsters, stern-looking barracuda, slippery eels, majestic turtles, and hundreds of tropical fish.

Get up early. Though the sun sets over Quintana Roo mainland, it rises over the Caribbean. Combined with the solitude and quiet of the early-morning hours, watching the sunrise is a spiritual and calming way to start your day. Next, head to your favorite café for a cup of coffee and some *pan dulce* (sweet pastries) as you watch the shops open up and the tourists start their rounds.

sidewalk tables and a large-screen TV for live sporting events and recorded concerts. Vacation camaraderie is especially strong here, making it a great spot to meet and socialize with other travelers. Rooms have private terraces with hammocks, air-conditioning, private bathrooms, and minifridges. Rates: $30–50.

Midrange Hotels

Located on or near Quinta or even on the beach, these hotels are sufficient for most travelers. Many have swimming pools, restaurants, bars, and other amenities. They generally have air-conditioning, and all have private bathrooms. Prices range from $60 for a standard hotel off the beach to $120 for a property with a premier location (on Quinta or the beach), air-conditioning,

and upgraded amenities. They are popular with travelers who want to stay somewhere comfortable and with a local feel, without spending too much money.

Acanto Hotel & Suites
984-873-1252 or 631-898-3026 (U.S.)
www.acantohotels.com
16th Street between First Avenue and Quinta

This small complex is on a quiet side street just off an upscale part of Quinta. The grounds have tropical gardens, a swimming pool, and a rooftop terrace with grill for guest use. The seven one-bedroom villas, in a modern hacienda-style setting, have a decidedly Asian/Zen influence and include a private bedroom with queen bed, roman-tic bedding, candles, ceiling fans, and a large tiled shower. Each unit also has air-conditioning, a full kitchen with appliances and supplies, cable TV, a dining room, and a living room with sofa bed and stuffed chair, as well as a terrace or balcony with table and chairs and a hammock. Rates: $115–175; include complimentary wireless Internet access. The New York owner also has several private apartments around town and near the beach available for weekly/ monthly rental. Recommended.

Adelia Maria Suites

984-879-3393
www.adeliamaria.com.mx
First Avenue between 24th and 26th Streets

This condo-style hotel has 18 rooms with traditional Mexican decor, air-conditioning, and cable TV. It's a bit reminiscent of *Melrose Place,* with a courtyard pool and a friendly, social atmosphere. Rates: range from $70 for a studio with kitchenette up to $190 for a two-room deluxe suite with living room, sofa bed, and kitchen.

Alhambra Hotel

984-873-0735
www.alhambra-hotel.net
Eighth Street at the beach

With 23 rooms right on the beach, Alhambra is part of the old Playa, before the development of large-scale condo projects that pushed the density restrictions to the max. Don't expect luxury, but you will find clean accommodations, air-conditioning, friendly service, in-room TVs, and a New Age atmosphere with an emphasis on peace and tranquility. There is a small pool and sundeck, massage service, and yoga classes. The best thing about Alhambra, though, is staying on the best beach in town, with close proximity to the town's best restaurants and nightlife. Rates: range from $50–80.

Blue Beach Hotel

984-873-1204
www.bluebeachhotel.com
On the beach between 12th and 14th Streets

This part of the beach is a bit rocky, and the shallows have many fishing boats with their anchors stretched to the beach. It's more relaxed than nearby beaches, though, and the hotel is set back from the ocean, giving guests plenty of room to stretch out and relax. This complex has 28 units in all, ranging from simple but contemporary beachside bungalows and a hotel building to a three-bedroom beachfront villa with all the luxuries. Rates: from $50 for a cabaña with no air-conditioning up to $275–420 for the villa, depending on the time of year.

Casa Tucan

984-873-0283
www.casatucan.de
Fourth Street between 10th and 15th avenues

Looking everything like a quaint European hideaway from the street, the Casa Tucan is a charming alternative to the corporate-run resorts that have led the explosive growth in the Riviera Maya. There is a small pool, some tropical gardens, and a street-facing café that was built around the trunk of a large tree. The rooms don't have air-conditioning, but they are usually clean and cozy. Its location in the Barrio Latino district puts it just a block from the excitement of Quinta. Rates: start at $60 per night.

Costa del Mar

984-873-0850
www.hotelcostadelmar.com
First Avenue between 10th and 12th Streets

One of the original beach hotels in Playa, the modest colonial-style Costa del Mar has kept up with the times but retained its simple and relaxing nature. It has a small pool, a great beach, and 38 rooms, most with air-conditioning, safes, ceiling fans, and TVs. At the beach, the on-site El Pirata bar and restaurant serves draft beer and snacks and has a wooden bar with swinging bar stools. It's directly adjacent to the Blue Parrot bar (see *Drinks & Dancing*), so guests have ready access to the nighttime revelry. Rooms near the beach can be a bit loud at night, so choose one near the street if you want to go to bed before the clubs close. There's also an on-site dive shop offering trips to the nearby reefs, Cozumel, and the freshwater cenotes of the Riviera Maya. Rates: $60–$85, depending on amenities and time of year.

Eclipse Hotel
984-873-0629
www.hoteleclipse.com
First Avenue between 12th and 14th Streets

This artsy 18-room hotel has themed rooms, including the two-story Robinson Crusoe Suite, the De Luxe Suite, and the Caribbean Palapa Suite. Each eclectic and casually rustic room features original decor and artwork, a unique floor plan, wooden furnishings, ceiling fan, satellite TV, and other extras, depending on the room. Some have air-conditioning. The courtyard has some large palm trees, hammocks, and gardens. It is a favorite of traveling artists, young couples, backpackers, and others who like some character and charm in their accommodations. An attached convenience store and Native Deli café (known for quality inexpensive breakfasts) are open to the public. Guests can borrow bicycles for free. The German owner speaks several languages, has been in the area for years, and is happy to dispense excursion-planning advice. Guests can book airport transfers at the hotel front desk. Rates: $50–150, depending on the room selected.

Fusion Hotel
984-873-0374
Sixth Street at the beach

Formerly known as the Hotel Alejari, the 29-room Fusion Hotel has a great location on the beach and is just a block from the most bustling part of Quinta. The rooms are oriented around a central courtyard and are reminiscent of a Spanish villa, with winding staircases and meandering sidewalks. Units are decorated in a traditional Mexican style and face the courtyard or the open ocean. Each room has a mini refrigerator, cable TV, and ceiling fan. Many also have air-conditioning and a private balcony. The on-site international restaurant serves tropical drinks and snacks on the beach, plus seafood, Mexican food, and pasta dishes. Rates: $70–$120, depending on the room class and season.

Hotel Coco Rio
984-879-3361
www.hotelcocorio.com
26th Street between Quinta and 10th Avenue

This 15-room hotel features colonial architecture and spacious rooms with air-conditioning, cable TV, in-room safes, and minifridges. The decor is tropical, with bright and airy rooms, and the staff works to make guests feel welcomed and secure. There is an on-site restaurant serving gourmet Italian food. Rates: $50–150, depending on the size of the room and time of year.

Hotel Lunata
984-873-0884
www.lunata.com
Quinta between Sixth and Eighth Streets

Though it's right on Quinta, Lunata seems somewhat secluded given its narrow entrance through a private hall, which

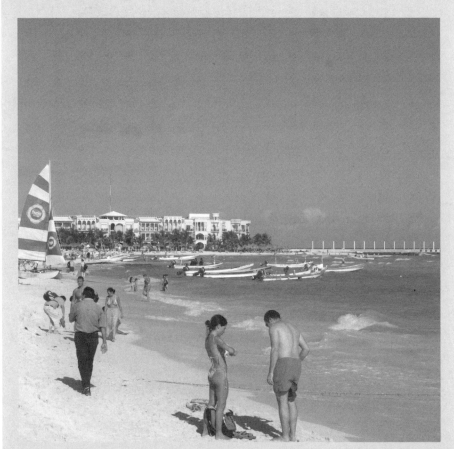

Mike Stone

Hit the Beach

Playa, plage, spiaggia, beach: However you say it, and in whatever language, the white powdery beaches of the Riviera Maya are undeniably—and justifiably—the region's main draw. Though not quite as flourlike as the shoreline in Cancún, the crushed-shell beaches in and around Playa del Carmen are world renowned for their softness, white color, and cleanliness.

All ocean beaches in Mexico are considered federal property and are open to the public. No hotel, land owner, beach bar, or other entity may legally restrict access to the beach. That being said, it is common for hotels to cordon off an area for the exclusive use of their guests, and this is generally accepted as it seems to do more good than harm for the most number of people. All-inclusive hotels, for instance, may serve food and drinks on the beach, and it is helpful to their servers if their guests are slightly removed from other beachgoers. Some beach bars set up a perimeter around their beach-front tables and do not allow minors to enter and can even have a cover charge, but the area cannot extend all the way to the water line, so nonpatrons can still freely pass by without being hassled. In some spots, resorts have set up a roped-in area where their guests can use beach chairs and beach umbrellas without being hassled by passing vendors or other nonguests.

Licensed vendors can set up chairs and shaded *palapas* and can legally charge for their use. The general rule is, unless you're staying at the hotel that owns the facilities, you are not allowed to use them. Still, though, many tourists successfully beach-hop and visit a number of different beaches and rarely have problems using any lounge chair they happen by. Sometimes ordering a drink can earn you access to a good beach spot, and having a beach towel that matches the color of the ones the hotel provides helps, too.

Many of the main beaches, including the beach just north of the ferry dock in Playa and along the shallow cove of Akumal, are secured by federal lifeguards, who are well equipped and well trained to handle most emergencies. The nature parks, including Xcaret, Xel-Ha, and Tres Rios (see chapter 4), have private guards on duty to keep an eye on bathers and assist with any problems. With the lack of undertow, little poisonous marine life, clear water, and well-marked swimming areas, accidents are relatively uncommon, though, and the beaches are considered quite safe.

Some areas, though, do require a bit more caution. Keep an eye out for submerged rocks, shallow reefs, and off-course WaveRunners. Be careful also to avoid the black spiny sea urchins, floating debris, and diving into shallow water. If you're exploring remote areas, it's a good idea to stay in a group and not wander off alone. It's also important to keep in mind that although the Riviera Maya is generally safe and most of the people are friendly and welcoming, every town has its bad apples, and you don't want to encounter them. Even though the beaches are government property, locals may not take too kindly to tourists wandering too far from the beaten path and encroaching on their home territory. Be careful not to enter private property that is adjacent to the beach and be respectful of locals who have claimed a beach area for themselves.

Petty theft can be a problem anywhere, including on the beach. Keep a watchful eye on your belongings if you stray from them or, better yet, take turns playing in the waves and leave someone on the beach to watch your things. And don't assume that just because you're on a remote spot and can't see anyone that no one can see you. Stories abound of snorkelers who come back to their beach blankets after a stint on the reef only to find their bags pilfered. Though some may choose to deny that there could be crime in paradise and instead blame the pesky and ever-curious white-faced monkeys, the thieves' penchant for cash, MP3 players, and digital cameras leads me to believe the culprits are looking for more than bananas.

The city police in Playa del Carmen sometimes patrol the popular beaches of town on ATVs. They are mainly looking for rowdy drunks and local drug users, so the average tourist, even a Corona-guzzling one, is almost never bothered. In some areas, generally remote beaches, the Mexican Navy performs foot patrols, presumably checking for drug runners and drop-off sites. Be respectful, and they will pass by with just a friendly wave.

To the north of the Reef Cocobeach (described later in this chapter), the beach (known as Chun-Zumbul) is still mostly deserted and is great for exploration and relaxation. Parking is available next to the Reef's main parking lot. Though there are other developments planned for the area, there's still a lot of virgin beach available, and intrepid adventurers will always be able to find a secret spot in which to enjoy the sand and the waves in relative seclusion.

lends an air of privacy and sophistication not found in other downtown hotels. The decor is contemporary hacienda style, designed by architect Angel Isles, with archways, earth tones and blues, river stones, dark woods, iron, and tile. The hotel has the feeling of an old-style guest house, with only 10 rooms, each with its own style and charm. All rooms have air-conditioning and private balcony with ocean, garden, or street views. Rates: $99 for a standard in low season to $145 for a junior suite in high season; includes continental breakfast. Highly recommended.

Hotel Quinto Sol

984-873-3292
www.hotelquintosol.com
Quinta at 28th Street

A Mediterranean/Mexican hacienda-style hotel in the heart of Quinta's international section, the midsize Quinto Sol has much of the same style and class as some of the area's more expensive hotels, yet its prices are more moderate. Rooms and suites have air-conditioning, minibars, cable TV, safes, and phones, and some have kitchenettes, balconies, terraces, living rooms, Jacuzzis, and business desks. Rates: $70–110 for a standard room and $100–150 for a suite, depending on the time of year.

Los Itzaes Hotel

984-873-2373
www.itzaes.com
10th Avenue between Sixth and Eighth Streets

A block back from Quinta, Los Itzaes is a haven from the rush of the downtown entertainment district. The hotel's 14 rooms and suites are casual, but quite soothing and even a tad elegant, at least for the price. Each has air-conditioning, ceiling fan, satellite TV, minifridge, safe, and private balcony. There's a well-stocked book exchange behind the front desk. The

complex has a rooftop swimming pool with a view of the city and the beach. Rates: average $60–80; continental breakfast included.

Luna Blue Hotel & Gardens

984-873-0990
www.lunabluehotel.com
26th Street between Quinta and 10th Avenue

Formerly known as the Zanzibar, this hotel was completely renovated in late 2005, partly with the help of Hurricane Wilma and partly with the help of the ambitious new owners from San Francisco. There are shaded hammocks and a lagoonlike sunken garden and waterfall, and the whole place is surrounded by jungle and tropical flowers, giving it a lost-in-time quality that's not always easy to find in a modern resort destination. Each of the 18 rooms at Luna Blue is a little bit different. All rooms have ceiling fans, private bathrooms, locally made furnishings, and a private porch, and some have air-conditioning and full kitchens. The treetop terrace penthouses have a private deck, air-conditioning, and refrigerator. Guests receive complimentary continental breakfasts and purified water. Rates: range from $40 for a standard room in low season to more than $100 for the treetop terraces in high season.

Mayan Paradise

984-873-2016
10th Avenue between 10th and 12th Streets

Set back from the street a bit, the Mayan Paradise is sometimes hard to spot: The dark-wood exterior blends peacefully into its surroundings. Each of the 40 rooms has air-conditioning, ceiling fan, TV, kitchenette, minibar, and private balcony. There is also a pool, a restaurant, and an off-site beach club. It's a good spot to stay if you're in town for a while and want to be close to the action but still want a quiet place to hide out when you need to. Rates: $130–200. Recommended.

Plaza Mariachi Hotel
16th Street at Quinta

Located just to the beach side of Quinta, this well-located hotel has a nice pool and sundeck and spacious rooms with kitchenettes, air-conditioning, and ceiling fans. There is an on-site bar, Internet access, and a snack bar. It's not particularly fancy, but if you want to be in the center of the action and don't want to pay too much, it can be a good alternative. Rates: starting at $55.

Posada Freud
984-873-0601
www.posadafreud.com
Quinta between Eighth and 10th Streets

Located above a busy restaurant and bar, the 14 rooms and penthouse suite at Posada Freud define funky chic. Rooms have two double beds or one king, tile floors, balconies, and traditional Mexican decor, and some also have air-conditioning. The multilevel, three-bedroom penthouse has a living room with entertainment center, air-conditioning, several private terraces, coffeemaker, sofas, and dining area, and it feels more like a private home than a hotel room. Rates: range from $35 for a single room with no air in low season to more than $200 for the penthouse in high season (four-night minimum). Highly recommended.

Riviera del Sol Hotel
984-873-3100
www.rivieradelsol.com
First Avenue and 40th Street

At the northern end of the tourist section of downtown Playa del Carmen, this 23-room family-run hotel is easy to spot, with a Mediterranean-influenced cupola crown-

Ocean Safety
Many beaches along the Riviera Maya use a colored flag system to alert swimmers of the ocean's condition:

Black: No swimming allowed. Used to denote swift current, dangerous tides, lightning, or other serious problems. Seldom seen and should be taken very seriously.

Red: Caution urged. Dangerous conditions possible. Used to mark crashing waves, presence of rocks, or other potential hazards. Common at high tide or on windy days. Good swimmers can still enter the water but should be careful.

Yellow: Stay alert. No known issues, but swimmers should stay aware. Most common flag flown in the area. Used on all but the calmest of days. Competent swimmers should not be dissuaded from enjoying the water.

Green: Ideal conditions. Safest swimming possible. Seen only on the best of days.

ing the main lobby. The hotel has Mexican decor and tropical furnishings, and it's a quiet respite from the bustling Quinta commercial district. There is a swimming pool and relaxing waterfall, plus an on-site international restaurant. The rooms have air-conditioning, ceiling fans, minibars, satellite TV, mosaic tile work, safes, and private balconies. Some also have kitchenettes. Rates: average $80.

Luxury Hotels
The best of the best, these hotels and resorts cater to international travelers who are accustomed to the finer things in life. Most have multiple swimming pools, restaurants, bars, fitness rooms, business centers, and concierge service. They generally have efficient air-conditioning, satellite TV, spacious rooms, well-designed

bathrooms, guest balconies, and on-site restaurants, and many also have room service, Internet access, and other amenities associated with a first-class hotel. Room rates range from $125 per night for a highly rated tourist-class hotel up to more than $500 per night for a room at a top-of-the-line all-inclusive resort.

Aventura Mexicana
984-873-1876
www.aventuramexicana.com
22nd Street at 10th Avenue

With 25 rooms, this boutique hotel is large enough to have a nice pool, two outdoor Jacuzzis, a gourmet restaurant, and other facilities, but still small enough to benefit from personal service, a tranquil atmosphere, and a dose of class. The decor is reminiscent of a Mexican hacienda, but with many modern upgrades. All rooms have stylish modern decor, air-conditioning, ceiling fan, satellite TV, Internet access, garden/pool views, and room service. It has multiple sundecks and is particularly popular with gay travelers. Rates: $135–230.

Blue Parrot Fifth Avenue
984-873-0083
www.blueparrot.com
Quinta between 10th and 12th Streets

This is the spot formerly occupied by Pancho's Hotel & Frida Bar, which was one of the most popular spots in town before being shut down by the government for not paying taxes. Open in late summer of 2005, Fifth Avenue is the newest location of the popular Blue Parrot franchise. Guests traverse a wooden bridge to get to the lobby, and there are 18 boutique-style upscale hotel rooms as well as a Thai-influenced restaurant and bar perched above a decorative pool and adorned with ornate *palapas*. The scene is much more serene and sophisticated than

at Blue Parrot's beachfront location. The spacious Asian-inspired rooms have cold air-conditioning, satellite TV, and safes. Guests have privileges at the nearby Blue Parrot beach club. Rates: $110 and up; more in high season. Recommended.

Blue Parrot Hotel
984-873-0083
www.blueparrot.com
12th Street at the beach

The Blue Parrot offers the quintessential Playa del Carmen experience. Owned by a native of Chicago, it's more of a tropical community center than a hotel. Even if you're not staying here, you'll most likely end up here at some point. Whether it's to eat breakfast at the beachfront restaurant, lounge in a beach chair and sip a cold drink, visit the Abyss dive shop to plan a tour, or stop by for a late-night swing at the bar, watch the fire dancers (show starts at 11 PM), and dance the night away, nearly all Playa visitors are touched by the Blue Parrot in some way. The hotel's 35 luxury rooms are housed in a condo-style complex a block away from the reception and bar area. There are spacious studios and one-bedroom suites with wicker furniture, contemporary/tropical decor, kitchenettes, Internet access, and soothing colors. A few have oceanfront views, but most are set back a bit from the beach, looking across at other units, with a partial ocean view to one side. There is a narrow pool between the buildings and a welcomingly shady courtyard. There is also a small group of rustic beachfront bungalows just north of the beach bar. Guests get a 20 percent discount at the hotel restaurant and free access to the beach chairs. Rates: range from $80 (for the beach cabañas) to $180 (for the suites). Highly recommended.

The Blue Parrot on Quinta is more subdued.

Blue Parrot Suites
984-873-0083
www.blueparrot.com
First Avenue at 14th Street

Though guests use the reception desk at the Blue Parrot Hotel on 12th Street, the Suites are in a separate building 1½ blocks away. The 28 studios and suites have modern amenities and name-brand furnishings, kitchenettes, and a Bahamas-like contemporary rattan decor. Since it is a bit removed from the rest of the Blue Parrot

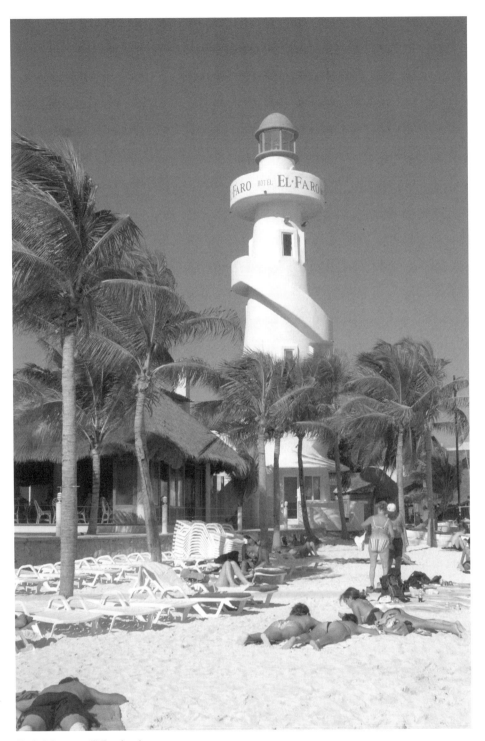

The lighthouse at El Faro hotel Mike Stone

property, it is quite calm and relaxing. There is a small pool, and the beach is only a block away. Rates: vary throughout the year, but studios start at $140 and suites at $250.

Deep Blue Hotel
14th Street at the beach

This beachfront boutique hotel has 35 rooms and features tropical decor, a trendy ambience, and a see-and-be-seen attitude. The vibe is positive, though, and the ready access to the backyard beach club makes it a great place to stay. Rates: $220–250.

El Faro
984-873-0970
www.hotelelfaro.com
10th Street at the beach

Home to Playa's landmark lighthouse (*faro* means "lighthouse" in Spanish), this hotel has 28 rooms and suites housed in low-rise buildings built around a beachside swimming pool and tropical gardens. Its central location and relaxing ambience have made it a favorite for years. A condo project behind the hotel is giving visitors a chance to own a piece of this local landmark. Rates: start at around $130. Recommended.

Gran Porto Real
984-873-4000
www.realresorts.com.mx
Constituyentes Avenue at the beach

Constructed on the site of Playa's original nudist beach, the Gran Porto Real was the first large-scale hotel built on the town's main tourist strip. It has Italian and Mediterranean decor and overlooks a waveless cove at the southern end of Playa's central beach. Guest have their choice of all-inclusive or European plan accommodations. There are five restaurants, four bars, a nice pool, a car rental desk, a day spa, and a kids' club. Rooms have satellite TV, premium bedding, minibars, and private balconies. Rates: start at $140.

Hotel Básico
984-879-4448
www.hotelbasico.com
Quinta at 10th Street

Básico is a concept hotel owned by the same company that runs Deseo, just down the road. It has 14 rooms, including three suites, housed on three floors and built above Quinta with an entrance on 10th Street. The beige facade owes its unusual color to the Caribbean sand that was mixed with concrete to form its solid walls. The design was conceptualized by a well-known avant garde design firm in Mexico City called Omelet, since, as its owner says, it takes "*huevos*" to do the kind of design they do. The theme is rooted in 1950s Mexico and Latin America, when oil production and construction boomed and beach vacations were a sign of prosperity. The building shines with the creative use of tile (imported from Mérida), glass, rubber, and latex. Rooms have high beds with built-in minibar and lighting system, exposed plumbing, corner rain shower, TV with DVD player, and colored neon accent light, plus air-conditioning and a security safe. The ground-level juice bar doubles as the front desk. The patio level features a Veracruz-style seafood restaurant, and the visually striking rooftop terrace features canopy sunbeds, a trendy bar, a projection movie screen, ocean views, hammocks, and two smallish plunge pools, modeled after holding tanks commonly found at Mexican oil fields. Rooms that overlook the street can get a bit loud, so consider this when choosing yours. Guests have complimentary use of the hotel's three-wheeled bicycles during their stay. Rates: range from $150 (patio view) to $210 (ocean view) and are slightly more in high season.

TEMAZCAL

The word *temazcal* means "bath house" in the Nahuatl language of the ancient Aztecs, and the centuries-old *temazcal* sweat-lodge ceremony hasn't changed much over the years. The ritual, performed by a shaman or trained healer, is designed to serve both spiritual and medical purposes. Native women were known to give birth inside the dark, warm environment of the *temazcal*, thus making the transition from the womb more gradual. The sweat-lodge ceremony takes place in a stone or adobe hut, dug into the earth and forming a dome large enough for about a dozen participants. Before entering the *temazcal*, all those who will participate reflect on the four cardinal points and are cleansed with incense. Volcanic stones are heated in a wood fire, carried into the *temazcal*, and placed in the center of the floor.

Each participant sits behind a clay pot full of water, and the door is closed and sealed, making the inside completely dark and very hot. The leader pours water onto the rocks, creating steam that fills the *temazcal* and helps partakers to liberate their minds, bodies, and souls. Ancient chants are repeated, songs are sung, and participants are led through a cleansing ritual. In some versions, regional fruits are passed around to be tasted and rubbed on the skin. Modern-day participants generally wear their bathing suits and can splash water on themselves to regulate their breathing and prevent overheating.

Many people have visions and even see an animal or other creature rising from the glowing rocks. The ceremony leader can help interpret whatever you may see. At the end of the ceremony, it is customary to run to the ocean and bathe in the shallows, letting the cool water wash away the sweat and complete the renewal process. Next, a soothing herbal tea helps lock in the benefits reaped during the ceremony. It's a wonderfully spiritual experience that can leave you energized and refreshed for hours afterward.

Spiritual healing awaits in the temazcal. Courtesy of Maroma Resort

Places in the Riviera Maya with *temazcal* facilities include Maroma Resort & Spa, Punta Maroma (see chapter 1); Ceiba del Mar, Puerto Morelos (see chapter 1); Tulum Dreams/Resort & Spa, Tulum (see chapter 3); Ikal del Mar, Playa Xcalacoco (see chapter 1); Ana y José Charming Hotel & Spa, south of Tulum (see chapter 3); Cabañas Copal, south of Tulum (see chapter 3); and Oasis Akumal, Akumal (see chapter 3).

Hotel Cohiba

984-873-2080
www.hotelcohibaplaya.com
First Avenue and 12th Street

If you want to be close to the party zone and prefer boutique style over a large full-service resort, Cohiba is a good choice. The three-story hotel's 20 rooms are tropically swanky, with decorative lighting, wood furnishings, and an intriguing sense of fashion. Standard rooms feature air-conditioning, ceiling fan, cable TV, and private balcony. There's also a thatched-roof rooftop suite with a spacious bedroom, kitchenette, and large terrace. Rates: $120–180, depending on the room and the time of year. Recommended.

Hotel Deseo

984-879-3620
www.hoteldeseo.com
Quinta and 12th Street

Think Miami Beach meets Beverly Hills meets the Riviera Maya. Built around a central pool and swanky bar, the hotel's 15 rooms are very minimalist, but very cool. The walls are a crisp white, and lounge music is piped in from the hotel bar. On the nightstand, you'll find incense, earplugs, and condoms. The beds are amazingly comfortable, and the rooms have stage lighting, so you can create your own shadowbox show, if you're so inclined. It's a good place to meet other travelers, and it's always a plus when there's a happening bar right outside your door. Best bet for the young and single crowd. Rates: start at $150. Highly recommended.

Illusion Boutique Hotel

1-866-460-3604 (U.S.)
www.illusionhotel.com
Eighth Street between Quinta and 10th Avenue

Opened in 2005, this swanky Mediterranean-style hotel has a central location and clean rooms opening into a central courtyard. The decor is decidedly European, and everything looks crisp and neat. Rooms have air-conditioning and ceiling fans, and some feature terraces with a partial ocean view. There is a rooftop pool and *temazcal*, plus an on-site spa and dive shop. Rates: start at $140 for a standard room in low season and go up to $328 for a master suite in high season.

La Tortuga

984-873-1484
www.hotellatortuga.com
10th Avenue and 14th Street

On a corner, just a block off Quinta and around the corner from the Calle Corazon district, this 45-room boutique hotel offers stylish rooms; an exclusive, welcoming pool; a pool table; and a private and upscale ambience. Rooms have air-conditioning, safes, fans, satellite TV, wireless Internet access, and phones. Many also have a mini-bar, private balcony, and views of the court-yard pool. The hotel has an entrance into the Spa Itzá Mayan-themed day spa (see *Spas, Gyms & Body Work*), and the hotel restaurant, Agora, serves Italian and international food in a casual sidewalk café atmosphere and boasts the best cappuccino in town. Rates: range from $85 for a standard room in low season to $189 for a suite in high season; complimentary beach club access and the use of a beach towel included. Recommended.

Las Palapas

984-873-0616
www.laspalapas.com
34th Street at the beach

One of Playa's original hotels is still one of its most revered. It's a bit north of the main strip, so the beach is a touch more secluded, and there are no rocks, making it a great place to play in the water. There is a shady pool, Mayan-inspired lawn art, and an interpretive walking trail through the jungle. The hotel's 75 rooms are housed in spacious individual cabañas near the beach or in two-story villalike buildings with *palapa* roofs and private porches, built around a pair of grassy courtyards. The beachfront rooms don't have air-conditioning, but most of the rest do. Rates: range from $125 for a standard room in low season up to $270 for a beachfront cabaña in high season. Highly recommended.

Mosquito Blue

984-873-1245
www.mosquitoblue.com
Quinta between 12th and 14th Streets

Though Mosquito Blue carries a Quinta address, it fronts 12th Street, and the entrance is not especially visible from Quinta. Composed of a mix of Mexican and Mediterranean architecture, it oozes a hip and cool style that you'll notice as soon as you enter the lobby. The 45 rooms in the two-story building face the interior courtyard and nautical-themed entrance. Amenities include a library, a lounge area, a courtyard pool, and an on-site restaurant that specializes in Italian cuisine and has imported wines. It's a great choice for couples and singles who may want to impress a guest. Rates: $100–180 for rooms; suites are more.

The Reef Cocobeach

984-873-4120
www.thereefcocobeach.com
40th Street at the beach

The all-inclusive Reef resort has a privileged location on the northern end of the last beach in Playa del Carmen. To the south are the two main coves of Playa, and to the north is a for-now deserted beach ideal for walking, swimming, and exploring. There are 200 rooms with air-conditioning,

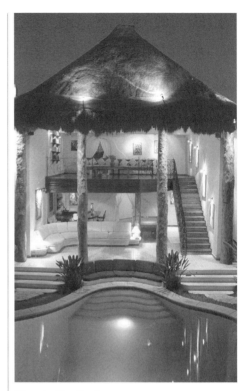

Mosquito Blue Hotel   Courtesy of Mosquito Blue Hotel

minibars, large-screen TVs, and private balconies. At meal time, guests head to the buffet restaurant or the Latin or Italian specialty restaurants. There are two pools, a kids' pool, a kids' club, a teens' club, nightly shows, a gym, pool tables, a tennis court, a basketball court, and a wide variety of water sports. Next to the hotel is a beachfront parking area, where many locals go to enjoy the beach, known to the locals as "Chun-Zumbul." Rates: start at $240.

Royal Porto Real

987-873-4000
www.realresorts.com.mx
Constituyentes between Quinta and the beach

This is the sister property to the Gran Porto Real, just across Constituyentes. With 418 rooms, it is by far the largest hotel on the

Playa del Carmen side of town. It has a grandiose portico reminiscent of Cancún or even Las Vegas. A large concrete dock stretches out from the beach in front of the hotel, which can be a bit distracting, but the sand itself is great, the water is calm, and it's one of the better beaches in the area. Rooms have flat-screen TVs, cold air-conditioning, Jacuzzi tubs, and private balconies with hammocks. It has six restaurants, four bars, a nice pool, a day spa, and a fitness center. Next door is Mamita's Beach Club, a popular day-tripping site for cruise passengers. Rates: start at $180.

Sandos Caracol Village

984-873-4444
www.caracolvillage.com.mx
Highway 307, km 295

A couple of miles north of Playa del Carmen, this 362-room, all-inclusive resort offers a contemporary Mexican atmosphere, lots of green space, two lively pools, three restaurants, three bars, a kids' club, volleyball, tennis, sailing, windsurfing, bocce ball, archery, nightly shows, and other activities. Rooms have cold air-conditioning, TVs, and private balconies. It is most popular for vacationing and honeymooning couples, young families, and singles who want to be a bit removed from the bustle of downtown Playa del Carmen. Rates: $195 per person.

Shangri-La Caribe

984-873-0611
www.shangrilacaribe.net
38th Street and Quinta

This beachfront hotel is laid out like an old Mayan village, with low-rise, thatched-roof cabañas housing most of the rooms. One of the original hotels in the area, it retains its local charm while keeping the facilities up-to-date. It is one of the last hotels on the northern edge of town, giving it a sense of privacy and remoteness. Each room has a ceiling fan, private porch with hammocks, and bottled water, and some rooms have air-conditioning. There are two pools, three restaurants, and a beachfront bar. Rates: range from $95 for a standard room in low season up to $300 for a top suite in high season.

Villas Sacbe

984-879-3918
www.villasacbe.com
First Avenue between 12th and 14th Streets

Villas Sacbe offers privately owned one- and two-bedroom condos, each with its own unique and very trendy decor. All condos have air-conditioning, full kitchens, living rooms, purified water, indoor parking, linens and towels, and satellite TV with DVD players. The complex has a narrow, meandering pool and Jacuzzi, and it's a great place to stay in luxury and still be close to the 12th Street party zone. Rates: range from $160 for a one-bedroom unit up to $250 for a two-bedroom villa; three-day minimum. Discounted weekly rates are available. Highly recommended.

DINING

Playa del Carmen offers an incredibly wide variety of cuisine types and dining establishments. From hole-in-the-wall taco shacks offering complete meals for less than $3 and traditional Mexican steakhouses serving fine cuts of Angus beef and live lobster to stylish lounge-style restaurants serving Mediterranean and international cuisine, Playa is sure to please.

Breakfasts are normally inexpensive, with many restaurants posting their specials on a chalkboard out front. Choices include traditional Mexican dishes such as *pan dulce* (sweet pastries), *huevos rancheros* (ranch-style eggs) and *huevos Mexicanos* (Mexican-style eggs), and there are also American favorites such as pancakes,

Playa del Carmen offers a wide variety of cuisine. Courtesy of Riviera Maya Tourism Authority

omelets, and steak and eggs and European choices such as bagels and lox, croissants, and crêpes.

Lunch is generally quite casual, with many travelers choosing to eat fresh seafood, sandwiches, or burgers on the beach or next to their hotel pool. Most restaurants in town are open for lunch, too, with happy-hour specials starting early and plenty of seats available at the sidewalk restaurants along Quinta.

Once the sun goes down and the stars come out, the lights of the restaurants, bars, and shops of Playa's main street start to twinkle, and candlelight glows from many eateries. The town begins to feel a bit like an international bazaar, with the restaurants competing for your business, hawking their specials, offering free drinks with a meal purchase, and tempting diners with live music, wafting smells, and attractive hostesses.

Choosing where to eat is sometimes half the fun, with many visitors making several laps along the entire 2-mile-long street, checking out the night's offerings and taking in the scene. Many restaurants put together sample entrées and place them on display next to their menus, showing you the exact size of their plump steaks, lobster tails, giant shrimp, or fish fillets.

If you're not sure what you're in the mood for or if you have a group of travelers with varied tastes, you're in luck, since many of the restaurants have extensive menus, spanning the range from tacos to pasta, from fish to steak, and from pizza to burgers.

Restaurants in this book are labeled as inexpensive, moderate, or expensive. The average meal price at an inexpensive restaurant is less than $7 per person. Moderate restaurant meal prices range from $7 to $20. Expensive restaurants offer meals starting at $21 and higher.

All of the locations in the *Budget Dining* section are ultracasual eateries catering to locals, students, and other budget travelers.

They are good places to sample the local fare and use your Spanish. They typically do not accept credit cards and may have restrooms that are not up to the cleanliness standards expected by some travelers. They are still regulated by the health department and serve only purified ice and water.

Budget Dining

Aca Los Tacos
984-803-3482
Constituyentes at Quinta

This popular taco spot is located on a busy street corner between the old and new sections of town. Like the busy taco stands near where the locals live, Aca serves fresh, hot tacos *al pastor* (cut right from the fire), beef tacos, and cheese tacos. There are tables along the patio, overlooking the traffic circle near the Royal Porto Real hotel. Open 11 AM–1 AM daily.

Bambu
Eighth Street between Quinta and 10th Avenue

This is the place for inexpensive Mongolian stir-fry. Pork, beef, shrimp, and vegetarian options are available.There are a few shaded tables facing the street, making it a fun spot to sit and watch travelers walk from the hotels west of Quinta to the beach.

Beer Bucket
Quinta between 10th and 12th Streets

This Playa veteran serves up inexpensive breakfasts, affordable lunches, and great dinner specials. Check the daily board to see the day's offerings. Favorites include burgers, fajitas, and shrimp. Open 7 AM–11 PM daily.

Bip Bip Pizzas
984-803-2888
Quinta at Constituyentes

Open for three meals per day, this casual spot is close to the traffic circle. It offers traditional breakfasts, smoothies, pizza, nachos, tacos, pasta, and seafood. Tables are covered by a shady *palapa*. Open 7 AM–11 PM daily.

Coctelería el Paisano Veracruz
Avenue Juárez, just west of Highway 307

Eat seafood with the locals. The restaurant specializes in shrimp cocktail but also serves fried fish, ceviche, and other dishes. It is located away from the tourist zone and you're likely to be the only travelers during your meal. Most of the waiters don't speak English, but don't let that dissuade you from going. Chances are you'll be able to communicate enough to order or someone at the restaurant will be able to help translate.

Dr. Taco
10th Avenue between Eighth and 10th Streets

In front of the Plaza Pelicano movie theater and mall, this tiny outlet serves tasty and inexpensive tacos and quesadillas. Diners sit on bar stools at the counter or at one of a

Hungry but don't want to go out? Delivery Express offers restaurant food delivery to hotels, condos, and other locations throughout Playa del Carmen. The service works with many local restaurants, including Hot Baking Company, Il Baretto, Maktub, Kabuki, 100% Natural, El Oasis, and Dr. Taco. There is a 15 percent service fee, and tips are not included. Delivery is available from 11–9. For more information call 984-803-5986.

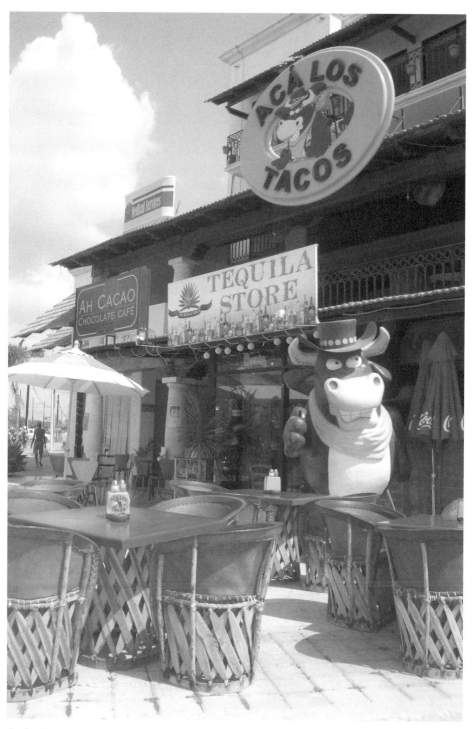

Aca Los Tacos

handful of plastic tables along the sidewalk. Many locals stop by on their way to or from work. Recommended.

El Amendro
984-803-1473
Fourth Street between Quinta and 10th Avenue

This typical Mexican restaurant is popular with area workers and budget travelers. The shaded dining room has plastic tables, and the menu includes selections from around the country, including *panuchos* (thick corn tortillas topped with chicken, lettuce, and cheese), quesadillas, and fried Mexican sandwiches called *tortas*. Daily lunch specials ($4) include a main dish, small salad, rice, beans, and fruit drink.

El Faisán y El Venado
Highway 307, just north of Avenue Juárez

This is a popular local spot for tacos, quesadillas, and seafood. At midday workers fill the plastic tables and order from the *comida corrida* menu, which offers hearty meals prepared and served quickly. Meals are served with fresh corn tortillas and spicy *pico de gallo* sauce.

El Fogon
30th Avenue between Fourth and Sixth Streets, in front of Harmon Hall

Located along the busy 30th Avenue strip of local restaurants, El Fogon serves a mixed-grill plate (*parrillada mixta*) big enough to serve three people. Also try the fried nopal cactus. Highly recommended.

El Fogoncito
30th Avenue between 28th and 30th Streets

Where do the bartenders and restaurant workers go when their shifts are over? Chances are, you'll find them at El Fogoncito, which is open 24 hours. Top

dishes include tacos *al pastor* (cut right from the fire) and fried meat sandwiches served on a toasted bun called *tortas de carne*. Very inexpensive and very good.

El Tropical-ito
10th Avenue between Sixth and Eighth Streets

This hole-in-the-wall lunch spot serves cheap tacos, fajitas, nachos, and sandwiches. Nothing on the menu is more than $4. Diners order at the counter and sit at plastic tables along the sidewalk.

La Loncheria de la Quinta
Quinta between 22nd and 24th Streets

This tiny restaurant has only four tables and does not serve alcohol, though they don't mind if you bring a drink in with you. Sit outside at a shaded table and watch the crowd go by on Quinta while enjoying tasty $1 fish or shrimp tacos.

Killer Taco
1st Avenue between 10th and 12th Streets

Located next to Litros bar, it's a good place for cheap tacos on the way to or from the 12th Street party zone. The menu is written on a chalkboard and features beef tacos, quesadillas, burritos, and even pork tacos *al pastor*, cut right from the spit. Everything on the menu is $5 or less. They don't sell alcoholic drinks, but feel free to stop next door and get a beer to go. No credit cards accepted. Open late.

Pizza Banana
984-803-1249
12th Street at 10th Avenue (and other locations)

Here you can get inexpensive pizza by the slice or pie, as well as combo deals with drinks and multiple pieces. Open late; delivery available noon–6 AM.

Pizza Pazza

Quinta at 14th Street
10th Avenue between Eighth and 10th
Streets

The Playa del Carmen Children and Family Services Department accepts donations for its health and literacy programs, so if you can save a bit of space in your luggage to bring donations, the residents of Playa would greatly appreciate it. For medical items, please do not bring outdated medicines or equipment.

Requested items include:

Kindergarten and primary-school workbooks (in Spanish)

Number 2 pencils, colored pencils, crayons

Coloring books

Children's books (in Spanish)

Educational toys (no batteries required)

Glucometers and glucose test strips

Stethoscopes

First-aid kits

Lumbar-sacral body supports

Neck collars

Tension wraps/bandages

Fiberglass cast kits

Arm slings

Infant and children's clothing

Blankets/children's blankets

Children's toothpaste

Eyeglasses (children's and adults', including prescription lenses)

Vitamins (children's and prenatal)

Items can be dropped off at the Ajua Maya restaurant on Fourth Street between Quinta and 10th Avenue. For more information call 984-803-1118 (Playa del Carmen) or 804-201-4142 (in the United States), or log on to www.americamaya.org.

At Pizza Pazza, which has a good reputation and seems to open more stores all the time, slices go for $1.50. (The gourmet pizzas are slightly more.) There are also combos with slices and drinks included. Open late, they are a favorite for satisfying after-party munchies.

Pizza 16

Quinta between 10th and 12th Streets

Open from lunch until very late at night, this is an inexpensive spot for pizza by the slice. There are a few stools at the counter, but most customers sprinkle on some Parmesan cheese, red pepper flakes, and hot sauce, grab a few napkins, and eat their pizza on the go.

Super Panaderia Aguilar

Quinta between Second and Fourth Streets

This is a great spot for inexpensive pastries, pizza, sandwiches, cold drinks, coffee, and snacks, and they also sell convenience-store items.

Tacos Arabes

984-803-5858
12th Street at 10th Avenue

Serves inexpensive tacos, lamb and seafood kebobs, and other light fare. Open 11 AM–3 AM daily.

Vagabunda

Quinta between 24th and 26th Streets

A favorite with locals and ex-pats, this *palapa*-shaded restaurant serves traditional American and Mexican breakfasts, crêpes, omelets, pastas, and cappuccino. Recommended.

Mexican & Mayan

Ajua Maya Lobster & Steak House

984-873-2523
www.ajuamaya.com

Carlos 'n Charlie's

Fourth Street between Quinta and 10th Avenue

With a great mix of authentic food, entertaining waiters, good service, and a great location, Ajua has become very popular with repeat guests. The owners are on-site most of the time and are great at remembering the names of customers they may see only once or twice each year. Food ranges from traditional Mayan dishes to lobster, fish, Black Angus beef, Caesar salads, pasta, fish tacos, and Mexican favorites. This is a popular place for wedding receptions and special-event meals. There is live music nightly and free wireless Internet access. An upstairs *palapa*-covered deck offers a more upscale dining and special-events room with hacienda-style furnishings. Prices range from $5.50 for fish tacos to $20–25 for larger dishes.

Open noon–2 AM daily. Highly recommended.

Asado de Manolo
Quinta between 24th and 26th Streets

This bustling local café features traditional Mexican lunches, sandwiches, coffee, and fruit juices. It is located in the international section of Playa and has a varied clientele, from hotel workers to the owners of the nearby nightlife hot spots. Great prices and a varied menu.

Carlos 'n Charlie's
984-803-3953
www.carlosandcharlies.com
10th Avenue at First Street

Occupying a prime corner at the northern edge of the Paseo del Carmen Mall, Carlos 'n Charlie's could be called the anchor tenant of the entire shopping plaza. This Mexico standard offers consistently good Mexican food, seafood, and pasta, though the main draw is the lively atmosphere, unique decor, and friendly waiters. There are several seats along the window, affording nice views of the plaza. Unlike some of the chain's other locations, this is more of a restaurant than a bar, so don't expect too much in the way of vacation revelry, drinking contests, or wet T-shirts. For that scene, check out C&C's sister property, Señor Frog's, located on the ferry dock, just a block away. Opens at 10 AM daily.

Don Diego
984-879-4493
Quinta at 22nd Street

This medium-size sidewalk café in the heart of "New Quinta" offers contemporary Mexican food (or "Modern Mex," as they call it), steak, and seafood. Open for dinner only, 5–midnight daily.

Don Emilione
984-873-2073
www.donemilione.com
Quinta at Second Street

Near the bus station and the town square, this restaurant is part of the Don Emilione hotel. There are tables along the sidewalk, plus an air-conditioned dining room. Popular dishes include soup, pasta, lobster tacos, calamari, steak, and shrimp, and vegetarian dishes are also available. A Latin or jazz band plays on some nights, and there's a nightly happy hour from 5 to 7. After your meal, order a flaming Mayan coffee and homemade cheesecake.

Doña Mary
30th Avenue at 28th Street

A local fave, it opens at 8 PM daily and stays open until the wee hours. Good pork tacos *al pastor* (cut right from the fire), quesadillas, and fajitas are served in a casual setting with traditional Mexican decor. It is located several blocks from the tourist strip and is frequented by expatriates and others who need a break from the standard tourist joints.

El Jardín del Jaguar
984-873-0650
Quinta at Eighth Street

With a red, black, and white color scheme, Jaguar seems to be stuck in the 1970s, except for the fact that almost none of Playa del Carmen even existed then. The restaurant serves seafood, steaks, and Mexican food. The tables border Quinta, making it good for people-watching.

El Pastorcito
30th Avenue between 28th and 30th Streets

White plastic tables and glowing yellow lights welcome diners to this local taqueria in the busy commercial district a few blocks from the tourist zone. True to the restaurant's name, tacos *al pastor* are the featured menu item, and they are served on small corn tortillas and topped with a slice of fresh pineapple. Other items include quesadillas, steak, guacamole, and hot salsa. Unlike many local taco restaurants, El Pastorcito offers a full bar.

El Templo
Eighth Street between Quinta and 10th Avenues

Serving typical Mexican dishes on a large second-story terrace on a busy side street, El Templo's dining area overlooks the pedestrian plaza, where travelers scurry to and fro. Since it's off the main road, it's an ideal spot for relaxing and sipping a cold beer.

Guadalupana
984-879-3717
10th Avenue at 12th Street

Popular with locals, this stand-alone restaurant has a two-for-one happy hour and traditional Mexican food such as tacos and fajitas, plus burgers, grilled fish, and shrimp. It also has cold air-conditioning, which patrons are grateful for on the hottest of days.

Hacienda Maya
984-873-2523
www.haciendamaya.com
Fourth Street between Quinta and 10th Avenue

Hacienda Maya offers upscale dining on a *palapa*-covered balcony above the Ajua Maya restaurant, which is run by the same owners. The menu features 19th-century French-influenced Mayan and Mexican cuisine, with dishes featuring Angus beef, venison, Cornish game hens, breast of duck, and prawns. The candlelit restaurant is a great spot for a romantic date or a group meal and frequently hosts wedding receptions. Recommended.

La Cueva del Chango
984-804-9190
38th Street between Quinta and the beach

The "Monkey Cave" restaurant is an eclectic spot that somehow manages to be rustic, funky, and romantic all at the same time—perfect for a special occasion or just a night out. The menu features several cuts of steak, fish, shrimp, fajitas, and other Mexican specialties. The candlelit tables are in a junglelike setting, making it very soothing and exotic. Recommended.

La Diez
984-803-5829
10th Avenue at Eighth Street

Known for having self-service beer taps at some of its tables, this cantina offers all-inclusive meal packages with all you can eat and drink, as well as a daily brunch. Menu items include traditional Mexican food, plus grilled meats, seafood, and pork. There are pool tables, board games, Foosball, and other games. Open 1 PM–2 AM daily.

La Parrilla
984-873-0687
Quinta at Eighth Street

With its Spanish-tiled roof and strolling mariachi bands, La Parrilla puts diners in the mood for good Mexican meals, and it delivers. The best dishes include beef fajitas, grilled shrimp, and chiles rellenos, and there are also fresh salads and vegetarian dishes. Save room for the flambé desserts and flaming coffees, prepared tableside. Open noon–1 AM daily.

La Taberna
984-803-0447
Fifth Street between Quinta and 10th Avenue

With a good mix of locals and tourists, this bar and restaurant combo is especially popular when there are live sporting events on TV. One wall has computer workstations, with Internet access going for $1.50 an hour. It's a good spot for cooling off since it's one of the few restaurants in the area with air-conditioning. It serves tacos, burgers, grilled chicken, nachos, steak, quesadillas, and seafood cocktails. Open 10 AM–4 AM daily. Recommended.

Las Delícias
984-803-1214
Quinta at 22nd Street

Located in the newer part of Quinta, this casual restaurant offers traditional Mexican food with a bit of Caribbean influence. The menu includes grilled shrimp, spicy pork tacos, and fried fish. Order beer by the bucketful for the best value. Open noon–11 PM daily.

Requesting a Mariachi Song

The strolling mariachis you see in the restaurants, walking down Quinta, or sometimes even on the beach work for tips. The typical price per song is $3–5, but ask ahead to be sure. Duos can cost less, and larger groups cost more. Not sure which song to request? Here are a few longtime favorites to choose from:

"El Son de la Negra." This raucous song is often the first song played when the mariachis make their grand entrance; it's also a lively, uplifting song to play anytime the room needs a lift.

"La Bamba." Everybody knows the words—at least some of them. This is an uplifting song of hope and can really get the crowd going.

"La Cucaracha." The sad tale of a bad day for a cockroach. It's a funny and entertaining song that's easy to sing along with. Kids love it, too.

"Las Golondrinas." A sad song known to bring grown men to tears. It tells the tale of the swallows flying on and is often played when someone is gone or going away.

"Las Mananitas." This is the song played for birthdays and celebrations. Request it for a friend who is celebrating something special.

"Maria Isabel." An easy song to sing along to, it tells the story of lovers on the beach. It has a happy tropical sound that you'll remember for a long time and is especially popular in Cozumel.

Las Mañanitas

Quinta between Fourth and Sixth Streets

This courtyard restaurant, in the part of Quinta near the town square, serves up inexpensive breakfasts, lunches, and dinners, specializing in Mexican, pasta, and seafood.

Las Manitas

984-873-0014
Quinta between Fourth and Sixth Streets

This jovial spot in the original part of Quinta serves traditional Mexican food (such as tacos and fajitas), plus seafood (shrimp, fish, octopus), spaghetti, baked pasta, steak, tuna tartare, carpaccio, and fresh salads. Open 7 AM–midnight daily.

Limones Café

984-873-0848
Quinta at Sixth Street

This subdued restaurant has an entrance on Quinta, but the eating area is down a flight of stairs and tucked in a sheltered courtyard away from the hustle of the street. The menu features traditional Mexican dishes, fish, shrimp, lobster, steak, and grilled chicken. Mayan replicas, candlelit tables, and a fountain add to the warm and welcoming ambience. Open noon–11 PM daily.

Los Aluxes

Quinta at 16th Street

Across 16th Street from Natural Spa and above a liquor store, Los Aluxes offers a quiet place to enjoy a good meal while still being near the hustle of Quinta. It has good happy-hour drink specials, and at night several tiki torches illuminate the alfresco dining area, giving the place an exotic and romantic vibe. The menu features such classic Mexican specialties as fajitas and tacos, plus seafood and steaks. Recommended.

Los Comales

984-873-0982
Quinta between Second and Fourth Streets

This cozy Mexican restaurant features steaks, fajitas, tacos, quesadillas, and some seafood. The waiters are longtime Playa residents and know a lot about the area and are happy to make suggestions and recommendations—on your dinner and on your tours.

Pez Vela

984-873-0999
Quinta at Second Street

This sports bar and Mexican cantina has several settings in one spot: There is a bar with swinging bar stools, a central dining area with plastic tables, a few sidewalk tables, and some TV-front tables, perfect for watching live sports games, which seem to always be on. There's even an upstairs Internet café. The menu, which includes tacos, grilled shrimp, and burgers, is inexpensive and good for the price. For the best deal, order beer by the bucket (five bottles).

Tecolote

984-803-1249
North side of the town square

This sidewalk restaurant offers traditional Mexican food, such as tacos, burritos, and quesadillas. It has frequent beer specials, and it's a great spot for watching the pedestrian traffic on the main square.

Mayan Cuisine

Contributed by Destination Riviera Maya *magazine*

Traditional Mayan cuisine integrates the delights of land and ocean: the beans, vegetables, and fruits cultivated, mixed with the products of fishing and hunting as part of the customs of a centuries-old society. Corn, chocolate, honey, and turkey not only are the main ingredients of delicious meals and beverages but also are an integral part of Mayan religious rituals, where chocolate became known as the "drink from the gods." Numerous spices such as peppercorn, coriander, achiote (similar to paprika), and cinnamon are used to make *recados,* special seasoning pastes that enliven chicken, fish, or beef dishes. Some traditional Mayan dishes include the following:

COCHINITA PIBIL. The word *pibil* means "to roast in a hole," and luckily, modern cooks have devised a method that requires no shovel. The dish is typically made with pork and marinated with red *recado* and bitter orange. It is wrapped in banana leaves with onions and steamed or roasted, and then served with onions marinated in vinaigrette.

POC CHUC. Char-grilled pork marinated in sour orange with black beans, purple onion, tomato, and Mayan spices.

PAPADZULES. Tortillas stuffed with hard-boiled eggs and covered in a pumpkin seed and tomato sauce.

FRIJOL CON PUERCO. Pork and black bean stew served with chopped radish, onion, tomato, and pieces of lime, eaten with a corn tortilla.

RELLENO NEGRO. Turkey, ground beef, and hard-boiled eggs in a blackened chile sauce.

TIKINXIC. A whole fish marinated in achiote and sour orange with tomato, white onion, and green pepper slices, then wrapped and grilled in a banana leaf.

PANUCHOS. A fried tortilla filled with refried beans, pieces of turkey or chicken, lettuce, tomato, onion, and avocado.

Xlapak

Quinta between 14th and 16th Streets

This small but friendly restaurant with whimsical Mayan decor is tucked in a narrow lot facing Quinta. Menu selections include chicken, fish, beef fajitas, spaghetti, and squid.

Yaxche

984-873-2502
www.mayacuisine.com
Eighth Street between Quinta and 10th Avenue

With seating along the sidewalk or in a gardenlike interior, Yaxche is one of Playa's most respected restaurants. It serves authentic Mayan cuisine, including fish, chicken, and turkey, all cooked with native methods and using traditional spices. Yaxche is the Mayan name for *la ceiba*, a green-leafed tree believed to bring good luck. Try the Mayan Kiss after-dinner drink, made with Xtabentun and Kahlúa. Dishes range from $15 to $25. Open noon–midnight daily. Recommended.

Italian

Agora

10th Avenue between 12th and 14th Streets

Located on the ground floor of the La Tortuga Hotel (see *Lodging*), this casual restaurant serves Italian food, pasta, fish, and inexpensive breakfasts under shaded *palapas* next to a busy street. It is Italian owned, and the food is authentic and good.

Café de la Luna

Fourth Street at 15th Avenue

Owned by the same folks who run the Posada Barrio Latino hotel, this authentic Italian eatery has great pastas, pizza, lasagna, cold beer, and a decent wine selection. There's also a pleasant outdoor seating area.

Idea Pasta

984-873-2173
Quinta between 12th and 14th Streets

Idea Pasta is all about choices: Diners can choose between sidewalk tables or a slightly more refined upstairs dining room, as well as from eight pastas and 12 sauces to create a unique dish. There is also lasagna, cannelloni, and ravioli. The meals are served hot and fresh, and it is some of the best pasta in town. Dishes are only around $8. No credit cards. Highly recommended.

Il Baretto

Quinta at 26th Street

Serving three meals a day, this sidewalk café and restaurant is somewhat of a headquarters for the Italians making the international part of Quinta their home. More than just ex-pats appreciate Il Baretto's pasta, pizza, seafood, and beef menu items, though. The restaurant also serves imported coffee drinks, espresso, and cappuccino and is known for sumptuous desserts.

Media Luna

984-873-0526
Quinta between 12th and 14th Streets

A casual spot for pasta, fish, grilled chicken, and other favorites, Media Luna offers seating in a small dining room or at sidewalk tables along Quinta or on the upstairs terrace. Daily specials are written on a chalkboard facing the street.

Ristorante Da Bruno

984-873-0048
Quinta at 12th Street

This is a longtime Playa favorite, for both its authentic Italian menu and its premium people-watching perch in the heart of Quinta. The owners and chefs are Italian, the pasta is made in-house, and the food tastes fresh and hearty. Top dishes include gnocchi, pizza, ravioli, antipasti, proscuitto, mahimahi, lobster, and, of course, tiramisu. Open 5 PM–1 AM daily. A typical entrée is $16. Recommended.

Rolandi's
984-803-4121
Paseo del Carmen Mall

Long a favorite in Cozumel and Cancún, Rolandi's now has a location in Playa del Carmen. There is indoor and outdoor seating, and the ambience is casual but with an upscale flair. Wood-oven pizzas highlight the menu, along with pastas and desserts. Open noon–midnight daily.

International

Amaris
984-803-4050
Paseo del Carmen Mall

Boasting an "eat, drink, lounge" concept, this fusion restaurant features decor and cuisine from Asia, Central America, and the Mediterranean. It has a marble bar, plasma TV, and indoor/outdoor seating. Best bets are the chicken satay—grilled chicken strips with peanut sauce. Open noon–midnight daily.

Apasionado
984-803-1100
Quinta at 14th Street

This terrace restaurant, above the Zoo Café (see *Cafés and Light Fare*), has unique lighting that gives it a bit of a magical quality. The decor truly adds to the dining experience, letting patrons know they are in for something special. Menu faves include grilled octopus in garlic sauce, sizzling beef fajitas, lobster, filet mignon, and grilled shrimp. Open noon–1 AM daily, with live jazz music nightly.

Aphrodesiac
12th Street at First Avenue

Flowing curtains, glowing candles, exotic music, and a delectable menu typify this unique Playa restaurant, located next to Salon Riviera in the 12th Street entertainment district. It may be one of the only places in all of the Yucatán to sample traditional African dishes. There is also a wide variety of desserts, after-dinner drinks, and coffees that tempt diners to linger when the meal is done.

Byblos
984-803-1790
14th Street between Quinta and 10th Avenue

A French-owned gourmet restaurant and wine bar, Byblos is one of the few spots in town where you can enjoy a delicious dinner in an air-conditioned dining room with white linen tablecloths. There's also an alfresco patio. Menu highlights include carpaccio, foie gras, pasta, risotto, grilled fish, flambéed lobster, veal chops, rabbit, New Zealand beef and lamb, duck, apple tarts, and crêpes flambéed with Grand Marnier. Open 6 PM–1 AM; closed Sunday. Highly recommended.

El Zocalo
Eighth Street between Quinta and 10th Avenue

The interior at this restaurant has a strong Mexican theme, but the menu is international fusion. The food is good, and the waiters are professional and accommodating. Popular dishes include chiles rellenos (stuffed peppers), Caesar salads, steak, and pasta.

Esparragos
984-803-2109
Quinta between Sixth and Eighth Streets

A two-level restaurant with a nice, dimly lit terrace overlooking Quinta, Esparragos' menu spans from mahimahi, lobster, and grilled shrimp to traditional Mexican favorites and Argentinean beef. Pleasant atmosphere, friendly waiters.

The Glass Bar
Quinta at 12th Street

An elegant bar and eatery on the Quinta side of Mosquito Blue hotel (see *Lodging*), the Glass Bar has cushioned chairs, linen tablecloths, and personable waiters. The menu features Italian and Mediterranean food, pasta, fish, and steak. Dishes range from $15 to $20. The outdoor seating is slightly less exclusive but still very upscale and comfortable, offering a great view of the goings-on along Quinta. There is an extensive wine list, featuring selections from Mexico, the Mediterranean, and beyond.

Kartabar
984-873-2228
www.kartabar.com
12th Street at First Avenue

Cool colors, flowing tapestries, dim lamplight, and flickering candles highlight the decor at this Mediterranean-style restaurant and lounge. The menu features Lebanese and Mediterranean cuisine and seafood, including beef carpaccio, Provincial Mussels (baked with Parmesan, garlic, olive oil, bread, olives, and parsley), calamari, falafel, stuffed grape leaves, tabouli, shrimp stew, lobster ravioli, and mahimahi. It's also a great spot for an after-dinner drink or for a romantic tête-à-tête. Meals average $21. Open 6 PM–3 AM daily. Recommended.

La Caprichoza
984-801-8034
Quinta between 12th and 14th Streets

A newer addition to the Quinta cuisine scene, this upscale eatery offers fish, lobster, steaks, pasta, and fresh salads. The restaurant is upstairs, and the decor is soothing and welcoming, making you want to take a break from Quinta and stay a while. There is live music most nights.

La Tasca
984-803-2891
Constituyentes between 10th and 15th Avenues

La Tasca offers typical Spanish food, including paella, tortes, and seafood, in a casual setting. There are several outdoor tables facing the street, which usually bustles with traffic and tourists walking through town.

Le Bistro
Second Street between Fifth and 10th Avenues

This casual French bistro serves seafood and vegetarian offerings, and there's live music. It's just off the main plaza, making it a good stopping point while waiting for the Cozumel ferry.

Los Tulipanes
984-873-1255
Quinta at 14th Street

Come for dinner, and then stay for the loungelike atmosphere and soothing decor. Soft music beckons passersby to stop in and stay for a while. The candlelit tables and icy margaritas add to the appeal and make it harder to leave. The menu features steak, fish, and pasta selections, plus a house specialty, Molcajete Azteca, which has chicken, beef, octopus, and baby onions. Another favorite is the grilled chicken with Xtabentun liqueur. Open 7 AM–11 PM.

Maktub Caffe
Quinta between 28th and 30th Streets

Located in the international section of Quinta, in a strip with other sidewalk restaurants, Maktub is known for its authentic Arabic menu. Highlights include couscous, hummus, pitas, gyros, and grape-leaf rolls. An indoor hookah bar has six low tables surrounded by pillows for lounging and smoking. Recommended.

Mandarina's Pizza & Champagne
984-803-1249
Quinta at 14th Street

The decor at this Argentinean-owned restaurant and nightspot is more reminiscent of champagne than of pizza, with a decidedly upscale look and feel. The tables are lit by flickering candles and are deftly arranged to give diners an extra bit of privacy. There is live music nightly, which adds to the timeless, faraway ambience. The menu ranges from Mexican breakfasts and crêpes, pizza, and pasta to octopus, mussels, and lobster. Most diners choose to lengthen their stay with dessert and coffee—or perhaps another mojito cocktail, a house specialty.

Maria's
Constituyentes at Quinta, in the Gran Porto Real (see *Lodging*)

This fancy eatery, which has an entrance from the street, serves international and Mexican cuisine in a casual yet upscale setting.

Palapa Hemingway's
984-803-0003
Quinta between 12th Street and Calle Corazon

One of the few air-conditioned restaurants on Quinta, Hemingway's is known for its varied menu and interesting decor. The interior is decorated with bold paintings and Cuba-inspired accessories. The food is Mexican and Cuban, with salmon in three cheeses, grilled steak, Caribbean shrimp, and lobster tail among the favorites. There are also patio tables for those who would rather people-watch than cool off. Open 8 AM–midnight daily.

Sol Food
Quinta between 20th and 22nd Streets

Sol, in this case, means "sun," as in, "fresh food from the sun," rather than a misspelling of *soul food*, an ethnic cuisine popular in the southern United States. The dining room is sharp and modern, and the menu features dishes from Italy and the Mediterranean. Favorites include cold salads, baked linguine, and grilled shrimp.

Sur Pizzeria, Grill & Wine Bar
984-803-3285
Quinta at Calle Corazon, between 12th and 14th Streets

This two-level restaurant offers fan-cooled dining overlooking Quinta. The decor is slick and mod, with indirect lighting, soothing lounge music, and a strong Mediterranean vibe. The affordable menu includes pizza, grilled steaks, fish, chicken, and steamed shrimp. Open noon–midnight daily.

Tintos y Tapas
Quinta between 28th and 30th Streets

In the center of the new section of Quinta, this Spanish-themed sidewalk café and bar serves a delicious paella several times per week, plus other regional specialties. It also has a respectable wine list. Open 1 PM–midnight daily.

Ula Gula
984-879-3727
Quinta at 10th Street

Highly recommended for its gourmet Argentinean cuisine and extensive wine list, Ula Gula features white linen tablecloths, candlelit tables, and a sultry but casual terraced dining room over Quinta. It is a favorite of trendy locals, American ex-pats, and visiting diners from around the world. Downstairs from the restaurant, there's a tiny bar on the street corner deco-rated in white and tan. It has a trendy vibe and a nice view of Quinta. Open 6 PM–midnight daily. Recommended.

Zas
Quinta between 12th and 14th Streets

The varied menu at this local upscale fave includes vegetarian dishes, fresh salads, pastas, fish, steak, and chicken. The dining room is air-conditioned, and in the evening there are candles on each table.

Asian & Sushi

Babe's Noodle House
Quinta between 28th and 30th Streets
10th Street between Quinta and 10th Avenue

This sidewalk restaurant, which has two locations, offers inexpensive and well-portioned Asian and Thai dishes for lunch and dinner. It serves chicken, beef, pork, vegetarian dishes, coconut rice, spring rolls, and egg rolls. Open noon–midnight daily. Highly recommended.

Geisha
984-803-0807
12th Street at First Avenue

Impress your date at this exclusive sushi bar and lounge in the heart of the 12th Street party zone. The dining room is rela-tively small, but there is an open floor plan with cozy, candlelit tables, and a couple sofas along the sidewalk, so it feels both private and roomy at the same time. In addition to sushi, the menu includes deli-cious noodle dishes, egg rolls, spring rolls, and other sumptuous delights. Recom-mended.

Kabuki
984-803-5816
Eighth Street between Quinta and the beach

Located on the beach side of the El Jardín del Jaguar hotel (see *Lodging*), Kabuki is one of the best spots in town for sushi. It's a small affair, with a couple of sidewalk tables and a small sushi bar. Delivery is available. Open 1 PM–11 PM daily.

Sushi Itto
984-803-4127
Paseo del Carmen Mall
10th Street at First Avenue

With only a few seats at the sushi bar, most diners sit at one of the sidewalk tables, where they can watch the goings-on of the busy mall. (There's also a second location on 10th Street.) The restaurant offers fresh sushi, plus a variety of cooked rice and noodle dishes. The shrimp and rice is especially good. Delivery is available. Open 1 PM–11 PM during the week and until mid-night on weekends.

Sushi Tlan
984-803-3838
14th Street at Calle Corazon, between Quinta and 10th Avenue
Quinta between 28th and 30th Streets.

Sushi Tlan serves artistic and well-presented sushi dishes. You'll find such sushi standards as tuna, salmon, and California rolls, plus special dishes made from local fish. Dine in or call for delivery.

Thai Mid
984-879-4186
Constituyentes at 10th Avenue

Located in a small shopping plaza just up from the traffic circle on Constituyentes, this moderately upscale restaurant serves traditional Thai noodle and rice dishes, soups, and spring rolls. It also has a decent wine list and a street-side patio ideal for lingering. The restaurant is part of a chain, with other locations in Mérida and Los Cabos.

Steak

John Gray's Place
984-803-3689
www.johngrayrestaurants.com
Quinta at Calle Corazon, between 12th and 14th streets

This dark restaurant, popular with ex-pats and regulars, has a first-floor bar and lounge area and an upper-level dining room with cozy tables, candles, and a sub-dued, upscale atmosphere. The menu is international, with great steak and seafood. Open 6 PM—midnight daily. Highly recommended.

Pancho Villa
4th Street between 10th and 15th avenues

This casual patio restaurant at the Hotel Plaza (see *Lodging*) offers surprisingly good steaks and seafood, considering its unassuming setting and budget-friendly menu. Since it's on First Avenue it's close to the beach, making it perfect for a quick bite between sunning sessions. Recommended.

Quinta Corazon
984-803-1872
Quinta at Calle Corazon

Formerly Captain Bob's Restaurant, Quinta Corazon still serves up high-quality meats, plus fish, shrimp, and lobster. The dining room is decidedly upscale, though there is no dress code, and the waiters are welcoming of anyone with a hint of civility in search of a meal. The tables are a bit removed from the hustle of Quinta, making it a nice spot to escape the commotion for a relaxing dinner. Open 6 PM—11 PM daily.

Seafood

Big Lobster
984-873-2026
Quinta between Fourth and Sixth Streets

This casual eatery offers two-for-one beers, whole fish, fajitas, surf and turf, and, of course, lobster. The waiters are friendly and provide a bit of entertainment during your meal. Sample dishes are on display at the front, allowing diners to preview the meals before they enter.

Blue Lobster
984-803-2651
Quinta at 12th Street

The Blue Lobster opened in 1991 and is one of Playa's older restaurants. The two-story eatery just off Quinta specializes in live lobster and seafood (including a daily $14.95 lobster special), plus such unusual dishes as octopus puffs and fish with curry and anisette, as well as coconut shrimp. The Key lime pie is a popular dessert. Open 11 AM—midnight daily; happy hour is noon—4:30 PM. There's live music in the evenings. Recommended.

El Oasis
984-803-2676
12th Street between Quinta and 10th Avenue

Across from the Santanera nightclub (see *Drinks & Dancing*), this inexpensive eatery has shrimp tacos, fish tacos, and other seafood and Mexican dishes. The dining room is large and softly lit, and the decor is decidedly Mexican. It is always lively with a preparty crowd. Recommended.

Fly
984-803-1350
Quinta at 12th Street

A swanky lounge/restaurant with indoor seating, a large fish tank, candlelit tables,

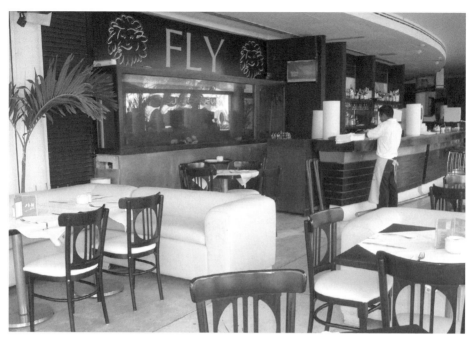

The dining room at Fly

leather sofas, and sidewalk tables facing Quinta, Fly has a menu offering such upscale options as grilled fish, steak, and lobster. (See also *Trendy Lounges*.) Open 1 PM—2 AM daily; happy hour is 5 PM—7 PM.

Hotel Básico Seafood Restaurant
984-879-4448
www.hotelbasico.com
Quinta at 10th Street

Even if you're not staying at Hotel Básico, you'll want some excuse to visit and experience the hotel's unique design, and the second-floor patio restaurant provides the perfect opportunity. Run by a staff brought in from a small town outside of Veracruz, the restaurant serves authentic Mexican Gulf Coast seafood in a style they call *maiz mariscos*, which means "corn and seafood" (though it sounds better in Spanish). The patio has a timeless quality, with 1950s-style concrete floors, lights twinkling in the trees, candles and lanterns around the tables, a market kiosk housing the food-prep area, and seating along a balcony overlooking the street. Menu favorites include shrimp empanadas, seafood cocktails, ceviche, stuffed blue crabs (*jaibas rellenas*), fried whole fish, grilled octopus, and lobster. It's also a good spot to sample some traditional Mexican desserts, such as *cocada con helado* (coconut ice cream), flan, and *budin de elote* (corn pudding). To make things more authentic, order your beer as a *michelada* and savor the salt and lime. Depending on the night, there are dance classes, tortilla-making demonstrations, or a marimba band. Highly recommended.

La Bamba Jarocha
984-803-0965
30th Avenue between 36th and 38th streets

Eat with the locals at this vibrant seafood eatery, a bit off the main tourist trail. It's safe and friendly, and the waiters will be happy to help you order. Favorites include fried or grilled fish, seafood cocktails, fresh oysters, and paella. A traditional baked rice dish called *arroz tumbada* is served on Sunday only. Recommended.

La Casa del Agua
984-803-0232
Quinta at Second Street

Located next to the Playa town square, this gourmet restaurant features European and Latin fusion cuisine, including fresh fish, shrimp, and shellfish, plus Angus beef and a few traditional Mexican dishes. Water features decorate the dining room, and the candlelit tables are covered in white linen, giving it a contemporary yet romantic feeling. Open 11 AM–11:30 PM daily.

La Morena
12th Street at First Avenue

In Playa's trendy 12th Street district, La Morena stands out with its upscale oyster bar concept, serving seafood, grilled fish, and other exotic dishes in a quaint *palapa-* covered dining room. The romantic, candlelit tables and soothing music lend a faraway vibe to the dining experience. Highly recommended.

Las Brisas
Fourth Street between Quinta and 10th Avenue

Popular with locals, this seafood restaurant specializes in shrimp cocktail and ceviche, and it also serves fried fish and grilled shrimp. Seating is in a covered dining room with open walls, allowing the breeze to flow through. Open 1 PM–11 PM daily.

Fast Food

Burger King
984-873-1523
South side of the town square, by the ferry dock

This walk-up eatery serves the same flame-broiled faves you're used to back home, using most of the same ingredients. Prices are comparable.

Even the McDonald's has a palapa roof!

Johnny Rocket's
Paseo del Carmen Mall

Mostly undistinguishable from the American chain's stateside locations, this casual fast-food joint serves up cheeseburgers, hot dogs, onion rings, french fries, and malts.

McDonald's
984-879-3450
Paseo del Carmen Mall
Quinta at Second Street
Highway 307 by Chedraui
On the ferry dock, across from Señor Frog's (take-out only)

Face it: After a few days of beer drinking, taco eating, and sensory overload, it's nice to be in the familiar confines of a McDonald's. The location near the town square and across from the bus station may be one of the only McDonald's locations with a *palapa* room. The entry is up a flight of steep stairs. The quality is comparable to the locations back home, and the prices are a bit better.

Subway
984-879-4553
Constituyentes at 10th Avenue
Paseo del Carmen Mall

Just like back home, this lunch spot has fresh bread, a varied menu, and custom-made sandwiches.

Cafés and Light Fare

Ah Cacao
984-803-5748
www.ahcacao.com
Constituyentes at Quinta

Facing the Olmec statue and fountain at a busy intersection, this small sidewalk spot makes all sorts of chocolate delicacies, including hot/cold drinks, brownies, ice cream, cookies, and old-fashioned chocolate bars. It also has gourmet coffees from around Mexico. Stop by and ask for a sample taste of chocolate every day between 7:45 AM and midnight.

Café Corazon
Quinta between 28th and 30th streets

This relaxing sidewalk café has a whimsical menu that's worth trying. Open 8 AM–midnight daily.

Café Sasta
Quinta between Eighth and 10th streets

Complete with espresso bar and sidewalk tables with seemingly permanent smoking patrons, this very European café has good coffees, pastries, and snacks. Recommended.

Café Tropical
984-873-2111
Quinta between Eighth and 10th streets

In front of the Maya Bric/Tank-Ha Hotel (see *Lodging*), this sidewalk restaurant serves inexpensive breakfasts and lunches. The menu features traditional American and Mexican egg dishes, smoothies, pastries, croissants, sandwiches, fruit, salads, hummus, falafel, and seafood. Open 7 AM–midnight daily.

Caffe-ina
Quinta between 20th and 22nd streets

This whimsically named kiosk café serves Illy-brand coffee, sandwiches, pastries, cookies, and other goodies. It is in the new stretch of Quinta, surrounded by boutique shops and restaurants.

Casa Tucan Restaurant
Fourth Street between 10th and 15th avenues, on the ground level of the Casa Tucan hotel (see *Lodging*)

At Casa Tucan, where a large banyan tree grows up through the middle of the restaurant, they serve an inexpensive breakfast that includes eggs, toast, coffee, and orange juice. Crêpes, sandwiches, steaks, and international entrées are also available. A small shop within the restaurant sells used books, perfect for beach reading.

El Espacio
10th Avenue between Sixth and Eighth streets

Located in the Los Itzaes Hotel (see *Lodging*), this small café with wooden sidewalk tables serves coffee, pastries, and sandwiches. The staff can prepare a meal to go for the beach or for a car trip.

Fresh Café & Pan
Quinta at Second Street

This small café offers fresh-ground coffee, gourmet pastries, homemade desserts, natural fruit smoothies, omelets, waffles, baguette sandwiches, and salads. Open 6 AM–11 PM daily.

Fruti Yogurth
Paseo del Carmen Mall

This eatery in the well-maintained Paseo del Carmen outdoor mall features fresh-squeezed juices, *torta* sandwiches, salads, and yogurts. Open 9 AM–10 PM daily.

Hot Baking Company
984-806-0781
10th Street between Quinta and 10th avenues
Calle Corazon at 14th Street

This casual café serves tea, coffee, fresh-squeezed juice, eggs, omelets, muffins, bagels, banana bread, carrot cake, cookies, pastries, and sandwiches. Open 6 AM–3 PM daily.

Java Joe's
984-876-2694
10th Street between Quinta and 10th Avenue

A good spot for espresso, cappuccino, and iced mochachino, Java Joes also serves bagels, cakes, pastries, sandwiches, and boxed lunches, perfect for a day trip.

Nature Deli
984-873-0629
www.hoteleclipse.com
First Avenue between 12th and 14th streets

Located at the entrance to the Eclipse Hotel (see *Lodging*), this casual sidewalk café is run by a chef who has put in time at some of the area's top hotels and now enjoys the more relaxed life of preparing meals for only a handful of tables, which are generally filled by regulars and hotel guests who have discovered the well-priced meals and gourmet tastes.

100% Natural
984-873-2242
Quinta between Eighth and 10th streets

Open for breakfast, lunch, and dinner, this is one chain restaurant that doesn't feel like it. There are several different eating areas, from the sidewalk and tables next to a waterfall to covered tables with ceiling fans upstairs. The menu has omelets, enchiladas, sandwiches, seafood, steak, and other dishes. The fresh fruit juices and smoothies are delicious and good for what ails you. Special concoctions exist for lowering chloresterol, boosting energy, curing hangovers, improving memory, and others. The prices are good, and the food is always fresh and delicious. Open 7 AM–11 PM daily. Highly recommended.

Sabor
Quinta between Second and Fourth streets

With its location close to the town square, this natural-foods café is popular with locals and others waiting for their bus or ferry. The menu offers homemade *pan dulce* (sweet pastries), sandwiches, juice, and coffee.

Tutto Dolce
984-803-4936
20th Avenue at 10th Street

Providing a nice air-conditioned respite from a hot day, this is a good spot for fresh breakfasts and lunches. The menu features empanadas, quiche, pizza, lasagna, fresh fruits, and coffee. Open 7:30 AM–8 PM daily.

Zoo Café
984-803-2377
14th Street at Quinta

A lively Internet and sports bar, Zoo is surprisingly inexpensive for how hip and stylish it looks. A bank of computers fills the center of dining room, while tables ring the outer edges, affording great people-watching along Quinta. Zoo offers Internet access, long-distance phone calls, newspapers, coffee, smoothies, sandwiches, and light meals. Open 7:30 AM–1 AM daily. Recommended.

Ice Cream

Baskin Robbins
Quinta between Second and Fourth streets

They have a good selection of ice cream (not quite 31 flavors) available in cups and cones, as well as frozen drinks and juices.

Häagen-Dazs
Quinta at 10th Street
Quinta at Fourth Street
Paseo del Carmen Mall

This international chain offers its signature ice creams, shakes, and other cold concoctions. The quality is the same as back home.

Go for the Experience

Alux
984-803-0703
Avenue Juárez between 65th and 70th avenues, just west of Highway 307

You've heard of cave diving, but this is cave dining: This restaurant and bar is housed deep within a natural cave, formed thousands of years ago. There is live music nightly, and it makes for a romantic spot for dinner or a drink. The food is not the best, but the novelty of eating in a cave more than makes up for it. Local promoters occasionally host all-night rave parties here, which can get extremely crowded and are best avoided if you're prone to claustrophobia.

Blue Parrot Restaurant
984-873-0083
www.blueparrot.com
12th Street on the beachfront

This is Playa's premier party location, but it's also a fun spot for a lively meal. Traditional American and Mexican breakfasts are served at the beachside *palapa*, and for lunch and dinner there are tacos, juicy burgers, grilled chicken, and seafood. Meal and drink service is also available at the chairs and bedlike lounges along the beach. At night, the lights go down and the music goes up as visitors fill the swinging bar stools that ring the bar. There is also a covered lounge area with DJ dancing. Food is served until 11 PM, when fire dancers descend on the main stage and beach area, and the restaurant turns into overflow bar seating. Recommended.

La Bodeguita del Medio
984-803-3950
Paseo del Carmen Mall

A Cuba-themed restaurant, bar, and late-night dance club (originally founded in Cuba in 1942) at the back end of the Paseo del Carmen shopping plaza, La Bodeguita del Medio has a few sidewalk tables and a fairly large indoor dining room. The slightly kitschy decor features Cuban artwork, flags, and a wall of fame with signatures and messages from previous diners. Ask for a marker and leave your own comments. A Cuban salsa band plays most nights. There is a back patio overlooking a steep, rocky arroyo. There are daily drink specials, free wireless Internet access, and free salsa lessons Tuesday and Thursday at 7 PM. Open 9 AM–1:30 AM daily.

Fire dancers practicing for the nightly show at the Blue Parrot.

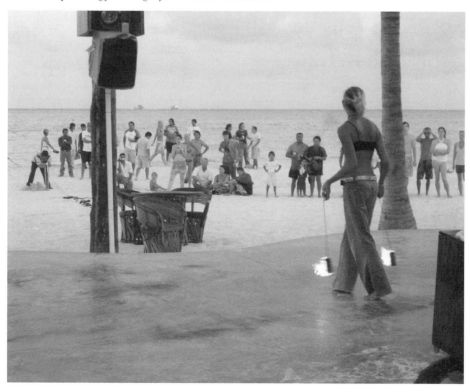

Mamita's Beach Club

984-803-2867
www.mamitasbeachclub.com
28th Street at the beach

This bustling beach club, on Playa's best beach, just north of Constituyentes, is a hot spot to be during the day. It's usually packed with day-trippers, cruise passengers, and sun worshippers staying in Playa, but not on the beach. Mamita's rents lounge chairs and umbrellas and offers beachside drink and meal service, with fish, shrimp, tacos, and other Mexican specialties topping the menu. There are lots of beach activities to enjoy, including Wave-Runners, parasailing, banana boat rides, and more. Recommended.

Pelicanos

Constituyentes at the beach

With white umbrellas and beach chairs, this beach club/restaurant serves traditional breakfasts, international dishes, steak, filet mignon, pasta, and lobster. It's a great spot for lunch or an early dinner while soaking up the sun or vicariously enjoying the antics on the beach.

Señor Frog's

984-873-0930
www.senorfrogs.com
Plaza Marina, at the ferry dock

You can't get off the ferry from Cozumel without first passing by Señor Frog's, situated at the end of the ferry dock and with a seating area on stilts right near the water's edge. It is very casual, and the waiters keep things lively. There is live music nightly and DJ dancing until the wee hours, and there are many audience-participation opportunities, including sexy body contests, drinking contests, and sing-alongs. The menu features Mexican standards, plus pasta, seafood, and burgers. It was completely destroyed by Hurricane Wilma in late 2005 but was rebuilt bigger and better than ever. Recommended.

NIGHTLIFE

When the sun goes down, the action on Quinta heats up. Tourists hit the town with their sun-kissed skin and newly purchased tropical outfits to enjoy the

The beach at Señor Frog's

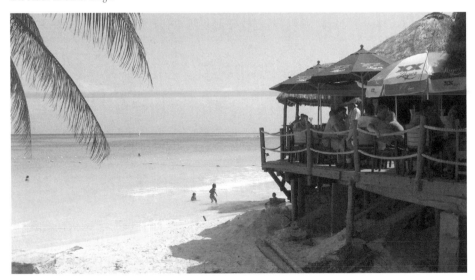

evening breeze, have dinner, gaze at the twinkling lights, and then, quite frequently, have a few drinks. Fortunately, there are plenty of options for nightlife on and around Quinta and the beach. Whether you're looking for a casual beach bar, live tropical music, TV sports, or a cosmopolitan discotheque, you'll find what you're looking for in Playa. There are clubs and bars all along Quinta and at various spots along the beach. Many travelers will take a few laps around town to see what's going on before settling on a place to go. As the night goes on, the crowd thins a bit and funnels to the after-hours clubs, some of which continue serving drinks until sunup.

The most popular area for nightlife is 12th Street, where bars and clubs line both sides of the road all the way from 10th Avenue to the beach.

Drinks & Dancing

Blue Parrot
984-873-0083 or 1-888-854-4498 (U.S.)
www.blueparrot.com
12th Street at the beach

The king of *palapa* bars in Playa, Blue Parrot is a sort of community center, with a hotel, popular beachfront with lounge chairs, and flowing beers, and at night, it's one of the best parties in town. The main bar is ringed with swinging bar stools, plus several tables and chairs leading all the way to the water's edge. At the back of the *palapa* is a stage and a cozy lounge area. Around 11 PM, local fire dancers perform, flinging sparks and ash dangerously close to the thatched roof, not to mention the entranced crowd, made up of Americans, Canadians, locals, and people from around the world. A covered lounge area offers romantic cushioned seating areas and a stage, where a DJ spins throbbing beats sure to set the mood for a fun night.

Help Support the Playa del Carmen Fire Department

The local fire department, Bomberos de la Riviera Maya, frequently sets up a kiosk in the Playa del Carmen town square near the ferry dock. They sell hats and T-shirts with the department logo to raise funds to buy updated equipment for the rescue squad. The department's various firehouses are welcoming to guests who want to take pictures and are eager to exchange patches with other fire departments around the world. Make donations and purchase souvenir merchandise online at www.bomberosdelarivieramaya.org.

As if the dual hurricanes of 2005 were not enough, the Blue Parrot burned to the ground in February 2006, when a fireball from one of the fire dancers landed on the thatched-palm roof and quickly spread throughout the club and surrounding structures. To the delight of Playa revelers, the bar rebuilt once again. Open 11 AM–4 AM daily.

La Bodeguita del Medio
984-803-3950
Paseo del Carmen Mall

La Bodeguita del Medio is a restaurant during the day and evening but its crowd gets more rowdy and the music gets louder as the night goes on. Live salsa music is featured most nights. For a break from the crowd, seek respite on the back patio. There are daily drink specials, free wireless Internet access, and free salsa lessons Tuesday and Thursday at 7 PM. Open 9 AM–1:30 AM daily.

Mambo Café
984-803-2656
www.mambocafe.com.mx
Sixth Street between Quinta and 10th Avenue

With live salsa music every night, Mambo Café has developed quite a following with the local crowd. Tourists are more than welcome to join in the fun, but some dancers take their moves very seriously, so try to keep up or at least stay out of the way. There's a $5 cover charge, depending on the day of the week and the band. All-you-can-drink, open bar available. On Wednesday, ladies enter and drink free 10 PM– midnight.

Playa 69
984-879-3217
Quinta between Fourth and Sixth Streets

This is the top gay bar in town: Look for the rainbow flag while walking down Quinta, and you'll know you've found it. There's live and recorded male entertainment, and it's a great spot to meet locals, ex-pats, and travelers from around the world. The scene gets going around midnight and lasts until about 4 AM.

Santanera
984-803-2856
12th Street between Quinta and 10th Avenue

Look for the brightly lit Vegas-style sign facing 12th Street and you'll find Santanera,

---

Cancún Pub Crawl Tour
If you're staying in Playa but want to check out the nightlife in Cancún, there's an easy way to do it without having to worry about the drive, finding the good places to go, or having friends to party with. Melsea Tours offers a Cancún party tour for $67, which includes round-trip transportation from your hotel, VIP cover charge, all-you-can-drink open bar, and guide at four Cancún clubs: The City, Dady O, Bulldog Café, and Daddy Rock. For more information call 984-803-3085.

---

the closest thing Playa has to the raging discos in Cancún. But don't worry, even this place has an unpretentious and down-to-earth atmosphere and a patio bar. The club's decor seems to pay equal homage to Mexican professional wrestling and the Catholic church. Downstairs, it's like a traditional nightclub, a bit reminiscent of the House of Blues, but without a stage. Upstairs, a large *palapa* roof contains the crowd of dancing, socializing, and margarita-drinking patrons. DJs spin the latest tunes, including American pop, Mexican rock, tropical music, and a bit of funk. The crowd is a good mix of locals and visitors. Opens at 8 PM, but it doesn't start hopping until at least midnight. Last call is 4 AM. Highly recommended.

Señor Frog's
984-873-0930
www.senorfrogs.com
At the ferry dock in the Plaza Marina center

Popular with day-trippers, cruise passengers, Mexico first-timers, and vacationers at hotels in the adjacent Playacar development, Señor Frog's is always a good bet for good cover bands, reggae music, audience-participation gags, goofy contests, and a bit of risqué fun. It is built out over the sand and has a great view of the Palace resort beach and the ferry dock. The restaurant serves Mexican food, seafood, and pasta and is open for lunch and dinner. It makes a good spot to dine while waiting for your ferry boat to Cozumel. Open 10 AM–2 AM daily.

Trendy Lounges

Básico Terrace Bar
984-879-4448
www.hotelbasico.com
Quinta at 10th Street

Enter through the hotel lobby on 10th Street and take the elevator to the top floor.

The trendy rooftop bar at Hotel Básico

If you're there in the daytime, you'll be treated to a breathtaking view of the ocean, and at night you can see the twinkling lights of Quinta. There are several seating areas, hammocks, canopy sunbeds, and unique aboveground pools.

Deseo Bar
984-879-3620
www.hoteldeseo.com
Quinta between 10th and 12th Streets

Here you can indulge in ultra-hip lounging in an atmosphere as nontraditionally Mexican as the $8 martinis they serve. You'll feel cool as soon as you crest the top stair that leads to the bar from Quinta. It's a lot like being in L.A. or Miami when you're at Deseo, but without the attitude that comes along with it. The glimmer of the pool, the glowing lights from the rooms ringing the deck, and the projection TV on the wall next door set a surreal stage for some serious lounging. Most of the patrons are hipsters from Mexico City, and they all seem to know each other, but find your spot at the bar, at a poolside bed, or at one of the lounge chairs near the hotel rooms, and you'll fit right in.

Fly
984-803-1350
Quinta at 12th Street

As the night goes on, diners swap out for drinkers, and the lounge scene begins. The swank factor multiplies, the lobsters in the large tank along the wall seem to start swimming in time with the bass beats, and the waiters develop a bit more attitude. The indoor couches become the favored seats, making an ideal spot for candlelit canoodling. Food is served until late at night, but you'll see more swizzle sticks than butter

Local Lingo—Out on the Town

2 X 1. Look for this sign at the entrance to a bar, and you'll know that their two-for-one happy hour has begun!

ANEJO CON COCA. Anejo is a golden blend of aged rum, and it goes great with Coke, making it a bit of an upgrade from a standard rum and Coke. To order one in a loud bar, grasp your chin and move your hand downward, as if stroking a beard. Then, with the same hand, hold your pinkie under your nose for a moment, then wipe it away, as if you're snorting a powdered Colombian export from under your fingernail.

BARRA LIBRE. Some bars offer *barra libre* nights, where your cover charge includes open bar, or basically all you care to drink. This normally includes bottled water, so it's a good chance to hydrate as well.

CANTINERO. Spanish for "bartender."

CHELA/CHELADA/MICHELADA. *Chela* is colloquially used to mean "beer." A *chelada* is a beer served in a glass of fresh lime juice and salt. For a real local treat, try a *michelada*—a *chelada* plus Worcestershire, Tabasco sauce, and tomato juice.

CONSUMO MINIMO. Translating from Spanish into "minimum consumption," it's a common policy at popular bars and clubs, where instead of a cover charge, your entry fee includes drink coupons equivalent in value to the amount you pay to get in. Such a policy keeps out patrons who just want to socialize and dance but not buy anything.

knives as the night goes on. Fly is not so much of a singles' scene as it is a conspiratorial hideaway for folks who may have been single the night before. It's also a great spot to woo a date or show your feelings for your special someone. Happy hour is 5–7.

Kartabar

984-873-2228
www.kartabar.com
12th Street at First Avenue, across from the Blue Parrot (see *Drinks & Dancing*)

This must be what lounge bars in the Mediterranean would be like. Cool colors, flowing tapestries, dim lamplight, flickering candles—it has all the trappings of a secret romantic escape. The scene is somewhat social, but folks tend to keep to their groups more than not. The dinner menu features Mediterranean and Lebanese cuisine, but things really get going around

midnight, when the dinner crowd yields to the late-night lounge scene, steeped in style and exclusivity. An upstairs boutique inn, Hotel Cohiba (see *Lodging*), plays on a similar theme. Open 6 PM–3 AM daily.

Lime Bar

984-100-6507
Quinta between 20th and 22nd Streets

This small and mod Euro-style bar in the Italian zone of Quinta is popular with Playa's chic international visitors. There are a few indoor tables, plus a lounging area on the sidewalk. There is no dance floor. Specialty drinks include the Kamikaze, Watermelon Cocktail, and Woo Woo.

Love Suites

12th Street at First Avenue

Located near the La Morena restaurant (see *Dining*) and Salon Riviera and operated by

CUBA LIBRE. "One revolution is still necessary: the one that will not end with the rule of its leader," wrote Cuban spiritualist Jose Marti, describing his desire for a free Cuba, which in Spanish is *Cuba libre.* It's also the name used locally for a rum and Coke, served with a wedge of lime. In the Riviera Maya, bartenders will still understand if you just order a "Cuba."

DESECHABLE. Remember, no bottles on the street, so if you want your drink to go, ask for it in a *desechable,* and it will come in a Styrofoam cup. Many bars also have a stack of them at the exit, so if you've got one for the road, leave your glass behind.

EN LAS ROCAS. Spanish for "on the rocks." Try your margarita *en las rocas* and earn a bit of respect from your *cantinero.*

FROG'S/CARLOS. Abbreviated versions of Señor Frog's and Carlos 'n Charlie's, it's how the locals refer to the popular drinking establishments.

LAGER. Used when ordering a Dos Equis (XX) beer in the green bottle, as opposed to the XX Amber, which is the dark beer in the tinted bottle. You can also hold your index fingers together to form an "X" in front of you, then pump your hands twice, indicating *dos equis,* or "two Xs." To order two or more Dos Equis, first flash the number of drinks you want with your fingers, then proceed to make the "X" sign.

NOHOCH. The Mayan word for "big." Order your favorite cocktail *nohoch,* and it'll be served in a tall glass.

the same company, these five ultraexclusive party suites have their own bars and Jacuzzis and are the perfect places to party with your celebrity friends. Each room has a theme, such as the Texas Cowboy Room, the Mediterranean Room, and the Jungle Room. Rates are around $400 for a night of partying.

Moon Dance Club & Sunset Bar
984-803-4125
Paseo del Carmen Mall

To find this hip nightspot, head up the stairs next to Rolandi's restaurant (see *Dining*), turn right at the top, and keep going up. The club is on two levels, with the top part called the Sunset Bar. It's one of Playa's tallest points and affords a great view of the jungle canopy, the ocean, and various celestial (and earthbound) bodies. It has a sand floor, orb lights, a lounge-music DJ, a decorative Jacuzzi, and a sultry vibe. The lower level, called Moon Dance Club, has a terrace with lounge beds and lounge chairs, DJ dancing, an amoeba-shaped bar, a waterfall, and several rooms with good corners for conversation. The crowd is mixed, with trendy locals mingling peacefully with status-conscious tourists. The bar opens at 6 PM, and the dance club opens at 10 PM. Cover is $5 for the dance club on busy nights.

Mushroom Bar
Quinta between 28th and 30th Streets

This stylish bar offers a unique serene and trendy atmosphere for lounging with locals and ex-pats. The music is a mix of electronic, funk, reggae, rock, and soul. There is a tiny "Kabaret" stage with live musical performances most nights and occasionally other shows. Open 6 PM–2 AM daily.

Party like a pirate at OM Bar. Mike Stone

OM Bar & Lounge
984-745-0584
www.omplaya.com
12th Street at First Avenue

Located just across the street from the entrance to the Blue Parrot (see *Drinks & Dancing*), this nightspot gets more busy as it gets later. The decor foretells what may happen if Martha Stewart were to make over a pirate ship, with dark wood furnishings, flowing red sails, candles, and well-maintained fixtures. International DJs spin lounge and chill-out music while patrons dance on the tables, conspire at dark tables, and enjoy watching the busy street scene. Open 5 PM–4 AM daily.

Salon Riviera I & II
984-813-1776
12th Street at First Avenue

On the off chance you were considering Ibiza and Las Vegas in addition to Playa del Carmen for your vacation, you'll be happy to know that there's a place in town where you can get a taste of each. Crowning the 12th Street entertainment district, Salon Riviera is the de facto see-and-be-seen nightspot in the Riviera Maya. It features one of the only air-conditioned party lounges in town, plus an upstairs open-air bar and rooftop sky bar with VIP rooms, bottle service, a sultry allure, glowing candles, and a decidedly trendy vibe. There are five luxury party suites with ultraexclusive amenities worthy of any celebrity party or special event. By the way, leave your Señor Frog's T-shirts, beach sandals, and hiking shorts at the hotel, or you won't get in. Open 10 PM–4 AM every day.

Casual Drinks

Bourbon Street
984-803-3022
Quinta between Sixth and Eighth Streets

This New Orleans–themed bar has live music, projection TV, beer specials, and a crowd of ex-pats and regulars who always make for good conversation. You'll hear much more English than Spanish here, making it a nice respite when you need a taste of home.

Captain Dave's
10th Avenue between Sixth and Eighth Streets

Offering live acoustic music, this has become a popular spot for early-evening drinks for many Americans. There's a tiled bar, and the walls are decorated with a variety of flags. Music starts at 8:30 PM nightly.

Casa Tequila–La Tequilaria
984-873-0195
Quinta between Fourth and Sixth Streets

This is primarily a liquor store, with hundreds of bottles ranging from $7 to $250. Most can be purchased by the shot, which makes for a fun experiment in tequila sampling. There are a few sidewalk tables, plus an upstairs balcony with a couple of tables overlooking Quinta—perfect for people-watching. Open 9 AM–1 AM daily.

El Pirata
On the beach between 12th and 14th Streets; enter through the Costa del Mar hotel (see *Lodging*)

Next door to the Blue Parrot, El Pirata has its own sound system, own crowd, and own vibe. The drinks are cheaper, the lines at the bar go faster, and the scene is a lot more relaxed. Kick back with a cold beer on a plastic table just feet from the Caribbean

Bourbon Street

and ponder the stars, or join the crowds near the bar for some first-class mingling and friend-making. Not to be outdone, El Pirata has its own fire dancers, performing nightly at the water's edge around midnight. Open 9 PM–3 AM daily.

There are plenty of beachfront restaurants and bars in Playa. Mike Stone

Dancing on the Sand: Top Spots to Have Sand between Your Toes and a Drink in Your Hand

Blue Parrot, 12th Street at the beach. Get there early to reserve a coveted waterfront table. If you fall out of your chair, you'll land on powder-white sand. Dancers spill out from the wooden dance floor all the way to the water line.

El Pirata, on the beach between 12th and 14th Streets. This no-frills beach bar offers a laid-back alternative to the Blue Parrot next door. The music is loud, the bar stools swing, and the tables on the beach are just steps from the lapping waves of the Caribbean. Fire dancers perform on the beach behind the club most nights at around midnight.

Mamita's Beach Club, 28th Street at the beach. Who says you can't go dancing during the day? The folks at Mamita's prove that getting your groove on by sunlight can be just as fun as by moonlight. The party gets going in the early afternoon and peaks just before sundown, then quickly dwindles. Arrive early to claim a coveted beach bed.

Señor Frog's, Plaza Marina, at the ferry dock. Built above the beach at the base of the ferry dock, this resort-town stalwart packs in a primarily American clientele in search of good Mexican food, pop music, and sometimes love. Dancing patrons can get their drinks to go and boogie on the beach below.

Karaoke Bar
Sixth Street between Quinta and 10th Avenue

This hole-in-the-wall karaoke bar is a fun spot to have a few beers and do something you wouldn't do back home—sing in front of a crowd of strangers! The song list features popular hits in English and Spanish.

La Crema
Fourth Street between Quinta and 10th Avenue

A good spot to sit and talk, this funky bar specializes in inexpensive draft beer. The interior is decorated with colorful tapestries along the walls and hanging from the ceiling.

La Cucaracha
Eighth Street between Quinta and 10th Avenue

Are you the next Riviera Maya idol? Located in front of Mambo Café (see *Drinks & Dancing*), La Cucaracha is a lively karaoke bar and a fun place to watch locals butcher American pop songs—or to take a shot of tequila and try it yourself.

La Jarra
10th Avenue at Fourth Street

This local hangout, known for draft beer and rock music, is a good place to ask locals about lesser-known area attractions.

La Taberna
984-803-0447
Fifth Street between Quinta and 10th Avenue

A good spot to watch a live sporting event on TV, La Taberna has a wall of computer workstations, with Internet access going for $1.50 an hour. There are dart boards, pool tables, and multiple TVs, and there's also cold air-conditioning, so it's a good

Common Beers of the Riviera Maya

Bohemia. Served in a dark bottle with gold foil on the neck, Bohemia is a bit more expensive than other beers, but it has a robust taste and is a bit of a status symbol.

Corona. Though it's brewed in Mexico, it seems to be more common in the States. Not all bars carry it, so if you're normally a Corona drinker, it may be time to expand your horizons. Normally served with a slice of lime.

Dos Equis. Advertised on billboards throughout the region, Dos Equis (XX) comes in lager (green bottle) and amber (tinted bottle). The lager is much more common and goes better with lime.

Leon Negra. A bit of a microbrew, this dark and flavorful beer is locally brewed in Mérida, the capital of the state of Yucatán. Sometimes hard to find.

Modelo. Sold by the single can in convenience stores, this light-bodied beer is favored by many locals and goes nicely in a cooler at the beach.

Montejo. Crafted at the same Mérida brewery as Leon Negra, this beer adds a touch of class to your bar visit. Not always available, though.

Negra Modelo. A dark beer sometimes sold at a slightly higher price than other beers. It's normally served in a glass and goes great with steak.

Sol. Commonly found at beach bars and nightclubs, Sol is what most Corona drinkers opt for when their usual beer is not on the menu. Frequently served with lime.

Superior. Served in a dark tinted bottle, which helps keep it from getting skunked in a cooler on a sunny day, this full-bodied beer is sold at a discount in grocery stores and is available mostly at bars favoring locals.

Tecate. Most commonly served in cans, Tecate is best enjoyed with plenty of salt and lime. Popular at sports bars.

Mucha Ropa, Mucha Ropa!

The equivalent to the English "take it off, take if off," *mucha ropa, mucha ropa* is just as cliché and out of fashion. In the Riviera Maya, the main gentleman's clubs are in Playa del Carmen, along Highway 307. They are generally considered safe for tourists, though like anywhere, it's best to keep your wits and not do anything that you think could get you in trouble. That being said, the law allows for quite a bit, and you're sure to find your choice of willing participants—for a price.

One such club is Baby's Hot (Highway 307 at Sixth Street). It's a small hangout for locals and doesn't see many gringos, so it can seem a bit rough around the edges to many foreigners. Cover charge is posted at $25, but they are flexible if they think you'll spend some money once you're inside, especially if you threaten to go down the road to visit their competitors instead. A few blocks south is Marlin Safari (Highway 307 and Avenue Juárez). It's the most stylish of the nonmembership clubs, featuring a pool table, laser light show, and multiple stages. Cover charge is negotiable. Farther down Highway 307, across from the southernmost entrance to Playacar, is Chilly Willy's, a *palapa*-roofed sister club to the longtime nudie institution in Cancún. Cover charge is posted at $20, and the club seems to open only certain times of the year. The most exclusive gentleman's club in town is La Cupula, adjacent to Chilly Willy's. It is open only to members and VIPs, so it's off-limits to most tourists. If you know somebody or you're willing to dig deep into your pesos, it's definitely worth a visit. It's the kind of place that rock stars and pro athletes would feel at home in, so if you have to ask how to get in, you probably can't.

Each club offers table dances in a private curtained room for $15–20, payable directly to your dancer of choice, waiter, or floor manager (who is eager to assist with your selection). More intimate encounters can be arranged for an additional fee (around $200 for the complete package), and each club has private rooms for rent by the hour.

Drinks are relatively inexpensive, though if a dancer asks you to buy her a drink, the fee is significantly higher—up to $15 for a single cocktail—so unless you're ready to drop a lot of money, you're probably best off saving your pesos for a dance since it's roughly the same price. Cash is the preferred payment method, so bring some bills and stay aware of your surroundings.

All taxis know these clubs well and will often recommend one to you since they get a kickback for dropping people off there. Negotiate your price in advance (it shouldn't be more than a few dollars from any Playa del Carmen or Playacar hotel), and if you want to try to get in without paying a cover, have them drop you off a block or two away so you're not obligated to your taxi driver in any way. No need to have your cabbie wait for you; there are plenty waiting outside when it's time to leave.

Be smart. Be safe. Have fun.

spot to go after a long day at the beach, when you just can't bring yourself to sit at a patio bar. They serve good tacos, burgers, grilled chicken, nachos, steak, quesadillas, and seafood cocktails. Open 10 AM–4 AM daily. Recommended.

Litros

First Avenue between 10th and 12th Streets

This primarily local hangout offers 33-ounce beers for $3 and equally large mixed drinks for $7. It's a good spot to sit on the sidewalk and watch the crowd gather for the Blue Parrot (see *Drinks & Dancing*). The small indoor area has funky lighting and Mexican rock music. Can't finish your drink? It's okay to get it to go, as long as it's in Styrofoam.

Puro Bueno
Quinta at 30th Street

This contemporary indoor bar is air-conditioned and relaxing, while its patio is more casual and kick-back. It's a good spot to sip a cold one and watch the endless parade of chic Italians along Quinta's international section.

Sharkey & the Jaime's Caribbean Shack/Beer Bucket
10th Street between Quinta and 10th Avenue

This American-dominated happy-hour favorite offers loud disco and rock music, beer specials, mixed drinks, and a come-as-you-are attitude. Seating is on the ground floor or on an upper deck overlooking the street. While not a great place to impress a date, it's a fun place to party with friends and make some new ones. As the night goes on, the scene gets crazier, leading to comparisons with the free-spirited Grupo Anderson's bars (Carlos 'n Charlie's, Señor Frog's).

Siesta Fiesta
984-803-1166
www.siestafiestahotel.com
Quinta between Eighth and 10th Streets

This courtyard bar and restaurant is a popular meeting spot where travelers congregate to watch live sporting events on the big-screen TV and listen to live music (several bands per night). After the live music, the staff puts live sports or recorded concerts on the TV, and the party keeps going. There are tables near the stage, several bar stools, and sidewalk tables for those seeking a bit more peace and quiet. Vacation camaraderie is especially strong here, making it a great spot to meet other travelers. Food is available all day long. There is also a quaint hotel offering comfortable and affordable accommodations (see *Lodging*).

Tequila Barrel
984-873-1061
www.tequilabarrel.com
Quinta between 10th and 12th Streets

A popular meeting point for message-board groups, the Texan-owned Tequila Barrel is a Playa classic. A dark wood bar gives a traditional hacienda feeling to the interior, while a large-screen TV near the back plays sports and news. When nothing good is on TV, there is live music. Sidewalk tables spill out onto Quinta, making this a great spot to sip a cocktail and watch the people walk by. The bartenders are friendly and welcoming, and the bar stocks more than 75 types of tequila (the owner's favorite is Centenario Anejo), plus a huge selection of imported cognacs, whiskeys, and Scotches. An air-conditioned sports bar on the bar's back side has a pool table and several TVs. The kitchen serves up traditional American breakfasts, including biscuits and gravy, plus burgers, fajitas, and bar food. The bar's web site has a live web cam and archives photos taken at the bar each night. Open nightly until 2 or 4 AM, depending on the night.

2 Dollar Drinks
984-803-3895
10th Avenue between Sixth and Eighth Streets

Despite the American name, this spot is popular mostly with locals who come for the cheap drinks (beer is $1, mixed drinks are $2), the soccer games on TV, and the camaraderie of friends. Tourists are welcome, though, so feel free to give it a try and maybe make a local friend. Open 11 AM–midnight daily.

Viva Margarita
Paseo del Carmen Mall, by Johnny Rocket's (see *Dining*)

This casual sidewalk bar features live and recorded music and serves tasty Jose

> **It May Be Paradise, but It's Still the Jungle**
>
> Don't forget, even though Playa del Carmen and the Riviera Maya are exotic and wonderful beach vacation destinations, they are still relatively undeveloped and are in close proximity to the jungle, and you should set your expectations accordingly. You should also remember that there are hassles and frustrations inherent to any travel situation. You're on vacation to have fun and celebrate life, so try not to let little challenges you encounter bother you.
>
> If a chicken walks into your beachfront restaurant and pecks at your crumbs, don't get mad—take a picture. If a gecko streaks across the wall of your hotel room, don't call the front desk—give him a name and consider him your pet. If your shower runs out of hot water, don't complain to the concierge—it's good for your sunburn. And most importantly, if you find yourself at odds with your travel partner, it's time to hit the nearest bar, order a margarita, feel the warm breeze, and remember why you came here in the first place.

Cuervo margaritas in a variety of flavors. Mango is a favorite of the regulars, and it comes with a salted and limed rim and light dusting of chili powder. Patrons can order sushi from the neighboring Sushi Itto location (see *Dining*).

A Classy Night on the Town

The Glass Bar
Quinta at 12th Street

An elegant bar and eatery on the Quinta side of Mosquito Blue hotel (see *Lodging*), Glass has cushioned chairs, linen tablecloths, and personable waiters. The menu features Italian and Mediterranean food, pasta, fish, and steak. (Dishes range from $15 to $20.) The outdoor seating is slightly less exclusive but still very upscale and comfortable, offering a great view of the goings-on along Quinta. There is an extensive wine list, featuring selections from Mexico, the Mediterranean, and beyond.

Ula Gula
984-879-3727
Quinta at 10th Street

This small lounge on the corner serves drinks until past midnight in a tiny covered area and at a few sidewalk tables fronting 10th Street. The interior is decorated with candles, making for a romantic spot to sit and watch the people walk by. There's also a much larger upstairs dining room. Open 6 PM–midnight daily.

SHOPPING & SERVICES

Watches, Jewelry, Sunglasses & Cosmetics

Diamonds International
www.welcometoourworld.com
Avenue Juárez at Quinta
Quinta at 14th Street

Especially popular with the cruise-ship crowd, this international chain retails rings, necklaces, watches, pendants, and gifts with a variety of gemstones and metals, including diamonds, emeralds, pearls, topaz, rubies, sapphires, tanzanite, silver, gold, and platinum.

Lightweight clothes are recommended year-round in Playa.

Effy Jewelry Factory
984-803-4100
www.effycollection.com
Paseo del Carmen Mall, 10th Avenue at First Street

This international brand has locations in Alaska, Aruba, Cozumel, Curaçao, New York, and St. Martin. The shop has cold air-conditioning and a broad selection of gold, silver, and diamond jewelry.

Etenoha
Quinta between Eighth and 10th Streets

This shop, which carries jewelry and accessories made from local amber, also has unusual lamps and interesting houseware.

Quarzos
Quinta at Fourth Street

This brightly lit shop has silver and gold jewelry, pre-Columbian re-creations, and souvenir jewelry.

Top 10 Songs to Load on Your iPod

The right song can help secure a memory, make good times even better, and share an experience with friends. Try some of these to capture the spirit of the Riviera Maya:

"Margaritaville" by Jimmy Buffett. Said to have been written on a flight from Cozumel to Houston, it's a song about a mythical island at the bottom of a Cuervo bottle.

"Mexico" by James Taylor. This is a classic tale of an extended vacation: "The sun's so hot, I forgot to go home."

"Stays in Mexico" by Toby Keith. A countrified reminder to keep your vacation exploits to yourself.

"Mexico" by Nash Girls. Young women having fun at the beach.

"Married in Mexico" by Mark Wills. A south-of-the-border romance complete with beachfront nuptials.

"I Got Mexico" by Eddy Raven. Sometimes, that's all you need.

"Blame It on Mexico" by George Strait. "Too much guitar music, tequila, salt, and lime." I know I've used this excuse before.

"Ten Rounds with Jose Cuervo" by Tracy Byrd. Crazy things can happen with tequila, especially after 10 rounds.

"Mail Myself to Mexico" by Buddy Jewell. Vacation fantasies go postal.

"One Step Closer to Cancún" by Elmer Thudd. Inspirational song about an upcoming vacation.

Sol del Mar
Quinta between Sixth and Eighth Streets

Sol del Mar sells jewelry and clothes from major designers and also local brands.

Sub Chrono
Paseo del Carmen Mall

At the back end of the mall, this upscale watch shop sells name-brand watches from leading designers, dive watches, and fashion watches.

Sunglass Island
Quinta between Eighth and 10th Streets

Offers decent prices on eyewear by Ray-Ban, Gucci, Chanel, Prada, Armani, and others.

UltraFemme
www.ultrafemme.com.mx
Quinta between 10th and 12th Streets

Duty-free prices, outside the airport. UltraFemme offers great deals on name-brand perfumes, cosmetics, and other merchandise. It carries Rolex, Cartier, Tiffany & Co., Brequet,

David Yurman, Mikimoto, Tag Heuer, Omega, Ebel, Roberto Coin, Mont Blanc, Corum, and Movado. Cosmetic brands include Lancome, Estee Lauder, Clinique, Clarins, Chanel, La Prairie, Shisheido, Hugo Boss, Ralph Lauren, and Calvin Klein.

For the Beach

Bazar Azul
Quinta between 10th and 12th streets

This large air-conditioned shop offers sportswear, hats, bathing suits, sandals, jewelry, picture frames, and souvenirs.

Beach Company
Quinta at 12th Street

A popular stop for cruise-ship passengers, this stylish shop has bathing suits, summer wear, hats, sandals, bags, and other accessories you may find useful on a tropical vacation

Bikini Palace
Quinta between 10th and 12th streets

Here you'll find trendy name-brand bikinis, thong bathing suits, and cover-ups.

Blue Planet
Quinta between 10th and 12th streets

This boutique shop sells wraps, bathing suits, casual wear for men and women, bags, hats, sandals, and accessories.

Crush
Quinta between Sixth and Eighth streets

This is the place for hip sunglasses and sportswear to help you look good at Playa's beaches and lounge bars.

Mare Swimwear
Quinta between Sixth and Eighth streets

Mare sells just what you'd expect from its name: bathing suits for men and women. National and local brands are available.

Marti
984-803-4083
Paseo del Carmen Mall

This large national chain store offers high-quality sporting goods, including diving and snorkeling gear, running shoes, water shoes, water toys, games, apparel, hats, jerseys, and other equipment.

Caracol

Miro

Quinta at Fourth Street

Known for its "everything is $10" prices, this chain store has T-shirts, shorts, sportswear, and other summery clothing.

Tank-Ha Dive Shop

Quinta between Eighth and 10th streets

While Tank-Ha offers dive trips and equipment rental/sales, and there is an electronic kiosk out front with information on area dining and nightlife, it's also a good spot to purchase masks, fins, and other gear for snorkeling and diving.

Zingara Swimwear

Quinta between Eighth and 10th streets

Here you can get name-brand and off-brand swimsuits, cover-ups, and accessories, mostly for women.

Clothing & Accessories

Caracol

Quinta between Sixth and Eighth streets

This small boutique store offers women's apparel, sandals, bags, hats, jewelry, and accessories.

Diesel

Quinta between Eighth and 10th streets

This medium-size showroom has casual wear, bags, shoes, sunglasses, and accessories. Its hip clothing can help you look like one of the stylish Europeans walking the streets of Playa.

Gold Duck

Quinta between Second and Fourth streets

You can't miss the big logo on the front of the building. This chain store offers mostly leather and canvas goods, including bags, backpacks, and hats.

Harley Davidson

Paseo del Carmen Mall

This shop has Harley-branded merchandise and apparel, including shirts, hats, jackets, leather goods, sunglasses, sport bags, and more. Harley Davidson motorcycle rentals are available at the rental office located on Highway 307 at Constituyentes Avenue.

Kin Mayab
Quinta between 10th and 12th streets

Kin Mayab has traditional men's and women's clothing, Mayan-inspired apparel, and clothing made of natural fibers.

La Casita
984-803-1249
Quinta between 10th and 12th streets

Sells tropical apparel, *guayaberas* (Mexican wedding shirts), *huipiles* (traditional embroidered Mexican dresses), and hand-stitched garments for men and women. There is also a selection of kids' clothing, silver jewelry, and accessories.

Mlueza
984-801-8001
www.mlueza.com
Quinta at 30th Street

This Spanish boutique offers jewelry, bags, shoes, wallets, cigarette cases, and other accessories.

Pygmee's
Quinta between Eighth and 10th streets

Here you'll find a funky selection of tropical sportswear, shoes, lamps, and accessories.

Roger's Boots
Second Street between Quinta and 10th Avenue

A popular regional chain, Roger's offers handmade leather boots starting at around $100. Custom boots are also available, if you're going to be around a while. They also sell leather bags, belts, fancy belt buckles, hats, holsters, and rifle cases.

Tita Sandalias
20th Street between First Avenue and Quinta

This unique boutique has a sand floor with wooden stepping-stones and cheery decor. On display are a wide variety of mostly handmade sandals for the beach, the disco, or strutting along Quinta. Bags and other accessories are also available.

Wayan Natural Wear
984-803-3543
www.wayan.com.mx
Paseo del Carmen Mall
Quinta at Second Street
Quinta at 16th Street
Quinta at Constituyentes

This successful chain, with stores in Cancún and Playa del Carmen, sells wraps, shirts, and other Mayan-inspired apparel, plus jewelry, bags, housewares, crafts, and accessories.

Handicrafts & Gifts

Caribbean Puzzles
Calle Corazon
Quinta at 20th Street (kiosk only)

This shop offers games, books, puzzles, and other fun stuff for kids. It's a good spot to find a gift for a child left at home or to find something to help keep a vacationing kid busy in the hotel room. Most of the stock is of the educational variety—nothing here makes loud noise or goes fast.

Le Best
Quinta between Second and Fourth streets

This large shop offers good liquor prices, souvenir bottles, T-shirts, lighters, tons of souvenirs, and—no joke—even a variety of hand-painted sinks.

PachaMama
Calle Corazon

On the south side of the short Calle Corazon strip, this shop offers Mayan and Mexican artwork, handicrafts, postcards, books, religious art, and great gift items.

Plaza la Fiesta
Quinta between Fourth and Sixth streets

This popular chain store is the largest souvenir store in town. It offers a vast array of gifts, personal items, and fun reminders of the area. There are T-shirts, sportswear, boots, sandals, leather goods, pottery, jewelry, hats, ashtrays, keychains, Mayan replicas, sculptures, and hundreds of other items.

Sacbe
Quinta between Second and Fourth streets

This interesting store has Mayan-inspired artwork, mostly from local artisans. There are artifact re-creations, home decor items, leatherwork, jade carvings, and natural fiber apparel.

Señor Frog's Gift Shop
Quinta at 20th Street
Second location at the ferry dock

Nothing like a T-shirt to prove you were there—or to rub it in the face of someone who wasn't. The *"world famoso"* bar and restaurant chain's off-site gift shop has hats, shorts, T-shirts, jackets, bags, and other items emblazoned with the happy frog logo. Great for gifts.

Bargains abound in Playa del Carmen. Mike Stone

Bargain Hunting in Playa

Contributed by Donna Loera

Playa del Carmen is a shopper's dream destination. Most shopping is confined to La Quinta Avenida (Fifth Avenue), which is paved with brick and restricted to foot traffic.

Shops are interspersed with restaurants and bars, so taking a break to drink a cool beverage and people-watch is all part of the day's fun. Exclusive shops can be found at the Paseo del Carmen Mall near the town square and on Calle Corazon, which intersects Quinta between 14th and 16th Streets. The local market is located on Quinta at 26th Street. The price and quality of goods is varied, so it is important to shop around before buying. It is appropriate to haggle over prices in the market and in lower-end stores, as well as with street and beach vendors, but not in the shops or boutiques.

Products are as varied as the ethnicity of the tourists who shop here and are priced for every pocketbook. Jewelry shopping is always fun, and in Playa the discerning shopper can find silver, turquoise, opal, and amber. In this resort town, swimsuits, sarongs, and other beachwear abound and can be had for a bargain even in the more exclusive shops. Hats are available in almost every color, fabric, and style and are affordably priced, so treat yourself to a newly purchased one instead of packing your own. Shoes, especially sandals and flip-flops, are another item you needn't take with you. They are trendy, cheap, and available in styles you're not likely to find at home. For example, you can find Brazilian Havaianas sandals in several shops and pay the same price for them as you would in Rio de Janeiro.

Shops are generally open from 10 AM until 10 PM or later, but the street becomes more congested as the day progresses. If you're a true shopping aficionado, you'll likely want to shop early, before the beach crowd decides to break for some shade and bargain hunting. Even if you are a sun worshipper, be sure to take at least one afternoon to browse the varied merchandise along Quinta and bring home a few memories from your trip to Playa.

Sample prices: Havaianas sandals: $22   Fake silver bracelets: $1 each   Mexican blanket: $5 Maracas: $2 a pair Sarong beach wrap: $4.50

Groceries, Liquor, Books, Music, Cigars & Conveniences

Bontan Book Store
Calle Corazon near Quinta

Bontan sells books, newspapers, and current-issue magazines in English and Spanish.

Casa Partagas
Quinta at 14th Street

This is a good spot to purchase real Cuban cigars. Ask the staff for an explanation of how to spot the fakes. T-shirts, smoking accessories, and gifts are also sold.

Casa Tequila–La Tequilaria
984-873-0195
Quinta between Fourth and Sixth streets
Quinta at 14th Street

This liquor store/sampling bar is a great spot to shop for tequila if you're looking for something specific. One-liter bottles range from $7 to $250. It has a few sidewalk tables, plus an upstairs balcony with a couple of tables overlooking Quinta. Souvenir bottles and flasks are also available. The bar serves many of the tequilas that it sells, plus some light snacks. (Salt and lime count as snacks, right?)

Market & Deli

Casita de la Musica
Quinta between Avenue Juárez and Second Street

They sell local and international music, including merengue, salsa, Cuban, Mayan, pop, mariachi, and lounge music. There's also a selection of nonmusical souvenirs available.

Chedraui Supermarket
Highway 307, adjacent to Playacar

This massive grocery superstore has fresh produce, meats, dairy, deli items, prepared foods, packaged goods, beer, liquor, cigars, clothing, electronics, furniture, and much more than you'd need on vacation. It has a great selection of domestic and imported goods and better prices than the convenience stores downtown.

Flower Shop
Avenue Juárez between 20th and 25th streets

Surprise your travel companion with a bouquet of fresh tropical flowers. This local shop has a wide assortment of tropicals, roses, and other flowers, plus premade bouquets, plants, and arrangements. Prices are about half of what you'd expect to pay back home.

Habana Cigars
984-803-1047
Quinta between 10th and 12th streets

Habana Cigars specializes in Cohibas (Cuba), Partagas, and Trinidad cigars, and it also sells lighters, newspapers, and gifts, as well as empty cigar boxes for $4. Though officially Cuban cigar boxes are still illegal to import into the United States, it's doubtful that U.S. Customs would hassle you for it.

Kodak
Quinta between Second and Fourth streets

This authorized Kodak dealer carries medium-quality cameras, plus simple point-and-shoots for travelers. Film, batteries, and CD creation are also available.

Market & Deli
Quinta at Sixth Street

A large store offering deli sandwiches, snack foods, some groceries, over-the-counter and prescription drugs, liquor, T-shirts, souvenirs, hot sauce, film, batteries, cold drinks, and many sundries.

Marsan Market
30th Avenue at South First Street

Six blocks straight back from the ferry dock, this local market has fresh meats and fish, fishing supplies, clothing, shoes, fresh fruits, and a wide variety of items found at a typical Mexican market. It's a good place for picking up a unique gift item or just strolling around to get a sample of the local color.

Top 10 Books for Riviera Maya Travelers

Try these great reads in preparation for your trip, while you're there lying on the beach, or to help ease your transition back to the real world.

Don't Stop the Carnival by Herman Wouk. This meandering tale may change your mind about wanting to open a hotel in the Caribbean.

Incidents of Travel in Yucatán by John Lloyd Stephens and Frederick Catherwood. Originally published in the 1840s, it's an amazing account of the life and times of the Mayans.

Cinnamon Skin by John D. MacDonald. A boat-bum detective travels to Cancún and the Riviera Maya to solve a crime for a friend.

A Salty Piece of Land by Jimmy Buffett. A cowboy moves to Sian Ka'an to become a fishing guide. Plenty of Riviera Maya and Buffett-song-inspired references.

A Tourist in the Yucatán by James McNay Brumfield. An action-adventure mystery set among the Mayan ruins.

Where the Sky Is Born: Living in the Land of the Maya by Jeanine Lee Kitchel. Thinking of moving to the Riviera Maya or just want to know what it would be like? Learn from someone who's done it.

Chaos in Cancún by Susan Murray. A detective novel for teens that takes the main characters on a whirlwind tour through the Riviera Maya. Includes some fun references to local spots that kids will find entertaining.

Wicked Spanish by Howard Tomb. This tongue-in-cheek language guide will teach you some naughty phrases and fun sayings to try out on bartenders and fellow bus riders.

Midlife Mavericks: Women Reinventing Their Lives in Mexico by Karen Blue. True stories of women who move to Mexico to start their lives over.

Captains Outrageous by Joe R. Lansdale. A comedic and bumbling tale of intrigue, with travels from east Texas to the land of the Mayans.

Morgan's Tobacco Shop

984-873-2166
Quinta at 6th Street

Morgan's offers cigars, cigarettes, T-shirts, smoking accessories, current magazines, and daily newspapers, including the *New York Times* and *USA Today*. Cigars are hand rolled in front of the shop each evening.

Mundo Bookstore

984-879-3004
First Street between 20th and 25th avenues

With more than ten thousand books in stock, Mundo is a great place to purchase a good beach novel, magazines, regional history books, Mayan literature, and other finds. The store also takes book donations to support local students. Open 9–9 daily.

Playa Mart
Quinta at Avenue Juárez

The busiest convenience store in town offers cold drinks, snacks, magazines, T-shirts, sunglasses, souvenirs, liquor, and beer to go. It is convenient to the ferry dock.

Sam's Club
Highway 307, adjacent to Playacar

Just like back home, Sam's has a massive selection of groceries and other items. A membership card is required, and your stateside card is valid.

San Francisco de Asis
30th Avenue at 12th Street

This Mexican chain–grocery store is not quite as well stocked as Chedraui on the freeway, but it's within easy walking distance of many Playa hotels. It has a good selection of beer and liquor, deli items, and snacks and also such basics as sandals, toiletries, batteries, and film.

Señor Habano
Quinta between Sixth and Eighth streets

One of several local stores offering regional and international cigars (including Cuban cigars), smoking accessories, lighters, T-shirts, and gifts.

Super Deli & Drug Store
Quinta between Second and Fourth streets

This big, modern store with several coolers and well-stocked shelves sells liquor, snacks, deli sandwiches, Gatorade, yogurt, cheese, cold cuts, tobacco, pharmacy items, personal hygiene products, and a fair range of souvenirs.

Super Ho
Quinta at 22nd Street

Its name may be funny, but the selection of cold drinks, snacks, fruit, and deli foods at this mini grocery store is fairly serious. It also has batteries, film, and other sundries.

Wal-Mart
8th Street at 30th Avenue

This full-size discount department store opened in early 2006 and quickly became a favorite of locals.

Spas, Gyms & Body Work

Area Body Zone
984-803-4048
Paseo del Carmen Mall

This modern gym is up the same stairs that lead to the Moon, next to Rolandi's Italian restaurant (see *Dining*). For a daily-use fee of $20, visitors can participate in Pilates classes, yoga, spinning, and Tai Chi. There are free weights, cardio equipment, workout stations, and clean locker rooms. Some classes and personal trainers are extra.

Cabellisimo Hair Style
20th Street between Quinta and 10th Avenue

This full-service hair salon offers tinting, cuts, and styling.

Muscle-Beach Gym
984-803-0478
Sixth Street between 30th and 35th avenues

They have a weight room and exercise machines, plus a climbing wall and steam room. Private instruction is available. Classes include spinning, Pilates, aerobics, Tae Bo, and kickboxing. Open 8–1 and 4–8 Monday–Saturday.

Natural Spa
984-879-3629
Quinta at 16th Street
Constituyentes between First Avenue and Quinta
Nikki Beach Club (massage only)

Here white-coated spa technicians provide a variety of relaxing and therapeutic services, including facials, pedicures, acrylic nails, massages, reflexology, body wraps, and other body treatments. They can also arrange *temazcal* visits at nearby centers. They are an authorized retailer of L'Oreal beauty products.

Playa Piercings
Quinta between 8th and 10th streets, in front of Pygmee's

Playa uses sterile needles and modern equipment and has a large selection of studs, earrings, and belly rings.

Screamink Tattoos
10th Street at Quinta

This tattoo artist offers tribal tattoos, Mayan designs, and custom jobs. T-shirts and piercings are also available.

Spa Ha
984-803-1564
www.spasmexico.com
10th Avenue between 38th and 40th streets

On the northern end of Playa's tourist zone, this "spa" is not recommended for serious patrons in search of quality therapeutic treatments as it seems to be more of a place to get rubbed by a pretty young woman than it is a serious spa. It offers massages, body treatments, steam baths, and a rooftop plunge pool. A 45-minute massage goes for $45. Additional "relaxation services" for men can be added for a $20 tip.

Spa Itzá

984-803-2588

www.spaitza.com

Calle Corazon/14th Street near Quinta, on the Calle Corazon pedestrian walk

Founded by veteran Californian holistic health practicioner Sharon Sedgwick, this modern spa takes a traditional approach to body treatments, accenting its services with ancient Mayan healing principles. Offerings include Mayan healing baths (aphrodisiac, milk, sea-weed, tonic rescue, sunburn relief, anti-itch), body treatments (Mayan salt exfoliation, cellulite treatment, black mud, Mayan clay), flotation chamber, oxygen bar, body waxing, facials, and manicures. Package deals are available for bride and groom, jet lag recovery, a mom's escape, and other specialties. The in-house boutique carries spa products from OPI, Fridda Dorsch, CV Aromatherapy, and Rain Forest Remedies. There is also a Mayan-themed terrace and rooftop sundeck. Open 10–9 daily.

Tatuajes La Suerte

Quinta between Second and Fourth streets

Here you can get artful tattoos and piercings, as well as T-shirts.

The terrace at Spa Itzá

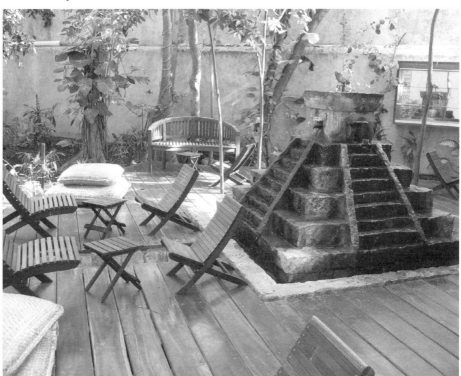

Veronica's Massage
984-807-5023
First Avenue between 24th and 26th streets

This boutique massage center offers sports, stone, Swedish, and deep-tissue massage, plus reflexology. Walk-ins accepted, based on availability. Excellent prices.

Yoga By the Sea
984-873-0735
www.morethanyoga.com
Eight Street at the beach

Operating out of the Alhambra Hotel (see *Lodging*), instructors Arielle Thomas Newman and Ellen de Jonge offer daily Hatha yoga classes, yoga retreats, specialized programs, and meditation and relaxation techniques. They also have special yoga programs for couples, divers, and golfers.

Shops at Paseo del Carmen Mall

Shopping Plazas

El Mercado Los Portales
10th Avenue at Sixth Street

With a pair of inexpensive restaurants (El Caguamo and Los Portales) serving typical local foods (such as *torta* sandwiches and tacos), plus a few T-shirt shops, souvenir stores, and junk shops, this is a good spot for budget travelers to get a quick bite or stock up on supplies. It is conveniently close to the youth hostel.

Paseo del Carmen Mall
First Street at Quinta

This modern outdoor shopping plaza has more than two dozen shops, restaurants, bars, and other attractions.

Plaza Maya
Highway 307, across from the southernmost entrance to Playacar

A massive shopping complex with restaurants, bars, boutique stores, a movie theater, discount stores, department stores, and a pedestrian plaza.

Plaza Pelicanos
10th Avenue between Eighth and 10th streets

This mall has a bank, Blockbuster, Papa John's, several clothing stores, a duty-free shop, and a three-screen movie theater, showing movies about two months after they are released in the United States.

3

The Riviera Maya—
South of Playa del Carmen

Travelers venturing farther south of Playa del Carmen will find a striking variety of options for lodging and recreation, and the farther south you go, the more remote, unspoiled, and adventurous things become. Playacar is a stone's throw from Playa del Carmen and home to nearly a dozen all-inclusive mega-resorts, where travelers from around the world visit to play golf, lie on the beach, and be pampered in every way possible. The beachfront towns of Puerto Aventuras and Akumal beckon scuba divers and fishing enthusiasts with excellent conditions year-round, while the abundant cenotes, hidden beaches, eco-adventure parks, and Mayan ruins provide venturesome travelers with the kind of vacation experiences that turn postcards home into exotic tales of intrigue and exploration.

Many of the hotels and resorts south of Playa are all-inclusives, with vast campuses featuring luxurious accommodations, multiple dining options, on-site nightlife, spas, recreational activities, and everything else guests need to spend a week of fun in the sun without ever getting into a car. Other lodging options in this area include local inns; eco-conscious cabañas with an emphasis on nature, rather than luxury; and low-cost hutlike properties fashioned from native materials and devoted to students, traditionalists, and other budget-conscious travelers who want to experience the splendor of the Riviera Maya much as the locals have been doing for hundreds of years.

Playacar

Just south of Playa del Carmen, off Highway 307, at km 285, the large-scale, gated resort community of Playacar surrounds the ancient Mayan ruins of Xaman-Ha and is composed of resort hotels, condos, private residences, shopping plazas, restaurants, a golf course, activities centers, and one of the most pristine stretches of beach in the whole Riviera Maya.

The creation of Playacar was the single most important event in the development of large-scale tourism in the Riviera Maya. Before that, travelers were content with small, locally owned hotels, relatively few services, and European plan (no meals included) rates. Aside from a few standouts, accommodations were generally simple affairs, with basic amenities and very few luxuries but a strong feeling of tradition and harmony with the surroundings. Strict density restrictions in Playa del Carmen made the town less than ideal

PLAYACAR

To
Playa del Carmen

N

Av. MUNICIPALIZADA

Ferry
(to Cozumel)

Playacar Palace

Plaza
Antigua

Mayan Ruins

PASEO XAMAN-HA

Aviary
Xaman-Ha

CARIBBEAN SEA

VILLAS PAKAL DRIVE

307

PASEO XAMAN-HA

Hacienda
Vista Real

PASEO XAMAN-HA

S. PLAYACAR ENT.

Club de Golf

The Reef Playacar

Riu Palace Riveria Maya

Viva Wyndham Azteca

Occidental Allegro Playacar

Playacar
Plaza

Royal Hideaway Playacar
by Occidental

Riu Playacar

Viva Wyndham Maya

Riu Tequila

Riu Palace Mexico

To
Tulum

PASEO XAMAN-HA

Riu Yucatán

Iberostar Tucan/Iberostar Queztal

0   1/4 mile
0   250 meters

© The Countryman Press

for large resort development, and had allowed the town to grow slowly and organically, unlike the rampant development seen in Cancún.

In the early 1990s, though, things started to change. Mexico's real estate conglomerate Grupo Situr purchased a huge plot of barren beachfront land just south of Avenida Juárez and christened it Playacar, a term deemed more marketable and English-friendly than the name of the town itself. Since it was out of the jurisdiction of the development restrictions, the Riviera Maya had its first opportunity to build international-class hotels, which needed a larger scale and higher volume of guests to turn a profit.

Today, there are more than a dozen large resorts owned by international corporations and averaging some three hundred rooms each. Unlike the small inns and guest houses of a few years ago, these resorts offer a vast array of services and luxuries, including imported linens, efficient air-conditioning, abundant hot water, water-sports centers, on-site scuba training, dry-cleaning service, Jacuzzi tubs, tennis courts, swimming pools, and kids' clubs. Most are operated as all-inclusives, where guests pay one price that includes accommodations plus all meals, drinks, and activities. Many hotels have on-site gourmet restaurants, multiple bars, and even amphitheaters and nightclubs.

The area has become a playground for tourists from the United States, Canada, and Europe. It is an extremely popular wedding and honeymoon destination, and the resorts are quite adept at catering to vacationing couples with welcome amenities (fruit baskets, chilled champagne, flowers), special dinner reservations, and couples' spa treatments. Other common Playacar visitors are families and budget travelers with flexible schedules, who compare prices weekly, waiting for a bargain. Frequently, these travelers will choose their resort based on what special offers are available and tend to be less loyal to the brands or specific hotel properties. Others have had a good experience at one of the resorts and become avid ambassadors for it, claiming that its services and amenities are unbeatable. These travelers wouldn't dream of staying anywhere else and pride themselves on returning year after year, sometimes bringing gifts for their favorite bartenders and waiters.

The main road through the complex, Xaman-Ha Avenue, is made of cobblestone and is lined with manicured tropical plants and an occasional actual Mayan ruin, lending a timeless quality to the otherwise modern resort community. The road parallels the beachfront and splits Playacar into two sides. Phase I, along the water, features a nearly solid line of hotels, though they are mostly low-rise buildings of two or three stories surrounded by tropical vegetation, so the area does not feel overdeveloped or crowded. Phase II, on the other side of the avenue, includes the golf course, hundreds of vacation villas and private homes, and several hotels that are not directly on the beach. These hotels shuttle guests to a beach club, so even though their rooms don't front the beach, their guests are still able to have a beach vacation. Craft stores, restaurants, bars, and tour agencies are housed in various shopping plazas along Xaman-Ha and at Plaza Marina, near the ferry dock. Most guests, however, either take their meals on-site at their all-inclusive resorts or venture into the neighboring town of Playa del Carmen to experience the abundant dining options offered along Quinta Avenida and throughout town. Shopping, nightlife, and other tourist attractions can be found in Playa as well.

During the day, the beach bustles with activity. Some guests stroll along the water, play volleyball, sail, kayak, windsurf, swim, Jet Ski, and enjoy the plethora of activities, while others seek respite in a lounge chair or hammock and read and snooze to the warm breezes. To the north of Playacar is the town of Playa del Carmen, reachable by bicycle (loaners available at most hotels) or a short taxi ride. To the south is a mile-long stretch of deserted beach decorated with massive boulders, which starts at the Gala Resort and ends at the Xcaret resort and ecopark.

Guests at Playacar resorts can spend an entire week without leaving the complex and have all their needs and whims catered to. Others, however, like to visit Playa del Carmen in the evening to go shopping, stroll the tourist plazas, try some local foods, and enjoy the nightlife.

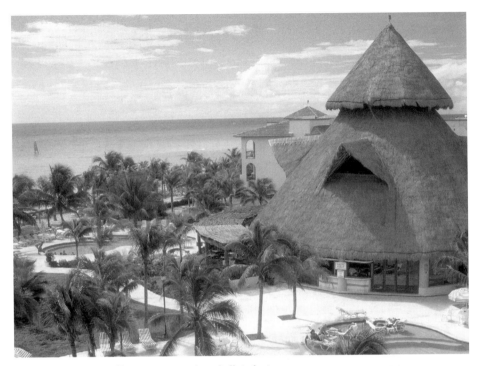

The accommodations in Playacar are upscale and all-inclusive. Courtesy of Riviera Maya Tourism Authority

LODGING

It can be a bit difficult to differentiate the all-inclusive resorts of Playacar. For the most part, the hotels share a common beach, which is just about perfect anywhere along the stretch. The hotels themselves are large-scale affairs, with comparable pools, gyms, restaurants, bars, and activities programs. Nearly all the rooms offer good air-conditioning, plenty of hot water, comfortable bedding, private balconies, minibars, and standard amenities. Most have bicycles for guest use, which makes the couple-mile trip into Playa del Carmen a breeze. The main considerations and differentiating factors are the size of the resort, whether or not the hotel is adults-only, whether it's on the beach or the golf course, and your budget. Rates range from $100 per person per night up to $250. As the price goes up, generally, the rooms are larger, the grounds are better maintained, the food and beverage quality is higher, and the vibe is more exclusive.

Allegro Occidental Playacar Resort
1-800-858-2258 (U.S.)
www.occidentalhotels.com
Paseo Xaman-Ha, Playacar

A family-friendly, beachfront, all-inclusive resort with 296 rooms housed in two-story villas scattered around the property, it was originally constructed in 1992 (it was the first all-inclusive in Playacar) and underwent $5 million worth of renovations in 2003, plus updates after Hurricanes Emily and Wilma in 2005. Rooms feature tropical colors, Mayan paintings, marble bathrooms, and private balconies. Casual and family-oriented, this moderately priced resort provides guests endless opportunities to have fun—and equal opportunities to be alone with the sun and the water. There is an activity pool, quiet pool, and children's pool; a kids' club; and an outdoor theater with live shows nightly. Rates: start at $225 per person per night and go up, depending on the class of room and selection of optional tours or amenities.

Hacienda Vista Real

984-803-1585
www.vistareal.com.mx
Paseo Xaman-Ha, Villas Pakal

This luxurious villa-style property has 78 rooms and is surrounded by the Playacar golf course, straight back from the Reef Playacar hotel. The decor is a combination of Mexican hacienda, Roman, and Mayan, with dark woods, marble floors, columns and arches, granite accents, and warm colors. Rooms have air-conditioning, satellite TV, safes, glass showers, original artwork, and amazingly soft sheets and duvets. Suites have up to three bedrooms and feature Jacuzzis, terraces, and large living rooms. The resort has a grill restaurant and pool facing several water hazards, the fairway of the first hole, and the clubhouse beyond. There is a massive fitness center with more than 30 LifeFitness machines, a kids' club, a convenience store, a bakery, a VIP TV lounge, an Internet café, and a Thai restaurant and sushi bar. Guests have access to the resort's exclusive beach club, located on Xpu-Ha beach, 15 minutes south of the hotel. The attached day spa is housed inside a recreation of a Mayan temple that is a marvel just to look it. It is the most lavish facility of its kind in all of Playacar, featuring a 30-foot waterfall, climbing wall, Mayan murals and stonework, and the most modern medical, therapeutic, and relaxing facilities available. Popular treatments include coconut-milk body wraps, aroma facials, Turkish baths, hot stone massages, Shiatsu, hydrobaths, and full beauty salon services. There is even an indoor *temazcal*, with upgraded seating and amenities from the traditional Mayan sweat lodges. Rates: around $225 per room EP (European plan). All-inclusive plans are available for an additional fee.

Iberostar Resorts

984-877-2000 or 1-888-923-2722 (U.S.)
www.iberostar.com
Paseo Xaman-Ha, Playacar

This complex near the southern end of Playacar includes the Tucan and Quetzal resorts, each with 350 rooms. Accommodations are all-inclusive, with unlimited food and drinks, nonmotorized water sports, nightly shows, and other activities. There is a great rock-free beachfront, multiple pools, outdoor Jacuzzis, restaurants, bars, scuba center, workout room, tennis courts, and nightly live shows. Water sports include windsurfing, kayaking, and snorkeling. Rates: average $250–$350 per night per room, double occupancy.

Occidental Royal Hideaway

984-873-4500
www.royalhideaway.com
Paseo Xaman-Ha, Playacar

Luxury and all-inclusives don't always go together. At this adults-only, 13-acre, 200-room resort, though, the two go together like piña coladas and sunset—which, by the way, are included in the all-inclusive room rate. The lavish property has meandering rivers, waterfalls, tropical gardens, and six pools (three reserved for quiet relaxation). There are several restaurants and bars, and men are required to wear long pants, closed-toe shoes, and collared shirts for dinner. There is a large fitness center, two tennis courts, a water-sports center, and a theater with live nightly shows. The rooms are housed in two- and three-story villas, with a mix of Spanish and colonial Mexican architecture. They have air-conditioning, ceiling fans, CD/DVD players, and marble bathrooms with jetted tubs. Internet access is complimentary in the business center. Tours, scuba diving, and a wide range of spa services (algae body wraps, massages, body scrubs) are available for an extra fee. Rates: start at $275 per person per night. Superior room classes, upgraded amenities, and preplanned tours are available for an additional fee.

Playacar Beach Properties
984-873-0418 or 1-866-862-7164 (U.S.)
www.playacarbeachproperties.com

This company has an inventory of more than 50 condos and villas in Playacar, including locations on the beach, on the golf course, and around the development. Their web site lists all of the properties and their amenities and helps you select one that may fit your needs. Rates: range from $650 a week for a basic one-bedroom condo up to $4,000 a month for an immaculate five-bedroom villa right on the ocean.

Playacar Palace
www.palaceresorts.com
North end of Paseo Xaman-Ha, Playacar

Previously the Continental Plaza Playacar, this was the first large hotel in the Playa del Carmen area and the flagship resort of Playacar. It was completely renovated and reopened in 2005 with 185 rooms, a chic lobby, and a beachfront pool. As it is adjacent to the Cozumel ferry dock and the Playa del Carmen town plaza, it's a good spot for travelers who desire the luxury of Playacar but still want ready access to the town of Playa del Carmen. Rates: start at $185 per night per room.

Reef Club Playacar
984-873-4120
www.thereefplayacar.com
Paseo Xaman-Ha, Playacar

This boutique all-inclusive property, located on the beach in the middle of the Playacar development, is within walking distance of the town of Playa del Carmen. With only two hundred rooms, it has a more exclusive feeling than its larger neighbors. It is a family-friendly property, with a kids' pool and Mayan and tropical design influences. Rooms have a private balcony or patio, air-conditioning, and ceiling fans. The rate includes meals at three restaurants (buffet, Italian, and snack bar), drinks at five bars (including a swim-up bar and beach bar), activities program (water aerobics, beach volleyball, water basketball), theme parties, kayaking, windsurfing, sailing, and snorkeling. There are two pools, an outdoor Jacuzzi, and a kids' club. Bicycles are available for guests who want to ride into Playa del Carmen. Rates: $225–$275 per person, all-inclusive.

Riu Hotels and Resorts
1-888-666-8816
www.riu.com
Paseo Xaman-Ha, Playacar

Spanish-owned Riu Hotels has five all-inclusive properties on the southern end of Playacar: Riu Palace Mexico, Riu Tequila, Riu Yucatán, Riu Playacar, and Riu Lupita. The Mexican Street shopping plaza adjacent to the resort complex offers a gym, hair salon, crafts market, clinic, tour office, and other attractions. Guests staying at one hotel can enjoy the facilities at the others, including the nightclub, which is located at the Tequila (well, that makes sense!). The Palace Mexico is the most upscale and has 434 rooms and a wedding chapel. The Tequila is the largest, with 664 rooms and an on-site nightclub; it appeals to the active crowd that's ready to party. The 507-room, hacienda-style Yucatán was renovated in mid-2005 and is just north of the Iberostar complex. The Playacar, which appeals to a young and budget-conscious crowd, has 396 rooms and 24-hour drink service. While the 300-room Lupita is in the middle of the golf course and not on the beach, guests receive complimentary transportation to the hotel's beach club, where food and drinks are included, just like at the resort. Rates: range from $150 per person per night up to $300, depending on the resort and the time of year.

Viva Wyndham Azteca
984-877-4100 or 1-800-WYNDHAM (U.S.)

www.vivaresorts.com
Paseo Xaman-Ha, Playacar

This relatively small property has 234 units, all within a short walk of the beach. The rooms have a bright and tropical vibe and are housed in low-rise Mexican colonial–style villas on either side of a central pool and courtyard. There is a buffet restaurant, plus an Italian and an Asian restaurant, open for dinner only. At night, guests head

VIDAS—Helping Pets and People in the Riviera Maya
A group of volunteer animal lovers called International Veterinarians Dedicated to Animal Health (VIDAS) travels each year to the Riviera Maya, providing education and free veterinary care in an effort to fight pet overpopulation, which can cause starvation, disease, and other health problems. They work with the local communities to improve the lives of pets and the people who love them. Their first trip, in 2002, involved two vets and six students and resulted in the sterilization of one hundred cats and dogs over five days in Playa del Carmen. Since then, more than one thousand animals have been sterilized and vaccinated in Akumal, Bacalar, Cobá, Chemuyil, Playa del Carmen, Tulum, Puerto Morelos, and Puerto Aventuras.

If you'd like to help the group by sponsoring a pet, making a contribution, or participating in a program, log on to www.vidas.org.

VIDAS volunteers take a break from helping area animals.

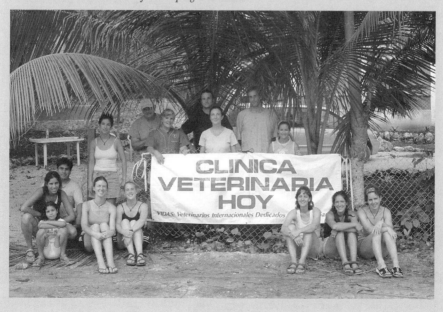

to the theater for live entertainment, then on to the on-site nightclub, where drinks are included. Guests can also enjoy the restaurants, bars, and other facilities of the adjacent Wyndham Maya property. There's even an affiliated Viva Café restaurant in Playa del Carmen, where guests can have a full dinner with wine, beer, and soft drinks for a surcharge of only $10. Rates: start at $260 per person.

Viva Wyndham Maya
984-874-4600 or 1-800-WYNDHAM (U.S.)
www.vivaresorts.com

The larger of the two Viva Wyndham properties has 13 acres of land and 400 rooms, with colonial and contemporary Mexican design. The rooms run on both sides of a central courtyard, where the pool, Jacuzzi, theater, and restaurants are located. Guests have their choice from three restaurants (international buffet, Mexican, and Mediterranean) and three bars and can also visit the eateries and bars at the nearby Wyndham Azteca resort. For a real change of pace, visitors can head into the town of Playa del Carmen to dine at the Viva Café and pay only a $10 surcharge for a multi-course meal and drinks. Rates: start at $225 per person per night.

Xcaret to Paamul

South of Xcaret, visitors get their first glimpse of the wild side of the Riviera Maya. No longer will you see souvenir stands, gas stations, and convenience stores every few miles. In this part of the region, a thick jungle canopy has kept tourism development at bay, while palm trees, unexplored Mayan ruins, and tiny traditional villages dot the landscape. To visit this part of the Yucatán, travelers either take a shuttle bus from the airport or rent a car so they can go where they choose. Public bus service is spotty and will let travelers off only along the main road, while most of the hotels and attractions are located along the beach, a few miles away. Tourists either take their meals on-property at their resort or, if staying at an EP (European plan) hotel or condo, stop off at the supermarket in Playa del Carmen to stock up on foodstuffs and other essential supplies.

LODGING

Occidental Grand Flamenco Xcaret
987-871-5400 or 1-800-858-2258 (U.S.)
www.occidentalhotels.com
Highway 307, km 282

Five minutes down the highway from Playa del Carmen, this 765-room, all-inclusive resort is on the beach and adjacent to the Xcaret ecopark. Narrow canals and rivers flow through the property, giving you the feeling that you're still in the park, even when you're back at the hotel. A second hotel, located within the Grand Flamenco,

is the Royal Club, which has 45 rooms, concierge service, a private pool, and an exclusive beach club. Rates: start at $410 per room, double occupancy, including admission for two to the park.

Paamul
984-876-2691
Highway 307, km 273

This RV haven is gaining in popularity with day-trippers who come by to see the sea turtles nest, go snorkeling or diving, or just lounge around the beach. The main road is lined with RV shelters, some of which have

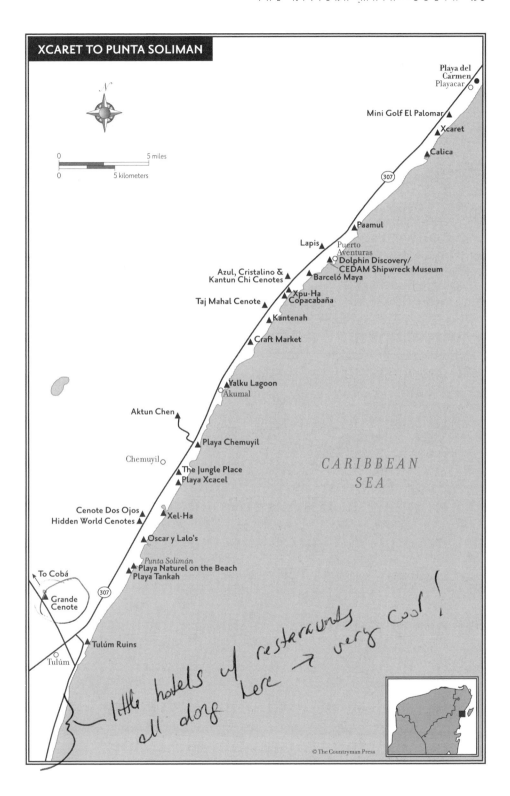

XCARET TO PUNTA SOLIMAN

N

0   5 miles
0   5 kilometers

Playa del Carmen
Playacar

Mini Golf El Palomar

Xcaret

Calica

307

Paamul

Lapis

Puerto Aventuras

Dolphin Discovery/
CEDAM Shipwreck Museum

Azul, Cristalino &
Kantun Chi Cenotes

Barceló Maya

Xpu-Ha
Copacabaña

Taj Mahal Cenote

Kantenah

Craft Market

Yalku Lagoon
Akumal

Aktun Chen

Playa Chemuyil

Chemuyil

The Jungle Place
Playa Xcacel

Cenote Dos Ojos
Hidden World Cenotes

Xel-Ha

Oscar y Lalo's

Punta Soliman
Playa Naturel on the Beach
Playa Tankah

To Cobá

Grande
Cenote

307

CARIBBEAN
SEA

little hotels w/ restaurants
all dong here → very cool!

Tulúm Ruins

Tulúm

© The Countryman Press

been there for years. Visitors can camp on the beach or stay at the small hotel. There are also a couple of super-casual beachside restaurants. ScubaMex has a water-sports center here and offers snorkeling and diving trips to the nearby reef. The beach along this shallow bay is rocky, so it's not the best for swimming. Rates:$75–$150.

ATTRACTIONS

Calica
Highway 307, km 280

Formerly used only as a commercial port and dock for the Cozumel car ferry, the Calica facility is becoming a popular stop-off point for international cruise ships as it is a lower-cost alternative to the busier ports at Cancún, Cozumel, and Playa del Carmen. A commercial plaza with shops, restaurants, and souvenir stands was recently added with the intention of attracting more and more cruise ships to the port. The Cozumel car ferry, operated by Transcaribe (987-872-7671), charges $25 per vehicle plus $1 per person for the 40-minute ride. It departs for Cozumel each day at 4 PM and 6 PM and returns at 6 AM, 10 AM, 4 PM, and 8 PM. See the "Practical Information" section for information on the pedestrian ferry.

There are still miles of deserted beaches in the Riviera Maya.

Get a Job and Stay a While

Though it's not always easy to make the transition from tourist to local, it can be possible. With a bit of determination and luck, you can find a job and live in paradise. The Mexican government requires that all foreign workers have an FM3 visa, which your employer must obtain for you. Fluency in Spanish is required, though exceptions are sometimes made. And don't expect to make anything near what you could earn back home: Minimum wage in Mexico is about $10 per day, and most jobs available to foreigners generally pay around $1,000 per month. Depending on the job, sales commission, bonuses, room and board, and other perks can help sweeten the pot. The cost of living can be much less, but only if you plan on living like a local. If you're looking for a permanent vacation and expecting to work during the day and then party at tourist clubs every night, you'll probably need additional financial resources.

Top 10 Jobs for Foreigners

- Bartender
- English teacher
- Hotel activities staff/animation (all-inclusives)
- Hotel front desk, guest services, or concierge
- Real estate sales
- Restaurant host/hostess
- Scuba instructor
- Time-share representative/sales
- Tour guide
- Waiter/waitress

Puerto Aventuras *(Highway 307, km 269)*

The exclusive resort town of Puerto Aventuras is the only true sheltered marina in the Riviera Maya. It was also the first major development south of Cancún, though it has not had the rapid growth that has been seen in Playa del Carmen. If you talk to the locals, they'll tell you that it's by design in order to retain the small-town feel and exclusive nature of the resort. Hurricane Emily passed directly over the marina in 2005, sinking boats, beaching others, and wreaking havoc across town, but thousands of palm trees have been replanted, and the area is quickly regaining its prestorm appeal. In fact, encouraged by the way the town survived the hurricane, condo sales have been booming, and the community's main challenge now is keeping its small-town luster. Visitors enter through a large security gate just off Highway 307. The road winds down to the beach and ends at the 250-slip marina, which is packed with fishing boats, dive boats, sailboats, and pleasure yachts. The marina channels wind through an open-air pedestrian plaza, which is lined with restaurants, shops, bars, pharmacies, Internet cafés (which are a little expensive at $1 for 10 minutes), and a few grocery/convenience stores. A Dolphin Discovery location is built into the marina, and visitors can stroll the plaza while watching the dolphins cavort, swim, and even jump out of the water. There are relatively few places to stay, given how pleasantly landscaped and maintained everything is. There is a nine-hole golf course, a museum, a crafts market, tennis courts, and a beautiful beach where the reef is close to shore, keeping the wave action to a minimum.

Spinning through Life on Spiral Island

A unique chapter in Puerto Aventuras history ended when Hurricane Emily rumbled through the marina in July 2005.

The story began in 1998, when British ex-pat, artist, and musician Richy Sowa (or "Reishee," as the locals call him) moved to the Riviera Maya with a dream of living a life of relaxation and simplicity while stressing recycling and low-impact survival. To that end he started collecting empty water bottles (he had accumulated more than 250,000 of them when the storm hit) and loading them into fishing nets, which were arranged in a spiral pattern to create an artificial island, which he cast adrift in Puerto Aventuras. He planted mangroves and fruit trees, added some 10 tons of sand, and built a house from discarded wood, bamboo, and thatched palm.

The island, sometimes called Bottle Island, reached the size of half a basketball court and could be maneuvered around the marina with an outboard boat motor attached to one end. It had a solar cooker (with reflectors laid out in a spiral) and a self-composting toilet and was home to several cats, dogs, and sometimes ducks. Richy's island was featured on *Ripley's Believe It or Not!* in 2000. His self-stated long-term goal for the project was to "use the waste from this world as a foundation to create a tranquil piece of paradise and sail around the earth on a floating island with the message of love and faith."

During the hurricane, Richy and his animal friends took shelter on the mainland. When morning dawned, his island lay in ruins, ripped apart and beached on the sand. He planned to transport the island by truck to nearby Soliman Bay and reconstruct it, thus keeping his island—and his dream—afloat.

Lodging

Aventura Spa Palace
984-875-1100
www.palaceresorts.com
Highway 307, km 270

With a romantic design inspired by a traditional Mexican hacienda but with a more contemporary flair, the 1,266-room Aventura Spa Palace is an adults-only, all-inclusive resort occupying 85 tropical acres along the beach. The entrance is separate from the main marina entrance and is well marked. The resort is built around a natural ocean inlet, making it ideal for protected-water snorkeling, swimming, and sunbathing. Most guests are vacationing couples celebrating a honeymoon, anniversary, or other special occasion. From the stone fountain in the main plaza to the ornate archways, tile floors, and locally crafted furnishings, the hotel embraces its Mexican heritage while surrounding guests with plenty of modern amenities and luxuries. Facilities and activities include four pools, seven Jacuzzis, scuba training pool, two gyms, theater, nightclub, volleyball, billiards, bicycles, rollerblades, beauty salon, activities program, cooking lessons, tennis courts, water-sports center, yoga, climbing tower, and meditation pond. All rooms have ocean or garden views, private balcony with hammock, minibar, coffeemaker, and bathrobes. There are even liquor dispensers, so you don't have to go to the bar to mix yourself a drink. The hotel provides complimentary transportation to the town square in Playa del Carmen and to Cancún once each day. Guests at any Palace Resort have access to the facilities, restaurants, and bars of all of the others. Rates:

$295–475 for two, based on double occupancy, all-inclusive.

Casa del Agua

984-873-5184
www.casadelagua.com
Highway 307, km 268

On a beach south of the marina and 1 mile from the main plaza in Puerto Aventuras, the very upscale Casa del Agua, formerly a private residence, has four rooms for rent, making it a good option for guests seeking simplicity, luxury, romance, and privacy. The house is contemporary Mexican, with handcrafted furniture, colorful Mexican textiles, and original artwork throughout. Rooms feature private garden bathrooms, minibars, and cold air-conditioning, and the rate includes a full breakfast served in a common dining room or in the privacy of your room. The El Arroyo room has a round bed, a large sunken bathtub, a double shower, and a stream of water that flows around the bed, cascades onto the floor, and then goes into the bathroom and behind the tub. The home is right on a perfect beach in a residential area with very little beach traffic. Rates: average $275 a night for two, including breakfast. Highly recommended.

Catalonia Riviera Maya

984-875-1020
www.cataloniarivieramaya.com
Avenue Xcacel, Lot 1 (off Highway 307, near km 271, just north of Puerto Aventuras)

An upscale and family-friendly all-inclusive, the 324-room Catalonia gives guests an authentic taste of the Mexican Caribbean while still providing the luxuries of a high-end resort. Hosting honeymooners, families, couples, and others in the mood for an active vacation, the hotel's location is great, with a calm-water beachfront surrounded by jungle. The property features several pools, a beach bar, a dance club, a kids' club, a tennis court, and a daily activity program that helps guests socialize and have fun all day long. There are also free scuba clinics, bicycles, and a gym. The hotel entry gate is located off the highway, separate from the marina entrance. Rates: average $195 per person per night.

Omni Puerto Aventuras

984-873-5101 or 1-800-THE-OMNI (U.S.)
www.omnihotels.com
Highway 307, km 269; behind the village center and on the beach

With only 30 rooms, the Omni offers personal service and boutique hotel–style comfort, along with the amenities and high standards normally associated with the Omni chain. Each room has a coffeemaker as well as a private balcony or patio with a Jacuzzi. Each morning the staff delivers coffee, juice, and Mexican pastries to a "magic box" built into the room. Since there's access from outside the room, you don't even have to get up to receive it. Just open your side of the box, and it's there waiting for you. The hotel features two restaurants, two bars, car rental, and a souvenir shop. Rates: $160 without meals or $360 all-inclusive, for two.

Sunscape Puerto Aventuras

984-875-3000
www.sunscaperesorts.com
Highway 307, km 269

With 294 rooms, the Sunscape resort is a medium-size all-inclusive on a pristine beach in the heart of Puerto Aventuras, within walking distance of the marina, museum, restaurants, and other attractions. Rooms have air-conditioning, satellite TV, and private balconies, most with a view of the marina or ocean. There are two pools, on-site restaurants, a bar, and nightly live entertainment. Rates: start at $225 for two guests, based on double occupancy. Higher rates for oceanfront, suites, or other room upgrades.

DINING

Most restaurants in Puerto Aventuras are located around the central marina plaza, overlooking the Dolphin Discovery waterway, and most have small interior dining rooms and a patio with shaded tables. They are all in close proximity, so it's easy to walk from one to the next, checking to see what looks good. Prices are a bit higher than in other areas of the region due to the exclusive nature of the resort and the lower volume of visitors.

Dos Chiles
At the Puerto Aventuras marina

This casual outdoor eatery offers a view of the dolphin shows, shops, and entertainment plaza. The menu offers good Mexican food, shrimp, fajitas, and tacos. Check the chalkboard for drink specials and featured menu items. Moderate.

Jones' Sports Bar
At the Puerto Aventuras marina

This café has pleasant alfresco dining at umbrellaed tables bordering the marina, in front of the Dolphin Discovery area. You can watch the dolphins jump and play while dining on nachos, tacos, burgers, steaks, and even grilled shrimp. Moderate.

La Caribena
At the Puerto Aventuras marina

This sidewalk café serves Caribbean and Mexican food. It has a view of the tree-lined marina and the many surrounding shops and attractions. The dining area is alfresco and overlooks the Dolphin Discovery area of the marina. Moderate.

The Pub
At the Puerto Aventuras marina

A popular spot all day long, the Pub is surrounded by shade trees and overlooks the marina, where diners can watch the dolphins cavort and play. The menu offers popularly priced breakfast, pizzas, fresh fish, tacos, enchiladas, and shepherd's pie. Inexpensive.

Tiramisu
At the Puerto Aventuras marina

Open for lunch and dinner, Tiramisu, as its name suggests, specializes in Italian food. Featured menu items include beef lasagna, pizzas, a variety of pastas, and a good selection of ice cream and desserts. Expensive.

ATTRACTIONS AND ACTIVITIES

CEDAM Shipwreck Museum
At the Puerto Aventuras marina

This museum, operated by the Club de Exploraciones y Deportes Acuáticos de México (Water Sports & Exploration Club), which is responsible for locating and protecting the region's wrecks, is free to the public (donations accepted) and displays a variety of artifacts recovered from shipwrecks in Mexico and around the world. It was founded in 1959 by Pablo Bush Romero, who is also the founder of Akumal. There are several rooms, and it's surprisingly easy to get disoriented given its relatively small size. Displays show how wrecks are excavated and how the materials are recovered and restored. There's also an interesting explanation of how the main cenote at Chichén Itzá was partially drained in a search for relics.

Dive Aventuras
984-873-5031
www.diveaventuras.com
In the Omni Puerto Aventuras (see *Lodging*)

This full-service dive shop offers all levels of instruction in multiple languages, including a 45-minute tune-up course for certified divers who have not been in the water for a while. It also offers complimentary lockers, equipment rental, camera rental, and gear sales. Dive boats depart for one- and two-tank dives at nearby reefs at 9 AM, 11 AM, 1 PM, and 2:30 PM, and the shop's shuttle can pick you up at any hotel in the region. There are also twice-daily dives at local freshwater cenotes. For nondivers there are one-and-a-half- and two-and-a-half-hour snorkeling tours, including sodas and a guide. One-tank ocean dives cost $38; two-tank trips are $74. Night dives are $65 and include a flashlight. Cenote dives are $65 for one tank and $110 for two.

Dolphin Discovery
At the Puerto Aventuras marina

You can interact with the dolphins at Dolphin Discovery, and there are several different packages, starting every hour. About half of the time is spent in orientation, and the remainder is with the dolphins. In the least expensive package, the Dolphin Encounter ($64), you touch the dolphins, and in the Dolphin Swim ($99) you get in the water with them. For $125 you can play a little more and even be propelled through the water by two dolphins in a maneuver called the foot-push.

Riviera Maya Parasail Adventures
984-873-5683
www.rivieramayaparasail.com
At the Puerto Aventuras marina

This well-respected outfit offers a variety of activities for vacationers seeking a bit of adventure, including "dry parasailing," in which tandem and solo riders take off from the back of a boat and soar high above the water, while taking in the view of the marina and surrounding beaches along the Puerto Aventuras bay and beachfront. The shop offers Sea Trek diving, which allows swimmers to don a helmet and breathe normally while sitting on the ocean bottom. It also offers Snuba, which is a type of forced-air snorkeling where participants swim freely underwater and breathe from a snorkel-like tube that is supplied with air from the surface. No scuba certification is required for either activity. Parasailing costs $65 for a solo ride or $99 for tandem.

SHOPPING

Itzcoatl
At the Puerto Aventuras marina

This small crafts and jewelry boutique specializes in handmade crafts and amber jewelry.

Lapis
984-803-2077
www.lapis.com.tr
Highway 307, km 270

On the highway near Puerto Aventuras is the Lapis jewelry factory, which offers handmade rugs, leather goods, silver, diamonds, gold, and precious stones from Turkey, Italy, Spain, and the Czech Republic.

Xpu-Ha (Highway 307, km 264)

Several different access roads lead from Highway 307 to Xpu-Ha beach, making for fun exploration of the various areas. The picturesque beach is very low-key, with a wide bay, coconut palms, and a shallow reef, making it a good spot for snorkeling. To find the best spots, walk to the north near the Xpu-Ha Palace Resort (see *Lodging*), where the water is calm and the access is easier. The beach to the south is not as sandy, with some rocks, vegetation, and seaweed. There are a few small family-run restaurants serving fresh fish and cold drinks on the beach. The main one, called La Playa, has snorkeling equipment for rent ($15), WaveRunners, and several tables in the shade or right on the beach. For overnight stays there are several major resorts, from the Xpu-Ha Palace to the north to the Club Maeva Tulum (see *Lodging*) to the south. There are also a handful of cabañas and villas for rent, as well as a small RV park. On the west side of the highway, across from the Xpu-Ha turnoff, are a pair of small but swimmable cenotes.

LODGING

Al Cielo Hotel
984-840-9012
www.alcielohotel.com
Highway 307, km 264.5

More like a private guest house than a hotel, this property has four rooms (two on the ground floor, two above) with private bathrooms, nice showers, and balconies or terraces. They are built right on the beach, with easy access to the water. There is a small beach club and a gourmet restaurant specializing in fresh seafood and meat. An on-site spa offers Shiatsu, Reiki, reflexology, and face and skin treatments. Rates: $150–260, depending on the time of year.

Barcelo Maya/Barcelo Maya Caribe
987-875-1500
www.barcelo.com
Highway 307, km 265, Xpu-Ha Beach;
direct entrance from the highway

The Barcelo complex offers two different hotels, which share some common facilities. The whole area is full of tropical plants, coconut trees, and flowers. All rooms in both properties have a private terrace or balcony, ocean views, high-powered air-conditioning, and stocked minibar. Restaurant choices include a beachside buffet, a Mexican specialty restaurant, a seafood restaurant, and a traditional Spanish eatery. There is a spa with Turkish bath, a sauna, a Jacuzzi, tennis courts, a gym, aerobics classes, several pools, and a daily activities program. Rates: average around $350 for two, all-inclusive.

Club Maeva Tulum

984-871-3000
www.clubmaeva.com
Highway 307, km 264, Xpu-Ha Beach

Surrounded by tropical gardens, this somewhat misnamed (it's more than 20 miles
from the ruins), 300-room, Euro-style, all-
inclusive resort was built as the Robinson
Club and has since changed. It has a large
central pool, fitness room, water-sports
center (snorkeling, kayaking), day spa,
shopping plaza, nightly entertainment,
dance club, two restaurants, three bars, and
enough activities to keep kids and adults
busy all day. There's also a rental car desk,
activities center, and tour desk so guests
who want to leave the resort and see the
local area have lots of choices, also. The
rooms have air-conditioning, ceiling fans,
stocked minibar, and private balcony.
Rates: around $200, for two people.

Copacabana Beach Resort

984-875-1800
www.hotelcopacabana.com
Highway 307, km 264, Xpu-Ha Beach;
direct entrance from the highway

With 288 rooms and suites, the Copacabana
is a medium-size beachfront hotel set amid
jungle foliage, tropical plants, swimming
pools, and other water features. The rooms
are laid out nicely, with plenty of open space
between the buildings, giving the resort an
exclusive feel throughout. Rooms have contemporary Mexican decor, premium bedding, and private terrace. There are also four
restaurants and four bars, including a *palapa*
bar right on the beach. An on-site tour office
and car rental desk help guests get out and
explore the region. Rates: $100–$250 per
person, depending on the time of year.

Hotel Esencia

1-877-528-3490 (U.S.)
www.hotelesencia.com
Highway 307, km 264, Xpu-Ha Beach

A unique resort built on 50 secluded acres
along the beach, Esencia is more like an
opulent private residence than a hotel. The
inn, once the home of an Italian duchess,
has 29 luxurious rooms and over-the-top
European decor. The property has large
breezy terraces, an idyllic beachfront, high
ceilings, an organic spa, a fitness center,
and an on-site cenote. The Sal y Fuego
restaurant specializes in seafood and is run
by a chef from the Four Seasons, and many
of its signature dishes use organic ingredients native to the area. The rooms have
premium bedding, liquor (which includes
full-size bottles, rather than the small sizes
typically offered in minibars), and iPods
for guest use. Rates: start at $325, double
occupancy, and go up fast.

Xpu-Ha Palace Resort

984-875-1010
www.palace-resorts.com
Highway 307, km 265

With 464 rooms, this large-scale, family-
friendly, all-inclusive resort was built from
the ruins of the defunct Xpu-Ha Ecopark. It
is located on a pristine and relatively
deserted beach, great for swimming and
playing in the shallows. Accommodations
are bungalow-like villas with *palapa* roofs,
jetted tubs, coffeemakers, stocked minibars, and private balconies with hammocks
and views. There are multiple restaurants
(Italian, Asian, seafood) and bars (lobby,
swim-up, beach), tropical gardens, two
swimming pools, workout room, and water-
sports center with snorkeling, kayaking,
and other activities. Parents can drop their
children off at the kids' club, where they
will enjoy activities, meals, and supervision
during the day. Scuba diving and area tours
are available for an additional fee. Rates:
start at $355, double occupancy.

DINING

Café del Mar
984-873-2194
Highway 307, km 264; near the Copacabana Beach Resort (see *Lodging*), on Xpu-Ha Beach

Great grilled fish and seafood await visitors at this no-frills beachside haven. Eat at one of the plastic tables under the shaded *palapa* or get your food to go and have an impromptu beach-towel picnic. This is a good place to park if you have your own car and want to visit the beach for a while. Inexpensive.

Restaurante Al Cielo
984-840-9012
www.alcielohotel.com
Highway 307, km 264.5; between the Xpu-Ha Palace and the Copacabana Beach Resort (see *Lodging*)

On the grounds of the Al Cielo hotel (see *Lodging*), this beachfront restaurant has a *palapa* roof and several tables right next to the sand. The internationally trained chef prepares shrimp, seafood paella, Angus beef, duck, quail, and lamb. The signature dish is a whole fish coated with salt and roasted. It takes 30 minutes to prepare and costs $25. Desserts include crème brûlée, chocolate mousse, and ice cream. No credit cards. Expensive.

Kantenah

A small sign on Highway 307 at km 262 points the way to Kantenah beach, which is a couple miles down a washboard road. There are many coconut trees and a quiet bay with a shallow reef for snorkeling. Near the beach, there is a large handicrafts market with much better prices than in Cancún or even Playa del Carmen, and there's another one on the highway, at km 259.5, with a large assortment of pots, rugs, and blankets.

LODGING

El Dorado Seaside Suites
984-875-1910
www.karismahotels.com
Highway 307, km 262

This adults-only, 133-room, all-inclusive resort is a popular destination for honeymooners, couples, and even families who want to experience the less populated areas of the Riviera Maya but don't want to do without the service, comfort, and convenience of a first-class resort hotel. The rooms are spread out along the ocean, which gives each room easy access to the beach. The buildings are all low-rise, lending a more relaxed, less urban feeling to the development. All rooms have private balconies with hammocks. Guests congregate on the hotel's wide white beach, which has calm water and a rock-free area for swimming and snorkeling. There are three restaurants, serving Asian, Mexican, and seafood specialties, and no buffets. There is a bar at the beach, one by the pool, and other one by the main restaurant, which is the main place to be at night, with live music, souvenir kiosks, and a bustling bar with seat swings. Guests of the El Dorado can pay a day-use fee to visit the clothing-optional Hidden Beach hotel next door. Rates: start at $280 for two people; include all food, drinks, activities program, and nonmotorized water sports.

Grand Palladium Colonial Resort & Spa
984-877-2100
www.fiesta-hotels.com
Highway 307, km 260

Sister property to the adjacent Grand Palladium Kantenah, this massive 836-room resort paradise was built in a Spanish colonial design by the architects behind the Iberostar and Paradisus chains. Though it is large and sprawling, special care has been taken to preserve the natural surroundings and allow guests to wander and explore without feeling crowded. There are four outdoor pools, including one meandering giant that seems more like a lagoon. Though the hotel welcomes families, there are designated areas for kids, allowing them to be themselves without disturbing the couples and honeymooners. There are seven restaurants, including Mexican, Asian, Mediterranean, and steak specialty à la carte restaurants, and the other three are buffets serving continental, regional, and Creole fare. There are 11 bars, including a *palapa* beach bar, swim-up pool bar, and dance club. There are also four tennis courts and a basketball court, water-sports center, scuba/snorkeling center, health club, and Turkish spa, which specializes in Mediterranean and local body treatments. The resort shares a huge stretch of beach with its sister property, with plenty of room for everyone.

The rate includes all meals, snacks, and nonalcoholic drinks (alcoholic drinks, including premium liquors, are included from 6 PM to midnight), as well as a workout room, a Jacuzzi, a sauna, and steam baths, plus nonmotorized water sports. Rates: $175–210, double occupancy.

Grand Palladium Kantenah Resort & Spa
984-877-2100
www.fiesta-hotels.com
Highway 307, km 260

With 414 rooms, the Grand Palladium Kantenah is about half the size of its sister property, located just next door. The all-inclusive, family-friendly resort features Mayan architecture, which blends harmoniously into the natural surroundings. In fact, there is a staff biologist who monitors the hotel's impact on the environment and makes recommendations on ways to preserve the native flora and fauna. As a result, there are many trees, tropical gardens, and native animals on the property. There is a ½-mile stretch of open beach, perfect for jogging, sunbathing, and sun worshipping. The rate includes all meals, snacks, and nonalcoholic drinks (alcoholic drinks, including premium liquors, are included from 6 PM to midnight), as well as a workout room, a Jacuzzi, a sauna, and steam baths, plus nonmotorized water sports. Rates: $175–210, double occupancy.

Hidden Beach Resort
984-875-7000
www.hiddenbeachresort.com
Highway 307, km 262

A 42-room, all-inclusive, clothing-optional resort, Hidden Beach is next door to the El Dorado Seaside Suites , is separated from it by a high stucco wall. Guests enter through a private lobby, where a security guard is on hand to ensure that no outsiders enter. The upscale resort is on the beach, with a pool, hot tub, and beach cabañas. All rooms are spacious suites, with ocean views, private balconies with hammocks, air-conditioning, CD/DVD players, and a stocked minibar (which includes full-size liquor bottles). The ground-floor suites offer swim-up access, allowing guests to enter the pool from their terrace and then swim to the restaurant or bar. Guests can enjoy nude dining, sunbathing, and ocean swimming (though it's mostly rocky). The hotel's gourmet restaurant

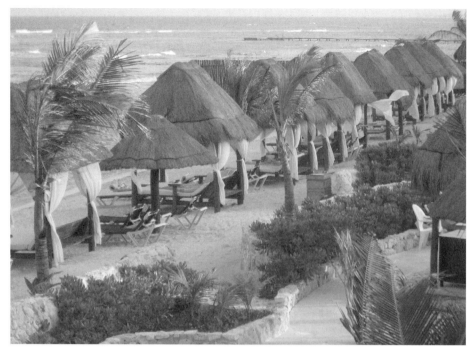

Hidden Beach Resort: clothing, optional; relaxation, mandatory

serves three meals per day, either in the shaded dining room or alfresco, next to the pool. There is a swim-up bar, where bartenders (clothed, for the most part) are more than happy to mix up special drinks for guests to try. An activities coordinator keeps you busy during the day, or you can sneak off on your own and camp out on a daybed at the beach and nobody will bother you, unless it's an attendant checking in to see if you need fresh towels, a bite to eat, or a cold drink. At night, guests head to the on-site mini-discotheque for nude salsa lessons, dance music, and socializing. This is not a swingers resort, and it does not allow any public displays of anything that's not allowed at a clothed hotel. Singles are welcome. Guests can use the facilities and take meals at the El Dorado Seaside Suites, next door, though they must be clothed to do so. Guests of the El Dorado can pay a day-use fee to visit the Hidden Beach. Rates: $195–300 per person, all-inclusive.

Akumal *(Highway 307, km 255)*

Five separate highway exits lead to this marina town, whose name translates into "Place of the Turtles." It is known as a family-friendly resort area with calm and shallow coves, dozens of nearby dive sites, superior sportfishing, pleasant pedestrian plazas, quality restaurants, lively bars, and a variety of accommodations options. The area consists of three separate bays: Half Moon, Akumal, and Aventuras. The late author John D. McDonald wrote several of the books in his famous Travis McGee series of boat bum/private detective novels while lounging on the beaches of Akumal.

The area is still a nesting ground for sea turtles, and they are now closely protected by the government and privately funded preservation organizations. Visitors can take guided tours to see the turtle nests and, if the timing is right, see the turtles lay their eggs or watch the hatchlings return to the water. An information center at the main entrance can book tours, provide directions, and reserve accommodations ranging from simple hotel rooms to large private villas. There are several grocery stores, an Internet café, a scuba diving center, a kiteboarding office, and handicrafts available near the main entrance. There is free parking if you're just visiting for the day. Turn into the lot on the right prior to entering the main gate. It's a safe area with lots of visibility, so you can feel fine leaving your car and walking through the gate and to the beach. The best beach within a short walking distance is just beyond the dive shop.

In 2005 Hurricanes Emily and Wilma passed through the region, uprooting hundreds of trees, tearing away roofs, and flooding the ground floor of many properties. Though it will take a while for all the vegetation to grow back, the town quickly rebuilt and is ready for an exciting future as one of the area's fastest-growing destinations.

LODGING

Akumal Beach Resort

983-875-7500
www.akumalbeachresort.com
Highway 307, km 255

Akumal aims to protect its beaches.

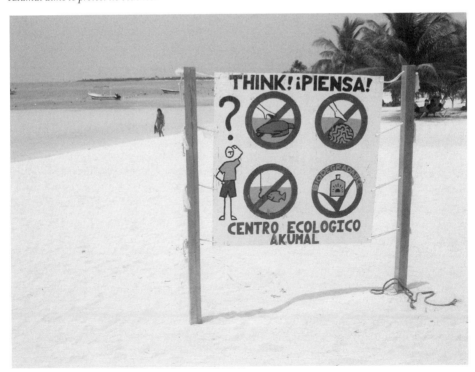

With 241 rooms and a broad white-sand beach, this all-inclusive resort is ideal for families and couples who are seeking casual and comfortable surroundings but can do without superfluous luxuries. The hotel operates as an all-inclusive, with all food, drinks, and nonmotorized water sports included in the rate. The beach is long, flat, and mostly private, and thanks to the off-shore reef, the water is calm, with tame waves. There are three eateries and a nice pool with a view of the beach. Like most all-inclusives, there is a theater where shows are performed nightly. Rates: $150–250 per room, double occupancy.

Gran Bahía Príncipe Akumal

983-875-5000
www.bahia-principe.com
Highway 307, km 254

This 1,440-room, all-inclusive hotel is the largest property in the region and has two separate sections: Tulum and Akumal. There is a private entrance off the highway, just before you reach the main Akumal entrance, if you're coming from Playa del Carmen. The resort is decorated with stonework, Talavera handicrafts, marble, native hardwoods, and thatched-roof *pala-pas.* Even with its immense size, it has a friendly feeling since the buildings are low-rise and grouped like homes in a small village. Many rooms have an ocean view, even though many of them are set back from the water in a junglelike setting. The resort's nine restaurants serve international, Italian, seafood, Mediterranean, Mexican, and Caribbean cuisine. There are also several bars, including a lounge bar, beach bar, and swim-up bar. The rate includes all food and drinks, shows, and a wide range of activities, including kayaking, sailing, windsurfing, biking, tennis, basketball, volleyball, aerobics, and even horseback riding. In addition, there is an on-site European-style spa, and the resort's tour desk can plan scuba diving, fishing, and other excursions. Rates: $85–200 per person.

Oasis Akumal

984-875-7300 or 1-800-521-5200 (U.S.)
www.oasishotels.com
Highway 307, km 254

This 180-room, all-inclusive resort is one of Akumal's longtime favorites, with many repeat guests. There is a private entrance located just south of the main Akumal entry gate. The accommodations have contemporary Mexican-style decor, and the rate includes all meals, snacks, drinks, nightly shows, activities, and sports. (Things like scuba diving and spa services are extra, of course.) The powdery-sand beach is on a wide, shallow cove, with very calm water and little current, making it great for swimming and snorkeling, even for beginners. There are several restaurants, serving international, Mexican, and Italian cuisine, and several bars, including a beach bar and a swim-up pool bar. Rates: $130–235 per person. There are also several suites available.

DINING

La Buena Vida

On the beach of Half Moon Bay

The ultracasual beach bar downstairs has chair swings, a long happy hour, and good music, and an upstairs dining room affords a nice view of the beach and serves three meals a day. Inexpensive.

La Lunita Restaurant

At La Tortuga Condos, Half Moon Bay

The road that winds around the marina leads back to the main road along the beachfront. Follow that about a half mile to the south and you'll come to La Tortuga Condos. Open to the public, this casual restaurant serves breakfast and dinner next to the beach. At night, the staff set up a few candlelit tables right on the beach. The menu features international and Mexican dishes. Moderate.

Lol Ha
On the beach next to the Akumal Dive Shop (see *Diving, Fishing, and Boat Tours*)

Lol Ha has a *palapa* beach bar with snacks and a good happy hour, and the kitchen serves pizza and pastas, plus Mexican dishes and seafood. Alfresco tables offer dining right on the beach. Moderate.

Que Onda
North side of town, near Yalku Lagoon

A small and romantic restaurant surrounded by palm trees and tropical plants, Que Onda is cheerfully decorated and serves gourmet Italian food and fresh seafood for lunch and dinner.

Turtle Bay Café
984-875-9136
www.turtlebaycafe.com
Just inside the main entry gate to Akumal and near the back of a cluster of thatched-roof buildings on the left side of the road

Just inside the main entrance to the left, you'll find a cluster of restaurants and shops. The Turtle Bay Café is housed in a small, homey building with a large palapa out frontwhich has several ceiling fans and is often one of the cooler spots in town. It is frequented by local ex-pats and villa owners and is home to an annual Thanksgiving party. They serve breakfast and lunch daily and dinner Wednesday to Saturday. The menu features a variety of specialty cocktails and smoothies, sandwiches, fresh salads, fish tacos, and more than 20 breakfast options, ranging from American classics to Mayan delicacies. The owner is an animal lover and even sells doggie treats.

DIVING, FISHING, AND BOAT TOURS

Akumal Dive Shop
984-875-9032
www.akumal.com
On the right, just after entering the main gate at Akumal

The Akumal Dive Shop offers several diving and nondiving tours, including a one-tank boat dive ($45), a two-tank boat dive ($60), a night dive (one tank, boat; $55), and a cavern

Live Like a Celebrity for a Week
If hotels and condos aren't your thing and you want to experience the Riviera Maya with first-class luxury and privacy, consider renting a beach house for your visit. Akumal Villas (678-528-1775, www.akumal-villas.com) manages a collection of some of the finest private rental homes and villas in the area, with properties in Puerto Aventuras, Akumal, Jade Bay, South Akumal, Soliman Bay, and Tankah. These homes have one to six bedrooms and feature swimming pools, hammocks, full kitchens, purified water, safes, balconies, satellite TV, DVD players, and other amenities. Full-time maids, caretakers, and on-call chefs and massage therapists are also provided.

Need some wine or spirits to liven up your house party? Akumal Wines (984-875-9287, www.akumalwines.com) offers more than 100 wines and liquors from around the world for delivery in the Riviera Maya.

dive ($65). There's also gear rental ($15/day), open-water certification ($420), and a scuba resort course ($100), which includes instruction and a shallow open-water dive. Non-divers can enjoy kiteboarding ($50 for one hour of instruction); sportfishing ($100 for the whole boat; additional hours cost $45) for barracuda, dorado, mackerel, and sailfish, on a two-hour trip that includes all refreshments, equipment, and bait; the Robinson Crusoe Cruise ($65/person), which departs at 10 AM and returns to the beach at 3 PM and includes catamaran sailing, fishing, snorkeling, hiking, drinks, and a stop-off at Xaak, a minor Mayan ruin site that was once home to a primitive lighthouse; or the Sunset Cruise ($35/person), a two-hour sailing cruise along the beach that includes drinks. (Remember, though, the ocean is to the east, so don't expect to see the sun fall into the Caribbean. Instead, it sets over Akumal's thick jungle canopy.)

Chemuyil *(Highway 307, km 249)*

Not really a touristy town, the dusty beachfront village of Chemuyil hosts many of the service workers for nearby Akumal and other developments. It has a gated entry, and the guards are not necessarily welcoming of foreign adventure-seekers, but if you can't get enough of the Riviera Maya beaches and you won't be content until you see them all, you should be able to talk your way in and make your way to the beach for a look.

The beach itself is relatively clean, and the water is very calm and shallow since the reef comes all the way to the surface and acts as a breakwater to keep out the waves. There are a couple of private campsites and some basic hotels to accommodate the few backpackers, naturalists, and escape artists who find their way here, and there is also a handful of beachside restaurants and local bars.

LODGING

The Jungle Place
www.thejungleplace.com
East of Highway 307, km 248; just inland from Chemuyil

Known in the native Mayan language as *kuxi k'aax*, the Jungle Palace offers two bungalows set on a 20-acre nature preserve, home to dozens of spider monkeys and royal toucans. The units are surprisingly upscale, with stone walls, hardwood furnishings, air-conditioning, full kitchen, satellite TV, Internet access, and a nature-friendly but contemporary vibe. Guests can watch and sometimes even cavort with the monkeys, depending on the monkeys' mood. Rates: average $130 per night.

Xcacel *(Highway 307, km 247; between Chemuyil and Xel-Ha)*

A popular nesting ground for loggerhead and green turtles, Xcacel has very few services and no electricity. The area is a nature preserve with skunks, snakes, and other protected animals, plus a combination of beaches, cenotes, mangroves, and jungle terrain. The turtles are most common in the warmer part of the year, from May to October. If visiting during this time, it is very important to avoid the nests and not bother any of the turtles. A cenote large enough to swim in is on the southern end of the beach (walk to the right, as you're facing the ocean). A small path leads from the beach to the cenote; look for a small wooden sign. To the north, the reef comes close to the beach, making it a good spot for snorkeling. A primitive camping facility offers a place to pitch a tent.

Punta Soliman (*Highway 307, km 240*)

A restful beach good for jogging, sunbathing, and shell collecting, Soliman is the kind of place where you feel compelled to arrange your Corona bottles and lime on the table and take a picture with the sundown in the background. In fact, this beach has become famous for being the site featured in a popular series of Corona beer commercials. The majority of the ads were taped in front of Oscar y Lalo's restaurant (see *Dining*), and the waiters are eager to point out the different areas used.

A small cenote is located behind Oscar y Lalo's. To find it, head away from the restaurant entrance, behind the kitchen, and it's slightly hidden in a grove of trees. It's a bit salty and murky, though it's still a nice spot to jump in and cool off. Just to the south is a much larger inlet from the ocean, which is full of fish even though the water isn't very clear. Alltournative Tours offers kayak trips to the area, but kayaks can also be rented on-site.

Oscar y Lalo's: a perfect spot for lunch

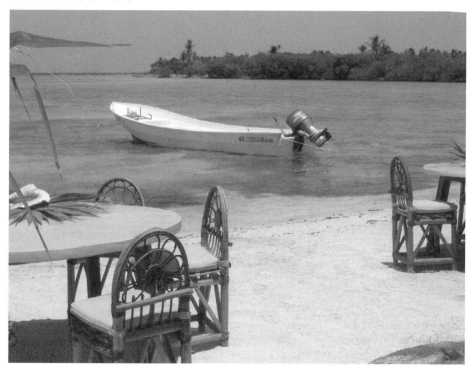

LODGING

Playa Naturel

984-871-2387
www.playanaturel.com
Highway 307, km 238, Playa Tankah (just
south of Soliman)

Turn right when the road from the highway
meets the road paralleling the beach, and
the inn is about a half mile down. It's a
simple four-room complex with nicely decorated rooms large enough for four. There
are bright furnishings and tropical decorations, giving it a cheery feeling. It's right on
the beach, though the sand is not raked like
at the big resorts, so it has seaweed and a
bit of trash, though it is still quite nice. As
its name loosely suggests, guests are free to
go au naturel anywhere on the property.
The central focus is a small swimming pool,
where guests socialize and relax the day
away. Rates: A one-bedroom costs $125 in
low season, up to $225 in high season;
lunch for two included. A two bedroom goes
for $150 in low season, $250 in high season;
lunch for four included.

DINING

Oscar y Lalo's

984-804-6973
Highway 307, km 240

Take the main road from Highway 307 to
the beach, and then turn left and wind
through the bumpy, sandy road. Oscar y
Lalo's is just about the only thing along that
stretch, so you can't miss it. The restaurant
is the unofficial home base for Alltournative Tours, which always seems to have its
tents up and its kayaks at the ready. There
are a dozen tables in a shaded *palapa* and a
dozen or so more stretched out along the
beach. The best thing on the menu is the
fried whole fish, large enough for two, and
there's also great ceviche and fish fillets.
Though this was the site of the filming of a
popular series of Corona beer commercials,
the restaurant has since stopped carrying
Corona, so order a Sol instead. Kayaks are
available for $8 an hour. Moderate.

Tankah *(Highway 307, km 237; between Xel-Ha and Tulum)*

Tankah is a small bay that was once an important ceremonial site for the ancient Mayans,
and there are minor ruins in the area, though they are still being explored and are not
open to the public. The main road parallels the beach and is home to several guest houses
and inns, and one of the largest is Casa Cenote, which is between the beach and a large
freshwater lagoon called Manatee Cenote, rumored to have a manatee living in it. The
cenote has a channel that leads underground, below the road and the hotel, and ends 100
feet offshore from the beach. Only experienced cave divers should do the swim, however.
Visitors can also stay at the Blue Sky Resort (see *Lodging*), located on the beach just north
of Casa Cenote.

LODGING

Blue Sky Resort

984-801-4004
www.blueskymexico.com
Highway 307, km 237; on the beach, just
past the cenote in Tankah

Less of a resort and more of a small inn,
Blue Sky has six rooms, each with a minibar,
ocean view, and direct access to a nearly
private beach. There is a small pool in the
courtyard, right by the beach. The decor is
thoroughly contemporary, and the rooms
feel like modern condos inside. An on-site

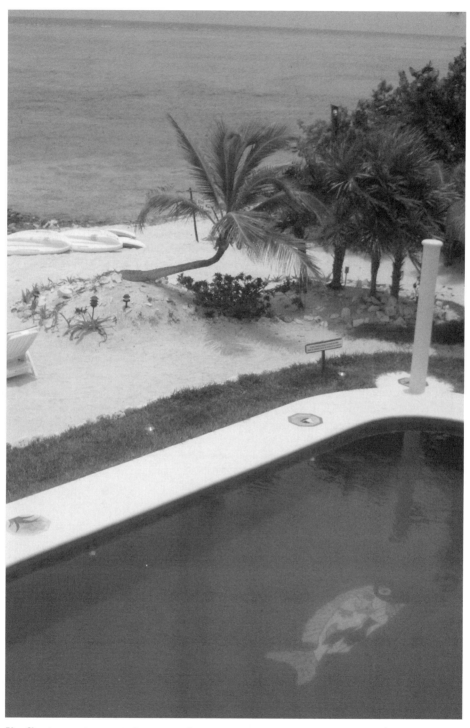

Blue Sky gives guests access to the ocean and a cenote.

restaurant serves a varied international menu and is open to the public. Across the street is Manatee Cenote, rumored to have a family of manatees living in it, though not even the locals have seen them in recent years. An underground tunnel connects the cenote to the ocean, which is a great dive for those with cave diving certification. (It should in no way be attempted by anyone else.) Rates: $75–$250, depending on room choice and time of year.

Casa Cenote
998-874-5170

This collection of charming casitas sits on the beach between the calm waters of Tankah Bay and a large freshwater lagoon called Manatee Cenote. The rooms are along the beach and have terra-cotta tile floors, local artwork, and ceiling fans; some also have air-conditioning. Nearby four-bedroom villas offer ocean views, outdoor grills, air-conditioning, and chef service on request. They rent for $2300–$3300 per week depending on the time of year. The main hotel has a small restaurant with a *palapa* roof and grill and several plastic tables on the beach. Popular dishes include cheeseburgers, nachos, fajitas, grilled shrimp, fried fish, and fresh lobster. The bar sells beer to go for day trips or lounging on the beach. Rates: $150–$200, double occupancy; includes breakfast, snorkeling gear for two, and kayak rental.

Freedom Paradise
984-871-3340 or 1-866-548-3995 (U.S.)
http://freedomparadise.com
Highway 307, km 237

Located on a pristine beach and accessible through a side entrance at the end of the main Tankah turnoff, or directly from a private access gate off Highway 307, just south of the Tankah road, this all-inclusive hotel is one of the world's only resorts catering to oversize guests. There are 112 rooms decorated in contemporary Mexican style, with cool tropical colors, wood furnishings, private balconies, satellite TV, ceiling fans, in-room safes, and tile floors. There are large armless chairs and beach loungers, safety steps into the pool, easy-access showers, and reinforced hammocks, and the staff has been specially trained to serve all guests with the dignity and respect that they deserve. There are four pools, several restaurants and bars, nightly live shows, and optional tours and activities available. Rates: about $250, double occupancy.

Tulum & the Mayan Coast

The dusty town of Tulum, which marks the official end of the Riviera Maya, lies along Highway 307 at km 230, about 80 miles south of the Cancún airport. The Mayan Riviera officially ends where Highway 307 intersects the road to Cobá, and just north of there is the turnoff to the Tulum ruins. Turn west at the crossroads, and the town of Cobá, a picturesque lagoon, and the Mayan ruins of the same name are about an hour away. For a traditional Mayan meal, stop at the Restaurante Campestre Las Cabañas, about 10 minutes before you get to town. Go south and you'll be in the Mayan Coast, also called the Sun Coast, where the road bypasses Laguna Bacalar as it skirts the Sian Ka'an biosphere and heads toward Kohunlich and on to Chetumal, and eventually to the beach town of Xcalak and the border with Belize.

Turn east at the crossroads, and where the road meets the beach there is a small hotel zone that is a backpacker's paradise and a real treasure for eco-conscious travelers who value privacy, serenity, and natural beauty over modern luxuries and pampering services.

Tulum has two bus stations along Tulum Avenue.

Many of the resorts do not have power-line electricity and rely on solar power or generators to keep the lights on and the beer cold. It is common for rooms not to have electric light and for hotel staff to light candles along the walkway, and even in the rooms. Guests at these hotels are encouraged to bring flashlights, mosquito repellent, and nature guides and to leave their mobile phones, laptop computers, and urban mindset behind.

To the left (north) are a few vacation homes and a couple of hotels, and to the right (south) is the notoriously bumpy road to Sian Ka'an. In the town of Tulum (called "Tulum pueblo," to differentiate it from the Tulum Mayan ruins) there is a gas station (Pemex, just before the crossroads), an ATM machine (at the HSBC bank), and several smallish hotels, restaurants, bars, and tour offices. At the Cobá turnoff there is a large San Francisco de Asis grocery store, a Hertz car rental office, and an El Point Internet and phone-calling office. The section of Highway 307 from the Tulum crossroads to the end of town is called Tulum Avenue. Along this 12-block stretch, travelers will find laundry services (Lava Easy, at Osiris Street), a huge gift shop and market (Plaza Fiesta Maya Mexican Outlet, at Jupiter Street), an Internet café (Internet Tulum, at Alfa Street), and a clinic with an English-speaking doctor (at Osiris Street).

Buses depart for Tulum from Playa del Carmen from the bus station near the town square every hour and cost $2. A *colectivo* shuttle van departs Playa from Second Street between 15th and 20th Avenues and will drop passengers off anywhere along the way between Playa and Tulum for $2, even if the drop-off is off the main road. The van fits eight people and departs as soon as it is full, from 7 AM—8 PM.

There are two bus stations on Tulum Avenue, across the street from each other on the

Tulum Avenue is lined with shops and restaurants.

southern edge of town, between Alfa and Jupiter Streets. Buses depart hourly for Playa del Carmen ($2, 1 hour), Cancún ($4.50, 2 hours), Mérida, Chetumal, Bacalar, and other towns in the region. From the Tulum bus station, taxi fare to the ruins or to the hotel zone is about $3–5.

Taxi Fares from Downtown Tulum

Tulum ruins: $3

Azulik, Copal, Zamas, Zahra: $3.50

Ana y Jose: $6

Tita Tulum: $7.50

Akumal: $16

Kantenah: $18

Cobá: $21

Playa del Carmen: $30

Puerto Morelos: $47

Cancún downtown: $62

Cancún hotel zone: $67

LODGING

Ana y José Charming Hotel & Spa

998-887-5470

www.anayjose.com

On the Tulum beachfront, 5 miles south of Tulum pueblo on the Punta Allen road

This 14-room inn, only 10 minutes from the town of Tulum, offers clean, comfortable, and well-designed rooms with ceiling fans, hot water, towels, and linens, as well as garden, pool, or oceanfront views—but no telephones or TVs. It has been open since 1985; its owners wanted to create a place that had homey comforts but that was still close to nature. There is a pool by the ocean and a beachfront restaurant known for its fresh seafood and lobster. The tour desk can arrange scuba, snorkeling, and fishing trips, and there are great beaches and swimmer-friendly cenotes within walking distance. The electricity stays on 24 hours. Rates: around $100–150, depending on the room choice.

The road from Tulum village hits the beach and runs north and south.

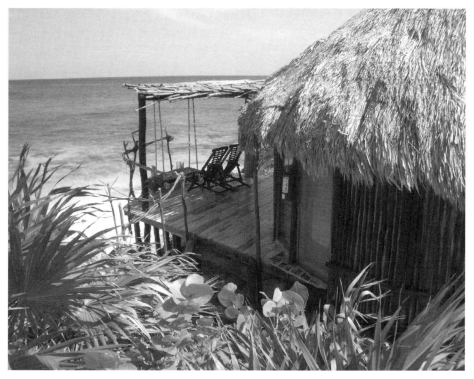

A beachfront cabaña at Azulik

Azulik
551-084-2820 or 1-877-532-6737 (U.S.)
www.azulik.com
On the Tulum beachfront, ½ mile south of
Tulum pueblo on the Punta Allen road

An adults-only, clothing-optional resort
with 15 rooms, Azulik features beachside
huts that are made from local hardwoods
and have waterfront decks ideal for sunning
and catching the ocean breezes. Each villa
has a private bathroom with hot water and a
wooden bathtub, but don't expect much
privacy since it's in the middle of the room.
There is no electricity in the rooms, but
candles and matches are provided. The
beach right behind the hotel is rocky and
has many sea fans, which are washed in
with the tide, and there are sandy access
points good for swimming just a short walk
away. The reef is only a couple hundred
yards from shore, and there is good snorkeling and kayaking in front of the resort
when the waves aren't too rough. The tour
desk also plans jungle hikes, ruins visits,
and cenote trips. Spa services at the adjacent Maya Spa include aromatherapy, massage, body scrubs, and Reiki. Though there
is no restaurant, guests can eat at the
neighboring hotels and can even order
room service, which is prepared at the villa.
Just raise the red flag on your deck to sum-
mon a waiter. Rates: range from $190 in a
Sea Villa in low season to $260 for the
Honeymoon or Romance Villa in high
season.

Cabañas Copal
551-084-2820 or 1-877-532-6737 (U.S.)
www.cabanascopal.com
On the Tulum beachfront, ½ mile south of
Tulum on the Punta Allen road

This 47-room, clothing-optional hotel is eco-conscious and rustic, yet romantic with candlelight. There is no electricity in the rooms, though the lobby and restaurant do have power. A beach bar serves cold drinks at the water's edge and has hammocks for guests to relax in while enjoying the day. Rooms are simple, with thatched roofs and heated water, but all water must be trucked in or pumped from an on-site well, so guests are encouraged to use it sparingly. The rooms are on a bluff above the beach (just like Tulum is) and are built to blend with the natural surroundings. The staff advises that geckos, hermit crabs, iguanas, and even nonpoisonous snakes are sometimes seen on the property, but that they are treated like guests and should not be feared. Guests are encouraged to embrace nature and to appreciate all of it, rather than work to shut it out, like in most hotels. The hotel is just steps from the ocean, and all rooms have direct beach access. Room classes include simple bungalows with shared bathrooms ($35), garden-view rooms with private bath ($75), ocean-view rooms with private bath ($95), and even a small casita ($210).

Cabañas Papaya Playa

www.papayaplaya.com
On the Tulum beachfront, just south of the turnoff to Tulum pueblo

This ultracasual hotel has 45 rooms, a restaurant, bar, and more than a third of a mile of pristine beachfront. Rooms range from sand-floor huts like the Mayans used to live in and cabañas with cement floors to villas with sealed walls, private bathrooms, and a touch of elegance. Electricity runs from sunset until 11:30 PM, with power in the rooms, restaurant, and bar. An on-site tourist information center offers free maps, a book exchange, and a tour office. Popular trips include a snorkeling tour with reef and cenote visits ($35), a two-cenote snor-

keling trip ($40), scuba diving in Akumal ($50 for one tank, $80 for two), and a cenote dive ($65 for one tank, $105 for two). Rates: rooms with sand floors and shared bathrooms cost $30, rooms with concrete floors and shared bathrooms cost $30 (extra beds are $10), and one-bedroom villas cost $100 per night and have private bathrooms.

Dreams Tulum Resort & Spa

984-871-3333
www.dreamsresorts.com
Highway 307, km 234

This all-inclusive resort is just five minutes north of the village of Tulum, and you can even see the cliffside Mayan ruins of the same name from the hotel beach. It features 238 rooms with air-conditioning, ceiling fans, 27-inch TVs, stocked mini-bars, CD players, coffeemakers, and private balconies or terraces with hammocks. There are four specialty restaurants (Mexican, Italian, Asian/sushi, and continental), plus a casual buffet. There are also five bars, including a pool bar and a beach bar. Included in the rate are the beachfront pool, freshwater lagoon, movie theater, wedding chapel, and fitness center. There's also an on-site Internet café, as well as a European day spa (complete with *temazcal*), golf, scuba diving, and tours (additional fees apply). Kids can spend the day at the Explorer Kids' Club and enjoy sports, swimming, and meals. Rates: $150 per person, based on double occupancy. Rates vary through the year.

Hotel Latino

984-871-2674
www.hotel-latino.com
In Tulum pueblo, Andromeda Street at Colonia Centro

Located 1 block off the main strip in Tulum pueblo, this small and stylish hotel has a facade that is vaguely reminiscent of Hotel

Deseo hotel in Playa del Carmen (see chapter 2). There is a small pool, and rates include free wireless Internet access and the use of a bicycle. Rates: $18–85, depending on whether you want air-conditioning and a larger room with more amenities.

La Vita è Bella

www.lavitaebella-tulum.com
On the Tulum beachfront, 1½ miles north of the turnoff to Tulum pueblo

La Vita è Bella is composed of 10 villas strung along the beachfront, each with a terrace with hammock and ocean view, a *palapa* roof, hardwood furnishings, showers with panoramic views, and original decorations. They are quite luxurious given the casual atmosphere of the Tulum beach area. The hotel offers in-room massage service, and there is an on-site restaurant serving Italian and Mexican food, plus wood-oven pizza, smoothies, and fruit juice. The staff can even set up a private table on the beach for a romantic candlelight dinner. There is also a beach club that offers lounge chairs, drink service, and snorkel gear rental. Rates: $80–150; include breakfast.

Los Lirios

998-850-6486
www.loslirioshotel.com
On the Tulum beachfront, 5¼ miles down the road from Tulum pueblo to Punta Allen

If you want to experience the Tulum beach hotel zone but you don't want to give up your air-conditioning, spa, and clean showers, Los Lirios is a good bet. The hotel's 32 rooms are housed in villa-style buildings built back from the sea. They have air-conditioning, private terraces with hammocks, canopy beds, bright tropical colors, private bathrooms, and phones. There is an on-site restaurant serving Mexican, vegetarian, seafood, and international dishes; a massage and yoga center; a tour desk; and laundry service. Rates:

$85–$150, depending on the time of year; include American breakfast.

Mezzanine

984-804-1452
www.mezzanine.com.mx
On the Tulum beachfront, 1 mile north of the crossroads from Tulum pueblo to the beach

Just a stone's throw from the Tulum ruins, this Thailand/Mediterranean-influenced beachfront hotel and lounge oozes with style. The owners are longtime friends and backpacking companions and traveled the world picking up ideas for how to build their dream resort. Whether you visit for an afternoon or a whole week, Mezzanine seems to seep into your soul, with its provocative decor and deep-rooted romantic appeal. It has four hotel rooms fronted by a smallish cenotelike plunge pool and a cozy bar and lounge. Hugging a cliff over the beach are a few lounge chairs, affording a great view of the ocean. The restaurant offers Thai food and fusion specialties, including shrimp satay, wraps, curries, Thai soup, pad thai noodles, and lobster, served at a handful of mod orange tables perched on the cliff or in the veranda dining room. At night, tiki torches and red and orange candles bathe the entire pool deck and dining room in a welcoming and sensual amber glow. The bar has developed into a trendy spot for traveling hipsters and locals alike. Every Friday, visiting DJs from Europe and around the world spin house- and chill-out music for crowds of up to 250 people. A hidden mezzanine level above the dining room houses the VIP area, with swanky lounge seating and a pool table. The rooms offer rich Caribbean colors, premium bedding, a loft with futon, in-room safes, ceiling fans, and great ocean views. Steps lead down from the pool deck to the one of the region's best powder-white beaches, which is practically devoid of

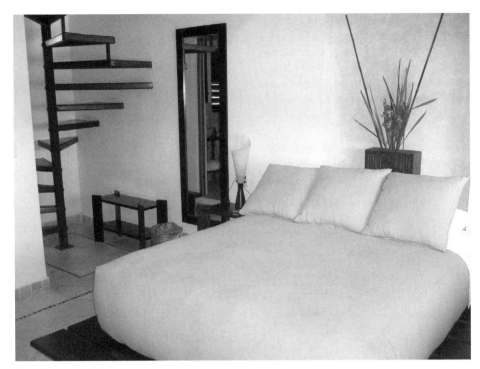

A swanky room at Mezzanine

people. A few minutes' jog to the north and you can see the ruins of Tulum looking like a fortress on the horizon. Snorkels, masks, and sea kayaks are available free for guest use and the reef is just a couple hundred meters offshore. Happy hour by the pool is 1 PM–4 PM daily. Rates: $150–225, depending on the season.

Tita Tulum
984-877-8513
www.titatulum.com
On the Tulum beachfront, 5 miles south of Tulum pueblo, on the road to Punta Allen

This small property has six cabins with *palapa* roofs, mosquito nets, solar power, and hot water, and each has a private patio with hammock overlooking the powdery white-sand beach. An on-site restaurant serves Mexican and Mayan dishes next to the beach. Rates: start at $40.

The Weary Traveler
Tulum pueblo, Tulum Avenue between Jupiter and Acuario Streets

This hostel and travel center is the center of low-budget info and activity for Tulum pueblo. There is a nice shaded courtyard and snack bar, a common refrigerator, and acceptable rooms with bunk beds. The hostel offers discounted tours, bike rental, snorkeling gear rental, and plenty of traveler camaraderie. It's also known to be a good place to party with other backpackers. Rates: $10 single, $18 double, including breakfast.

Zahra
984-806-4406 or 1-877-532-6737 (U.S.)
www.zahra.com.mx
On the Tulum beachfront, 1 mile south of Tulum pueblo on the Punta Allen road

The 22 rooms at Zahra have thatched roofs, but they are not completely rustic, with ceiling fans, electric lights, hot water, in-room spa services, and even room service and wireless Internet access. Some rooms face the gardens and others face the ocean, and there are beaches on two sides of the hotel and lots of palm trees. An on-site restaurant serves traditional Mayan and Mexican food and often has live music, and there is an on-site Internet café open when the power is on. Rates: range from $25 for a small cabin without ocean view or private bathroom in low season to $250 for a two-level family suite with room for five, private bathrooms, and an ocean view. Other room classes are available. A small convenience store is right across the street. Highly recommended.

Zamas Beach Cabañas

415-387-9806 (U.S.)

www.zamas.com

Three miles south of Tulum pueblo on the Punta Allen road

Zamas, which means "sunrise" in Mayan, was the original name for Tulum, which is only five minutes away. This beachfront inn has 15 *palapa* bungalows built in the traditional Mayan manner. Wind- and solar-generated power stays on until late at night. The complex has a few interesting touches, such as Mexican tile work, private shaded porches, and handmade hammocks. An open-air restaurant features Mayan-inspired dishes, Mexican specialties, wood-oven pizza, and fresh seafood, including lobster. The hotel sits on a small and quiet beach, ideal for beachcombing, swimming, and snorkeling. The hotel can organize dive trips, expeditions to the ruins, fishing, and bird-watching. Rates: average $115 a night.

DINING

Buenos Aires Grill

984-871-2708

Tulum Avenue at Calle Beta

This restaurant claims that it's the only steakhouse south of Puerto Aventuras. It serves Angus beef, grilled lobster, shrimp, fish, and vegetarian food. Open 1:30–11:30 daily. Moderate.

Il Giardino

984-806-3601

Satelite Avenue at Sagitario Street

Italian food served in a garden setting. The tables are surrounded by tropical plants and stone carvings. The menu features lasagna, pasta, and fresh fish. Open 1 PM–1 AM daily. Moderate.

La Palapa del Chino

984-804-3647

Tulum Avenue between Osiris and Beta Sur

This casual spot, which serves Chinese and Mexican food, is open 7 AM–11 PM daily. There are a few plastic tables with a view of the street. The menu offers a variety of rice dishes, chicken tacos, and other budget fare. Inexpensive.

Taqueria Gringa

Tulum Avenue between Jupiter and Acuario Streets; across from the Weary Traveler hostel

A typical local restaurant serving very inexpensive food for breakfast, lunch and dinner. The plastic tables are along the sidewalk and the menu offers tacos, chicken enchiladas, quesadillas, and other local fare.

Diving

Acuatic Tulum
984-100-7122
www.hotels tulum.com/acuatic_tulum. htm
At the beach-side Cabañas Don Armando hotel, ½-mile north of where the main Tulum crossroad intersects with the beach road; second location is on Highway 307 at the Tulum crossroads.

Tulum's first dive shop, in operation since 1993, offers snorkeling, ocean diving, and cenote diving trips each day. It also has gear and bike rental.

Spas

Maya Spa
551-084-2820
www.maya-spa.com
Next to Cabañas Copal in the Tulum beach hotel zone (see *Lodging*)

At this beachfront retreat with open-air massage huts and a candle-lit indoor spa, there are daily yoga classes, lucid dreaming courses, and a *temazcal*, a Mayan-style sweat lodge ($29 per person). The spa serves fresh fruit and tropical meals. Local shamans perform traditional Mayan treatments, and local healers use native plants and herbs to perform various healing ceremonies. Other services include body wraps, Reiki, aesthetic treatments, Mayan massage, and flotation chamber therapy. Highly recommended.

Boca Paila, Sian Ka'an & Punta Allen

Very few travelers will ever have the chance to visit a place as remote—and as starkly beautiful—as the Sian Ka'an biosphere reserve in their entire lives. Meaning "gift from the sky" or "the sky's beginning" (depending on which translation you believe), Sian Ka'an was officially designated a nature reserve in 1986. It spans more than 1.25 million acres, which is 10 percent of the land in the state of Quintana Roo, and it is an official UNESCO World Heritage site. Don't expect to find picnic tables, public bathrooms, concession stands, or beach bars—this is not a nature park like Xcaret or Xel-Ha. This land is remote and does not have any of the facilities or services that one sometimes associates with a "park." Once Sian Ka'an became a federal reserve, all development was frozen, and all activities are strictly regulated, which is designed to protect the wild diversity of flora, fauna, and geography encompassed in the reserve. There are more than three hundred species of birds (including herons, ibis, roseate spoonbills, and parrots), one hundred types of mammals (such as wild cats, monkeys, coatimundis, and deer), and such land features as barrier reefs, mangrove swamps, lagoons, marshes, and tropical forests. There are also more than two dozen Mayan relics, small native villages, and ruins of abandoned ranches, hotels, restaurants, and homes.

The goal of the reserve is to provide a place where nature can thrive on its own, without the negative impacts that come with the presence of humans and the development that always seems to follow. A portion of the biosphere is completely restricted, but much of it is open to exploration, as long as visitors follow the reserve's strict rules of low- or no-impact

What I Like about the Riviera Maya

Contributed by Ellen Hloben

Exquisite beaches, glorious sunsets, turquoise aqua-teal colors of the Caribbean Sea, exciting nightlife, enjoying an all-inclusive resort with all you can eat and drink, exploring Xcaret, diving in a coral reef, enjoying a relaxing massage on the beach under the soothing shade of a palm tree or a day at a soothing spa, exploring azure cenotes.

Drinking Dos Equis beer, taking the ferry to Cozumel, feeling a balmy breeze on my face, hanging out with friends at the lobby bar, swimming with dolphins, climbing to the top of the pyramid at Chichén Itzá, watching a folkloric performance, eating tacos *al pastor,* enjoying the sidewalk entertainers, visiting Mayan ruins.

Parasailing, visiting the Xaman-Ha Aviary, dancing all night in a resort disco and then going into Playa for more music, playing at a championship golf course in Playacar, exploring historic archaeological sites, enjoying a traditional strolling mariachi band, getting a green light at the airport, dining on spectacular international cuisine, visiting the Hekab Be Biblioteca (a charming one-room library/schoolhouse in Akumal) and meeting the students, dancing to soca music, buying from beach vendors with their brightly colored wares.

Strolling quaint Fifth Avenue in Playa del Carmen and stopping at every cantina; getting braids in your hair; eating guacamole; visiting Tres Rios; exploring jungle lagoons; getting a henna tattoo like a teenager; strolling through craft-filled open-air marketplaces, buying straw hats, silver jewelry, and serapes; being surrounded by bougainvillea; taking a side trip to the Ruinas El Rey; buying Cancún perfume at the airport; basking in an oversize hot tub; riding in a *colectivo;* exploring the Yucatán Peninsula; witnessing breathtaking sunrises; spending a day at the historic city of Tulum and standing on a cliff overlooking a beautiful beach; scuba diving; drinking frosty, cold, salt-rimmed margaritas; seeing Cozumel at night in the distance under the glow of a Mayan full moon.

Listening to Venga Boys tunes by the pool; white powdery sand; spending a day at beautiful Xel-Ha; snorkeling in sparkling, crystal-clear waters; dining in gourmet restaurants; taking a siesta in a thatched *palapa;* visiting Sian Ka'an; swinging in a hand-knotted hammock; driving south of Playa del Carmen and stopping at a new beach, cenote, or city; hearing the sweet swishing sound of swaying palm trees; exploring the ruins at Cobá; listening to salsa music; watching the WaveRunners dart by; visiting ecological reserves and natural aquariums; sipping a chilled Corona with lime; lolling in a Jacuzzi; taking a lobster cruise; making footprints in the sand; visiting Crococun Zoo.

Renting Jet Skis; catching a glimpse of a flamingo, peacock, or howler monkey on your resort grounds; shootin' tequila slammers; seeing lush red tropical hibiscus; peeking at iguanas sunning atop the ruins; smelling coconut and cocoa butter suntan-lotion scents wafting in the air; playing tequila volleyball; driving thunder boats; hearing a marimba band by the pool; eating warm tortillas; witnessing the sea turtle release program; and, my favorite thing of all: reexperiencing my pleasures by writing in my journal at the end of a glorious day in paradise.

ELLEN IS FROM ST. LOUIS, MISSOURI, AND IS A FREQUENT TRAVELER TO THE RIVIERA MAYA. HER ZEST FOR THE AREA IS TYPICAL OF TRAVELERS WHO ARE DEEPLY TOUCHED BY THEIR TRAVEL EXPERIENCES.

adventuring. A rocky and sometimes sandy road passes through the area, and vehicles may not depart from the path. There is no inland fishing or scuba diving, though snorkeling is allowed since it has less impact on the reefs. A handful of fishing lodges and rustic hotels operate in the reserve, though they must provide their own water and electricity since there are no utilities in the area.

There is a $2-per-person fee to enter the park, and all travelers must stop at the visitors center to check in. Jeeps and four-wheel-drive vehicles are recommended as the road is heavily rutted, rocky, and sometimes muddy. Taking a regular rental sedan on the road makes for slow going and may violate your renter's agreement, nullifying any sort of insurance you have purchased, so it's best to check in advance. There are plenty of picturesque and totally deserted beaches where you can stop for a bit of beachcombing, picture-taking, and stretching. Unfortunately, since the beach is not tended to like at the resorts, years of washed-up trash remains piled at the high-tide mark, making a silent yet very compelling case for the need for more awareness of garbage-dumping in the world's oceans.

At the southern end of the road, you'll reach the tiny village of Punta Allen. And no, some gringo named Allen doesn't own the town. The name comes from the Mayan word *allin*, which means "crocodile." The village is home to 600 inhabitants, said to originate from 90 original families. Most work as fishing guides in the area lodges or at the nearby lobster farm (which covers some 300,000 acres). There are a handful of lodges, a couple of restaurants, a bar, and a general store called Tienda Socorro, where travelers can purchase basic supplies.

With mangrove swamps, shallow lagoons, and a barrier reef that comes quite close to the beach, this region is a favorite for birdwatchers, anglers, and shell collectors. Crocodiles and manatees also make their home here, which adds to the excitement and your chance for a once-in-a-lifetime natural encounter. Jimmy Buffett fans will recognize this area as the setting for the singer's novel *A Salty Piece of Land*, which chronicles an American expatriate cowboy who sails with his horse to the fictitious island of Punta Margarita (sound familiar?) in Ascension Bay and becomes a fishing guide.

Speaking of fishing, the shallow flats, coves, and tiny coastal islands of Sian Ka'an, Punta Allen, and Ascension Bay offer some of the best fly- and light-tackle fishing in the world. Popular catches include barracuda, bonefish, and the coveted permit, which range from 2 to 20 pounds. Many of the lodges host fly-tying sessions for anglers who want to tie their own flies. If you're not familiar with fly-fishing techniques, local guides can teach you how to do it. If that's not your thing, you can fish in many of the same spots using light tackle. Most fish are caught by sightcasting, where the guide or the angler stands on the boat and searches the water for signs of fish, and then makes pinpoint casts to land the fish. At other times, anglers will wade into the waist-deep water and cast into the schools.

Getting There

Take Highway 307, the main highway along the Riviera Maya, south from Playa del Carmen to the town of Tulum, about 45 minutes away. At the main Cobá crossroads, one stoplight past the turnoff to the Tulum ruins, turn east and follow the paved road a couple of miles to the end, and then turn right, to the south, and parallel the beach. After passing the Tulum beach hotel zone (which includes Cabañas Copal, Azulik, Ana y José, etcetera), you'll cross a usually empty guard post marking the unofficial beginning of the Sian Ka'an biosphere reserve. Three miles later, you'll come to an arch across the road and the official, always-manned biosphere entrance. All vehicles must stop to be logged in and pay a $2-per-person fee to

The twin bridges of Boca Paila

enter. Once inside the park, follow the road along the beach for another 10 miles (about 45 minutes' worth of bumping up and down), and you will reach Boca Paila, marked by twin bridges (one wooden, one concrete, built in 2005) over the lagoon. Twenty miles into the trip, you'll come across a small unmarked Mayan temple partially hidden in the scrub brush next to the road, on the west side of the road. Several miles later, the road ends at the town of Punta Allen. Once you've left Tulum, the next gas station is in Punta Allen, which is 40 miles and about an hour and a half away (in good conditions), so be sure to gas up before you leave.

Colectivo shuttle service is available from Tulum to Punta Allen departing from a garage on Highway 307, two blocks north of the Weary Traveler. It leaves daily at 2 PM.

LODGING

If you thought Playa del Carmen was the antidote to Cancún's consumer-driven frivolity, this area quickly reminds you that even Playa's relative calm is wildly more developed and bustling than the region was in yesteryear. Around here, you won't find the margarita-fueled party scene, boutique bikini shops, or European spas of the resorts farther north. There are no ATM machines, gas stations, or money exchange booths, and no convenience stores, public bathrooms, or taxi stands. There's not even much running water or electric utilities. What you will find are miles of virgin beaches, awe-inspiring tropical landscapes, spectacular bird-watching, world-class flats fishing, and a timeless and relaxed atmosphere that helps to rejuvenate the soul and clear the mind.

Accommodations are eco-friendly "lodges," which means simple, no air-conditioning, no bathtubs, no swimming pools, and few luxuries. Travelers in these parts tend to be nature enthusiasts, backpacking adventurers, serious anglers, and others who are comfortable in tents, wooden cabañas, and other no-frills accommodations. For the hearty few that are up to the task, staying the night in the biosphere can reveal wondrous parts of the jungle that are rarely seen by others. The hotels in the area offer shuttle service from Cancún or the Riviera Maya, with advance notice required.

Ascension Bay Bonefish Club
984-877-8532 or 1-800-819-0750 (U.S.)
www.ascensionbay.com
On the edge of Ascension Bay, in Punta Allen

This private lodge hosts only six anglers per week, in a small house built right on the beach. The rooms are spacious and have ceiling fans, 24-hour electricity, and private bathrooms with hot water. Accommodations packages include meals, drinks, and fishing. A Friday–Friday package goes for $2,600 per person and includes transfers from Cancún, lodging, meals, and six days of fishing with a private boat and guide. Credit cards accepted on advance reservations.

Bonefish Bum Lodge
984-877-8532 or 1-888-584-1453 (U.S.)
www.bonefishbum.com
Northern edge of Ascension Bay

Clean rooms, Mayan-style meals, and world-class bonefishing make this one of the world's best places to spend a week on the water, watching for the telltale flash of a bonefish as it turns to take a fly. After a full day of fishing, guests are welcomed back to the lodge with appetizers and cold drinks. Sample rates: four nights with three days of

fishing is $1,200 each for two anglers sharing a room and boat; seven nights $2,400. Day-fishing trips are available for non-guests for $390 per boat, for up to three anglers. Alcohol, ground transportation, and equipment are extra. An ecotour package consisting of four nights' lodging and three days of tours (including snorkeling, boat trips, and Mayan ruins) goes for $875 per person, based on two participants, including room, meals, boat, and guide. Credit cards accepted on advance reservations.

Casa Cuzan
983-834-0358
www.flyfishmx.com
On the southern edge of Punta Allen

Casa Cuzan is a rustic hotel that offers 12 fan-cooled, thatch-roofed cabañas; a restaurant (think lobster, fish, Mexican/Mayan cuisine); and great access to the area's best fishing spots. All rooms have hot water, decent beds, 24-hour electricity, and patios with hammocks. They are a short walk to the beach, and the boats leave from right in front of the hotel. Rates: $40–80 per night, with all-inclusive fishing packages going for $1,999 per week. No credit cards.

Casa Sirena
984-877-8521
www.casasirena.com
Punta Allen

This simple inn offers cabaña-style rooms with hot water, thatched roofs, and walls that stop short of the ceiling to let in the breeze. It may not offer a lot in the way of luxury, but it's a friendly and relaxing spot to get away from the hustle. Rates: range from $30 for a simple hut and $40 for a small cottage to $50 for the main house. The inn also offers snorkeling trips for $40 and fly-fishing trips for $65, based on two people booking together. No credit cards.

Cesiak

984-871-2499
www.cesiak.org
Two miles north of the Boca Paila bridge on
the road from Tulum to Punta Allen

This eco-friendly lodge is located on a 15-acre ranch that once housed an upscale resort until it was abandoned in 1982. Cesiak opened in 2000 with a more eco-conscious approach. It has a learning center, tour office, and central kitchen for guest use. The rooms are housed in tents on wooden platforms and have terraces, hardwood furniture, and great views. Rates: range from $90 for a standard cabin to $105 for a deluxe waterfront cabin.

Let It Be Inn

984-877-8506
www.letitbeinn.com
Punta Allen

With a maximum of six anglers at a time, Let It Be is about as secluded and private as it gets. Hosts Rick and Rosie Montgomery run the tiny lodge, cook the meals, help plan the fishing trips, and take care of anything else that guests may need. The restaurant serves up delicious meals, and there is a beachfront bar and fly-tying station where guests can make their flies and sip cocktails. Standard rates include all meals and drinks, plus transportation to and from the Cancún airport. Rates: start at $1,495 for three nights' lodging for two and two days of fishing, based on double occupancy. No credit cards.

Pesca Maya

998-845-6501 or 1-800-894-5642 (U.S.)
www.pescamaya.com
Three miles north of Punta Allen

Just when you think you can't take the bumps of the road through Sian Ka'an anymore, you arrive at Pesca Maya. Due to its close proximity to Punta Allen, guests can go into town for supplies or a tiny taste of civilization if they need it. Most visitors don't see another car once they arrive, though, and that's part of the charm. The lodge is built on the land of the Chenchomac (Mayan

Pesca Maya has cabins right on the beach.

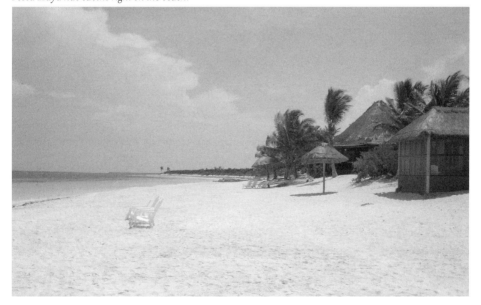

for "land of the foxes") ranch, which formerly operated as a coconut plantation. It has a large, well-built *palapa* restaurant and bar, which also serves as the library, fly-tying station, and social center. Guests get up at the crack of dawn, have breakfast at 7 AM, and leave by 8 for a full day of fishing. Each angler is assigned to a boat and a guide, with no more than two guests per boat. The boats return between 2 and 4 PM, and then it's off to the beach to relax or to the restaurant to recount the day and swap stories. Dinner is served family style each evening, and the bar stays open until 10 PM, though by that time most guests have retired to their rooms, exhausted from the day and excited for the next one. Nonanglers also enjoy Pesca Maya, since the beach is absolutely pristine and perfect for sun-bathing, beachcombing, and relaxing. It's also a great place to snorkel, with frequent sightings of barracuda and other large fish. There's an old rusted anchor, about 5 feet long, half buried in the sand. Jorge, the on-site manager, says it's from a 1950s-era Cuban shrimp boat. A day-fishing package for two anglers, which includes eight hours of guided fishing, tackle, water, sodas, beer, sandwiches, snacks, and round-trip trans-portation from hotels in the Riviera Maya, is $450. Pickup is at 6–6:30 AM, with a return at 7 PM. Half- and full-week fishing/lodging packages are also available.

Rancho Sol Caribe
Km 48 on the Punta Allen road, 5 miles north of Punta Allen

There are only four rooms available at this secluded and well-kept inn. Each has a private bathroom, hot-water shower, terrace with hammock, and 24-hour electricity. Given the simple nature of accommodations in this region, this inn's special touches give it a casually elegant feeling and a touch of romance not necessarily found at the average fishing lodge. Each evening, the staff lights dozens of candles around the property and the bartenders are always at the ready to mix drinks, give tips about the area, and make everyone feel at home. Rates: $135 per person, double occupancy; includes all meals and drinks (including alcohol). For $350 per day, the rate includes a full day of fishing (deep sea or flats). Room-only rates are available for just $95 per night per room.

ACTIVITIES & TOURS

Cesiak Centro Ecologico
984-871-2499
www.cesiak.org

Housed at the Cesiak eco-lodge camp in Boca Paila (see *Lodging*), this tour operator offers two primary trips. The all-day Sian Ka'an tour ($68 per person) includes a boat trip through the biosphere, a visit to Mayan ruins, a float down a freshwater river, a glimpse of sea turtles, bird-watching, snacks, and refreshments. The sunset bird-watching tour ($60 per person) includes a boat trip through the biosphere, with swimming, snorkeling, bird-watching, and a stop at a Mayan ruin. Each tour includes round-trip transportation from Playa del Carmen.

Friends of Sian Ka'an Tour
998-884-9583

This tour includes a bilingual guide, a driving tour through the reserve, a boat trip through the mangroves, and a visit to a freshwater spring. It departs daily at 9:30 AM from Ana y

José in Tulum's northern hotel zone (see *Lodging*) and returns at 3 PM. The tour costs $50, including drinks and snacks.

Sian Ka'an Ecotourismo
984-871-2363
siankaan_tours@hotmail.com
Tulum Avenue between Beta and Osiris Streets, Tulum pueblo

This tour company's main offering is a biosphere tour, which includes a tropical forest walk, Mayan ruin visit, boat tour through the wetlands, bird-watching, and cenote swimming. The trip includes entrance fees, equipment, transportation from Riviera Maya hotels, and a boxed lunch. The company also offer skayak tours, fishing trips, and other expeditions.

VEA Excursions
866-646-6202 (U.S.) or 984-875-5040
www.jeep-safari.com

If you have only one day to visit Sian Ka'an but want to fit in as much as possible, try the VEA Jeep Safari. It includes a Jeep ride to the biosphere entrance, a boat tour to see dolphins, swimming, snorkeling, beachside lobster paella lunch, bird-watching, beachcombing, and a chance to see crocodiles. The cost is $95 per person. The company also offers an all-terrain vehicle tour through the jungle roads of Tulum and the surrounding area. It includes a dip in a freshwater lagoon and a nature tour with tamed jungle animals. The trip lasts four hours and costs $62 per person sharing a bike or $77 for a solo rider.

THE MAYAN COAST—SOUTH OF THE RIVIERA MAYA

Laguna Bacalar
About two and a half hours south of Playa del Carmen and 90 miles from Felipe Carillo Puerto is Laguna Bacalar, a freshwater lake just east of Highway 307 that feeds into Chetumal Bay. With crystal-clear water and gleaming white sands, it is a rare jewel in the jungle. The lake has a dramatic setting and varying depths, which causes the colors to change from spot to spot—hence its nickname, the "Lake of Seven Colors." It is a prime spot for snorkeling, bird-watching, swimming, and photography.

LODGING

Hotel Laguna Bacalar
983-834-2206
www.bacalarmosaico.com
Twenty-five miles north of Chetumal, just off Highway 307

A full-service hotel with air-conditioning, suites, and incomparable views of the laguna, Hotel Laguna Bacalar is a great spot if you want to spend a couple of days exploring the area. There is a terrace restaurant overlooking the lagoon and a sundeck with direct access to the laguna itself. Rates: $80 per night.

Mahahual

When you arrive in Mahahual you'll immediately notice a laid-back atmosphere, but with a sense that things could be changing. More villas and small inns are being built all the time, and the town is developing a rustic yet upscale tone, similar to the early days of Playa del Carmen. There are a few sandy streets and several open-air restaurants, and the hotels and private homes are stretched out along the beach.

The shallow reefs of the Chinchorro Banks are known for being the healthiest in the area, with huge sea fans, sponges, anemones, sea cucumbers, arrow crabs, and seahorses. There are also hundreds of species of fish (including large barracuda), sea turtles, and even dolphins, which sometimes follow the dive boats and play in the wake.

In 2000 Mahahual completed construction of a cruise ship terminal, and each month there seem to be more arrivals, which is steadily changing the face of the town. The cruise dock is only 5 blocks from the town center, and the street is becoming lined with new restaurants, bars, and souvenir shops. When the boats are in town, the beach is full of day-trippers snorkeling, swimming, riding WaveRunners, and enjoying the day. The rest of the time the village is more mellow, with locals talking in the storefronts, tourists lingering in the beachside restaurants, and only a few people relaxing on the beach.

GETTING THERE

To get to Mahahual by car from anywhere along the Riviera Maya, take Highway 307 south toward Chetumal. Fill up with gas when you go through the town of Carillo Puerto, as there are not many stations in this area. Once you pass the village of Limones (about two and a half hours south of Playa), you will go about 2 more miles, and then you should see a sign for Mahahual and the Cafetal exit. Turn left and start heading east to the beach. From this point, Mahahual is still about an hour away. About halfway down this road, you'll arrive at a military checkpoint, so don't be alarmed if you see men in uniform carrying machine guns. They may search your car for drugs, but they are courteous and will not cause any problems—as long as you don't. The road is a fairly straight shot through the jungle, finally arriving at the small beach town of Mahahual. Most hotels, restaurants, dive shops, and other attractions are close to the area where the main road meets the beach.

To get to Mahahual by bus, from the Cancún bus station take a bus to Limones, either a direct or a bus to Chetumal that stops there. Be sure to ask, as not all buses to Chetumal stop in Limones. From there transfer to a Mahahual bus, which leaves every hour or so from Limones.

LODGING

Balamku Inn

983-838-0083
www.balamku.com
Three miles south of the Mahahual town square

To get to Balamku, take the main beach road south of town for about five minutes, and the hotel will be on your left. It's surrounded by trees and flowering plants, making it a great escape for nature lovers and others who want to get away from the hustle and bustle for a few days. The beach is perfect for tanning and relaxing. The large rooms feature colorful designs, dark wood furniture, hot-water showers, and ceiling fans, and Internet access is available.

Guests have access to several sea kayaks. Rates: around $70; breakfast and use of sea kayaks included.

Forty Cannons Hotel

www.los40canones.com
On the beach in the center of Mahahual

Right in the center of town, this 10-room hotel may seem bustling for the area, but if you compare it to the more touristy destinations up the coast, it is still ultrarelaxed. All rooms have ceiling fans, 24-hour electricity, and hot-water showers. The other main attraction is the hotel restaurant, which fronts the beach and serves pasta, seafood, and other international dishes. Rates: $35–100 (higher prices are for suites with air-conditioning).

KaiLuumcito

1-800-538-6802 (U.S.)
www.mexicoholiday.com/destinations/kailuumcito.html
Rìo Indio

From the military checkpoint on the main road into Mahahual, go east a couple of minutes until you see a sign for Tampalam. Turn left and travel for 6 miles. Turn left again at the sign for Rio Indio, and follow that road along the beach for 2 more miles. The last stretch is completely unpaved, but just when you feel like you can't go any farther, you'll arrive at the hotel. There are 10 canvas tents set up on wooden platforms and surrounded by palm trees and a deserted beach, which leads to a shallow and very calm cove. Even though the accommodations are not luxurious, the service is very personal, and the staff does a great job of making sure you feel cared for. Meals are set up on an open-air deck, and the food is great. Rates: $95–190.

Mayan Beach Garden

El Placer, 15 miles north of Mahahual

On a remote beach up the coast from Mahahual center, this solar-powered inn offers suites and beach cabañas that feature ceiling fans and direct beach access. There are also kayaks available for guest use and a lounge area. An on-site restaurant offers three meals per day, and there's excellent beachcombing, snorkeling, and relaxing to be had at the hotel beach. Rates: $90–120; include full breakfast. Ask about the suite with a king bed and two singles, plus a dining room and private *palapa* terrace.

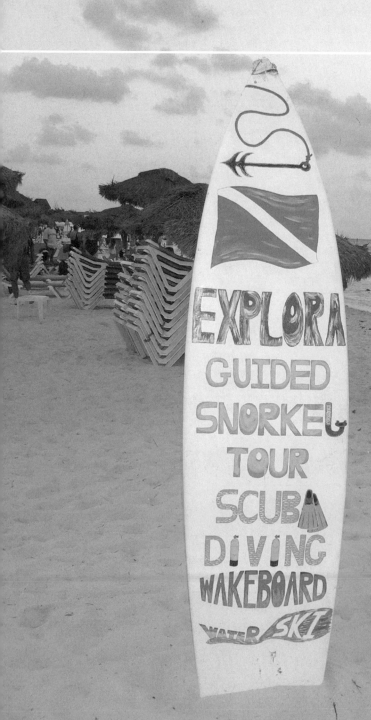

4

Activities

These are the primary attractions in the Riviera Maya, and they are no more than an hour away from any hotel in the area. Nearly every hotel tour desk can sell you tickets that include round-trip transportation. They're also easy to get to by rental car or even bus, so they make for good self-guided outings as well. Note: Secondary and local attractions are discussed in other chapters in this book, based on the area where they're located.

NATURE PARKS, AMUSEMENT PARKS & ZOOS

Aktun Chen
998-877-8550
www.aktunchen.com
Highway 307, km 107, between Akumal and Xel-Ha

Atkun Chen, whose name means "underground river cave" in Mayan, is a 1,000-acre nature park with a large cave and jungle tour. The main cave (600 yards long) is said to have been a natural bunker for the native Mayans, who sought its protection during serious storms. An hour-long guided walk through the park reveals badgers, iguanas, spider monkeys, tropical birds, and wild turkeys. There is also a motorized ATV tour, if you'd rather ride than walk. Along the way, you'll see many tropical flowers, coconut palms, and a gum tree called the *chicozapote*. The cave itself has amazing formations of stalactites and stalagmites, and an amazing underground cenote that is more than 35 feet deep. Though the cave winds its way several hundred yards through the ground, there are frequent openings and areas where fresh air and the sun shine through, so it's not as claustrophobic as it may sound. A restaurant at the cave exit serves fresh fruit drinks, traditional Mayan and Mexican dishes, and cold drinks. Open 9–5 daily. Adults $19, children $9.

Crococun Crocodile Farm & Zoo
998-850-3719
Highway 307, km 323, near Puerto Morelos.

If you're more into fauna than flora, you'll enjoy the Crococun zoo. Formed in 1985 as a commercial croc farm where the animals were raised for their skins and skulls, it has been transformed into a preserve, where visitors' admission fees go toward rescuing the crocs rather than killing them. The park now has dozens of other animals, including white-tailed

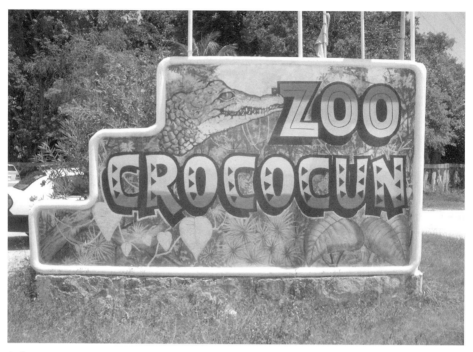

At Crococun you can see crocodiles, iguanas, birds, and more.

deer, spider monkeys, snakes, spiders, and birds. Except for the zoo's three hundred crocodiles, many of the animals are tame enough to pet, which is a real kick for the kids. There is a souvenir shop with T-shirts, maps, and videos, as well as a small snack bar. Open 9–5:30 Monday–Saturday. Adults $16, kids $10; admission includes a one-hour guided tour through the park. Tours leave continually.

Kantun Chi
984-873-0021
www.kantunchi.com
Highway 307, km 266.5; 14 miles south of Playa, 1 mile south of Puerto Aventuras

The entrance to Kantun Chi ecology and adventure park is marked by a small replica Mayan temple, across from the Barcelo Maya Hotel. The park, whose name means "yellow stone mouth" in Mayan, has nature trails, swimming holes, caves, and an animal sanctuary. There are hundreds of plant species, including many rare mushrooms. For fauna there are raccoons, spider monkeys, and white-tailed deer, along with several endangered local species, which the park is helping to bring back.

There are four cenotes large enough for swimming and snorkeling, including one called Uchil Ha, or "ancient water," which is said to have been an ancient Mayan religious site. Visitors can go horseback riding, mountain biking, or hiking. A *palapa* restaurant serves Mayan and Mexican food. Open 9–dusk daily. Entry is $35 for adults and $30 for kids, including the grotto tour, snorkeling gear, guide, and cenote hike. Fees are $20 for adults and $10 for children without the grotto tour, gear, or guide.

Parque Nizuc

998-881-3000

www.parquenizuc.com

Boulevard Kukulcán, km 25, Cancún

Just across the highway from the Cancún airport, as you head to the Cancún hotel zone, you'll come across the 18-acre Parque Nizuc water park. You can't tell from the road, but it's actually on a huge stretch of perfect white-sand beach. There are wave pools, water slides, a lazy river, tube rides, and many other freshwater attractions. There are also three bars and a large restaurant serving burgers, pizza, nachos, sandwiches, and ice cream. Dolphin-swim programs are offered through Atlantida, which is located at the back end of the park. Open daily, 10–6 May–October and 10–5:30 November–April. Entry is $29; the dolphin program costs extra.

Tres Rios

998-887-8077 or 1-800-714-3643 (U.S.)

www.tres-rios.com

Highway 307, km 300, 7 miles north of Playa del Carmen

A 370-acre activity and nature park, Tres Rios, which underwent a major renovation in 2005, is a place to learn and also have fun. There are mountain bikes for cruising through the jungle, canoe trips, jungle rivers, sea kayaks, snorkeling beaches, freshwater swimming holes, and beach hammocks. Hiking tours and horseback expeditions are offered and take participants through the dense jungle to see cenotes, tropical flora, wild animals, and deserted beaches. If you're interested in scuba diving, you can take a resort course that includes an hour of instruction and then an actual open-water dive, with an instructor at your side. The areas of the park are left as untouched as possible, giving visitors the feeling that they are seeing the land much as the Mayans did hundreds of years ago. An on-site restaurant serves Mexican lunches and snacks, and lockers are available for rent. Open 9–6 daily. Entry is $22 for adults and includes biking, canoeing, and kayaking. An all-inclusive option is available for $75 and includes unlimited food and drink, plus horseback riding and snorkeling.

Xaman Ha Aviary

Paseo Xaman Ha, behind Plaza Playacar, Playacar

Popular with families and other nature buffs, this privately run aviary exhibits more than 50 species of tropical birds, including flamingos, toucans, macaws, and other favorites native to the region. Some are caged, while others roam free in their natural habitat. There are also lots of iguanas, butterflies, turtles, brown squirrels, and freshwater fish. Open 9–5 daily. Entry is $15, with one child free with each paying adult.

Xcaret

www.xcaret.com

Highway 307, km 287, 3 miles south of Playa del Carmen

Once a sacred Mayan site, the Xcaret Mayan-themed recreational park is far and away the top attraction in the area. There are ads for it everywhere—on nearly every city bus in Cancún, at every hotel tour desk, on placards at the airport, in every tourist publication, in the newspaper, and on dozens of billboards along Highway 307. True to its roots, it has several native ruins on-site, and each evening native dancers put on an incredible show of Mayan dances and rituals. There is an interactive museum, miniature models of many Mayan sites, and a petting zoo.

Visitors can go tubing or snorkeling through an underground river, watch horsemanship exhibitions, see native fish in a saltwater aquarium, watch butterflies in their natural habitat, swim with dolphins, and even visit a re-creation of a native Mayan village. Near the village, an ancient ball court is set up where games of *pok-ta-pok* are played, with rules similar to those that were used more than a thousand years ago. In the game, players try to bounce the ball through an overhead hoop without using their hands or feet. It is said that in ancient times the losers were sacrificed to the gods. *Xcaret* means "inlet" in Mayan, and the park is right on the beach, so snorkeling, scuba diving, swimming, and sunbathing are popular as well.

At dusk, the wooden Mayan drums called *tunkules* start to play, signifying the start of the nightly show, complete with fire dancers, native costumes, and regional music. The Mayans originally called this area P'ole, which means "merchandise," since it was a popular trading village. Today visitors can shop for Mexican blankets, leather goods, glassware, and other souvenirs. Tour buses from Cancún come in hourly, so it's best to arrive early to

Caring for the Dolphins at Xcaret

The biologists of Xcaret and area veterinarians meet all the needs of the park's dolphins. They monitor their health, weight, and food, and in some facilities they conduct research on their behavior. At Xcaret dolphins are treated with care and respect, and their well-being is always the main priority. In fact, biologists claim that the life expectancy of a dolphin, which is about 40 years, increases when it is placed in captivity or semicaptivity (in extensive areas of its natural habitat). Dolphins have actually been born in captivity at Xcaret, and the way in which baby dolphins are brought into this world is quite an experience. They come out of their mother's womb tail first so as not to drown, and they emerge like torpedoes to the surface as they take in their first breath. Their first year is a delicate time, because dolphins are born without antibodies; however, their mothers feed them for one to two years, providing them with these defenses.

Qualified dolphin trainers, who are constantly learning new skills, spend long hours with the dolphins. At this time, the magic goes well beyond expectations: The relationship between trainers and dolphins is as close as that found in a family, where every single approach of the dolphin trainer receives an answer from the dolphin. A jump that soars more than 2 meters up in the air, a tail dance, a flipper greeting, a friendly sound, and underwater tricks are some of the ways in which dolphins show their fondness and approval. Due to their high cognitive ability, these animals understand every instruction their trainers give them. Dolphins have the ability to associate, and this allows them to translate signs and develop a series of perfectly synchronized movements. With a so-called target pole, which functions as an extension of their trainer's hand, dolphins learn to identify instructions until they develop a language that allows them to establish a sophisticated way to communicate with their trainer.

Ancient Mayans saw the dolphin as a sacred animal and a source of inspiration for the creation of myths and legends. Today, dolphins contribute to aquatic therapies and humanities disciplines, and experience has shown that all they lack is the ability to talk.

Sights and Activities Included in Basic Admission to Xcaret

WATER ACTIVITIES:
Beach, snorkeling cove, tidal pools
Coral reef aquarium
Manatee lagoon
Mayan river tube ride
Paradise river tube ride
Sea turtle farm
Underground river tube ride

SHOWS AND CULTURAL EXPERIENCES:
Archaeology sites
Flying Men of Papantla
Horse-riding show
Live theater performances
Mayan village
Museum of Culture and Archaeology
Observation tower
San Francisco of Assisi chapel
Spectacular Nights folklore festival (at dark on Sundays)

EQUIPMENT AND FACILITIES USE:
Beach chairs and umbrellas
Hammocks
Inner tubes
Life vests
Lock bag

FLORA AND FAUNA:
Beekeeping exhibit   Monkey island
Butterfly pavilion   Mushroom farm
Crocodile exhibit   Orchid greenhouse
Deer island   Puma and jaguar island
Ecology tour   Wild bird aviary
Jungle walk

Xcaret eco-adventure park Courtesy of Riviera Maya Tourism Authority

Hard-hat diving at Xcaret

experience the park before it gets too crowded. This trip is offered by nearly every tour operator in the area, so if you can't get there on your own, that may be a good option. Open daily, 8:30 AM–9 PM in winter and 8:30 AM–10 PM in summer. Basic admission is $59 for adults and $29.50 for kids 5–12. Numerous other pricing packages are available.

Xel-Ha

998-883-3143
www.xel-ha.com
Highway 307, km 245, 8 miles from Tulum

This nature park was once a Mayan seaport, and later it became a popular snorkeling cove, frequented by the adventurous few who cruised the coast looking for new spots. Today it is one of the largest attractions in the Riviera Maya. Xel-ha, whose name means "where the waters are born," features underground rivers where fresh and salt water come together, an animal nursery, cliff jumping, a tubing area, a dolphin discovery center, massage huts, ocean snorkeling, mountain bike trails, and a hiking area. An all-inclusive package is available, which includes unlimited food and drinks, plus most activities (no dolphins or massages). The park is open 9–6 daily; dolphin swim is 9–3. Get there early for the best experience. Adults $29 weekdays/$22 weekends, children 5–12 $15 weekdays/$11 weekends. All-inclusive: adults $56, children $28. Other activities include Snuba (surface-fed air snorkeling) and SeaTrek (helmet diving) for $45 each. The dolphin discovery program costs $115, which includes a one-hour swim.

Yaax-Che Jardín Botánico (Botanical Garden)
Highway 307, km 37, just south of Puerto Morelos

A fun stop-off between Cancún and Playa del Carmen is the 150-acre Jardín Botánico. Set up like a museum, with everything clearly marked and explained, this nature preserve has hundreds of species of plants, trees, and flowers. A long path snakes its way through the jungle, with everything growing in a natural setting. There is a hilltop overlook where you can see the jungle canopy and the ocean beyond, and a small Mayan ruin called *el altar* that dates from the 1400s. There is also a mock-up of an ancient Mayan homestead, as well as a chicle camp, where farmers would work to process the rubber gum from the chicle tree.

Also worth seeing is a native tree called the ceiba, which the Mayans called *yaax chen*. For the natives, this tree was a spiritual icon and was said to grow from the core of the earth, connecting the three levels of the universe. Many spider monkeys and other animals make their home in the gardens and can often be spotted by visitors. Open 9–5 Monday–Saturday. Admission is $5.

Xel-Ha   Courtesy of Riviera Maya Tourism Authority

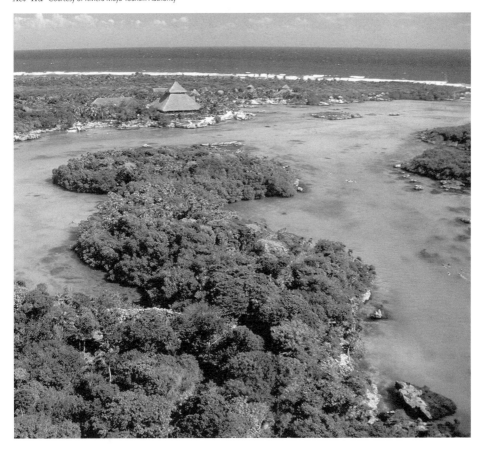

A Mayan Legend

Following the great flood, the world was dark and full of chaos. Nothing moved and nothing existed. The sea and the sky were empty. On the second day, the gods became tired of dancing over cold waters, so they created a thin layer of solid land where they could rest while they finished their work. "Let there be land," they said, and a beautiful layer of earth rose from the ocean. On the third day, the gods called upon Chaac, the god of rain, who poured rich water into the cracks of the land, giving life to the plants, flowers, and trees. As the rain continued on the fourth day, water filled all the cracks and basins, producing amazing lagoons and cenotes. On the fifth day, Kukulcán, the god of wind, flapped his wings, blowing warm breezes over the land, giving all living things a gentle dance. On the sixth day, Kukulcán turned his winds toward the sea, creating waves and forming Ixchel, the goddess of the moon and womanhood. Ixchel rose to heaven and gave birth to Itzámna, the lord of the skies, who created the day and the night and then painted the night with thousands of stars. "Let the trees have their own guardians," the gods ordered on the eighth day, and birds were created in astonishing varieties, including Mo, the scarlet macaw, who became the guardian angel of the skies. On the ninth day, Hunab-Ku buried a white knife in the land, and from it flowed all sorts of animals, including reptiles, jaguars, monkeys, and Huh, the iguana, who was the guardian of the land. Like a falling star, Ixchel descended from the night sky on the tenth day. She dove naked into a cenote, and the waters came alive with millions of fish, of all colors and sizes. The gods then picked the parrotfish, or Kay-Op, as the guardian of the waters. The gods rested on the eleventh day, but they were feeling cold, so they asked the sun god to help them. He came from the skies with his magic fire and heated the waters of the sea, the lagoons, and the cenotes, thus creating a warm and gentle climate. On the twelfth day the gods created humans, the most perfect of living creatures. With their intelligence, speech, sight, smell, taste, hearing, and touch, they were the ones gifted with the right to enjoy all the magic the gods had made for them. The gods danced and sang, full of joy for what they had created, and then they returned to the heavens. Pleased with what they saw and the world they had created, they decided to name it Xel-Ha, or the place where the waters are born.

Cenotes

Cenotes are relatively small and the water does not circulate, so it is important that all swimmers and divers rinse off any mosquito repellent or sunscreen before entering the water.

Camino de Cenotes

Across from the main entrance to Puerto Morelos, a gravel road heads inland, under a tall archway etched with CAMINO DE CENOTES at the top. This road is a fairly straight shot for 25 miles, passing through the blue-collar town of Central Vallarta, past several cenotes, and on into the interior of Quintana Roo. There are dozens of cenotes in the area, though most of them are still unaccessible. The largest is Selvatura, which has established an ecopark complete with bike rentals, zip lines, and canopy tours. On the way to Selvatura, the road passes other cenotes in various stages of tour-readiness. Check for signs as you travel the road, and you could be the first to visit one of the newly opened ones. A few of the most established ones are:

Boca del Puma, Ruta de Cenotes, km 14. A small sign marks the turnoff to this medium-size cenote, which has a camping area and room for snorkeling and swimming. Admission is $7; slightly more for overnight stays.

Cenote Verde Lucero, Ruta de Cenotes, km 16, has several different cenote openings, with undergound caverns connecting them. There's not much to see for snorkelers, but trained divers can traverse underground to the connected lagoons. The owner is happy to introduce you to his dogs and show you around. There are some nice birds, a big nopal cactus plant, and other interesting sites. The cenote is about a quarter mile from the entrance. You can park and walk or, if you want to brave it, drive your car right up to the edge. Admission is $7.

Selvatura (998-898-1423, www.selvatura.com.mx), Ruta de Cenotes, km 19, runs adventure tours from hotels in Playa del Carmen and the Riviera Maya. The trip includes a visit to a 247-acre preserve, with bike riding, zip-lining, canopy tours, and lunch. Impromptu visits can also be accommodated. The park boasts a zip-line circuit that has 24 platforms and is more than 2 miles long, making it the longest circuit in North America. There is also a 160-foot-wide cenote, perfect for cooling off and swimming. Adults $59, children $42, including transportation; adults $42, children $29, entry only. Admission includes the zip-line canopy tour, biking, cenote swimming, lunch, drinks, and lockers.

Siete Bocas, Ruta de Cenotes, km 13. There isn't yet a road connecting the cenote to the main road, so visitors have to walk 25 minutes down a jungle path to reach it. As the name

Cenote diving: It's like being in outer space. Courtesy of Riviera Maya Tourism Authority

Cenote water is as clear as air. Yibran Aragon

suggests, there are seven different lagoons, though only a couple of them are large enough for swimming. Admission is $7.

Other Cenotes around the Riviera Maya

Aktún-Ha—The Carwash, just south of Akumal, off Highway 307. One of the better known cenotes in the region, frequented by scuba-diving groups from the United States and beyond, the Carwash is only 50 feet deep, but the caverns are wide and long (nearly 2 miles long), making it very popular for certified cave divers. During the summer the surface is covered with algae, but in the cooler months snorkeling is possible.

Cenote Azul, Highway 307, km 266. This cenote, half the size of a basketball court, is on a small ranch that borders the highway, and the family who owns it operates it as a private park. Look for the hand-painted sign along the road and slow down fast to avoid slipping on the gravel entryway. The lagoon is a short walk from the parking area and has a rope swing and 10-foot-high cliff, perfect for jumping into the water. You can climb the face of the cliff or take the less treacherous path to the left, which leads up the hill to the jump-off point. You can bring a cooler, but remember to leave the sunscreen behind. The water is cool and clear, and it's only about 10 feet deep, so it's good for snorkeling but not diving. An adjacent cenote, El Jardín del Eden, offers a similar experience and is a frequent stop for tour groups.

Cenote Dos Ojos, Highway 307, km 242. Part of an immense nature preserve and ranchers' cooperative, this ecopark offers several cenotes for exploring, snorkeling, and scuba diving. It was first discovered in 1985 by dive maven Mike Madden and has been extensively explored and mapped. Most of the cenotes connect through underground caverns, which require advanced cave-diving certification to experience. If you have your own gear and are comfortable poking around on your own, you can enter for $8 per person. A snorkeling tour, complete with equipment and guide, costs $40, and scuba diving costs $65 for one tank or $95 for two tanks. Dive gear can be rented for $8. These cenotes are popular spots to spot a local bird known as the toh, which has two long tail feathers and sits on exposed rocks deep in the cenote, where the air is dark and cool, wagging its tail back and forth. Every minute or so it will let out a loud cry, almost like a howler monkey. Locals tell tales of people being lost in the jungle listening for the call of the toh, which they knew would help lead them to water. There are also bats found in some of the caves. An on-site photographer has some incredible pictures of the cenotes and tunnels and offers photography services during snorkel and dive trips. The photos are delivered on CD, along with some stock images of the area, plus general information on cenotes ($35).

Cenote Ponderosa, Highway 307, 3 miles south of Puerto Aventuras. This cenote and cavern dive is made up of two separate cenotes, connected through an underground channel. The depth ranges from 25 to 55 feet, and the visibility is more than 300 feet. The water is a mix of fresh and salt water and hovers around 77–79 degrees. The cenotes have mostly small fish, but they're very brightly colored. The wide caverns are easy to maneuver and swim around, which helps prevent any feelings of claustrophobia. The main feature is an underground air dome called the Chapel, where divers can submerge and breathe natural air, even though they are under the water level. Most dive shops in the region can take divers on expeditions through the cenote. The price is $50 per person per dive.

Chaak Tun Ts'ono'ot, Avenue Juárez at 120th Avenue, Playa del Carmen. From downtown Playa, take Avenue Juárez across Highway 307 and keep going for about 5 miles. You'll pass several housing communities and get a firsthand look at how the local workers live. This cenote, whose name translates from Mayan as "rain rock cenote," has multiple caverns and a stunning cave formation. It's a good spot for snorkeling and just lounging in the water while you gaze in awe at the geology. Admission is $5. Open 9–5.

Grand Cenote. Take Highway 307 to the main intersection in Tulum and turn right, away from the coast, on the road to Cobá. Just 2 miles down that road, you'll see the signs for Grand Cenote (or Gran Cenote) on your right. You'll pay an $8-per-person fee and then hike about 100 feet through the jungle to the palm-ringed cenote. Popular with snorkelers and divers, the Grand Cenote features amazing underwater stalactites, stalagmites, and other limestone formations. You can swim a ring around the middle island sundeck area. The water is cool (77 degrees) and clear (400 feet of visibility), with a maximum depth of less than 25 feet. It makes for a great stop-off after a trip to the beach or a long drive back to Playa from Cobá. There are benches and plenty of room for sunbathing. Open until 4 PM daily.

Hidden Worlds Cenotes
984-877-8535
www.hiddenworlds.com
Highway 307, 30 miles south of Playa, 2 miles south of Xel-Ha

This site covers nearly 10,000 hectares of land, and the cave system runs for 42 miles, most of it underground. It was discovered in 1986, and the park has been in business since

1994. It was the site of the filming of the IMAX film *Journey into Amazing Caves* and operates as a private scuba and snorkeling park, affording visitors an incredible underwater
experience that feels more like being in space than being underwater. Visitors choose from
several different cenotes and caves, depending on their experience, the amount of time
they have available, and whether they want to scuba or snorkel.

The lobby area is located just off the highway, and from there participants are driven on
the park's rugged and odd-looking homemade four-wheel-drive truck. The first site is
called Dos Ojos (Two Eyes), and it's essentially two separate cenotes connected by a channel. This is the main site where most of the IMAX footage was shot, and it is the third
largest underwater cave in the world. Basic dive certification is required, and there is natural light the whole way, which adds a nice feeling of security. The water stays a constant 75
degrees, the depth ranges from 25 to 150 feet, and there is more than 1,500 feet of naviga-
ble space. Small groups of divers follow the dive guide as the group enters one cenote and
swims through the channel and then on to the enormous chamber of the other cenote
before surfacing 45 minutes later. The water is unimaginably clear, and if not for the air
bubbles, it really would seem like outer space, especially given the otherworldly scenery,
unlike anything you would ever see on the land.

The next dive, the Caverna de los Murcielagos (the Bat Cave), has been known to bring
divers to tears with its awesome beauty. The cave is as dramatic as it is exquisite, with a
sublime combination of steep drop-offs, Disney-worthy stalactites, and elaborate features
that have taken millions of years to develop. There are also hundreds of brightly colored
tropical fish, elusive cave shrimp, and other critters. The depth is only 35 feet, making it

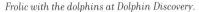

Frolic with the dolphins at Dolphin Discovery.

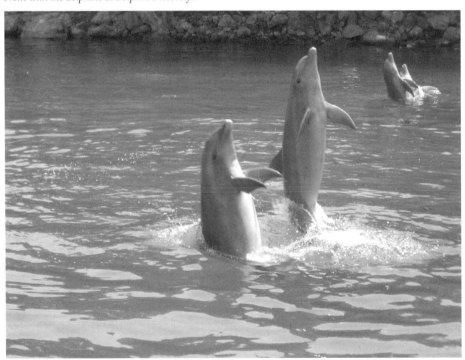

an especially safe dive that even scuba newcomers will enjoy. Since the water is so clear and the aboveground portions of the cave are as amazing as the underwater ones, snorkelers can easily appreciate the cave's grandeur.

The closest cavern to the reception area is called Hilario's Well. Given its relatively small size and shallow depth, this cenote is the best one for snorkelers. During a one-hour guided tour, snorkelers encounter stalagmites, stalactites, and other formations that are truly awe-inspiring. If you have enough time and you're up for a real Mayan-style adventure, sign up for the Tak Be Ha (Cave of Hidden Waters) jungle expedition. On this half-day outing, participants travel deep into the Mayan jungle in the four-wheel-drive Jungle Mobile to see secret cenotes, nearly virgin caves, and an assortment of the area's plant and animal life, including tropical birds, orchids, and mosquitoes. Led by an expert and multilingual guide, the group will explore the area, learning about the history, geography, and ecology of the region. Next, it's on with the mask and fins and into the cenote to see for yourself the amazing gin-clear waters and incomprehensible cave formations.

Scuba tours depart at 9 AM, 11 AM, and 1 PM, and snorkeling trips depart at 9 AM, 11 AM, 1 PM, 2 PM, and 3 PM. Snorkeling tours are $25 for adults and $20 for kids (8–12 years) for Hilario's Well only, or $45 for a visit to three different cenotes. Diving is $50 for one tank or $90 for two tanks. All equipment is included for snorkelers, but divers need to either rent or bring their standard equipment, light, and wet suit. Rental is $15 for all gear. There is an on-site snack bar.

Taj Mahal
Highway 307, 3½ miles south of Puerto Aventuras, just past Xpu-Ha

A group of four cenotes and caverns, the Taj Mahal averages around 50 feet in depth and the water is as clear as air, making it good for both snorkelers and scuba divers. Known for a cavern called the Beam of Light Room, this spot is less crowded than many of the others, making it a good place to linger over a picnic lunch. The connected Sugarbowl cenote has a large cavern open to the daylight, which creates mind-numbing rays of light under the water. Dive shops around the area lead trips to the cenote for $50 per person, per dive.

WATER SPORTS & ACTIVITIES

Atlantis Submarines
987-872-5671
Carretera a Chankanaab, km 4, Cozumel

See the amazing reefs of Cozumel, including Santa Rosa and Palancar, while in the comfort of a chair. The air-conditioned sub goes up to 100 feet deep and passes by many of the same dive sites that scuba divers visit. Trips depart every hour from 9 to 2 Monday–Saturday. The fee is $40 per person.

Dolphin Discovery
1-800-417-1736 (U.S.)
www.dolphindiscovery.com
Villa Pirata, Isla Mujeres (998-877-0207)
Avenue Juárez, downtown Cozumel (987-872-6605)
Puerto Aventuras, on the marina (998-849-4757)

At Dolphin Discovery, you can interact with live dolphins, and there are several packages from which you can choose. In the Dolphin Encounter, participants gather around a trainer, and the dolphins swim up to join the group. You are allowed to touch the dolphins while you learn about their habits and life in the wild. The dolphins perform stunts while you watch from close up. The experience lasts 45 minutes and costs $75.

For the Royal Swim package, the group receives an orientation from the trainer and then actually gets to enter the water and participate in the stunts, including being propelled through the water by a dolphin. The group is limited to eight people, so each person gets plenty of time with the dolphins. This activitiy lasts 45 minutes and costs $130.

In the Swim & Snorkel Adventure participants enter the water wearing masks and snorkels and swim around the dolphins. They will come up to you, and you can touch them and interact with them. You will even be able to do what they call a "belly ride," where you hold the dolphin by the fin, close to the body, and get pulled through the water. This activity lasts 45 minutes and costs $99.

For all the dolphin adventures, the minimum age is eight, and children ages eight to 11 must be accompanied by a paying adult. No pregnant women or people with physical or mental limitations are permitted. Open 8–6 daily.

Ikarus Kiteboarding

984-803-3490
www.ikaruskiteboarding.com
Quinta at 20th Street, Playa del Carmen
Quinta at 16th Street, Playa del Carmen

Ikarus, which is PASA and IKO certified, offers lessons, equipment rental, and sales of windsurfers, skateboards, and kiteboards, and it also has bathing suits, backpacks, T-shirts, and other beach games. Lessons are $55 an hour with two or three students, or $65 an hour for private sessions.

Learning to Kitesurf with Ikarus

Ikarus, named for Ik, the Mayan wind god, and Icarus, the Greek god who took to the sky, has successfully taught more than seven hundred people in the Riviera Maya, and they claim that the most important prequalification a student can have is experience flying a two-line stunt kite. That, they say, is even more important than having experience hang gliding, wakeboarding, snowboarding, windsurfing, or even aeronautical engineering.

The first 45 minutes are spent talking about weather patterns, safety, kite dynamics, and kite control. Next, there are hands-on lessons covering kite and line setup, launching and landing techniques, and safe flight patterns. After that, it's into the water, armed with a life jacket and radio helmet for a bit of body-dragging and self-rescue practice. The next step is to stand up and sail through the water. Most students get to this point after two days of three-hour classes.

Requirements for successful kitesurfers:

• Love of nature, comfort in the water, and desire to harness the power of the elements

• Time, patience, and respect for nature

• Equipment designed for stability, safety, and ease of use

• A qualified and experienced instructor

• A safe beach zone in the water

• WIND

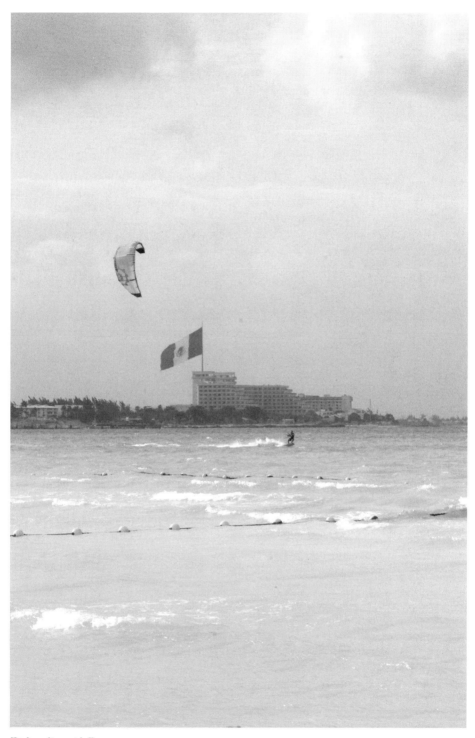

Kiteboarding with Ikarus   Dr. Joseph Will and the Ikarus crew

Great snorkeling abounds. Courtesy of Riviera Maya Tourism Authority

Snorkeling Tours
984-879-3427
www.tankha.com
Tank-Ha Dive Center, Quinta between Eighth and 10th Streets, Playa del Carmen

This is a great trip for snorkelers of all levels who want to wet their fins in the Caribbean. The three-hour adventure departs on a 25-foot boat with a sun shade, which leaves daily at 9:30 AM and/or 1:30 PM, and includes all snorkeling and safety gear, refreshments, and dive master. Advance reservations are highly recommended and can be made by phone or by stopping by the shop. The cost is $30 per person.

Sub See Explorer
988-848-8300
www.aquaworld.com.mx
Boulevard Kukulcán, km 15.2, Cancún

Take an underwater ride through the reefs and undersea channels off the coast of Cancún. You can see living coral reefs, sea sponges, sea fans, angel fish, parrot fish, grouper, rays, sea turtles, moray eels, and other marine life. The trip, which includes lunch and drinks, departs every hour 9–3 daily. The price is $45 per person.

Yalku Lagoon
North end of Akumal Bay

One of the top snorkeling spots in the area, this ocean inlet has a mix of fresh and salt water, which provides a habitat for a wide variety of fish, including triggerfish, wrasse,

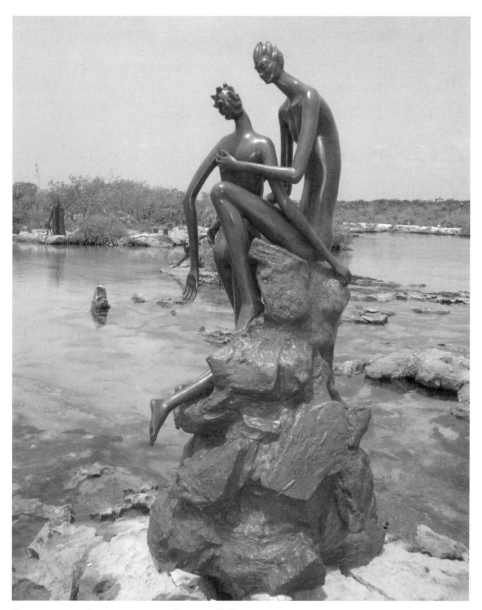

Contemporary sculpture meets ancient lagoon at Yalku. Courtesy of Riviera Maya Tourism Authority

parrot fish, needlefish, and sometimes sea turtles. The shoreline has several metal sculptures imported from Mexico City, plus a few picnic tables and stairways to the water. The bottom and sides are more rocky than sandy, so walking can be treacherous, but a pair of water shoes and a careful eye make it worth the effort. Float along in the cool water, watch the colorful fish, and listen to the tropical birds singing from the trees.

To get there, head through the main Akumal entrance and then turn left, paralleling the beach after the artificial-grass tennis court. You'll cross an abandoned checkpoint, but there is no need to stop. Keep going for about 2 miles, turning to the left wherever it's unclear, and the road will end at the lagoon. The cove is ringed by private homes, unreachable beaches, and a private park. Unless you're friends with one of the local homeowners, you'll need to enter the private park. Adults $6, kids $3. The park is open 8–5:30 daily.

Equipment rental and snacks are available from a small hut near the water, though visitors are welcome to bring their own gear, including coolers, drinks, and picnic supplies. A table with *palapa* roof makes the perfect spot for lunch. Follow the lagoon shoreline to the left to find it. Visitors are encouraged to use only biodegradable sunscreen, which is available for sale at the park entrance.

HORSEBACK RIDING

Rancho Loma Bonita
988-887-1708
Highway 307, km 315,
Along Highway 307, at km 315

This huge private ranch houses more than 150 horses and is a popular spot for tour groups and cruise-ship passengers. Typical packages include round-trip transportation, soft drinks, and a ranch-style buffet; two hours of horseback riding; and two hours of ATV riding. The horseback rides go through the ranch and to the beach, where you can even take the horse in the water for a swim in the waves. The price is $65 per person. Other events, such as donkey polo and soccer matches, can be custom designed.

Rancho Punta Venado
998-898-1331
www.puntavenado.com
Along Highway 307 in Paamul, 10 minutes south of Playa del Carmen

Once part of one of the largest and most prosperous commercial ranches along the Yucatán coast, Punta Venado is now open to visitors. Occupied by Mayan natives 1,500 years ago, the ranch still exhibits evidence of their existence through stone fences, small dwellings, and other minor structures. In the 1950s cattle baron Miguel Joaquin Ibarra purchased nearly 10,000 acres of land at this site and ran more than 600 head of cattle, in addition to farming coconuts, watermelons, limes, and cucumbers. In the 1970s blight struck the coconut crop, and Ibarra sold all but 2,000 acres. In 1988 Hurricane Gilbert hit, thinning the herd down to only 40 head. Some 10 years later the ranch opened as a tourist destination, turning the working cowboys into riding instructors and expedition guides. Better care was taken during Hurricane Emily in 2005, and the only losses were to the structure and were quickly repaired.

The ranch has 30 cenotes, caves, pristine beaches, and unexplored jungle, and three main expeditions are offered:

Horseback riding: This hour-and-a-half tour takes riders on a guided trip through the jungle and to a long stretch of beach where you and your horse can roam around, loosely following the trip leader. You can even take the horse into the shallows for a quick swim in the ocean. Groups are limited to 20 people. Departs at 9 AM, noon, and 3 PM; includes soft drinks. The price is $35 per person.

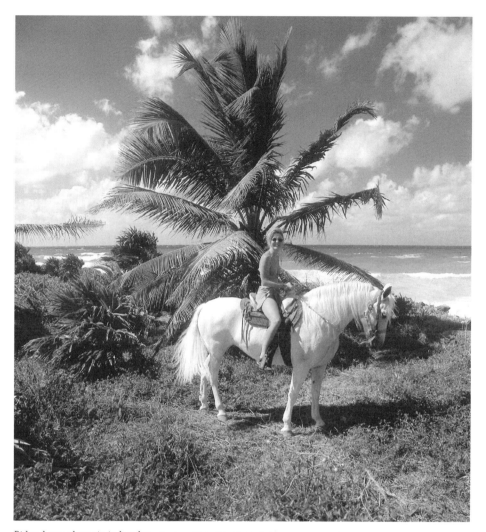

Ride a horse along virgin beaches. Courtesy of Riviera Maya Tourism Authority

Horseback riding and snorkeling: For two and a half hours, you can enjoy all of the wonders of the ranch, both in and out of the water. The trip starts with a one-hour horseback ride through the jungle and down to the beach. Once there, you'll be given snorkeling gear and have 40 minutes to swim in the ocean and snorkel along the reef. After that, the group rides the horses back to the ranch. Groups are kept small, with a maximum of 20 people. Expeditions depart at 9 AM, noon, and 3 PM; they include snorkeling equipment, snacks, and soft drinks. The price is $50.

ATV adventure: If you're more into adrenaline than nature, you're probably best off choosing the ATV tour over the horses. On this expedition, participants ride four-wheel-drive ATVs and visit several of the park's diverse attractions. You will motor through the jungle, trounce through the woods, explore an underground cave with flashlights, hike over ancient rock formations, cruise around a cenote, ride along the beach, go

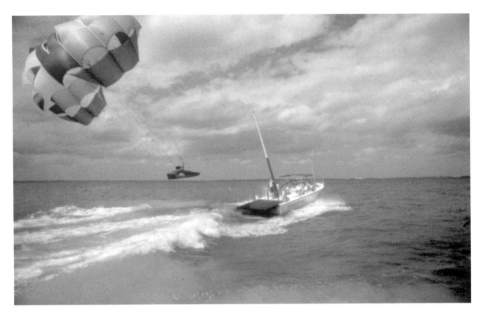

Parasailing gives riders a great view. Courtesy of Riviera Maya Tourism Authority

sea kayaking, and snorkel around the reef. This trip is limited to 14 riders, either one or two per ATV. Departs at 9 AM, noon, and 3 PM; includes all required gear and equipment, plus snacks and soft drinks. The price is $40.

With any paid expedition, guests can stay at the ranch all day and enjoy the other facilities, including the beach club, hiking trails, and snack bar.

BIKE RIDING

Akumal Travel Services
984-875-9030
www.akumaltravel.com
Akumal Marina

Take a 5-mile bike ride on a private ranch just west of Akumal. The tour stops at a cenote and an underground river, and there's beautiful scenery. Advance reservations are required and can be made at the Akumal Travel Services offices in the Akumal Marina. The tour, which lasts three and a half hours and costs $35, departs at 7 AM and 2 PM Monday–Saturday.

EuroBike Rentals
984-803-4733
30th Avenue at 26th Street, Playa del Carmen

EuroBike offers a variety of motorbike rentals, from Vespa and Piaggio scooters to Gilera, KTM, and Ducati motorcycles. Hourly and daily rentals are available.

PARASAILING, SKYDIVING & PLANE TOURS

Aerosaab
www.aerosaab.com

Services Playa del Carmen, Cozumel, Holbox, and Chichén Itzá and offers sightseeing tours, private transportation, and air taxi service. Rental rates range from $280–350 per hour.

Riviera Maya Parasail Adventures
984-873-5683
Oasis Hotel, Puerto Aventuras

This well-respected outfit offers tandem and solo rides around the Puerto Aventuras bay and beachfront.

Sky Dive Playa
984-873-0192
www.skydive.com.mx
Plaza Marina, Playa del Carmen

The facility, which offers tandem and solo jumps, is certified by the U.S. Parachute Association. Its rectangular parachutes have ram-air canopies, which allow for a very stable and controlled decent. Dives include instruction and transportation to the airport near the town square. Each dive has about 45 seconds of freefall, plus a six- to seven-minute

Tandem skydiving   Courtesy of Riviera Maya Tourism Authority parachute descent. Landings are on the main beach of Playa del Carmen. The cost is $200, plus an additional $95 for photos.

Ultralight Flights—Alas Sky Tour
984-871-4020

Small lightweight airplanes take off from an open field near Xcaret park, head north along the coast to Playa del Carmen, and then circle out over the water and back to the landing strip. The trip takes about 20 minutes. Standard rate is $99 per person.

BEACH CLUBS

Coco Maya Beach Club
14th Street at the beach, Playa del Carmen

This exclusive beach club next to the Blue Parrot Hotel (see chapter 2) is the preferred daytime hangout for stylish beachgoers showing off their new bathing suits, new boobs, or new gym results. It's a great place to sunbathe, listen to lounge music, and feel cool.

Deep Blue Beach Club
16th Street at the beach, Playa del Carmen

Located behind the Deep Blue Hotel (see chapter 2), this beach club has a waterfront bar and restaurant, beach beds, and plenty of beachy activities.

Mamita's Beach Club

Mamita's Beach Club
984-803-2867
www.mamitasbeachclub.com
28th Street at the beach, Playa del Carmen

Just north of Nikki Beach Club is Mamita's, which attracts a more trendy crowd that gathers every afternoon to soak up the sun and sip cold beers and frosty margaritas. There is a small pool and several cabaña-style beach beds, available on a first-come, first-served basis. A DJ spins lounge and pop music suitable for bar-top dancing, while other patrons join in a game of group soccer-ball juggling.

Nikki Beach Club
26th Street at the beach, Playa del Carmen

This family-friendly beach hangout, just north of the Royal Porto Real hotel (see chapter 2), is popular with day-trippers, cruise passengers, and beachgoers staying in Playa's downtown hotels. There are lounge chairs and beach umbrellas for rent, plus a kids' pool, a restaurant serving seafood and Mexican food, and, of course, cold beer right on the beach. Active folks can play beach volleyball and soccer, ride WaveRunners, or go parasailing, banana-boat riding, kiteboarding, or body surfing. Massage service is provided on the beach or in a rooftop hut by Natural Spa.

ORGANIZED TOURS

There are only a few group tour and travel providers servicing the Riviera Maya, and they own the vehicles, employ the guides, set the itineraries, negotiate rates, and provide the actual tour services. Sometimes they sell directly to the public, but primarily they rely on tour resellers to represent their tours to the public and book the majority of the reservations. Nearly every hotel has a tour desk, and there are tour offices on nearly every block of Quinta in Playa del Carmen. There are also tour kiosks at the entrance of some restaurants, and tour representatives even walk the beaches carrying a notebook describing the trips they can sell. Authorized agencies and individuals have licenses and ID cards, and it is recommended that you verify tour representatives' credentials before giving them any money. Most sellers have the same catalog of 20 or so tours, though there can be some variation in the selection. Prices are generally fixed and do not vary much from one operator to another.

Most tours require advance reservations so that transportation and meals can be planned accordingly. If you're interested in a spur-of-the-moment trip, your choices may be limited, but there's usually something available. When a tour is reserved, a deposit or even full payment is normally required, and you'll receive a voucher that proves you have paid and tells you when and where to go for the trip. Most major tours include hotel pickup and drop-off, while others begin at a predetermined location. The balance of the fee is paid at the start of the tour if you have only put down a deposit.

Many tours and adventures can be purchased well in advance, through your local travel agent, through the web site where you booked your flight, or directly with the tour operator. This can be a good way to guarantee availability and set your itinerary before your trip even begins, but prices are generally the same whether you book in advance or not.

Tour Operators

Alltournative Expeditions
984-873-2036
www.alltournative.com
Various locations along Quinta, Playa del Carmen

Alltournative specializes in natural and cultural tours, eco-adventure, and alternative adrenaline-rush activities. Activities include bird-watching, canoeing, cave exploring, cenote swimming, four-wheeling, hiking, rappelling, scuba diving, sea kayaking, snorkeling, zip-line rides, Mayan ruins tours, and even overnight camping trips deep into the jungle. Custom-designed trips can be put together for large groups, incentive trips, or team-building outings. The company's buses or signature Mercedes Unimog all-terrain vehicles pick up guests near their hotels and transport them to the location of the tour. Groups are matched with a guide, based on their language and similarity with other travelers. Depending on the tour, there are stops at the company's crafts shop, where profits are shared with the indigenous communities who offer their land to be used for the adventure trip. The tours are adventurous and educational, and they are a great way to meet other travelers. Most of the activities require participants to be in relatively good physical shape. Many of the locations for the tours are on private land and cannot be visited any other way. Trips can be reserved online, on the phone, or in person at one of their outlets. Most local tour agencies can book these trips, also. Prices are $50 and up and include lunch, snacks, water, and all necessary equipment. Participants should bring comfortable clothes, sport shoes, a bathing suit, and extra money for souvenirs, tips, and photos.

CancúnVista Tours
998-898-4312 or 1-800-860-5917 (U.S.)
www.cancunvista.com
Avenue Cobá, #31, Cancún

This tour operator offers some great combination tours for travelers who want to see and do a bit of everything during their stay. It also represent many of the standard water sports, adventure, and Mayan ruins tours offered by other agencies. All tours can be reserved in advance through the company's toll-free number or their web site.

EcoColors
www.ecotravelmexico.com

Environmentally conscious travelers who want to experience and enjoy the Riviera Maya but don't want to alter it will find those with a similar philosophy at this eco-friendly tour operator. Adventures include boat trips through Sian Ka'an, bird-watching, biking, kayaking, cenote swimming, and jaguar discovery trips. The company also offers guided trips to Chichén Itzá, Cobá, and the lesser-known ruins of Muyil. Tours can be booked direct or through an agent.

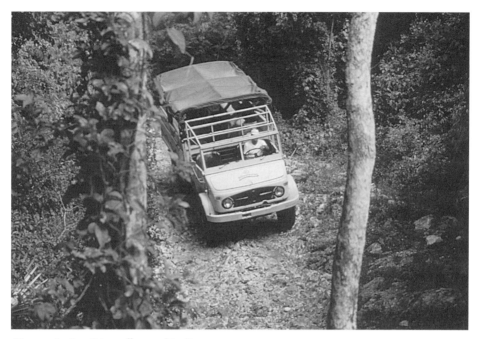

Alltournative Expeditions offers eco-friendly tours. Courtesy of Riviera Maya Tourism Authority

SeaMonkey Business Tours

984-876-3306 or 954-323-8227 (U.S.)
www.seamonkeybusiness.com

This budget tour office offers many of the same tours as other agencies, but often at a discounted rate. The company's web site has destination information, travel resources, and photos and descriptions of dozens of tours and activities.

Popular Tours

Unless otherwise specified, these tours can be reserved through the above tour operators or through local agencies. Availability, times, and prices can vary.

ATV Tours

984-873-1606
www.atvexplorer.com
Highway 307, between Playacar and Xcaret, Playa del Carmen

An active adventure tour, this outing includes a two-hour ATV ride through the jungle, stopping at a freshwater lagoon, caves, Mayan ruins, and other attractions. Participants should bring walking shoes, a bathing suit, and a towel. Departs at 9 AM, 11 AM, 1 PM, and 3 PM daily. Rates are $38.50 per person riding double or $48.50 per person riding single; refreshments included.

Captain Hook Dinner Cruise

Though there's no pillaging and plundering, there is plenty of eating, drinking, and laughing on this swashbuckling dinner cruise. Board a 93-foot Spanish galleon replica and sail the waters of Cancún while enjoying a pirate-themed show and dinner. The boat leaves the dock at 6:30 PM nightly, returning at 10 PM. The price for adults is $63 for steak and $73 for lobster and steak, including open bar, and children 5–11 cost $31.50 for steak and $36.50 for lobster and steak. There is also an additional $4 port fee per person. Transportation from any hotel in the Riviera Maya is $12 extra.

Catamaran Sailing Adventures

984-876-3316
www.fatcatsail.com

Live the dream of sailing through the Caribbean, playing in the water, sipping cocktails on the deck, taking pictures, snorkeling, fishing, and exploring hidden Mayan ruins. You'll enjoy all this and more aboard a 41-foot catamaran: the *Fat Cat*. The trip departs between 9 and 10 AM, depending on your hotel. The first stop is the hidden beach of Xaac, where you can go snorkeling, climb the Mayan ruins, play on the beach, and grab a bite to eat. Next, it's back on the water for some real sailing adventures and goofing around in the boom net. The boat returns to the dock in Puerto Aventuras at 3 PM. The trip is available Monday–Saturday and includes food, drinks, water, transportation to/from the dock, and all equipment. Adults $80, children $55.

Chichén Itzá Deluxe

If you're looking for a first-class way to visit Chichén Itzá, this tour is a good bet. The trip includes transportation, bilingual guide, continental breakfast on the bus, bottled water and soft drinks, a pass through the colonial city of Vallodolid, entrance to Ik-Kil nature park, entrance to the Chichén Itzá ruins, buffet lunch at a Mexican hacienda, and a traditional folkloric show. Departing from Plaza Antigua in Playa del Carmen, with stops at Plaza Playacar, Puerto Aventuras, and hotels along the Riviera Maya, the tour is available Tuesday, Thursday, and Sunday and runs from 9 to 7. Adults $77, children 5–12 $47.

Cobá & Chimuch

For a mix of Mayan history and modern adventure, this trip is a good choice. It includes a two-hour visit to the Cobá ruins, an authentic Mayan lunch buffet, and a trip to two different eco-parks for kayaking, rappelling, and zip-lining. This trip operates daily. Adults $90, children under 12 $81.

Dos Palmas Mayan Ceremony Night

984-803-2462
www.dospalmas.info

This unique educational and entertaining tour includes Mayan cultural lessons, a Mayan jungle ritual with bonfire and torches, a *temazcal* steam bath ceremony, and cenote swimming. This activity must be reserved as a group and can accommodate groups of 10 or more. Prices vary according to menu and bar options.

Eco-Tour Nohoch

Your ride will pick you up at your hotel and take you to the jungle, where you will be met by a Mercedes Benz Unimog four-wheel-drive truck. The group is transported to Rancho San Felipe and the Nohoch Nah Chich cenote system. Includes snorkeling, hiking, and all transportation. Adults $98.

Fly-Fishing or Light-Tackle Fishing in Ascension Bay

You don't have to spend the night in a sweaty, un-air-conditioned lodge to experience the incredible fishing in Ascension Bay. This trip starts with a pickup from your hotel at 5 AM for the adventurous drive past Tulum and down the bumpy road through the Sian Ka'an biosphere. You'll arrive at around 8 AM and have breakfast before boarding the boat at 9. Spend the day fishing for bonefish, permit, tarpon, snook, barracuda, and other game fish, plus have lunch on the boat. You'll return to the dock at around 4 PM, and then it's back in the van for the ride back to your hotel, where you'll arrive by 8. The trip includes all necessary tackle, food, drinks, and transportation and costs $450 for one or two anglers.

Marina Maroma Paradise

www.maromaparadise.com

Adventure seekers will find a variety of exciting tours at Marina Maroma, including an ATV/speedboat combo trip ($65), snorkeling at Paradise Reef ($50), deep-sea fishing ($105 for four hours), snorkeling/horseback riding/lunch ($105), and the Paradise Combo, which includes horseback riding, ATV excursion, Jet Skiing, and lunch ($130).

Mayan Canopy Expedition

For an all-day trip combining water fun and jungle adventure, try the Mayan Canopy tour. The trip includes a bike ride through a Mayan farm, zip-lining, a visit to the Xtabay cenote, snorkeling in Chikin-Ha cenote, and a visit to Aluxes cenote for a purification ritual, plus snacks and drinks for the entire day. Runs daily, departing at 8 AM. Adults $67, children $58.

Pac-Chen Tour

This is an eco-friendly trip deep into the Yucatán jungle. The first stop is Cobá, where you will have a guided tour of one of the most dramatic of all the Mayan ruins. Next stop is the traditional village of Pac Chen, a lagoon-side town of one hundred residents living much as their ancestors did hundreds of years ago. The trip costs $98.

Rio Lagarto and Ek Balam Tour

This tour lasts a full day and takes travelers to the traditional town of Tizimin and to the Ek Balam ruins in the northern part of Yucatán State. The highlight, though, is the visit to Rio Lagarto, a remote river where hundreds of flamingos make their home. You will also see pelicans, falcons, and crocodiles. The tour includes a glass-bottom boat ride through the river, lunch (fresh fish in a traditional village), guide service, and hotel pickup. Advance reservations are required. The tour departs at 7:30 AM and returns at around 7 PM, and it costs $90 per person.

You can see an actual bullfight in Cancún

Tulum & Cobá

If you're interested in seeing a couple of Mayan sites but don't have much time, this is a good trip for you. The air-conditioned tour bus picks you up at your hotel and transports you to two of the best-known Mayan sites: Tulum and Cobá. The trip includes transportation, bilingual guide, entrance fees, and lunch. Pickups are available from Plaza Antigua in Playa del Carmen or at any hotel in the Riviera Maya. It departs Monday–Friday at 7:30 AM, returning at around 5:15 PM. Adults $62, children 5–12 $38.

Tulum & Xel-Ha

For travelers who want to see the ruins but also want something a bit more active, this combo trip is a good compromise. Since both sites are relatively close to Playa del Carmen, it's also a good way to minimize the amount of time you'll spend on a bus. The first stop is Tulum, where visitors will have a chance to see the cliffside ruins and the ocean below. Next, the bus heads to the Xel-Ha water park, where you can play in the water, snorkel, or lie on the beach. The trip includes air-conditioned bus transportation, bilingual host, entrance fees, lunch, drinks, and snorkeling equipment, and pickups are available from Plaza Antigua in Playa del Carmen or at any hotel in the Riviera Maya. Departs daily at 8 AM and returns at around 5 PM. Adults $103, children 5–12 $62.

Whale Shark Tour

Swim and snorkel with the docile 50-foot-long whale sharks at Isla Holbox, north of Cancún. The tour includes transportation to a dock north of Cancún and then the boat ride to Isla Holbox, and it costs $120 per person. Please note that this tour is not available year-round, and it must be scheduled in advance, based on availability and presence of the sharks. For more information contact the Holbox Adventures tour office at 10th Street between First and 10th Avenues in Playa del Carmen. Other tour agencies in the region can also sell this tour.

OTHER ACTIVITIES

Bullfights
Plaza de Toros, Bonampak Avenue, downtown Cancún

Bullfights are every Wednesday at 3:30 PM and sometimes on Sunday. Depending on the day, there will either be a tourist-oriented show with folkloric dancing, Mexican rodeo, and a single bullfight, or a full bullfighting competition with two matadors and six bulls.

Mini Golf El Palomar
984-803-2606
www.minigolfelpalomar.com
Highway 307, km 285.5

Just south of Playa del Carmen, before you get to Xcaret, you'll find a "Mayan-style" mini golf course on the west side of the road. There are 18 holes surrounded by fruit trees, water fountains, bridges, and tropical flowers, and there are also video games, a shooting gallery, and a snack bar. Open 10–9 daily.

Movie theater
Plaza Pelicano, 10th Avenue between Eight and 10th Streets

This three-screen, air-conditioned theater shows fairly new releases that are usually in English with Spanish subtitles. Some older films and kids' movies are dubbed in Spanish.

Dribbling in Paradise
Each year, in mid-December, the Playa del Carmen Municipal Gym hosts the Fun in the Sun Shootout men's and women's college basketball tournament, an early-season invitational that includes four teams for each division. It is televised in the United States on Fox College Sports Network. The players stay in the area and enjoy tours to Xcaret, Xel-Ha, and other attractions during their visit. The tournament is open to the public, and tickets are available at the door for $20. For more information log on to www.funinthesunshootout.net.

Mike Storie

5

Mayan Ruins

If you could travel back in time and see the Riviera Maya as it was hundreds of years ago, you would see a thriving civilization with a complex social, political, and religious community. From the Cancún hotel zone to the Playa del Carmen shoreline to the beaches and jungles of the Riviera Maya, there were hundreds of structures, religious temples, dwellings, stone roads, and even recreational facilities. When the Mayans abandoned their cities, their buildings were reclaimed by the jungle, and many of them deteriorated. Some sites retained their spiritual significance and were occasionally used as ceremonial sites by the local population until not long ago.

Archaeologists began uncovering the sites in the early 1900s, and little by little, more sites were rediscovered, studied, and, in some cases, restored to their original splendor. Many of the sites have been declared federal property by the Mexican archaeological institution and have been turned into public parks where locals and tourists can visit to learn about the Mayan culture and history and to experience firsthand the places where the ancient Mayans lived, worked, prayed, and played. Many other sites remain buried, shrouded by jungle, sometimes just out of view, and some are too remote to be easily discovered, but new sites are being uncovered all the time.

If you can't make time to visit any of the major sites in the area, you can always peek through the fence on the east side of Quinta Avenida at 14th Street in Playa del Carmen to see an authentic, though quite unassuming, bit of Mayan history. Surrounded by a chain-link fence and official-looking signs declaring it a federal archaeological site is a small temple built at the base of a tree. It's not labeled, but it's rumored to be a small ceremonial site or even an ancient dwelling.

Chichén Itzá

Mexico's best-known Mayan ruin site is 128 miles southwest of Cancún, a two-and-a-half-to three-hour drive from either Cancún or Tulum. To get there, visitors can take the toll road, Highway 180D (cost is about $40 each way), out of Cancún or take the road from Tulum and head inland past Cobá and through Valladolid. The drive through the jungle is interesting, with many picturesque places to stop along the way. The beautiful town square of the colonial city of Valladolid is worth a few minutes' diversion.

Chichén Itzá is the jewel of the Mayan sites that are easily reachable from the resorts of the Caribbean coast, and its grandeur makes it the obvious choice if you have time to visit only one of the ancient cities. The site is amazing, and for first-time visitors it can be a bit overwhelming. The structures are awe inspiring, and the restoration work makes it easy to picture what the city must have been like at the height of its splendor.

The area covers more than 6 square miles and is divided into two very distinct parts, and you can see classic Mayan as well as later Toltec-influenced structures. Be sure to get a glimpse of a map and see both—many tours cover only the later structures that are typically seen on postcards (the Pyramid of Kukulcán and the *pok-ta-pok* ball court, for example). These structures are the largest here, in particular the ball court (270 feet long and one of 22 on the entire site), which is the largest in Mesoamerica. However, the newer city is an area that is large enough that you could easily spend all your time in it if you were not aware of the older structures. These older structures also include examples of the softer *pu'uc* architecture (the church and its annex in particular) and display beautiful carvings not seen on later structures—they are not to be missed. A good plan is to head over to the older area and work your way back to where you started.

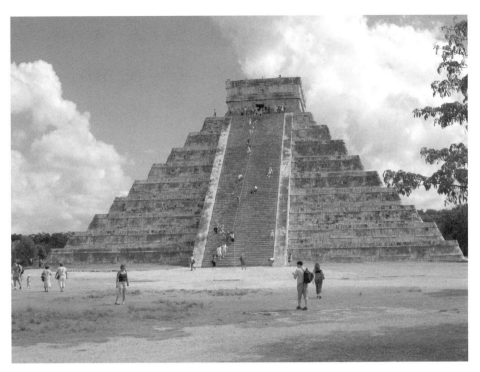

Chichén Itzá's main pyramid has 365 steps. Mike Stone

If you are investing the time to make the visit, it is also worth the trouble to read an article or two about the Mayans. Many tour guides seem to want to stimulate the crowd with tales of human sacrifice (which did indeed occur) at the expense of broader aspects of Mayan culture. Climbing the Pyramid of Kukulcán gives one a breathtaking view of most of the site, but be aware that there is an equally challenging set of stairs inside the temple as well, which fewer people take the time to see. This and the Nunnery (where an explosion was used in the 19th century to access one side of the structure) are the two places where you can really see that the Mayans built these structures in successive additions in their religious time cycle. The temple interior is interesting as long as you are not claustrophobic, but don't spend your time standing in line for it if you haven't seen the rest of the site, because the exterior features are more impressive.

There is a museum on the site that displays some of the small artifacts that were not taken to other museums around the world, which is interesting but not mentioned on many tours. If you are coming on your own, it is worth seeing, but if you are on an organized tour, your limited time is likely better spent outdoors.

There are night shows here with light and sound, but most of these are not practical for the traveler from the coast due to the long drive back after dark. Finally, make sure you bring some water and a hat when you visit these or any of the other ruins. The humidity and the sun will get to you more quickly than you think.

The entrance fee is $10 per person, and tours (including transportation, snacks, and drinks) can be arranged through any local travel agency or tour desk.

The pok-ta-pok *ball court at Chichén Itzá*

Tulum

Given its proximity to the hotels of the Riviera Maya, Tulum is one of the most frequently visited Mayan sites. It is located 2 miles east of Highway 307, 40 miles south of Playa del Carmen.

Tulum is unlike any of the other major Mayan ruins in Mexico in that it is right on the coast. Originally called Zama, which means "sunrise" in Mayan, it faces due east. The beauty of the Caribbean Sea enhances the structures, and many people say that this is what makes Tulum appeal to them. The site, known as the Walled City, rose to prominence during the post-Classic period (A.D. 1000–1500), and it is the polar opposite of Chichén Itzá in terms of the reasons behind its beauty.

While Chichén Itzá has a sense of isolation about it because of its distance and the thick jungle surrounding it, Tulum has a sense of openness and airiness brought on by the ocean itself, and the ocean views are amazing. At the same time, being next to the ocean leads to a great deal of erosion, and between this and the many hurricanes that hit the Caribbean, most of the detail of Tulum's structures has been lost. Some restoration work has been done, but the structures do not at all bear the crisp lines of those at Chichén Itzá. Instead, they are well-rounded, bleached limestone, and the few detailed carvings that remain are protected by woven structures to keep the rain off.

Since it is so close to the population centers, there are many more tourists for the size of the area than you would see elsewhere (this is also in part because it is a small area, and it is more difficult to find a place to retreat from large groups). The fact that it is easy to get

TULUM

Wall

Cenote
House

Harbor

Wall

Great
Palace

Temple of the
Descending God

The
Castle

To
Parking Lot
←
West
Door

Exit

The Temple
of the Frescoes

CARIBBEAN
SEA

Wall

Southeast
Door

Southwest
Door

© The Countryman Press

to also means that many of the tourists are not particularly interested in the Mayans and come because it is close and worth looking into. This can make for a somewhat less sacred atmosphere than one sees at the other sites.

Tulum is a relatively small site, and there is no problem finding time to see all the major elements of the ruins. This makes it a good first ruins site to visit if you have time to visit several, and it is also a choice to consider if you are traveling with small children or anyone with limited mobility. In fact, if you have your own vehicle, you can start off at Tulum early and go to Cobá the same day. The small size also means that the time it takes to tour the ruins is not generally long enough to make it worthwhile for a commercial tour to visit only the ruins themselves, and so you will typically see this site combined with some other activity on a day tour. This may not interest you if your focus is purely on the Mayans, but it is a good way to fit other activities into a packed vacation schedule.

Free parking for Tulum is available at the back gate. To get there, head south of the main highway entrance to the ruins and turn east at the Tulum crossroads, by the San Francisco de Asis grocery store. After 2 miles, the road will dead-end at the Tulum beach road. Turn left and the ruins are straight ahead, 2 miles down the road, past a wonderful public beach at Playa Maya. This gate is used for bicycle and walking access by travelers staying at hotels along Tulum beach. Park along the side of the road and walk the half mile to the entrance booth.

Tulum is perched above a beautiful beach. Don't forget your bathing suit and towel!

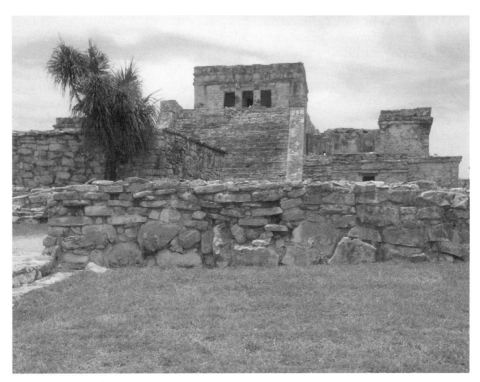

Go to Tulum early to find some solitude.

Tulum is well worth your time because of its unique features, but since it is so time-worn you will not get an accurate picture of the Mayans if it is the only ruin you see. Many of the structures at Tulum tend to look similar because they have been reduced to their most basic components, and partly because of this, you do not see the architectural variety so readily apparent at the other sites. It is a very good contrast with Chichén Itzá and is a good choice if you would like to combine an interest in the Mayans with a beautiful ocean view, but if you are interested in seeing less-restored ruins, Cobá has more to offer than Tulum.

Entrance is $5, and bilingual guide service is available.

Cobá

In its heyday, Cobá city had 44 miles of urban sprawl, making it one of the largest cities in the Mayan civilization. It is located an hour inland from Tulum, on the road that starts at Tulum pueblo, and it passes several popular cenotes, such as Grand Cenote and the Carwash (see chapter 4), before yielding to the jungle.

The city of Cobá flourished during the Classic period (A.D. 300–1000) and was once home to more than fifty thousand inhabitants. It is the least excavated of the major ruins on this side of the Yucatán. The site is surrounded by thick jungle, which lends an atmosphere of discovery to the site (Chichén Itzá is also surrounded by jungle, but the area around the structures themselves has been largely cleared). A number of the ruins at Cobá are partially reconstructed, but not in the finished way that one sees at Chichén Itzá, so the effect is that the ruins look like ancient unrestored buildings, as opposed to what one would see in Chichén Itzá or Tulum. Because of this, things appear more as they would have looked to the European explorers at the time of their arrival rather than a modern excavation.

The city of Cobá was very large, and the excavated ruins are in groups that are spread across the jungle. Bicycles come included with many commercial tours (or can be rented for $2.50; tricycle taxis for two go for $7.50) and are advisable. If you are on an organized tour you will have limited time here, and more of it can be spent exploring the ruins if you can move between the groups more quickly. That said, the jungle walk is also pleasant and relaxing if you can devote the time.

The highlight of Cobá is Nohoc Mul, the largest pyramid in southern Mexico (138 feet tall), and it is considerably larger than the Pyramid of Kukulcán at Chichén Itzá. The fact that it is surrounded by jungle rather than open space further exaggerates the size difference. Like the Pyramid of Kukulcán, this structure can be climbed, but take great care: While the stone steps are stable, they are very irregular compared to the climb at Chichén Itzá. The view from the temple atop Nohoc Mul is beautiful, and you can see the tops of many other structures, the lake (rare in the Yucatán) on which Cobá sits, and also a vast canopy of surrounding jungle. The ball court here, one of the smallest in the Mayan world, is also an interesting comparison to the main court of Chichén Itzá.

There are also several other very significant structures, including Xaibe (the Crossroads Pyramid), which is a rounded, tiered structure that is very different from any of the structures on this side of the Yucatán and is more reminiscent of Uxmal. There are also many stelae (standing stone markers) here that note important events in the history of the Mayans, and many are still detailed enough to see the forms carved onto them.

Tours to Cobá are still less common than to the other ruins, and so the area can be less crowded than the others. If you are looking for a place with fewer tourists, this is likely your best choice. A number of commercial tours combine a visit to Cobá with a tour of a local Mayan village, intending to both show the ancient architecture and give the visitor exposure to the Mayans in their modern lifestyle.

Entrance is $5, and guide service is available. Open 9–5 daily.

Chunyaxche/Muyil

Fifteen miles south of Tulum on Highway 307 and 7 miles from the coastline, the ruins of Chunyaxche/Muyil are located within the Sian Ka'an biosphere and are significantly less visited than the better-known temples of the Caribbean coast. Some researchers believe, however, that the site will one day rival Tulum in its scale and importance to the historical record. The site was inhabited from 300 B.C. until the Spanish conquest, and there are some 75 individual structures believed to still be hidden beneath the jungle vegetation. Excavation of the site is being led by the University of the Yucatán, though funds have been scarce, which has significantly delayed the project. Archaeologists have found evidence that the site was built to pay homage to Ixchel, the Mayan god of fertility.

The site is built on La Laguna freshwater lake and has narrow canals that lead to the ocean and once served as passageways for seafaring adventurers and traders.

Entrance fee is $5, and guide service is available.

6

Diving & Snorkeling

The Riviera Maya is home to some of the most unequaled dive sites in the world. It's one of the few places where you can swim with a green moray eel on a 100-foot wall dive in the morning, go free-diving and snorkeling with dolphins after lunch, explore virgin caverns on a freshwater cave dive in the afternoon, and then pet sleeping sharks on a shallow-water dive that same night.

The Great Mayan Reef is the second longest living barrier reef in the world, and only Australia's Great Barrier Reef is larger. It starts in Cancún and extends just offshore along the eastern tip of the Yucatán Peninsula and all the way down to Honduras. From many towns the reef is only a short swim from the beach, making for excellent snorkeling without the need for a boat or special equipment. You can usually see the water breaking over the reef, which helps to pinpoint its location. The reef itself is razor sharp and extremely delicate, so touching it, bumping it with your equipment, or even kicking sand onto it can cause serious damage from which it takes years to recover. It is home to hundreds of species of live corals, fish, anemones, eels, rays, and other life forms, small and large.

The water itself is gin clear, with horizontal visibility up to 150 feet in some areas. The prevailing current is north to south, though it varies widely depending on the weather and local geographic conditions. Water temperature ranges from a low of 75 in the winter months up to the mid-80s in the height of the summer. Many divers choose to dive without a wet suit, which lessens the amount of weights they are required to carry, making for a less-encumbered dive and more bottom time. Other divers opt for a spring suit, shortie, or Farmer John–style wet suit, which provides a good layer of warmth while still allowing for freedom of movement.

There are a variety of open-water dives available. Divers in Cozumel and Akumal frequently go on shore dives, either in small independent groups or with a dive master. In these locations the reef comes within 100 yards of the shore, enabling divers to reach excellent dive spots with a short underwater or surface swim. Cozumel is also known for its wall dives and drift dives, where the dive boat will stop at one end of a reef and let the divers out, follow the divers' bubbles as they drift along with the current, and then be waiting to pick them up when they surface at the end of the dive. This type of diving can be very relaxing for the divers, who hardly need to swim as they are swiftly drawn along with the current, which travels up to 5 mph.

On other dives, when there isn't as much current, such as off the coast of Puerto Aventuras, Isla Mujeres, or Playa del Carmen, the boat will anchor, the dive master will lead the group on a dive, and then all divers will return to the entry point. Diving this way requires all divers to stay in sight of the others to ensure that nobody gets lost underwater. If you don't have a dive buddy, you will be assigned one on the boat before the dive begins.

A surprise to many first-time Riviera Maya divers is the presence of many freshwater dive spots that are just as close and accessible as the saltwater ones. Throughout the Yucatán Peninsula, there are caverns and spring-fed lagoons called cenotes that offer unique dive opportunities for both amateur and experienced divers. The word *cenote* comes from the Mayan word *dzonot,* which was used to describe the sinkholes that formed after the collapse of the thin limestone earth revealed a cave underneath, which then filled with freshwater from the water table (which is quite near the ground in the porous crust of the Riviera Maya). Once a major source of drinking water for the ancient Mayan villagers, these cenotes range from the size of a kiddie pool up to that of a large lagoon covering several acres of land. Some are on private ranches and have been recently opened to visitors, and others are commercially operated as recreational parks and have resident dive operations and on-site instructors and tour guides.

The water in the cenotes is crystal clear and remains a fairly constant temperature of around 72 degrees. Most cenotes are fairly shallow, making even snorkeling and free-diving quite rewarding. Others have deeper holes, up to 50 feet deep, and are best explored with scuba gear. Since they are relatively small and the water does not circulate, it is important that all swimmers and divers rinse off any mosquito repellent or sunscreen before entering the water. The fish are colorful but fairly small, giving snorkelers and divers the feeling that they are diving inside an aquarium. The bottom is rocky and sometimes covered in algae, and the sides are craggy, making entry and exit a bit tricky, especially in areas that are less frequented by visitors. The major sites, though, have wooden docks and ladders and can be easily entered, even by divers in full gear. With their shallow depth, clear water, and easy accessibility, cenotes make for great dives for beginner divers. They are sometimes even used for training classes since there is no wave action and no current, and it's easy to keep track of where all the divers are.

Caves and caverns, on the other hand, offer a completely different scenario. Diving in these situations should be done only by experienced and certified cave divers since they often require the use of specialized equipment, including redundant air systems, lighting systems, and navigation aids. Cave and cavern diving requires the diver to leave the openwater realm and enter restricted areas where there is no easy escape and no way to surface without retracing your path to the entry point. Without the proper precautions, this type of diving can be extremely dangerous, though it can also be rewarding for divers who know how to do it properly.

The Riviera Maya and the Yucatán are home to some of the world's best spots for this type of diving, and it's an amazing feeling to be surrounded by water as clear as air and to see the incredible cave formations, the underwater stalactites and stalagmites, and the fish that call this realm their home. Some of the dives involve entering the cave at ground level and swimming through a series of caverns prior to entering the more enclosed caves, which twist and turn their way for several hundred yards, sometimes opening up into wide rooms where divers can congregate and rest before continuing the adventure. With the proper preparation, equipment, training, and guide, it's easy to see why this can be one of the most incomparable diving experiences you will ever have.

Each town has its own local dive shops, located around the town square, on the touristy streets, on the beach, or on-site at the larger hotels. Depending on the location, they offer

The author descending into an underground cenote near Cobá

NAUI and PADI training and certification, boat dives, shore dives, drift dives, reef dives, wall dives, night dives, cenote dives, and cavern/cave dives, as well as name-brand equipment and gear for sale or rent. All reputable dive shops and tour operators require divers to have a current certification, commonly called a C-card, prior to renting equipment or going on any guided trip.

Instruction and certification are offered at most shops, and many of the larger hotels offer free scuba introduction classes at their on-site pools. In this confined and safe environment, people new to the sport can practice using a mask and fins, snorkeling, and even breathing underwater from the scuba tank through the regulator. This can be a great way to experience the thrill of scuba diving for the first time, and it just may convince you to take a class and do it in the ocean.

Most dive operators offer a "resort course," which includes a bit of instruction on scuba theory and techniques, some time to practice in the pool, and then an actual scuba dive in open water with a certified dive master right by your side. Though the diver will not receive certification with this type of training, it is the best way to go from having no experience to going on an actual dive in only half a day. For safety reasons, the dive master will keep the dive above a depth of 30 feet and will monitor the diver throughout the adventure.

Many dive shops in the area offer full certification classes and even private certification classes. Though normal dive classes are spread out over a few weeks, a private instructor can take the student through a legal certification program in just a matter of days, including classroom lessons, pool practice sessions, and the open-water checkout dive. Some student divers take the classroom and swimming pool portions of the class at home and then just do their open-water certification dives while on vacation. If you plan on doing this, your home instructor will need to fill out a training referral form, and then your instructor in the Riviera Maya will complete the course with you and issue your C-card.

Experienced divers can go on self-guided dives right from the shore at many hotels, particularly in Cozumel and Akumal. You can bring your own gear or rent it at the hotel dive shop. Most shops have tanks available for less than $10, allowing you to custom-create the dive profile that you want and then go for it. On these dives, the maximum depth is usually around 50 feet, but divers can see just as much variety and just as much beautiful underwater scenery as on boat dives.

Organized boat trips are another way to go. These trips are normally booked at least one day in advance so that the boat captain can ensure that all the gear will be ready and that there will be enough assistants on the boat to handle the group. These trips offer either one or two dives and can be in the morning, afternoon, or even night. Most boat rides will be 30 minutes to an hour long, giving you plenty of time to prepare your gear, document the trip in your log book, socialize with other divers, and even do some sight-seeing along the way. The boats range from 14-foot, open-hull "pangas" that carry just a couple of divers all the way up to 40-foot yachts that can accommodate more than a dozen divers and have air-conditioning, a galley, a shower, and other luxuries. Divers can choose to go on a private trip or can join a group trip with other divers. Nondivers can accompany divers on the boat trip for a nominal fee, though this must be arranged in advance so the captain can plan for the extra space and refreshments.

Most boats require divers to enter the water by performing a back roll or giant stride entry. The water is normally fairly calm, making either type of entry relatively simple for experienced divers. If you have less experience and need additional assistance, just let the

A giant stride entry into a cenote Courtesy of Riviera Maya Tourism Authority

boat captain and the dive master know, and they will do everything they can to accommodate you. Depending on how strong the current is, the group will assemble either on the surface or at depth, and then the dive master will lead the group on the dive while the other divers, paired up with buddies, follow along. Oftentimes there is a safety diver who will stay behind the group to assist with any problems and to make sure everyone stays safe.

There are several types of open-water dives common in the area. One of the most common is a reef dive, where divers swim or drift along the top of the reef. Off many beaches there is a steep wall within a few miles of shore, where the depth drops from around 80–100 feet to more than 1,000 feet, almost straight down, and on these dives either the divers swim along right at the edge of the drop-off, with the reef below them and the vast depths of the blue ocean just beyond, or they swim along the wall itself, with the reef to the side and the depths straight below them. When wall diving this way, it is important for divers to watch their depth gauges closely since it's deceptively easy to go deeper and deeper without even noticing it. For recreational scuba diving the maximum depth is usually considered to be 120 feet. Plus, the deeper you go, the shorter amount of time you can stay, so most divers prefer to keep their maximum depth to around 80 feet, which gives them 30–40 minutes of underwater time.

Most dive boats carry sodas, water, and juice, and many stop for lunch between dives. Lunch can be taken on the boat, or the boat will pull up to the beach, where buffet meals are served. This is most common in Cozumel, though it is being done in other areas as well.

Diving at night is a completely different experience than diving during the day, and it is a real thrill. All divers carry their own lights and backup lights and also wear glow sticks to make them visible, even if their lights should fail. Octopuses, sharks, rays, squid, and other marine life are more prevalent at night since this is the time they normally feed. The same dive site will look totally different at night, with different colors on the coral, different types of fish swimming around, and a different sense of depth for divers since they can see only where they point their lights. On a clear night with a big moon, the divers can also see light from above and can sometimes see large fish or the dive boat silhouetted against the moonlight.

Though some divers like to boast that the only reason to dive in freshwater is to rinse your gear off, others appreciate the difference between freshwater and open-water saltwater diving and consider them to be equally rewarding experiences. This is certainly true in the Riviera Maya, where the cenotes and underwater cave systems present unique diving opportunities that are unparalleled anywhere else in the world. Since most cenotes are fairly shallow, novice divers and even snorkelers find them great places to spend the day in the water. The Riviera Maya's underground river system is only 10 percent explored and holds many amazing and surprising sights. Even experienced cave divers revel in the number of possible dive spots and marvel at the variety of the dives, the clarity of the water, and the beauty of the natural formations.

In cave and cavern diving, divers carry extra air tanks and lights since they do not have the luxury of surfacing at any time should something go wrong. They also run lines of rope from their entry point so that they can always retrace their paths and will never get lost.

You'll see some breathtaking sights while scuba diving in the Riviera Maya. Courtesy of Riviera Maya Tourism Authority

Some caverns are quite narrow, requiring divers to actually remove their tanks from their backs and carry them in front of them so they can fit through. Others are wide enough to allow several divers through at a time and can even be enjoyed by relative newcomers to cave diving, as long as an expert guide is close at hand.

On group tours the depth and bottom time will be recorded by the dive master, and there will be time after each dive for participants to note the details in their log books. Dive operators use the recreational dive tables to plan the dives, the maximum depth, the required surface interval, and the available bottom time. Divers using their own dive computers may plan alternate dive profiles as long as they communicate with the dive master and boat captain so they know what to expect. The crew performs a head count at the start and end of each dive to ensure the safe return of everyone in the group.

While ascending from a dive more than 30 feet in depth, it is customary to perform a safety stop at 15 feet for three minutes. This is a precaution to help eliminate any cases of decompression sickness. If anyone does experience symptoms of "the bends," the crew will take quick action to get the diver to a medical facility and even to a hyperbaric chamber, if necessary. There are several chambers in the Riviera Maya, usually within a 30-minute drive from shore. Most dive operators charge a $1 insurance fee for every dive, which ensures that divers will be covered if they need to enter the chamber. Divers should remember not to dive within 24 hours of flying on an airplane, since doctors say the risk of decompression sickness and other diving ailments increases if you do so.

For most dives, except for extensive cave and cavern diving, no special training or licenses are required beyond the basic open-water scuba diving certification. However you decide to dive, remember what you learned in dive training class: plan your dive, then dive your plan.

Cancún

Known across the world as a mecca for water sports, Cancún is at the far northern tip of the Great Mayan Reef and does not have as much coral growth as the areas farther south. The water is as clear as a shot of tequila *blanco*, though, and some five hundred species have been documented. Most of the dives are fairly shallow and can be enjoyed by both snorkelers and scuba divers.

DIVE SITES

La Bandera
Accessible from either Cancún or Isla Mujeres, this reef stretches out for hundreds of feet at a depth of 40–50 feet. It is home to angelfish, parrot fish, barracuda, lobsters, moray eels, anemones, and living coral, including elkhorn and staghorn. The large Mexican flag (or *bandara*) that is on Cancún is due south of the dive spot.

Punta Cancún
This open-water dive is near the eastern tip of Cancún, offshore from the Hyatt Regency, Dreams, and Riu hotels. Divers see lots of colorful fish, sea urchins, sponges, and sometimes sharks. The average depth is 45 feet.

Punta Nizúc

This shallow bay is offshore from the bridge that connects Cancún to the mainland near the airport, close to the Club Med Hotel. There is an artificial island here, where snorkeling tour groups make their home base.

Isla Mujeres

With an average underwater visibility of up to 100 feet and nearly 50 different dive sites within range of a 30-minute boat ride, Isla Mujeres, whose name translates to "island of the women," is also the island of the snorkelers and divers.

DIVE SITES

Camaronero

The site of a sunken shrimp boat that went down in a storm in the late 1990s, this dive spot ranges from 55 to 70 feet in depth and has become an artificial reef, home to brightly colored corals, Christmas tree worms, anemones, and tiny coral-dwelling fish.

Cave of the Sleeping Sharks

Discovered by local lobster diver and fisherman Carlos Garcia Castilla in the 1950s, the site was visited by Jacques Cousteau in his survey of the area in the 1960s. An underwater cave at 65–70 feet is fed from a fresh spring and has a swift current carrying enriched water through the gills of the resident sharks, allowing them to temporarily halt the perpetual swimming normally required to oxygenate their bodies. The sharks fall into a type of stupor and appear to be sleeping, though their eyes remain open. In this state, the sharks seem not even to notice their human visitors, sometimes allowing themselves to be touched or petted. Most of the sharks are nurse sharks, but bulls, blacktips, and reef sharks have also been spotted.

Garrafon National Marine Park

A national marine sanctuary, Parque Garrafon is open to sunbathers, swimmers, snorkelers, and scuba divers. Two dive sites are just offshore of the park: the Arch and the Bridge. The average depth is 60 feet, and the dives feature healthy coral gardens in spur and groove formations, with several swim-throughs, which makes it an intermediate to advanced dive. Visitors can also try Snuba, a sort of combination of snorkeling and scuba diving where the diver breathes air from a tube into which air is pumped from the surface, without the need for heavy equipment.

Hondureño

Popular with intermediate and advanced divers, this site's main attraction is a 120-foot shrimp boat that sunk in stormy waters during a direct hit by Hurricane Gilbert in 1988. The average depth is 75 feet, and the wreck is home to several large green moray eels, which sometimes leave their protective holes and swim freely above the boat's rusty hull.

Los Manchones
Located close to shore in Mujeres Bay, on the Cancún side of Isla Mujeres, Manchones is about 35 feet deep, making it ideal for novice divers and for long bottom times. The reef is a half mile long, with elkhorn, staghorn, and brain coral, plus many sea urchins, parrot fish, angelfish, trunkfish, and large schools of wrasses and grunts. In the mid-1990s a large bronze cross was attached to the reef to mark the founding of the island and as remembrance to sailors lost at sea, and each year, on Isla's founding day of August 17, an underwater mass is performed at this site.

Los Marinos
Lying at only 70 feet, a sunken Mexican Navy boat can be explored by intermediate and advanced divers. Divers can enter the hull and see the interior compartments of the ship, plus the gun mounts, railings, and exposed deck. Encrusted in coral and sea sponges in parts, the wreck is also home to many species of fish.

Punta Negra
Recognized as one of the northernmost sites along the Great Mayan Reef, Punta Negra is 60 to 70 feet deep and benefits from little to no current, making it a good spot to practice underwater navigation skills while observing the sea turtles, groupers, barracuda, and moray eels that call it home.

Punta Sur
This lively dive at the southern point of Isla Mujeres averages 40 feet and has strong currents, making it best for intermediate divers and above. Many visitors like to think of it as the meeting point of the Caribbean Sea and the Gulf of Mexico, though the exact spot is rather arbitrary. The dive features the coral-encrusted remnants of a shipwreck and a four-hundred-year-old rusted anchor. Dolphins, sea turtles, groupers, and even sharks are known to swim by.

Tavos Reef
A less visited site, Tavos is a shallow reef that features twisting and turning coral formations, huge sea sponges, swim-throughs, overhangs, and bridges. Common sightings include sea urchins, arrow crabs, groupers, rays, barracuda, lobsters, and sharks.

The Ultrafreeze
Eight miles east of Isla, this dive is at the site of a 100-foot-long sunken cargo ship. The bottom is at 100 feet, which makes it an advanced dive. Groupers, sea turtles, manta rays, jewfish, moray eels, barracuda, and sometimes sharks call the wreck their home.

Isla Contoy
With white-sand beaches, shallow bays, and open-water drop-offs, this tiny island offers big variety for snorkelers and divers. Since Contoy is not sheltered by the mainland, the water can be rougher than in other areas along the Yucatán coast.

DIVE SITES

Ixlache Reef

A very shallow reef, Ixlache is popular with snorkeling tours and beginner divers. The coral is in good condition, with large sea anemones, brain coral, and Christmas tree worms. An extension of the reef juts out into deeper water, up to 50 feet deep, so it is possible to start your dive at the deep end and then slowly work your way to the shallows.

Las Calderas

This reef, whose name means "boiling pot" in Spanish, is so named for the wave action that occurs when the ocean swells crest on the exposed reef. The reef is virtually untouched and is home to many spider crabs, sea urchins, sponges, and anemones. Most dives are done at about 50–60 feet.

Costa Maya

The Costa Maya starts an hour south of Playa del Carmen and extends nearly to Mexico's border with Belize. The reef is especially healthy in this section because it sees fewer divers and cruise ships. The coral is healthier, the colors are brighter, and the fish are larger. Unfortunately, it is also harder to reach, so expect longer boat trips as well.

DIVE SITES

Banco Chinchorro

A thriving and expansive coral reef that is just off the pristine beach, Chinchorro has various dive sites available. Popular sightings include hundreds of species of fish, playful arrow crabs, colorful coral, rays, lobsters, and anemones. Because parts of the reef are so shallow, this site was affected by Hurricane Wilma, which pulled water from this area and pushed it ashore near Cancún. The reef was left exposed in some areas and parts of it died. The deeper dives are still as vibrant as ever and it is still a great spot.

Sian Ka'an

Part of the protected biosphere reserve, which was named a UNESCO World Heritage Site, this area has dozens of viable dive sites, many of which are so remote and seldom visited that they don't even have names. For divers who prefer untouched reefs and virgin dive sites, it is definitely worth the challenges of getting there.

Cozumel

One of the most popular dive destinations anywhere, Cozumel has enough world-class dive sites that you could stay there for a week, diving every day, and never go to the same spot twice. It is home to Palancar Reef, regularly ranked as one of the top five dive sites in the world. From shallow-water snorkeling spots to sheer walls that drop thousands of feet, Cozumel has superb dives for every skill level. The most popular type of diving is drift diving, which can take some getting used to but brings a whole new dimension to the diving experience. Most dive sites are on the island's southwest coast, facing the Riviera Maya mainland, where the reef runs parallel to the beach and the water is relatively calm since it is sheltered from the open ocean.

DIVE SITES

Chankanaab
Chankanaab is a nationally preserved beach and underwater park whose name means "small sea" in the native Mayan language. There are several dive sites, both near the shore and several hundred yards from shore, where the water is deeper and the fish tend to be larger. The park also has a freshwater lagoon, botanical gardens, a dolphin show, restaurants, a museum, and a designated snorkeling area. This area was slammed hard by Hurricane Wilma in 2005 and the shoreline was heavily damaged. It has since been rebuilt and is once again one of Cozumel's favorite sites for snorkeling and diving.

Palancar
Cozumel's largest and most celebrated reef, plastered on T-shirts, sweatshirts, and hats sold across the island, is famous for good reason. The coral is healthy and brightly colored, and the marine life is incredibly diverse and abundant. Depths range from 20 to 120 feet, and there are several distinct sites, depending on the part of the reef you dive. The Gardens is a shallow reef bed, the Caves offer swim-throughs and steep overhangs, and Palancar Deep features huge coral formations, sheer drop-offs, and large fish.

Punta Sur
This dive at the southern tip of Cozumel Island is generally offered by special request only. It is deeper than most dives, averaging up to 120 feet, and often has swift currents, making it the exclusive realm of advanced divers. This is one of the most common dives to see gray sharks and reef sharks, in addition to nearly virgin reefs, large barracuda, manta rays, huge groupers, and massive coral heads.

Santa Rosa Wall
A popular boat dive with an average depth of 90–100 feet, Santa Rosa is frequently the first dive visited on a two-dive tour. There are spur and groove formations and a steep drop-off where the depth increases dramatically. Divers should watch their gauges and be careful not to go too deep. Many large groupers, wrasses, rays, parrot fish, and angelfish can be seen here.

Tormentos
With the top of the reef at about 60 feet deep, this site is popular with intermediate divers and others who would gladly dive a little shallower in exchange for more bottom time. A resident green moray eel, more than 6 feet long, can usually be spotted, and it is known to eat fish right from the dive master's hand. While hiding in its hole in the reef, it slowly opens and closes its mouth as if anticipating its next meal. In actuality, it's just keeping a flow of oxygenated water through his gills. Sometimes this beautiful green monster leaves

its lair and swims freely above the reef, occasionally swimming straight at divers who aren't sure whether they should swim away or stay and watch. There are also many rays, sea urchins, Christmas tree worms, and large groupers and barracuda.

Puerto Aventuras

Boats depart from the Puerto Aventuras Marina several times per day, shuttling divers to the nearby reefs. Though it's always best to book ahead, dives can sometimes be planned at the last minute if a boat has extra space available.

Dive Sites

Brisa Caribe
A steep drop-off in front of the Brisa Caribe condos between the public marina and the Oasis beach, this dive can be done as a shore dive or boat dive. The reef features deep crevices and overhangs, along with plentiful parrot fish, angelfish, and sea urchins.

Los Caniones
One of the deeper dives available in Puerto Aventuras, this reef lies at around 75 feet, making it best for intermediate and advanced divers. The visibility is more than 50 feet. Los Caniones features steep canyons and groove formations with elkhorn, staghorn, and brain coral. There are plenty of fish, including grunts, wrasses, barracuda, parrot fish, and angelfish.

Mook-Che
Just off the beach near Playa Xcalacoco, this dive site is accessible by boat from either Puerto Aventuras or Akumal. The average depth is 35 feet. The reef is colorful, and there are many small species of fish. An occasional barracuda lurks just above the reef.

Akumal

Akumal is a shallow bay with calm water, slow currents, and coral beaches. There are many good spots to dive in the 20- to 40-foot range, making it a good spot for beginning and intermediate divers who want the thrill of an ocean dive but aren't quite ready for deep walls and cave systems. More advanced divers will appreciate the deeper sites such as Gonzalo's Reef, which reaches 85 feet in some spots.

Dive Sites

Dick's Reef
Named for the retired owner of the Original Akumal Dive Shop, this bump dive ranges from 20 to 50 feet and features large coral heads and patches of white sand. There are also several swim-throughs and large overhangs.

Gonzalo's Reef

A fairly deep dive bottoming out at 85 feet, Gonzalo's Reef is famous for being one of the spots where divers can usually count on a close encounter with a sea turtle. There are several species native to the area, and they frequently make the rounds at the reef, looking for a bite to eat.

Las Redes

This 50-foot dive, whose name means "the nets" in Spanish, features high concentrations of stingrays, lobsters, angelfish, sea urchins, Christmas tree worms, and anemones and an occasional barracuda or sea turtle.

Motorcycle Reef

A sunken motorcycle lies in the sand at one end of this reef, which sits at 60 feet. There are abundant sponges, rays, grunts, and angelfish.

Shark Cave

Similar to the Isla Mujeres dive site with a similar name, this 30-foot dive features a healthy reef with large overhangs that funnel the current and shelter a group of resident nurse sharks. The current carries oxygen-rich seawater through the sharks' gills, allowing them to stay motionless in a sleeplike state.

Tzimin-Ha

Named for the remnants of a 20-foot fishing boat that sank here, this dive site is a good spot to see enormous blue jewfish, hungry groupers, and barracuda.

Yal-Ku

A good spot for snorkelers and shallow-water divers, this spot is on the ocean side of Yal-Ku Lagoon, where the water from the lagoon mixes with the water from the open ocean. There are elkhorn and staghorn coral, sea urchins, sponges, and anemones, as well as lots of Caribbean lobsters.

Paamul

This relaxing beach is home to some of the best diving in the area. With little in the way of tourism development, the reefs are still in pristine condition, and the sea life is prolific. The shallow bay also offers excellent snorkeling since the reef is healthy and full of life, even in just a few feet of water.

DIVE SITES

Horst's Reef

With a maximum depth of only 45 feet, this dive spot is good for all certified divers and even offers some small swim-throughs for an added bit of excitement. It's a popular site to see spotted drums, groupers, parrot fish, and an occasional sea turtle.

Paamul Mini Wall

With an average depth of more than 100 feet, this wall dive is for advanced divers only. Lobster, huge groupers, nurse sharks, green and spotted moray eels, and barracuda can usually be spotted.

Paraíso Shallow

Good for intermediate divers, Paraíso lies at about 60 feet and features large coral heads, sea sponges, Christmas tree worms, and abundant marine life.

Xel-Ha

A government-regulated ecotourism park, Xel-Ha offers several shallow-water snorkeling sites where the coral reef comes nearly to the water's surface, so even novice snorkelers can see the amazing sea life.

Xel-Ha Reef

Offshore from the park, the reef is open for exploration provided that divers follow the preservation rules of the park. Dive boats depart from the park itself and from nearby beaches. The depth ranges from 35 to 55 feet, depending on the part of the reef selected. Your dive master will choose a spot based on the experience of the divers, the prevailing currents, and the advice of the boat captain.

Tulum

Known for its Mayan ruins and relaxed atmosphere, the Tulum area also has some great snorkeling and diving sites.

DIVE SITES

Las Ruinas

The beach right behind the ruins doesn't offer much in the way of reef life, but the water is clear and the waves are small, which makes it a popular swimming spot.

Tulum Reef

Offshore from the ruins, the barrier reef is in great condition, and many snorkelers and divers enjoy the thrill of diving while in the shadow of the great Mayan temple. Dives range from 15 to 60 feet.

Playa del Carmen & Playacar

The unofficial capital of the Riviera Maya is also home to the greatest concentration of diving and dive-related activities and services. There are more than a dozen dive shops along Paseo del Carmen and in the water-sports centers of the larger hotels, particularly those in Playacar. Dive sites accessible by boat from Playa range from shallow reefs good for snorkeling to deep-water drop-offs best reserved for advanced divers. The Buceo Mexico hyperbaric chamber, the leading facility in the treatment of diving accidents, including cases of "the bends," is open every day and is well known by all major dive operators.

DIVE SITES

Chen Zubul
This is a shallow-water dive averaging only 40 feet, and it is frequently visited by novice divers and for night dives.

La Tortuga
La Tortuga, whose name means "the turtle" in Spanish, is one of the more adventurous dive sites given the large schools of grunts and wrasses that let you swim with them, the friendly moray eels, the huge groupers, and, if you're lucky, a curious sea turtle or two. There is usually a fairly strong current, which can turn the dive into a drift dive. The reef depth is 60–70 feet.

Las Barracudas
A short boat trip from Playa del Carmen, this site is offshore from the Xcaret ecological park. The depth is 40–50 feet, and there are many tropical fish, including—of course— several large barracuda.

Los Cerebros
A middle-range dive averaging around 65 feet, this site is known for a large amount of brain (*cerebro* in Spanish) coral, towering coral heads, spider crabs, anemones, and plenty of angelfish and parrot fish, which can be seen hungrily chomping on the reef.

Moche Deep
With an average depth of more than 100 feet, this is one of the more advanced dives in the area. The reef is in good shape, and there are lots of big fish.

Punta Maroma
A few miles north of Playa del Carmen, this site offers several different dives within a close distance of each other. The reef isn't much, but there are lots of turtles, eels, lobsters, arrow crabs, and other sea life. Depths range from 60 to 120 feet.

PLAYA DEL CARMEN DIVE SHOPS & HYPERBARIC CHAMBERS

The Abyss
abyss@playadelcarmen.com
Blue Parrot Hotel, 12th Street and the beach

They offer PADI and NAUI instruction, open-water dives, and cenote trips.

Buceo Mexico Hyperbaric Chamber
987-873-1365
10th Avenue and 28th Street

Buceo Mexico offers diagnosis and treatment of the most common diving ailments, including decompression sickness and reef rash. The chamber is supported through a mandatory $1-per-dive donation, which is collected by dive operators. No other fees are charged for services, including x-rays and exams.

Cyan Ha Divers
987-873-0978
buceocyanha@playadelcarmen.com
North of town, between Hotel Las Palapas and Hotel Shangri La

Open since 1983, Cyan Ha has several boats, an on-site training pool, and PADI instruction. The shop specializes in small groups, cenote dives, and reef dives.

Explora Divers
Tukan Beach, 28th Street at the beach

Explora specializes in cenote and cave dives, but it also offers windsurfing instruction and board rental, sailing tours, and motorcycle tours.

Go Cenotes
First Avenue between 24th and 25th Streets

They offer cenote trips, open-water dives in Playa and Cozumel, snorkeling tours, and trips to Holbox Island.

Scuba Playa Dive Shop
984-803-3123
www.scubaplaya.com
Second Street between Quinta and the beach
10th Street between First Avenue and Quinta

This dive shop offers a variety of open-water and cenote dives, including a one-tank ocean dive for $35 (two tanks is $55), a two-tank trip to Cozumel for $95 (plus the price of the ferry), night dives or wreck dives for $45, a snorkel tour to reefs near Playa for $25, and a cenote dive package, including two cenote dives at two separate locations, transportation, lunch, and drinks, for $95. It also offers a three-day open-water certification course for $295 and a referral course for $190.

Studio Blue
984-873-1088
First Street between the beach and Quinta

On the north side of the town square, Studio Blue is a full-fledged dive shop with retail showroom, dive school, and snorkel and dive tours. It offers daily boat trips to local reefs, excursions to Cozumel, and cenote diving adventures.

Tank-Ha Dive Shop
984-873-0302
www.tankha.com
dive@tankha.com
Fifth Avenue between Eighth and 10th Streets

Tank-Ha has PADI and NAUI instruction and an on-site training pool and offers cenote dives, open-water dives, and reef dives, with hotel/dive combination rates available. Sample prices: two-tank dive, $60; one-tank dive, $40; two-tank cenote dive, $100; night dive, $55; open-water certification, $350; referral course, $220. There are two other Tank-Ha locations: at the Hotel Royal Albatros in Playa and at the Club Maeva in Xpu-Ha.

Yucatek Divers
984-803-1363
www.yucatek-divers.com
15th Avenue between Second and Fourth Streets
Quinta between Sixth and Eighth Streets

Yucatek offers a variety of dives, including one-tank dives for $40 and two-tank dives for $60, night dives for $55, and cavern and cave dives for $100, including transportation. It also offers scuba instruction, with discover diving courses ($80), refresher courses ($90), open-water certification (three days, $350), and open-water referrals ($220).

7

GOLF

Though the Mayans never used the wheel, they did have the ball, and it is believed that they took great pleasure in playing various games. Their most famous ball game was called *pok-ta-pok*, and it was serious business. The ball was about the size of a kickball, and the game was played on a large field about the size of a basketball court. Similar to basketball, the game's object was to shoot the ball through a hoop mounted above the playing surface. Considering that players weren't allowed to use their hands, though, scoring was quite rare and was considered a tremendous feat. Large numbers of villagers turned out to watch the games, which had great religious and ceremonial importance. Fans sang songs, acted boisterously, and even bet on who would win. The winners of the game were given a hero's welcome, and a celebration was held in their honor. As legend has it, the losers were put to death.

Today, the open fields, beachfronts, and carved-away jungles of the Riviera Maya make a perfect backdrop for the more "civilized" ball game of golf. There are a dozen places to play within a short distance of the Riviera Maya, including courses in Cancún, Cozumel, and the town of Bacalar (south of the Riviera Maya). Some of the courses are par 3, but others are par 72 championship courses designed by some of the best golf architects in the business, including Jack Nicklaus, Robert Trent Jones Jr., and Robert Von Hagge.

Most of the courses have beautiful views of the ocean and the tropical jungle. Iguanas, colorful birds, and other animals are commonly sighted. Most have multiple water and sand features, and a couple even have actual Mayan ruins next to the fairways.

Most courses have clubs for rent, and unless you're a real pro or planning on playing multiple rounds, the loaners are normally sufficient. Balls can be expensive (and the loss ratio can be high), so it's usually best to bring some of your own since they're cheap back home and fairly easy to pack. The larger courses have full-service pro shops with name-brand equipment and apparel, club repair, and instruction.

Some of the courses operate with an all-inclusive concept, where the greens fee includes a cart, range balls, and all the food and drink you care to consume during your round. To keep the costs down, consider playing in the afternoon to take advantage of discounted twilight rates. Just make sure to bring a hat, sunscreen, and plenty of water.

The Riviera Maya is becoming more of a golf destination each year. More than 15 courses are currently under construction or are in the design/approval/development stages. For information on all area golf courses, log on to the Mexican Caribbean Golf Association's web site, www.cancungolf.org.

Golf Courses

Cancún Country Club—Pok-Ta-Pok
998-883-1230
www.cancungolfclub.com
Kukulcán Boulevard, km 7.5, Cancún hotel zone

Designed by Robert Trent Jones Jr., Cancún's original course (opened in 1976) is 6,636 yards long, with 18 holes and a par of 72. It has several holes along the beach and a few Mayan ruins scattered about. High-season (December 18–April 30) rates are $100 before 2 PM and $75 after. In the low season (May 1–December 17) it's $75 before 3 PM and $50 after. Rates include use of the practice tee and putting green and a shared cart. Club rentals are $40, shoes are $16, and nonplaying riders are $30. Reservations and discounts are available through the Fiesta Americana Coral Beach, Holiday Inn Express, and Marriott CasaMagna hotels. An on-site restaurant serves sandwiches, salads, and Mexican food. Open 6–6, with the last tee-off at 4.

Cancún Oasis Golf Club
998-885-0867
www.oasishotels.com
Kukulcán Boulevard, km 16.5, Cancún hotel zone

This nine-hole par 3 course is between the Oasis Cancún hotel and the main road through the Cancún hotel zone. It covers nearly 900 yards and has a practice putting green. The greens fee is $40 per person.

Cozumel Country Club
987-872-9570
www.cozumelcountryclub.com.mx
info@cozumelcountryclub.com.mx
Carretera Costera Norte, km 6.5 Interior, Cozumel

Designed by Nicklaus Design in 2001, this course has four sets of tees, with the longest being 6,734 yards. There are many sand and water features to contend with as the course skirts native mangroves and tropical swamps. Standard greens fees are $155.

Golf Club at Mayakoba
1-800-540-6088 (U.S.)
www.fairmont.com
Highway 307, km 297, north of Playa del Carmen

Managed by Fairmont Hotels, this is the first course in Mexico to be designed by Greg Norman. Dubbed the Camaleon course, it curls around the Fairmont Mayakoba hotel and along the beach of the 1,600-acre tourism development. Players enjoy unusual hazards such as cenotes, mangrove swamps, and other tropical features. The course spans more than 7,000 yards and has five sets of tees. Two of the holes are right along the beach, while 15 holes have some sort of water hazard. There is a driving range and putting green, plus a well-stocked pro shop and a steakhouse overlooking the 18th hole. A novelty in Mexico, all carts have GPS navigation and yardage systems, allowing players to keep score, monitor other players' scores, and order refreshments while on the course.

Golf Club Moon Palace Cancún

984-873-0624 or 1-800-525-5025 (U.S.)
www.moonpalace.com
teetimes@palaceresorts.com
Highway 307, km 340, Cancún

This 7,165-yard course, set along the beach and the tropical jungle, is par 72. The showcase hole is the 141-yard 17th, a challenging par 3 with an island green. Greens fees are $250, including a shared cart. The twilight rate (after 2 PM) is $150, nonplaying riders are $55, rental clubs are $32, and caddies are available for $30 per group. Guests of Palace resorts get a $50 discount. Fees include unlimited food and drinks during your round, plus transportation from hotels in the Riviera Maya. Email or call to make reservations.

Hilton Cancún Beach & Golf Resort

998-881-8016
www.hiltoncancun.com
Kukulcán Boulevard, km 17.5, Cancún hotel zone

This course near Cancún's southern end has 18 holes, par 72, and 6,767 yards of play and was designed by Isao Aoki and built in 1994. It features holes along Nichupté Lagoon, with peacocks, an occasional crocodile, and lots of iguanas. From the 15th and 16th holes, players have a great view of the Ruinas El Rey, Cancún's largest and most important Mayan ruins site. The standard rate for non-Hilton players is $175, with hotel guests paying $125. Twilight rates are $90. All rates include cart. Club rental is $25 (Mizuno and Precept) or $50 (Titleist and Calloway). There is a practice tee and practice green, plus a European day spa and the 19th Hole restaurant. No pull carts allowed.

Iberostar Playa Paraíso Golf Club

984-877-2800
www.iberostar.com
golfparaiso@iberostar.com.mx
Highway 307, km 309, Playa Paraíso

Part of the massive Iberostar complex, this course, designed by P. B. Dye and opened in 2005, is convenient for guests staying anywhere in the Riviera Maya. It features 18 holes stretched across 6,800 yards, with wide fairways, deep sand traps, and undulating greens. Rental equipment from brands such as Titleist, Nike, and Mizuno is available. Email or call for pricing and tee-time reservations.

Las Velas Golf Club

998-883-2222
Highway 307, km 350, Bacalar

A little-known course near the border of Belize, it has 18 holes and is par 72. It is part of the Club Las Velas Gold resort. The greens fee is $120 per person.

Melia Cancún Golf Club

998-883-1230
www.solmelia.com
Kukulcán Boulevard, km 16, Cancún hotel zone

Stretching more than 1,800 yards, this course, next to the Gran Melia Cancún hotel, has 18 par 3 holes and a nicely manicured putting green. It's a fun place to practice your chips and get in a round without spending all day. The greens fee is $40 per person.

Playa Mujeres

998-843-1078
www.playamujeres.com.mx
Bonampak Avenue, Punta Sam

Part of the newly developed Costa Mujeres region, just north of Cancún and across the channel from Isla Mujeres, this 18-hole course was designed by Greg Norman and snakes through tropical mangroves, the beachfront, and a saltwater lagoon. It's set to open in late 2006.

Playacar Club de Golf

984-873-0624 or 1-800-635-1856 (U.S.)
www.palaceresorts.com
teetimes@palaceresorts.com
Paseo Xaman-há, 26 Fraccionamiento Playacar, Playa del Carmen

Play golf around Mayan ruins at Playacar. Courtesy of Riviera Maya Tourism Authority

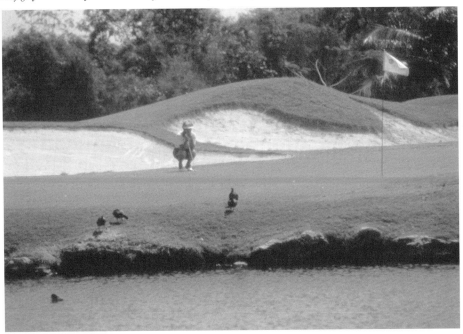

Opened in 1994, the Playacar golf course was designed by Robert Von Hagge and was acquired by Palace Resorts in 2005. The course runs 7,202 yards and has many jungle, sand, and water features to keep golfers challenged and entertained. There are even a few actual Mayan ruins along the fairways and greens. The standard greens fee is $160, including a shared cart and unlimited drinks and snacks while on the course. Twilight fees (after 2 PM) are $100. Clubs are available for rent for $30 (steel shaft) or $40 (graphite shaft), and transportation from Riviera Maya hotels is only $20. There is also a pro shop offering instruction, equipment, and apparel, plus a swimming pool, driving range, putting green, and on-site restaurant. Email or call to make reservations.

Puerto Aventuras Club de Golf
984-873-5109
www.puertoaventuras.com.mx
Highway 307, km 269.5, Puerto Aventuras

This nine-hole, 3,236-yard, par 36 course, part of the Puerto Aventuras marina, tennis, and golf club, was designed by Thomas Lehman and built in 1990. Greens fees are $49 and include unlimited play and access to the practice green. Cart rental is $34 (walking is allowed), and clubs are $23. The first tee time is 7:30 AM and reservations are not required. Astroturf tennis courts are available for $20 per hour. No credit cards.

Puerto Cancún
www.puertocancun.com
East of Bnampak Avenue, near where Kulkulcán Avenue meets downtown Cancún

Currently in development just north of Cancún, the 808-acre Puerto Cancún resort will feature more than 2,000 condos, 435 private homes (including 40 fronting the golf course), a 350-slip marina, 5 hotels, and a large shopping plaza. The golf course, designed by Tom Wesikopf, features 185 acres of water features, sand traps, and manicured greens. An additional course, designed by Tom Fazio and Nice Price, is being contemplated.

Riviera Maya Golf & Tennis Club—Mayan Palace Golf Club
984-206-4000
www.mayanresortsgolf.com
Highway 307, km 310, Playa Paraiso.

This rare Jack Nicklaus–designed par 3 course opened in 2003. It spans 2,823 yards and has lots of water and sand features. The signature 17th hole skirts a large lagoon and has an island sand trap, making your approach shot a crucial factor. The standard greens fee is $157, which includes shared cart and unlimited food and drinks. Club rental is available for $35. The first tee time is at 6 AM.

8

FISHING

Fishing has been a way of life in the Riviera Maya since the indigenous inhabitants paddled their dugout canoes through the shallows, plunging their wooden spears into the water to snare their catch. They also fished with reed baskets or nets, woven with the same techniques that were used to make hammocks. In some areas fish were also caught with bows and arrows or with poisons, which were thrown into the water, killing the fish, which then floated to the surface to be harvested. Later, the Mayans even used a pole and line, possibly even making a sport out of it.

With its variety of good fishing locations in such a relatively small geographic area, the Riviera Maya is one of the top spots for sportfishing and deep-sea fishing in the world. The waters off the northeastern coast of the Yucatán are prime for finding numerous fish species and a wide variety of fishing conditions. From deep channels to wide flats and shallow reefs to rocky points, there's always a spot that's producing, no matter the time of year and the weather conditions, unless a major storm keeps the boats in port.

Fishing options range from a do-it-yourself wade-fishing expedition to a full-day excursion trolling on a luxury yacht, complete with meals, drinks, guides, gear, and a video recording of all the action. From your hotel in Playa del Carmen or elsewhere in the Riviera Maya, several distinct fishing spots are within easy reach. From the deep waters off Cancún to the north, through the reefs of Puerto Morelos, to the shallows of Cozumel, to the drop-offs near Playa, to the bays of Akumal and Puerto Aventuras, and all the way down to the flats of Sian Ka'an, each area holds something unique and exciting for fishing. And whether you're a novice who just enjoys being out on the water and reeling one in, a regular enthusiast in search of your first marlin, or an old pro going for a coveted grand slam, you can find what you're looking for in the Riviera Maya.

There is great fishing year-round, but if you're looking for a specific type of fish, then you'll need to take note of the seasons to make sure the fish you're looking for is around when you plan to visit. Many visitors come to Playa seeking the majestic billfish, which produces a thrill like no other when it takes the bait and then jumps in the air for all to see. These beautiful creatures, weighing up to 500 pounds, are seen throughout the year, though the prime time is from March to July, when they ply the deep waters between Cozumel and the Yucatán mainland in abundant numbers. Each year, there are several billfish grand slams recorded, when a single group manages to boat a blue marlin, a white marlin, and a sailfish on the same trip. When fishing for these beauties, a strict catch-and-release policy is followed, so make sure to bring your video camera to capture the moments for bragging rights.

Fish	Jan	Feb	Mar	Apr	May	Jun	Jul	Aug	Sept	Oct	Nov	Dec
Amber jack	high season	high season	high season	high season	high season	high season	high season	high season	some catches	some catches	some catches	some catches
Barracuda	high season	high season	high season	high season	high season	high season	high season	high season	high season	high season	high season	high season
Blue marlin	off season	off season	some catches	some catches	high season	high season	high season	high season	high season	some catches	off season	off season
Bonefish	some catches	some catches	high season	high season	high season	high season	high season	high season	some catches	some catches	some catches	some catches
Bonito	off season	high season	high season	high season	high season	high season	high season	high season	some catches	some catches	off season	off season
Bottom fish	high season	high season	high season	high season	high season	high season	high season	high season	high season	high season	high season	high season
Grouper	high season	high season	high season	high season	high season	high season	high season	high season	high season	high season	high season	high season
Kingfish	high season	high season	high season	high season	high season	high season	high season	high season	high season	high season	high season	high season
Mackerel	high season	high season	high season	high season	high season	high season	some catches	some catches	some catches	some catches	high season	high season
Mahimahi	off season	some catches	high season	high season	high season	high season	high season	high season	high season	off season	off season	off season
Permit	high season	high season	high season	high season	high season	high season	high season	high season	high season	high season	high season	high season
Sailfish	off season	some catches	high season	high season	high season	high season	high season	high season	off season	off season	off season	off season
Shark	high season	high season	high season	high season	high season	high season	high season	high season	high season	high season	high season	high season
Snapper	high season	high season	high season	high season	high season	high season	high season	high season	high season	high season	high season	high season
Tuna	off season	off season	some catches	high season	high season	high season	high season	some catches	off season	off season	off season	off season
Wahoo	off season	off season	high season	high season	high season	high season	high season	high season	high season	off season	off season	off season
White marlin	off season	off season	some catches	high season	high season	high season	high season	high season	off season	off season	off season	off season

Tuna, mahimahi, bonito, bonefish, and wahoo prefer the warmer waters and generally are more active from March to August or September, though catches of each have been recorded in every month of the year. Due to the varied underwater terrain and the year-round temperate climate, however, many fish species can be caught all through the year, such as barracuda, grouper, kingfish, shark, skipjack, snapper, and other reef and bottom fish. They are so abundant, in fact, that many chartered boats promise to prepare a meal on the boat or on a hidden beach, and they rely exclusively on the day's catch to supply the main course. Though certainly it has happened that bad luck strikes and the group is left to dine on crackers, salsa, and sides, the trips almost always end with a bounteous feast of ultrafresh ceviche or fried fish.

A Mexican fishing license is required for boat fishing, and the fees go toward worthwhile conservation and regulation programs. Reputable tour operators, such as those listed in this guide, include all required licensing in the prices of their tours.

PRIZED CATCHES OF THE RIVIERA MAYA

Barracuda
Often seen while snorkeling, hovering nearly motionless next to the reef, seemingly watching every move you make, the barracuda is one of the most feared of all ocean creatures. Given its muscle-packed body, large eyes, gaping mouth, and razor-sharp teeth, it's easy to see why. Barracudas' fearless nature makes them great fighters, and they are commonly caught while drift fishing or bottom fishing, all across the shallows and deepwater cuts of the Mayan Riviera. Caught year-round.

Blue Marlin
The largest of the billfish, the blue marlin can reach up to 1,800 pounds in the deeper Atlantic waters, though they seldom grow to more than 500 pounds in the local region. Average catches are in the range of 80–120 pounds. Caught while trolling using artificial baits, the blue marlin will be landed only if the angler is strapped in tightly to the fighting chair and ready for an exhaustive struggle. Keeping tension on the line is the only way to keep the blues from spitting the hook while jumping into the air. Best months: May to September.

Bonefish
Noted for their exceptional fighting strength given their relatively small size, bonefish are taken with light tackle, generally fly-fishing, though spinning tackle can also be used. The angler normally casts when the fish breaks the surface or is swimming just below. The strike is hard and fast, requiring a high level of skill and making for a thoroughly entertaining day of fishing. One of the best spots in the world for finding bonefish is in Ascension Bay, at the southern end of the Sian Ka'an biosphere. Best months: March to August.

Grouper
A member of the sea bass family, groupers are strong fighting fish and are quite abundant in the warm Caribbean waters. They come in various colors, from dark gray to bright orange. Scuba divers are fond of watching groupers eat, a process that involves a slow

circling around the prey, followed by a quick kick of the tail fin and a hard swallow, which lets them suck in large pieces of food at one time. They are generally caught while bottom fishing. Caught year-round.

Mahimahi

One of the best-tasting fish in the Caribbean, the mahimahi (sometimes called dorado or dolphin fish) has a big face with a high, protruding forehead and beautiful blue dorsal fin running the length of its back. The body is thick and strong and seems to glow with every color of the rainbow. Can be caught trolling or bottom fishing, depending on the water depth. Best months: March to September.

Permit

Members of the jack family, permit are broad fish with silvery blue bodies that range in size from 3 to 30 pounds. Great fighters with fierce striking power, they can be taken with flies and light tackle. They are common in the shallow flats of Ascension Bay and near Isla Holbox, and since they stay in the warm, shallow water, fishing is good year-round.

Sailfish

One of the most exciting sport fish around, the sailfish is known for its long, protruding dorsal fin, which looks like a sail. It is also known to fly through the air once it's hooked, offering up superb picture-taking opportunities. Sailfish, mostly 30–50 pounds, are caught by trolling through the drop-offs and deeper channels, and they can be very hard to land since they twist and turn a lot while jumping and fighting. Best months: March to August.

Shark

The Mexico Department of Tourism's supercomputer that picked Cancún as the next tourism megadevelopment neglected to factor in the high number of sharks that live in the region's warm waters, feeding off the abundant baitfish. Though attacks are very infrequent, sightings are somewhat common, especially by local fishermen and others who spend a lot of time on the water. Long prized by natives for their liver oil, sharks are still commercially fished for their meat, teeth, and jaws. The English word *shark* is said to come from the Mayan *xoc*. A year-round catch, they can be caught while trolling, bottom fishing, or even wade fishing.

Tuna

The Riviera Maya is home to yellowfin, blackfin, and skipjack tuna, and each is quick and strong and can put up a great fight. Most often caught while trolling, tuna can be served grilled, in lime-marinated ceviche, or even raw. Can't beat that for fresh sushi! Best months: April to July.

Wahoo

Wahoo are long and thin, with a barracuda-like face and sleek body that can cut through the water at an incredible 45 mph. When a wahoo hits the bait, you better make sure the pole is fastened in the rod holder or securely in someone's arms, or you'll end up losing your whole rig to the depths. Most often caught while trolling, wahoo can be cut into large steaks and are great for frying. Best months: March to September.

White Marlin

White and blue, with a beautiful pointed "horn," the white marlin (50–80 pounds on average) is famous for long fights and high jumps, often twisting its body when it's out of the water. Found in the highest numbers in the Cozumel channel, between the island and the mainland. Best months: April to August.

TOP FISHING DESTINATIONS

Akumal

Akumal has been a sportfishing town for more than 30 years. One of the top guides in the area, Pillo, who has been a resident for 20 years, offers two-hour trips for up to four anglers (and up to four others) for $100, including tackle, bait, and drinks. Four-hour trips cost $200. Reservations can be made in person at Lot 40, near the Nah Kin Condos.

Ascension Bay

Recognized as the best place in the world for a permit, tarpon, and bonefish grand slam, Ascension Bay and Boca Pila are also a prime spot for snook, barracuda, Spanish mackerel, and permit. The bay has various inlets, ensuring that your boat captain can find fishing no matter the wind direction. Anglers can visit on a day trip from the Riviera Maya or can stay overnight at one of the many lodges found between Boca Paila and Punta Allen.

Cancún

A 55-foot boat accommodating 18 anglers departs out of Cancún on night-fishing expeditions to the reefs not far from shore, between the coastline and Isla Mujeres. Common catches include grouper, hogfish, mackerel, and snapper.

The trip includes five hours of fishing, all equipment and bait, an open bar, and a buffet meal featuring the fresh fish that is caught during the first part of the trip, plus lasagna, white rice, and steamed vegetables. It operates on Monday, Wednesday, and Friday and departs at 7 PM, returning at midnight. Adults $50, children under 12 $25. For more information call Cancún Vista Tours at 998-898-4312 (in Mexico) or 1-800-860-5917 (in the United States).

Cozumel

The lagoons, jagged shorelines, and flats of Cozumel Island offer up excellent bonefishing, which is most often done using fly-fishing tackle or a lightweight spinning reel. There is good bottom fishing along the northern coast near Passion Island and on the island's east coast, where the coral reef is not part of the federal reserve. Farther from shore, in the Cozumel channel, anglers troll for marlin, sailfish, and other large game.

Puerto Aventuras

The fishing mecca of Puerto Aventuras is the southernmost deep-water marina in the Riviera Maya, with many sportfishing and deep-sea fishing charters available. A walk around the marina reveals the dozens of well-equipped boats waiting for their next expedition.

One tour operator is Tours Cancún (998-887-3414; www.tours-cancun.com; Calle Lima, #18, Sm. 2-A, Mz. 2, Cancún), which offers share-fishing trips and chartered boat trips departing out of the Puerto Aventuras Marina. Boats are 30–35 feet and accommodate up to eight anglers and observers. The trip includes tackle, bait, drinks, water, license, and port fees. A four-hour trip is $90 for each angler and $50 for each observer; eight-hour trips are $180 and $75; and full-boat charters are $375 for four hours and $650 for eight hours. The half-day trip departs at 9 AM and 1:30 PM; the full-day trip departs at 9 AM.

Another option is Captain Walter of the Puerto Aventuras Fishing company (984-873-5463; www.puertoaventurasfishing.com; Puerta del Mar 1, Depto. 14, Puerto Aventuras), featuring half- and full-day charters aboard the 34-foot *Tanya* fishing boat, which accommodates up to 10 people. Trips include snacks, drinks, fishing gear, and bait, and the full-day trip includes lunch (including fresh ceviche) and snorkeling equipment. Fishing starts as soon as the boat leaves the marina. The crew will pack your fish fillets so you can take them home. Half day is $350, full day is $600.

Index

LODGING BY PRICE